Portraits of Pioneers in Psychology

VOLUME III

Portraits of Pioneers in Psychology

VOLUME III

Edited by

Gregory A. Kimble
Michael Wertheimer

AMERICAN PSYCHOLOGICAL ASSOCIATION
Washington, DC

LAWRENCE ERLBAUM ASSOCIATES, PUBLISHERS
Mahwah, New Jersey   London

BF
109
.A1
P67
V 3
apr 2000

Published by

American Psychological Association
750 First Street, NE
Washington, DC 20002

Lawrence Erlbaum Associates, Inc., Publishers
10 Industrial Avenue
Mahwah, NJ 07430

Library of Congress Cataloging-in-Publication Data

Portraits of pioneers in psychology / edited by Gregory
A. Kimble and Michael Wertheimer
    p. cm.
    "Sponsored by the Division of General Psychol-
ogy, American Psychological Association."
    Includes bibliographical references and index.
    ISBN 0-8058-2619-X. ISBN 0-8058-2620-3
(pbk.)
    1. Psychologists –Biography. 2. Psychology –
History. I. Kimble, Gregory A. II. Wertheimer,
Michael. III. American Psychological Association. Division of General Psychology.
    BF109.A1P67 1991
    150'.92'2–dc20

[B]

                                          91-7226
                                          CIP

Printed in the United States of America

    10 9 8 7 6 5 4 3 2 1

Portraits of Pioneers in Psychology: Volume III has
been published under the following ISBNs:
        APA: 1-55798-477-8
            1-55798-479-4 (pbk.)
        LEA: 0-8058-2619-X
            0-8058-2620-3 (pbk.)

British Cataloguing-in-Publication Data
A CIP record is available from the British Library.

Contents

Preface

The chapters in this book, like those in the two previous volumes in this series, present informal portraits of some of the giants in the history of psychology. The individual chapters offer glimpses into the personal and the scholarly/professional lives of these pioneers. As in the previous volumes, most of the chapter authors are experts in the same fields as those of their pioneers, are students of the history of psychology, or both.

The references to *Pioneers I* and *Pioneers II* throughout this book are to Volumes 1 and 2 of *Portraits of Pioneers in Psychology* (Kimble, Wertheimer, & White, 1991; Kimble, Boneau, & Wertheimer, 1996). One difference between this volume and the others is that almost all of the chapters in the first two volumes were revisions of papers presented at psychological association conventions. That is true of only two chapters in the present volume—chapter 10, on Duncker and chapter 17, on Spence.

All three volumes will be of interest to psychologists generally and to scholars in related fields. The resourceful teacher could use a selection of chapters from these volumes as supplementary readings to enhance almost any course in the discipline, as well as courses in related disciplines, such as anthropology, biology, and sociology. The major purpose of *Portraits of Pioneers in Psychology*, however, is to provide source materials for students and their teachers in undergraduate and graduate courses in the history of psychology. The most obvious use is in history of psychology courses, but they could also be used to help make the pioneers in the various subfields of psychology come more vividly alive for students and teachers in other standard courses in the psychology curriculum.

As stated earlier, the references to *Pioneers I* and *Pioneers II* throughout this book are to Volumes I and II in the series. Listed next are some of the chapters that are available in the three volumes. They are organized in a way that matches the categories that are apt to correspond to widely offered courses and major topics in course syllabi. Chapters in *Pioneers I* are separated from those in *Pioneers II* by a single slanting line (/); those in *Pioneers II* are separated from those in *Pioneers III* by a double slanting line (//):

Schools and systems: Carr, Freud, Heidbreder, Hull, James, Jung, Köhler, Pavlov, Sullivan, Titchener, Tolman, Watson, Wertheimer/Dewey, Guthrie, Sechenov //Duncker, Hickok, Lewin, Piaget, Rogers, Skinner, Spence, Wundt

Biological (Physiological) Psychology: Galton, Hunter, Lashley, Pavlov, Tryon/Burks, Graham, Hebb, Schiller, Yerkes//Darwin, Festinger, Krech, Kuo, McGraw, Nissen

Animal Behavior: Hull, Hunter, Köhler, Lashley, Pavlov, Thorndike, Watson/Schiller, Yerkes//Darwin, Kuo, Nissen

Sensation and Perception: Köhler, Wertheimer/Fechner, Gibson, Graham, Hebb, Rhine//Duncker, Festinger, Piaget, Wundt

Conditioning and Learning: Calkins, Hull, Hunter, Köhler, Lashley, Pavlov, Thorndike, Tolman, Wertheimer/Blatz, Guthrie, Hebb, Sechenov//Duncker, Ebbinghaus, Krech, Skinner, Spence, Krech, Underwood

Cognitive Psychology: Calkins, Köhler, Lashley, Tolman, Wertheimer/Dewey, Stern//Duncker, Ebbinghaus, Hickok, Piaget, Underwood, Wundt

Motivation: Freud, Hull, James, Jung, Köhler, Sullivan, Tolman/Milgram, Schiller, Tomkins, Yerkes//Erickson, Festinger, Lewin, Spence

Developmental Psychology: Freud, Leta Hollingworth, Puffer, Watson/Blatz, Doll, Murchison, Witmer//Binet, McGraw, Piaget

Individual Differences and Psychometrics: Galton, Leta Hollingworth, Pavlov, Tryon/Burks, Doll, Milgram, Stern//Allport, Binet, Thurstone

Personality: Calkins, Freud, Jung/Tomkins//Erickson, Rogers, Thurstone

Women in Psychology and the Psychology of Women: Calkins, Heidbreder, Leta Hollingworth, Puffer/Burks, Dix//Allport, McGraw

Applied Psychology: Jastrow, Puffer, Watson/Dix, Gilbreth, Harry Hollingworth//Skinner, Thurstone

Abnormal Psychology (Psychopathology) and Clinical Applications: Freud, Leta Hollingworth, Jastrow, Jung, Sullivan/Dix, Doll, Tomkins, Witmer//Binet, Duncker, Erickson, Rogers

Social Psychology and Psychology in the Social Context: Puffer/Dix, Milgram, Murchison//Allport, Festinger, Krech, Lewin

This selection is somewhat arbitrary because scraps of materials in other than the listed chapters are relevant to these topics and the number of the topics might be more or fewer.

All of the books in this series owe their existence to the contributions of many people. We want to acknowledge the moral and financial support of the Division of General Psychology (Division 1) of the American Psychological Association, the sponsor of the series. The publishers, in the persons of Lawrence Erlbaum and Gary VandenBos, provided sound advice and great patience as the manuscripts developed. For this third volume, Nicole Bush, a Book Production Editor for Lawrence Erlbaum Associates, did a remarkably thorough job of overseeing the production of this manuscript. Hazel Carpenter at Duke managed the details involved in dealing with authors and preparing the manuscript for publication. Sue Kreger-Edgerton and Troy Regan, also at Duke, handled all of the computer problems. Vivian Schneider helped construct the index.

Gregory A. Kimble
Michael Wertheimer

REFERENCES

Kimble, G. A., Wertheimer, M., & White, C. L. (1991). *Portraits of pioneers in psychology: Volume I.* Washington, DC: APA; Mahwah, NJ: Lawrence Erlbaum Associates.

Kimble, G. A., Boneau, C. A., & Wertheimer, M. (1996). *Portraits of pioneers in psychology: Volume II.* Washington, DC: APA; Mahwah, NJ: Lawrence Erlbaum Associates.

Portraits of the Authors and Editors

John K. Bare, who wrote the chapter on Laurens Perseus Hickok, received his undergraduate education at Oberlin College. He studied for the Ph.D. degree at Brown University, where he learned from Walter S. Hunter, Carl Pfaffmann, Joseph McVicker Hunt, Clarence Graham, Lorrin A. Riggs, Donald B. Lindsley, Harold Schlosberg, and Gregory A. Kimble. After his Ph.D. he taught for 9 years at the College of William and Mary in Williamsburg, Virginia. He then moved to Carleton College in Northfield, Minnesota, where he stayed for 25 years, until his retirement in 1983. He is currently Emeritus Professor of Psychology at Carleton. In writing a history of the psychology department at Carleton, Bare discovered that Hickok's *Empirical Psychology* was the first text to be used there. His intrigue with the title, the author, and the early date of that publication led him to write this chapter.

Victor W. Bergenn, co-author of the chapter on Myrtle McGraw, was born in New York City and attended Columbia University. He received his M.A. and Ed.D. degrees at Teachers College. He worked at the New York State Psychiatric Institute on Biometrics Research and then taught at Briarcliff College, where he was a colleague of Myrtle McGraw. He then became executive director of the Council on Educational Psychology in 1972. McGraw served as the first president of the Council from 1972 to 1988. The Council is actively engaged in the reform of educational testing policies affecting students in the greater New York metropolitan area. Bergenn is a co-author of several articles on McGraw's life and work and co-editor of a book of her collected essays, *Beyond Heredity and Environment: Myrtle McGraw and the Maturation Controversy*.

Daniel W. Bjork, author of the chapter on Burrhus Frederick Skinner, received his B. Ed. and M.A. degrees from the University of Toledo and a Ph.D. degree in American intellectual history from the University of Oklahoma, where he developed an interest in the history of psychology. He has published four books, three of which combine intellectual history and the history of psychology: *The Compromised Scientist: William James in the Development of American Psychology* (1983); *William James: The Center of His Vision* (1988, reprinted by APA Books, 1997); and the first major biography of Skinner, *B.F. Skinner: A Life* (1993, reprinted by APA Books, 1997). He has taught at the University of Alabama, Birmingham; the University of Oklahoma; and the Mercy College of Detroit. Since 1991 he has been Chair of the Department of History at St. Mary's University in San Antonio, Texas. There he lives with his wife Rhonda and two children.

Arthur L. Blumenthal, who wrote the chapter on Wilhelm Wundt, was born in Wyoming and grew up and was educated in several western states. He received his Ph.D. degree from the University of Washington and did postdoctoral work at Harvard and MIT, specializing in the history of psycholinguistics. His research on that topic culminated in the publication of a book, *Language and Psychology: Historical Aspects of Psycholinguistics*. That book was followed by a historically oriented text on cognitive psychology, *The Process of Cognition*. Most of Blumenthal's more recent historical research has focused on Wilhelm Wundt, whom he has struggled to rescue from the distortions and mistranslations that have confused Wundt's work with Titchener's structuralism and have left his voluntaristic psychology unknown. Blumenthal has taught at Harvard University and the University of Massachusetts. He now lectures at The New School in New York. Blumenthal is a Fellow of the American Psychological Association and the American Psychological Society.

C. Alan Boneau, author of the chapter on Hermann Ebbinghaus, received his doctorate with Gregory A. Kimble at Duke University in 1957. Subsequently he was on the faculty at Duke for 9 years. During that time he published articles on the effects (trivial) of violating the assumptions underlying tests of statistical significance (e.g., the t-test). He also explored the applicability of the theory of signal detectability to the behavior of pigeons in a discrimination-learning situation. Following a sabbatical leave at Stanford University, Boneau accepted a position with the American Psychological Association (APA) in Washington, DC, where he was Acting Executive Officer for a time. Currently, he is on the faculty at George Mason University in Fairfax, Virginia, one of the Washington suburbs. Boneau considers himself a generalist. He has served as President of APA's Division of General Psychology and as Editor of the Division's Newsletter, *The GENERAL Psychologist*.

Jack W. Brehm, author of the chapter on Leon Festinger, obtained his Ph.D. degree in psychology at the University of Minnesota under Festinger's direction. His dissertation research was one of the early experiments designed to test the theory of cognitive dissonance. Subsequently, first at Yale University and then at Duke, he worked with Arthur R. Cohen on a number of experimental tests of dissonance theory and, together, they wrote a book entitled *Explorations in Cognitive Dissonance*. Within a few years, this edition was followed by an updated version, *Perspectives on Cognitive Dissonance*, co-authored with Robert A. Wicklund. After a few more years of work on dissonance, Brehm turned his attention to the question of how people respond to threats to freedom and published a research monograph entitled *A Theory of Cognitive Reactance*. Eventually this monograph was updated and published as *Psychological Reactance: A Theory of Freedom and Control*, co-authored with Sharon S. Brehm. After moving to the University of Kansas, Brehm initiated a program of research about the motivational and other psychological effects of the difficulty of instrumental behavior. More recently he proposed a theory about the intensity of emotion.

Michaella Cox, co-author of the chapter on Karl Duncker, became interested in the history of psychology while she was a student in Brett King's undergraduate course on that topic. She received her B.A. in psychology from the University of Colorado at Boulder in 1991 and her M.B.A. from the University of Phoenix in 1996. Throughout her academic career, Ms. Cox has been a member of numerous honor societies and a participant in several research projects including projects on Karl Duncker and the Fragile-X Syndrome. Currently, Ms. Cox and her husband Greg live in the Denver area, where she pursues her career as a New Business Development Manager/Marketing Specialist.

Thomas C. Dalton, co-author of the chapter on Myrtle McGraw, is a Senior Research Associate and Lecturer, College of Liberal Arts, California Polytechnic State University, San Luis Obispo. Born in Ann Arbor, Michigan, he grew up in Toledo, Ohio and attended Ohio University. He holds a Ph.D. from the University of Massachusetts. He worked in the Governor's Office of the State of Washington from 1976 to 1978 before becoming Director of Research and Lecturer in the Institute of Public Service at Seattle University from 1978 to 1982. He is the author of three books, including co-editor of *Beyond Heredity and Environment: Myrtle McGraw and the Maturation Controversy*. He is completing an intellectual biography of John Dewey. He has written extensively on the history of psychology, which has included documenting John Dewey's collaboration with Myrtle McGraw and the history of Division 7 of the APA. Dalton was a consultant from 1994 to 1995 to the Public Broadcasting System program, *Scientific American Frontiers*, which featured the research of McGraw and her successors.

Donald A. Dewsbury, author of the chapter on Henry W. Nissen, is a Professor of Psychology at the University of Florida. Born in Brooklyn, New York, he grew up on Long Island and attended Bucknell University. His Ph.D. is from the University of Michigan; it was followed by postdoctoral work with Frank Beach at the University of California, Berkeley. Through much of his career, Dewsbury has worked as a comparative psychologist with an emphasis on social and reproductive behavior. In recent years, his work has shifted so that his primary focus is on the history of psychology, with work in comparative psychology remaining a secondary interest. He is the author or editor of nine books, including *Comparative Animal Behavior* and *Comparative Psychology in the Twentieth Century*. He is editing a series of volumes on the histories of the divisions of the American Psychological Association, *Unification Through Division*. He has also published over 280 articles and chapters, including the chapters on Paul H. Schiller and Robert M. Yerkes in *Portraits of Pioneers in Psychology: Volume II*. His interest in Henry Nissen has emerged from a current project, a history of the Yerkes Laboratories of Primate Biology as they existed in Orange Park, Florida, from 1930 to 1965.

Raymond E. Fancher, author of the chapter on Alfred Binet, is Professor of Psychology at York University in suburban Toronto. In the early 1980s, he was a founding faculty member of York's unique graduate program in History/Theory of Psychology, which allows psychology students to write M.A. theses and Ph.D.

dissertations on historical topics. He served from 1990 to 1996 as Executive Officer of CHEIRON (The International Society for the History of Behavioral and Social Sciences) and was President for 1996–1997 of the APA's Division 26 (History of Psychology). The third edition of his book, *Pioneers of Psychology*, appeared in 1996; he is also author of *Psychoanalytic Psychology: The Development of Freud's Thought*, and *The Intelligence Men: Makers of the IQ Controversy.* Current projects include a new, full-length biography of Francis Galton.

Joel S. Freund, author of the chapter on Benton T. Underwood, entered Northwestern University as a chemistry major and premedical student in September 1962. In the fall term of 1964, however, he enrolled in Underwood's Experimental Psychology course and that changed his life forever. Underwood typically invited some students from his course to work as research assistants and Freund was offered and accepted such a position. When not sitting behind a memory drum collecting data, these undergraduate assistants checked data and performed other routine tasks, often in Underwood's research office, which was the hub of Ben's research activities. In that setting, Freund spent 2 years listening to such Ph.D. candidates as Bruce Ekstrand, Gordon Wood, and Bill Wallace discussing theoretical issues in psychology. When Freund returned to school for his senior year, Underwood told him that Bruce Ekstrand, his current research assistant, would be graduating and that if he wanted to go to graduate school in psychology he could have that position. Because he had applied to several medical schools, Freund declined, but that brought on a postdecision dissonance: He spent the remainder of the term trying to decide what to do with his life. Finally, after having been accepted at two medical schools, he went to Underwood and asked if his offer was still open. Ben said, "I've started negotiations with someone, but they are not so far along they cannot be stopped." When Freund completed his Ph.D. in 1970, he was hired at the University of Arkansas, the home of the Razorbacks, where he has been a faculty member ever since.

Elizabeth Gilman, who co-authored the chapter on Jean Piaget, is an Associate Research Scientist in the Department of Psychology at Yale University and a fellow of the Bush Center on Child Development and Social Policy. As an undergraduate psychology and philosophy major, she served as a VISTA volunteer, working with teens involved in the Juvenile Court in Michigan. She received her M.A. in psychology from the University of Chicago, completing her thesis on the topic of motherhood motivation and self-esteem. Subsequently, she practiced as a social worker with a focus on child abuse in families and on adolescent behavioral problems. Testifying on behalf of her young clients in court led Ms. Gilman to pursue a law degree, which she completed at the University of Connecticut. After practicing law for several years, she returned to an academic environment in an effort to utilize her dual background in addressing social policy questions affecting children. In her present role at Yale, she coordinates research, drafts speeches and testimony, and serves as instructor in the child development and policy seminar led by Professor Zigler. She writes frequently on policy-oriented topics including child care, violence, child abuse, mental health, and early childhood intervention programs.

Gilbert Gottlieb, who wrote the chapter on Zing Yang Kuo, is a Research Professor of Psychology at the University of North Carolina, Chapel Hill. His research is aimed at achieving a synthesis of thinking between the fields of developmental biology and developmental psychology. In particular, he is interested in demonstrating the influence of prenatal experience on postnatal behavior—a topic that Kuo also considered to be of the highest importance. Gottlieb received his Ph.D. degree from Duke University. He has been President of the International Society for Developmental Psychobiology, a guest of the Czechoslovak and USSR Academies of Sciences, an Advisor to the German National Science Foundation, and U.S. delegate to the International Ethological Congress Committee. He has held invited academic appointments at the University of Minnesota, the University of Colorado, the University of Bielefeld (Germany), and the Neurosciences Institute, San Diego. His most recent book is *Synthesizing Nature–Nurture*, published by Lawrence Erlbaum Associates in 1997.

Nancy K. Innis, author of the chapter on David Krech, was born in Toronto and grew up in Petersborough, Ontario. She received her A.B. and M.A. degrees from the University of Toronto and her Ph.D. from Duke University. Her dissertation, supervised by John Staddon, described research on timing behavior in pigeons. Returning to Canada, Innis worked briefly at the Addiction Research Foundation in Toronto before she moved to Dalhousie University in Halifax, Nova Scotia for postdoctoral research in Werner Honig's laboratory. Following her postdoctoral appointment, she remained at Dalhousie for a year as a visiting faculty member. Innis then accepted a position in the psychology department at the University of Western Ontario, where she continues as a faculty member teaching motivation, animal learning, and the history of psychology. Her interests in animal learning and the history of psychology came together during a sabbatical leave when she began a biography of Edward C. Tolman. To increase her expertise in history, she spent a leave with the history of science group in the history department at Duke University and, at the same time, reestablished her ties to John Staddon's laboratory. She currently holds a joint appointment as a visiting scholar in the psychology department at Duke. Innis has been active in the International Society for Comparative Psychology and has just completed a 6-year term as Associate Editor of the *International Journal of Comparative Psychology*. She has been publishing articles on the activities and ideas of Tolman and his colleagues, including David Krech, as her work on the biography of Tolman continues.

Blair T. Johnson, co-author of the chapter on Floyd H. Allport, is Associate Professor of Psychology at Syracuse University, where he directs its Social Psychology graduate program. Johnson completed his baccalaureate degree at Moorhead State University in 1983, with majors in psychology and philosophy. For his graduate work he journeyed to Purdue University, taking a master's degree in 1985 and a Ph.D. degree in 1988 under the direction of Alice H. Eagly. Johnson's work focuses on attitude and stereotype change as well as on the application and science of research synthesis. He has served on the editorial boards of the *Journal of Personality and Social Psychology* and *Personality and Social Psychology Bulletin*. Interested in the history of psychology since he took an undergraduate course on the subject with Phillip L. Rice, Johnson learned about Allport and Katz during his graduate work on attitudes. Johnson became acutely interested in the history of social psychology when he became the director of a program on social psychology, the same program that Allport started in 1924 and that graduated Katz as its first Ph.D. in 1928. It was because of Katz's close involvement with Allport that Johnson approached Katz about writing the current chapter. Johnson continues an active scholarly involvement in matters surrounding the history of the social sciences.

Lyle V. Jones, who wrote the chapter on L. L. Thurstone, is Research Professor of Psychology at the University of North Carolina, Chapel Hill, where he has also served as Director of the L. L. Thurstone Psychometric Laboratory and as Vice Chancellor and Dean of the Graduate School. Born in Grandview, Washington, Jones grew up in Seattle, attended Reed College, and, after 3 years in the Army Air Corps, received B.S. and M.S. degrees from the University of Washington and a Ph.D. degree in psychology and statistics from Stanford University. He was an NRC Postdoctoral Fellow and then a faculty member at the University of Chicago. He has been President of the Association of Graduate Schools, the Psychometric Society, and the APA Division of Evaluation and Measurement. A member of the Institute of Medicine and a Fellow of the American Academy of Arts and Sciences, he twice was a Fellow at the Center for Advanced Study in the Behavioral Sciences at Stanford. He is author of 16 books and monographs and has published more than 100 articles and book chapters. Among his recent publications are several that focus on historical trends in U.S. school achievement, with special emphasis on the trends for minority students.

Daniel Katz, senior author of the chapter on Floyd H. Allport, is Professor Emeritus of Psychology at the University of Michigan and Research Scientist Emeritus at the Michigan Institute for Social Research. After receiving his A.B. degree from the University of Buffalo in 1925, Katz became Syracuse University's first Ph.D. in social psychology, completing his dissertation in 1928 under Allport's direction. Katz then taught at Princeton University (1928–1943) and Brooklyn College (1943–1947), where he served as the chair of the psychology department. During World War II, Katz was the Director of the Office of War Information's Survey Division and a Senior Analyst for the War Department. In 1947, he moved to the University of Michigan as a program director of its Institute for Social Research with a joint appointment as professor of psychology. As a Fulbright Scholar in Norway in 1951–1952, Katz helped organize a program of cross-cultural studies. He conducted further research abroad at the University of Oslo, as a fellow of the National Science Foundation for research on nationalism in Greece and Yugoslavia, and at the Institute of Political Science of the University of Aarhus, Denmark. He served as editor of the *Journal of Abnormal and Social Psychology* and its continuation as the *Journal of Personality and Social Psychology*. He also served on the editorial boards of *Public Opinion Quarterly, Journal of Conflict Resolution, Journal of Social Issues, Personnel Journal,* and *Journal of Cross-Cultural Psychology*. Katz's numerous awards include the Distinguished Senior Scientist Award from the Society of Experimental Social Psychology (1979), the Gold Medal Award from the American Psychological Foundation (1977), and recognition as Fellow of the American Academy of Arts and Sciences.

Gregory A. Kimble, editor and author of the chapter on Kenneth W. Spence, was born in Iowa and grew up in Minnesota. His A.B., M.A. and Ph.D. degrees were from Carleton College, Northwestern University, and the University of Iowa, respectively. At Iowa, Spence was his major professor. Kimble's major academic appointments have been at Brown University, Yale University, Duke University, the University of Colorado, and Duke University, again. He is currently Professor Emeritus of Psychology at Duke. Kimble served as Director of Undergraduate Studies and Director of Graduate Studies at Duke, and as Chair of the Department at Duke and Colorado. He has been President of the APA divisions of General Psychology and Experimental Psychology. Kimble was the last editor of the now-discontinued APA journal, *Psychological Monographs*, and the first editor of *Journal of Experimental Psychology: General*. His books include *Principles of General Psychology*, which appeared in six editions (all but one with Norman Garmezy and Edward Zigler as co-authors) and *Portraits of Pioneers in Psychology: Volumes I and II*, with C. Alan Boneau, Charlotte White, and Michael Wertheimer as co-editors.

D. Brett King, author of the chapter on Karl Duncker, obtained his Ph.D. in cognitive psychology from Colorado State University. He has been a faculty member in the Department of Psychology at the University of Colorado at Boulder since 1990. Among the courses he has taught are history of psychology, social psychology, cognitive psychology, personality, and introductory psychology. King has been the author or co-author of many articles and conference presentations in the history of psychology, and co-authored with Wayne Viney the second edition of *A History of Psychology: Ideas and Context*. King and Michael Wertheimer are preparing a book-length biography of the Gestalt psychologist Max Wertheimer, and the two recently co-taught a graduate seminar on Gestalt theory and Max Wertheimer. King is currently co-archivist with Cheri King for the Rocky Mountain Psychological Association.

Martin Lakin, author of the chapter on Carl Rogers, was born in Chicago, where he received his early education. After serving in the armed forces in World War II, he studied in Israel (then Palestine) and received his undergraduate education at the Hebrew University. Following his Ph.D. at the University of Chicago, Lakin did postdoctoral work at the University of Illinois Medical School. Subsequently, he joined the faculty of the Department of Psychiatry at the Northwestern University Medical School and served as the Assistant Chief (Psychology Section) of the VA Research Hospital in Chicago. In 1958, Lakin took a joint appointment in the

Departments of Psychiatry and Psychology at Duke University. He remained at Duke, where he is now Professor Emeritus of Psychology. Lakin has been particularly active in the training of clinicians for therapeutic interventions and in group dynamics. These converging interests are reflected in his book, *The Helping Group*. Lakin's other publications deal with the purposes and effects of human relations training experiences and the ethical issues that therapeutic processes involve. In the former category are a book and a monograph: *Interpersonal Encounters*, and *Arab and Jew in Israel: Case Study in Human Relations*. The latter are represented by numerous articles and two books that consider ethical dilemmas that may emerge in the course of psychotherapeutic relationships.

Miriam A. Lewin, who wrote the chapter about her father, Kurt Lewin, was born in Germany but emigrated with her family to the United States while she was still an infant. She received her A.B. degree from Swarthmore and her Ph.D. from Harvard—actually Radcliffe because, in 1957, Harvard was still refusing to grant degrees to women although the curriculum was the same for members of both sexes. Lewin has taught at several different colleges but her most important appointment has been at Manhattanville College, where she currently is Professor of Psychology. Lewin is the author of two books, *Understanding Psychological Research* and *In the Shadow of the Past: Psychology Portrays the Sexes*. In 1992, she was co-editor and a contributor to an issue of the *Journal of Social Issues*, which carried the special title, "The Heritage of Kurt Lewin: Theory, Research, and Practice." She has raised three children and has five grandchildren. In recent years she has given the keynote address at the dedication of the Kurt Lewin Institute in Amsterdam and spoke on Kurt Lewin at Tübingen University in Germany.

R. Bruce Masterton, who wrote the chapter on Charles Darwin, was born in Chicago, Illinois. He obtained an M.A. degree in mathematics and education at the University of Chicago. After a brief career as a mathematics instructor, he went to graduate school at Duke University and received the Ph.D. in Biopsychology in 1963. Masterton taught at Vanderbilt University for 3 years and then joined the faculty of The Florida State University, where he remained until his untimely death on December 7, 1996. Bruce Masterton held offices in several professional organizations; was a Fellow of the American Psychological Association, the American Psychological Society, and the American Association for the Advancement of Science; and was a member of the Cajal Club in the American Association of Anatomists. He was the author of more that 80 publications, which were widely recognized for the brilliance of their prose as well as the importance of their contributions. The following excerpt from an evaluation ("pink sheet") of one of Masterton's grant applications to NIH catches the sense of the esteem in which he was held: "It was indeed a pleasure to read this application. Dr. Masterton in probably the pre-eminent evolutionary neuroscientists in this country.... His... assessments of current trends in functional neuroscience....are impressive in their elegance, impressive in their quality, and impressive in their insightfulness." Those attributes also characterize his contribution to this volume [Eds.].

Diana R. Nichols, co-author of the chapter on Floyd H. Allport, is a graduate student at Syracuse University, studying social psychology under the direction of Blair T. Johnson. Prior to beginning her graduate work at Syracuse, Nichols knew of Allport only as Gordon's older brother. After she began her graduate studies with Johnson, he directed her interest toward Floyd Allport's life and career, and she and Johnson are collaborating on further studies regarding the history of social psychology. Nichols earned her undergraduate degree in psychology from Houghton College in 1996, where she completed an honors thesis examining whether people make self-reference judgments faster than other types of judgments. Her current research interests continue to involve the nature of the self as well as factors in attitude structure and change.

Harold Schiffman, author of the chapter on Milton Erickson, began his career as an electrical engineer working on feedback mechanisms. He completed his graduate work at Princeton University, earning a Ph.D. in Psychology. While at Princeton, he worked with Harold Gulliksen. After graduating, he worked with Silvan Tompkins on affect dynamics at the Philadelphia Psychiatric Hospital. He then accepted a position at the Educational Testing Service, working with Sam Messick on the development of a multidimensional scaling of the dimensions of personality. In 1962, he accepted an appointment at Duke University, where he remains today on the faculty as a Professor Emeritus. He remains active and continues to teach courses in statistics, the history of psychology, and introductory psychology. He is the author of numerous publications on the attribution of cause as a function of affect, early childhood memories, mathematical formulations of various memory processes, and other diverse topics. He first became interested in Milton Erickson while supervising and training clinical graduate students in the 1960s. Presently, he has been attempting a formulation of a concept of a working awareness as it relates to hypnotically altered states.

Michael Wertheimer, co-editor of this book (and of the previous two volumes in this series) and third author of the chapter on Karl Duncker, is Professor Emeritus of Psychology at the University of Colorado, Boulder. Born in Germany, he came to the United States as a youngster. He obtained his B.A. from Swarthmore College, his M.A. from The Johns Hopkins University, and his Ph.D. from Harvard University. After teaching at Wesleyan University for 3 years, he joined the Colorado faculty in 1955 and has been in the psychology department there ever since. He is a former President of Psi Chi, the national honor society in psychology, and several divisions of the American Psychological Association (general psychology, teaching of psychology, theoretical and philosophical psychology, and history of psychology). For almost four decades, he directed the departmental honors program in psychology at the University of Colorado, Boulder. His publications range from experimental and social psychology through psycholinguistics and philosophical psychology to general psychology and the history of psychology. Among his recent books, in addition to the first two volumes in the *Portraits of Pioneers in Psychology* series, are *A Brief History of Psychology, History of Psychology: A Guide to*

Information Sources, and *No Small Part: Histories of Regional Organizations in American Psychology.*

Edward Zigler, co-author of the chapter on Jean Piaget, is Sterling Professor of Psychology and Director of the Bush Center on Child Development and Social Policy at Yale University. He also serves as head of the Psychology Section at Yale Child Study Center. Professor Zigler was a member of the National Planning and Steering Committee of both Project Head Start and Project Follow Through. In 1970, he was named by President Nixon as the first Director of the Office of U.S. Children's Bureau. After leaving government, he served on the President's Committee on Mental Retardation and, at President Ford's request, served as chair of the Vietnamese Children's Resettlement Advisory Group. In 1980 President Carter called on him to head the 15th Anniversary Head Start Committee—a body charged with charting the future course of Head Start. Professor Zigler's scholarly work cuts across several fields, including mental retardation, child abuse, intervention programs for economically disadvantaged children, the effects of out-of-home child care, and the formulation of child and family policy. He is the author or editor of 25 books and has received numerous honors and awards.

Chapter 1

Laurens Perseus Hickok: Philosopher, Theologian, and Psychologist

John K. Bare

In his history of psychology, Robert I. Watson (1963) began his chapter on William James as follows: "In the United States before the 1880's there were two major psychological traditions—phrenology and Scottish psychology.... Scottish psychology had been the heir to the associationistic tradition...[and] it was used as a defense of revealed religion" (p. 317). Hunt (1993) echoed Watson: "The only forms of psychology then taught [in 1875] in the United States were phrenology and Scottish mental philosophy, an offshoot of associationism used chiefly as a defense of religion" (p. 150).

Laurens Perseus Hickok, (1854), author of the college text *Empirical Psychology*, might have accused both Watson and Hunt of committing an error of omission, and other historians of psychology would agree. Evans (1983) described Hickok as "perhaps the most widely read early American textbook writer of the German Idealist tradition" (p. 47); Harms (1972) referred to him as "America's first major psychologist" (p. 120); and Viney, Wertheimer, and Wertheimer (1979) described the second edition of Hickok's Empirical Psychology as "a typical pre-Jamesian U.S. psychology text" (p. 88).

EVALUATIONS OF LEARNING PERSEUS HICKOK IN HIS OWN TIME

The May 8, 1888 edition of *The New York Times* carried an obituary of Hickok, which is quoted here in part:

Laurens Perseus Hickok, formerly President of Union College, and widely known throughout the world as a metaphysician of profound learning, died in Amherst, Mass., on Sunday, in the ninetieth year of his age. Dr. Hickok was born in Bethel, Conn., Dec. 29, 1798, was graduated from Union College in 1820, and was licensed as a preacher two years later. He served as Pastor in Newton, Kent, and Litchfield, Conn., until 1836, when he was elected Professor of Theology in the Western Reserve College, Ohio, a position which he held until 1844, when he became Professor of the same branch of the Auburn Theological Seminary. In 1858 he was elected Professor of Mental and Moral Science, and vice-president of Union College, Schenectady. He assisted Dr. Nott in the government of the college for eight years, had sole charge during the succeeding eight years, and was made President March 1, 1866, a post which he resigned in 1868, when he removed to Amherst, retiring from public life at the advanced age of 70. (p. 2, column 4)

At its Founders Day celebration at Union College on March 20, 1947, Herbert W. Schneider (Larrabee, Schneider, & Bixler, 1947), Professor of Philosophy at Columbia University, an editor of the *Journal of Philosophy*, and author of *A History of American Philosophy*, said:

Laurens Perseus Hickok expounded by far the most elaborate, extravagant, and ambitious system of philosophy ever conceived by an American philosopher. He believed confidently that he had combined into a single, coherent body of self-evident truth, over and above empirical sciences of which he was also a master, the essential truths of the Bible, Plato, Kant, Hegel and Herbert Spencer. Those of us who today try to swim the deep waters of his system soon come to the conclusion that Hickok's own mind had been drowned in the boundless ocean of pure reason. But Hickok himself had no such fears; he could move in ever larger circles, never coming up for air, and always landing with a sure foot on the further shore of eternity, as though he had steered straight for it all the time. (p. 11)

He...lived in an environment in which it was fashionable to profess faith in revelation, in reason, and in righteousness...and to [try] to unite [them] into a single system, not in the spirit of compromise or toleration but as a rational system.... Faith in reason meant something more technical in Hickok's day than in ours; it meant that there must be an adequate reason for everything, not merely in the sense that every event must have a cause, but in the sense that every cause must have a reason. Pure science was conceived to be the knowledge of necessary relations, and to be rational meant more than to have a reasonable acquaintance with causes and their effects; it meant to know the principle or law in virtue of which each fact was not mere fact, but an instance of universal rule. (pp. 12–13)

TWO PSYCHOLOGIES

Given this description of Hickok's approach to knowledge, it is not surprising to find that, prior to his *Empirical Psychology*, Hickok (1849/1973) had authored *Rational Psychology*. The differences between the two books reflect a distinction first made by Christian Wolff (1679–1754). Wolff, perhaps adopting the claim by Leibniz (1646–1716) that the forms of knowledge are innate and the contents acquired by experience, defined *empirical psychology* as "the science of what experience tells us about the soul" and rational psychology as "all that is possible to the human soul[,]...a branch of metaphysics...that provides necessarily true statements regarding the essence and the nature of the soul" (Leary, 1982, p. 19).

In his *Critique of Pure Reason*, Immanuel Kant (1781/1934), employed the rational-empirical distinction to cover knowledge in general, proposing that "knowledge is made of what we receive through impressions and of what our own faculty for knowing...supplies from itself" (p. 25). What the faculty for knowing supplies itself "is entitled a priori, and is distinguished from the empirical, which has its sources a posteriori, that is, from experience" (pp. 24–25). Kant also concluded that a rational psychology is not possible, because knowledge of the nature of the soul is "beyond the power of human reason"; and that even empirical psychology "could never be a natural science proper...based on a priori principles because it could never employ mathematics, which provides the rational relation-ships between empirical data"; and finally that psychology could not even be a good empirical discipline because it could not control its phenomena (Leary, 1978, p. 115).

Hickok sided with Wolff and, in the introduction to his *Rational Psychology* (1849/1973), compared the empirical and the rational psychology in these terms:

> Psychology is the Science of Mind. *Empirical Psychology* attains the facts of mind and arranges them in a system. The elements are solely the facts given in experience, and the criterion of their reality is the clear testimony of consciousness. *Rational* psychology is a very different process for attaining to a Science of Mind.... In this science, we pass from the facts of experience wholly out beyond it, and seek for the *rationale* of experience itself in the necessary and universal principles which must be conditional for all facts of a possible experience. We seek to determine how it is possible for an experience to be, from those a priori conditions which render all the functions of an intellectual agency themselves intelligible. In the conclusions of this science it becomes competent for us to affirm, not as from mere experience. . . that this *is*—but from those necessary and universal principles, that this *must* be. The intellect is itself investigated and known through the a priori principles which must necessarily control all its agency. (pp. 17–18)

As an illustration of what such a science of mind might be, Hickok chose astronomy and, apparently with Copernicus, Galileo, and Newton in mind, said:

> Astronomy has its sublime and astonishing facts, gathered through a long period of patient and careful observation. Experience has been competent to attain the appear-ances and movements of the heavenly bodies, the satellites of some of the planets and their relation to their primaries.... The general relationships of different portions of our solar system have in this way been found; the sun put in its place at the center, the planets put in their places in their orbits around it, with the direction, distance and time of periodical revolution accurately determined. A complete diagram of the solar system thus may be made from the results of experience alone, and all that belongs to *formal* Astronomy be finished. In this process, through experience, we are compe-tent to affirm, *so the solar system is*. But if now on the other hand beyond experience,

we may somehow attain to the conceptions of an invisible force, operating through the system directly as a quantity of matter and inversely as the distance, we shall be competent to take this [conception] as an a priori principle, determining experience itself, and quite independently of all observation may affirm, *so the solar system must be.* (p. 19)

By analogy, empirical psychology consists of the facts of mind; rational psychology consists of the insights into principles that make those facts inevitable.

HICKOK'S RATIONAL PSYCHOLOGY

Although Hickok adopted Wolff's general position, he was obviously aware of Kant's assertion that both rational and empirical psychology are impossible. In response to that criticism, Hickok (1849/1973) posed three controversial philosophical questions, examined some of the answers given in the past, and indicated how *common consciousness* judges rational psychology to be justified.

1. If "the objects given in sense are out of, and in some cases, at a distance from the knowing agent[,]…how may the intellect know that which is out of, and at a distance, from itself?" Hickok replied that, if it is agreed that there must be some *representation* of the object, then knowledge of the outer world is mediate. Given that knowledge is mediate, with confirmation by "the universal decision of consciousness…we immediately know the outer material world in the perceptions of sensations to be the truth" (p. 43).

2. If we can be convinced that we gain knowledge of the world through perception, how do we put the perceived qualities together to form a thing in itself? How do we "put several qualities not merely into one group in the same place but into one substance existing in the same thing?" (p. 46). How do we come to think of "events not merely as successive in time but as originating in one cause at the same source? [H]ow come we by the notions of substances and causes, and especially how come we by their perpetual order of connection?" (p. 46). Hickok suggested that, if one can find the a priori principles—principles that are givens or intuitively obvious—of the operation of understanding and of the processes of the intellect in its thinking in judgments, then we may "demonstrate also the validity of their being" (pp. 56–57) as objects for the understanding.

3. Is there anything beyond nature that can be known? Is it possible to know whether there is a soul; whether there is a God? Hickok concluded that rational psychology provides the only method for reaching "a final stand on this last and highest point where science and skepticism may grapple in conflict" (p. 84). It does so by attaining "the…laws of the faculty of reason, and by knowing reason in its law, may thus lay the foundation for demonstrating the valid being of the Soul in its liberty, and God in His absolute personality" (p. 85).

HICKOK'S EMPIRICAL PSYCHOLOGY

The introduction to *Empirical Psychology* (Hickok, 1854) began with a description of "the difficulties and tendencies to error in the study of mind" and a demonstration of how each is to be overcome. The first difficulty is the one that Titchener (chap. 7, *Pioneers I*), later on would call the *stimulus error* in psychology: The mind "from its conscious apprehension...turn[s] its attention outwardly to the phenomena of nature [but, to deal with this difficulty] the facts we now need...[require that] the mind...make its own phenomena its study and turn the attention inward upon its own action" (pp. 15–16).

The second difficulty arises from the ambiguity of language: "The common language of mankind is...only an expression of what they find in their daily experience (p. 18). But in mental science [a word] cannot be [a] reference to sensible objects but must carry its meaning over to another mind by inducing the conception of the same mental fact in his own consciousness" (p. 19).

The third difficulty comes from "inadequate conceptions of mental being and [phylogenetic] development," (p. 21) arising primarily from mechanical and vegetable models. Hickok proposed a view of such development that came from Aristotle. Plants "spontaneously work out [their] organic development" (p. 22). Animals have:

> super-added forces of appetitive craving, an instinctive selection of [their] particular food, with the faculty of locomotion to bring [themselves] to it, and the capacity for mastication, digestion, assimilation and incorporation into [their] own substance and thus a growth in the whole system of the body and [their] members. (p. 22)

Human beings, with their:

> faculty of judging from sensible experience and thus acting from the dictates of prudence, [with] the distinctive and far more elevated endowment in *kind* of rational faculty, in its artistic, philosophic, ethic and religious capacities, [thereby have] the prerogatives of action in liberty and moral responsibility, ... lifting [them] from the bondage of all necessitated things into the sphere of personality. (p. 22)

In his introduction to Kant's *Anthropology From a Pragmatic Point of View* (1797/1974), the translator recognized that this volume "is generally referred to as Kant's work in empirical psychology" (p. ix). Perhaps to show some agreement with Kant, Hickok included in his introduction a chapter on anthropology, subtitled "The Connections of Mind and Body," which was a condensed version of Kant's position. It described three influences that have determined the makeup of the human mind: (a) *external nature*, which has produced "three races from the descendants of Noah"; (b) *constitutional organization*, which has produced "radical and abiding differences between male and female intellect" (p. 45) as well as the different temperaments (sanguine, melancholic, and choleric); and (c) *bodily weakness.* The chapter presented Hickok's only treatment of both the relationship between physiology and behavior and the effects of environmental variables on behavior.

In common with many more recent introductory textbooks, Hickok covered methods in chapter I of his text, imploring the student to be attentive of single facts, "to compare facts with one another and find their true relations" (p. 63), and to analyze complex facts carefully. When facts are disputed, they are to be settled by "the common consciousness of mankind or COMMON SENSE" (p. 67).

The central role of common sense in determining the truth has a history, as Windelband (1901) reminded us. The Stoics taught "that the surest truth is to be sought in those ideas which develop uniformly in all men with natural necessity." They took "as their starting point the *communes notiones*," having "a predilection for appealing to the consent of all men" (p. 204). St. Augustine, using doubt as a vehicle, established to his own satisfaction that there is "immediate certainty of inner experience" (p. 277). Leibniz argued that philosophy must search out that which is *immediately and intuitively certain* [italics added]. Aristotle concluded that there are two kinds of intuitive knowledge: "universal truths self-evident to reason and facts of experience, " (p. 398) the first being a priori and the second a posteriori.

Chapter II describes the "General Facts of Mind." Mind "permanently is, in its unchanged identity.... It does not appear and disappear as do the phenomena presented to it.... It retains it self-sameness through all change" (p. 75). That is, "it perdures through time," is "essentially self-active" (p. 77), and "discriminates itself from its objects" (p. 79).

Chapter III identifies "The Primitive Facts of Mind," which "must precede all conscious activity,...[for without them] no awakening in self-consciousness would be possible" (p. 82). The primitive facts are sensation, consciousness, and the mental states, which provide for our capacities of knowing (the intellect), feeling (susceptibility), and willing, each of which was treated in one of three of the four major divisions of the text. A fourth division was entitled "Mind Competent to Attain Its End." Given Hickok's Christian orientation, the major goal of this section was obviously religious.

THE INTELLECT

The Intellect is "the entire capacity for knowing" and has three functions or faculties: "The Sense, The Understanding, and The Reason" (pp. 111–112).

The Sense

The Sense is more than mere receptivity, because it also includes the intellectual processes of observation and attention. It is "the faculty for attaining cognitions *through sensation*" (p. 114). Observation gives a particular sensation "a distinct appearance and the previously undistinguished content becomes a quality" (p. 115). When observation and attention have determined that a sensory experience is visual, that the quality of this experience is color, and that the color is a particular one, (e.g., red), "I have fulfilled the whole work of observation" (p. 116).

With the quality of the sensory content established, attention determines its quantity in space, its intensity, and its duration—the properties that Titchener later called *extensity*, *intensity*, and *protensity*, making these attributes of experience the fundamental dimensions of consciousness. Thus, "a complete object is before the mind [, we are said to *apprehend* it, and] it is termed a perception" (p. 120) Hickok noted that perceptual phenomena are not "the things in themselves, ... not yet put together as attributes of one substance" (p. 121). Anticipating William James' conception of the "stream of consciousness," he added that "the impressions on sense organs are a series and not a constant" (p. 122). Like a river, the mind's stream is perpetual yet never the same. Without another intellectual process, there would be "only a medley of coming and vanishing appearances" (p. 122).

The Understanding

The Understanding "connects qualities [into] substance, and events [into] cause" (p. X). Thus,

> single phenomena become…known as connected qualities of a common substance. The redness, the fragrance, the smoothness etc., which have been separately attained by different senses are successively thought into one thing and the mind forms the [judgment] that the rose is red, and is fragrant, and is smooth, etc. (pp. 127–128)

This substance (e.g., the rose) is more than a perception; it is "a wholly new conception in the understanding" (p. 128).

There are "several particular faculties that belong to the province of the understanding" (p. 132), which Hickok then described.

Memory.   Anticipating the modern conceptions of *engram* and *the representation of information in memory*, Hickok asserted that memory "follows perception but is preliminary and auxiliary to all processes of thinking." Phenomena "apprehended in consciousness…pass from the mind and leave their semblance, or representative, behind them." Memory "is the faculty for retaining these representatives, and recalling them into consciousness is recollection" (p. 132).

Conception.   Hickok's discussion of conceptions reads like a 20th-century definition of *a prototype*:

> A representative of…a house is a resemblance of that house. With resemblances of many particular houses…the mind spontaneously makes a general scheme, which is

not a resemblance of any particular house but…includes that which is common to all houses. Such a generalized representative is properly termed a conception…. Conceptions are the materials for forming new judgments, and may be used…in thinking to carry the mind onwards … to the most comprehensive conclusions. (pp. 135–136)

Association.   Under this heading, Hickok presented a modern-sounding account of the organization of memory, in which he called on the standard laws of association: temporal and spatial contiguity, similarity, and contrast. When representatives are retained in memory, they lie in clusters, "attached to one another by some law of connection peculiar to the case." In recollection, one representative brings "a whole cluster" with it, and the attachment:

of representatives in the memory to one another is called association. A number of different modes (laws of association) account for the attachment: the phenomena may have been together in both place and time and thus are associated before they go into memory; the likeness or contrast between things can put them together; or the mind can voluntarily put its conceptions together. (p. 137)

Hickok also recognized that there are individual differences in association, noting that people vary in the speed with which things are associated and that the quality of their associations differs. Thus "different trains of thought, general habit, and manners must differ among men, and the particular air, address, and characteristic demeanor must be determined from the peculiarity of mental associations" (p. 140). Although the language now sounds archaic, Hickok's dealing with the rest of his proposed attributes of understanding provided that process with many of the constructive intellectual capabilities that contemporary cognitive psychology has adopted.

Abstraction.   Abstraction, "the taking of one [conception or train of thought] from many, or a part from a whole, and fixing it particularly in the consciousness[p,]…. is the chief operation in all analysis" (p. 140, italics omitted).

Reflection.   Reminding the reader of the importance—and difficulties—of introspection, Hickok remarked that reflection occurs "when the mind *turns back* on its passing train of conceptions, and takes up any one for more deliberate examinations" (p. 140). Sometimes that attainment is difficult, however, because of the "onward flow of the associated thought" (p. 141). "No conception that the mind may have can be accurately and adequately known except as it has been made the subject of steady and repeated reflection" (p. 142).

Judgment.   In reflection, the "mind determines" the "various peculiarities of conceptions" (p. 142). A judgment is the connection of two conceptions as in grammar. One conception is the subject, its characteristic is a predicate, that which connects the two is a copula. Thus, the house [subject] is [copula] white [predicate].

Deduction.   The conclusion of a deduction is based on the principle that whatever is true of the whole must also be true of its parts.

Induction.   Induction inverts the deductive syllogism and proceeds from the parts to the whole.

Imagination.   Imagination is not simply the faculty for making images, because an image in true imagination "has a concrete being and has grown into completeness in the active conception" (p. 153).

Reason.   Hickok was clearly aware of what today is called *metacognition*. He noted (pp. 156–161) that without reason mind would not examine "how it perceived or how it thought" and thus would be without comprehension and insight. Without reason, both space and time would be lost from consciousness. Both the "outer objects" and the "inner objects" of experience would be limited to the time and place of their occurrence.

THE SUSCEPTIBILITY

Hickok began this second division of his text with a definition. *Susceptibility* is "the capacity to have feelings produced by an impression or affection," either antecedent to consciousness, as in organic sensations, or subsequent to conscious perception, as in all emotions. In that capacity "lie all the joys and sorrows incident to humanity, and where must be found all our subjective motives to voluntary action" (pp. 176–177). Hickok observed that "most writers on mental science" have not made it a "distinct capacity and have confounded its facts with those of the will." He saw it as his task "to classify accurately the leading distinctions of feelings…as they stand related to the will and look toward moral responsibilities" (p. 177). In the fulfillment of this obligation, he treated animal susceptibility, rational susceptibility, and spiritual susceptibility.

Animal Susceptibility

Sensations, whether from external or internal sources, are antecedent to consciousness and might be called mere blind feeling. These blind feelings are not aimless or "indifferent to some end." They have "an intrinsic congeniality to certain results." They represent "impulses in very determinate directions" (p. 178) and are known as "instincts". As representative examples, Hickok included "the preservation of life, the shrinking from pain and death…the whole actions of infancy…the delirium of a fever…and the marvelous exhibitions of mesmerism" (p. 188).

When a feeling becomes conscious, the "[individual] no longer waits on instinctive prompting, but seeks guidance of conscious perception" (p. 179). Thus sensation becomes an appetite. Hickok cited hunger and thirst as eminent examples and proposed an explanation for hunger that would later be known as the *local stimulus theory of drive*: When the stomach is empty of food and the gastric juices act directly on its substance, the result is a peculiar sensation that requires some congenial object to relieve it. As "sensations seeking such gratification" Hickok included fatigue, protracted wakefulness, the longing for health in sickness, and the longing for shade in the heat.

The discussion following the presentation of these ideas was less empirical and largely definitional, serving to introduce new concepts. "When the object that gratifies is known, the sensation has...become a *desire* " (p. 180). Among these inclinations, there is, in parents, a deep propensity to nurture the welfare of the child. In the mother, to be destitute of this inclination is simply unnatural. In the father, its strength and constancy depend mainly on the action of connubial love. If the father does not love the mother, his love for his children "will be easily overcome by opposing considerations....One condition of natural parental affec-tion is that the child be not only the parent's own, but known to be so" (p. 192).

Feelings are of two kinds. The first are *self-interested* feelings, which provide an appreciation of any object that brings happiness. In the possession of an object there is joy and in its loss there is grief. These feelings include hope and fear, pride and shame, tranquility and anxiety, animation and despondency, and patience and perplexity. "Immoderate" amounts of the feelings, (e.g., in securing possessions or in an eagerness to hoard them) may result in covetousness and avarice, respectively. Human beings and animals can learn from experience that certain gratifications are followed by a greater evil, desire may be suppressed, and "a provident foresight awakens a new inclination" (p. 196).

The second kind of feelings are *disinterested feelings* arising from strong ties to society. These feelings "find their end in the welfare of others" and "are exclusive of self interest" (p. 197). These feelings lead people to rejoice with the joyous and weep with those who weep, and to feel pity or fellow-pleasure, condolence or congratulation. The disinterested feelings also "prompt...the denial of self-gratifi-cation for the happiness of others. All the feelings of kindness, or natural benevo-lence and philanthropy, are here exhibited" (p. 198).

Rational Susceptibility

Rational susceptibility is a "higher order of feelings" produced by "some insight of reason." These feelings (emotions) come in "many varieties."

Aesthetic Emotions. "The...Fine Arts...awaken no feelings of appetite nor the cravings of desire" but are produced by "the contemplation of that which the insight of reason finds within them" (p. 202). The aesthetic "feeling is the love of the beautiful. From the thousands of sounds of nature, and from painting, statuary, and music, the sentient spirit catches the sentiment of the supernatural, and our souls read the feelings of an approving or offended God" (pp. 202–204).

Scientific Emotions.   The feeling that drives the search for a priori scientific principles is the love of truth. God has put necessary and universal laws in all nature, and all the emotions excited by the successive degrees of insight into nature are among the enobling prerogatives of our rational being over our animal nature. The same organ that reads God's sentiments in art and music also detects the inner laws of nature; but one is seen as beauty, whereas the other is seen as truth.

Ethical Emotions.   The source of all of our ethical feelings is in one particular susceptibility known as conscience, which creates a feeling of constraint or obligation. "Conscience [is] the susceptibility which is reached by the insight that determines a rule of right" (p. 209; italics omitted). When I view my conduct as conforming to the rule of right, I feel approbation; when my conduct is contrary to this rule, I feel self-condemnation (p. 211). "[C]onscience must be the controlling susceptibility. Truth and beauty are higher than sensual gratification but duty is higher than philosophy and art, and thus virtue is above all. Where the conscience fully controls, the agent is virtuous" (p. 216).

Theistic Emotions.   "[T]he rational mind of man sees the eternal power and Godhead of the Maker. Nature is comprehended in a personal Deity, who originates it from Himself and consummates it according to its eternal plan. Such recognition of a God at once occasions its own peculiar emotions. Feelings are awakened that could arise from no other object in the insight....The very source of all beauty and truth and right is here [providing] an occasion for faith and love and worship, when the willing spirit shall joyfully yield itself in full devotion." (pp. 216–217)

Spiritual Susceptibility

With rationality "comes self-law, conscience, responsibility, and proper immortality. . .[and] there is in this personality perpetual spiritual activity" (p. 221). As this activity " goes forth" toward its object, it " determins character," and when "the disposing of the activity comes under the approbation or condemnation of conscience, the disposition has a moral character..." (p. 221). The Spiritual susceptibility has its source in the personal disposition..." (p. 222).

The disposition may be deliberately formed, as in choosing between law and divinity as an occupation. In choosing the ministry one is " perpetually energized...in that direction." The disposition induces "a susceptibility to [the] feeling and emotions...appropriate to the choice" (p. 224). Or, the disposition "may have been produced gradually, insidiously, and almost imperceptibly" (p. 224). In either case, a particular disposition is permanent. It produces feelings that one with a different disposition cannot have.

Shared dispositions create "the ties of the class...and produce an esprit de corps...variously named as sectarian feeling, party spirit, denominational sentiment, class sympathy, etc." (p. 227). When two or more individuals have "kindred interests, pursuits, and constitutional temperaments [and when in addition is] the sentiment of friendship is experienced" (p. 227). "When this mutual commitment of soul is between two persons of different sexes, and to the end of exclusive connection and cohabitation for life, the sentiment is that of connubial love" (pp. 227–228). If "a man commits his spirit to the highest advancement of the liberties and civilization of his country he has the disposition of the patriot [and thus]...the susceptibility of every patriotic sentiment" (p. 228).

To have truly virtuous sentiments, "one's spirit must be disposed toward the [rule of] right exclusively, comprehensively, and permanently" (p. 229).

When a man recognizes the being of a personal Deity; absolute in his own perfections; maker of himself and all things, and perpetual benefactor; and also recognizes his own dependence and accountability;...[there comes a disposition] to the feelings of religious confidence, divine gratitude and love, adoring praise and worship...and I have all the glad experience of a truly religious man. (p. 230)

When the man as a conscious sinner, helpless and hopeless in his condemnation, recognizes the crucified and ascended Redeemer; and knows that all his own morality and all his religion is induced by His gracious interposition, that through repentance and faith pardon and justification with God may be applied for his sake, and this consistently with every claim of God and his whole government; there is then an occasion for a disposition more than merely religious. And when a disposition, directly going out and fixing upon this crucified Savior, as the only source of help and hope, is truly possessed; it has in it a susceptibility to feelings, which no merely religious devotion to God in the man's own name can ever attain. The love that has much forgiven; the gratitude for grace imparted; the confiding constancy, which owes all and commits all to this only Savior; all these Christian sentiments now come out, and the spirit glows with emotions to which angels must themselves be strangers. (pp. 229–230)

THE WILL

In opening this third division of his text, Hickok distinguished between knowing and the will. In knowing, the intellect finds no alternative to what is known, and in perceiving no alternative to the perceived. However, in willing, at the point of "going out to one end [there is] an open way to a different end" (p. 239). Therefore, "the definition of the human will is a capacity for electing.... An act of will must have its end [and]...this end must also have an alternative in kind and not merely in degree" (pp. 255–256). In all acts of human will there is an alternative and thus avoidability. Without the presence of alternatives, no conception of liberty is possible.

Certain direct inferences follow from the conception that people have free will and that they exercise that ability.

1. "Man knows himself responsible for his character and actions ... and not responsible for anything utterly inevitable; he has thus both a character and a life" (p. 261).
2. "There is, to man, an alternative to his whole animal nature, and that he should live under the law of highest happiness, like the brute [Freud's 'pleasure principle'], is clearly avoidable" (p. 263).
3. People do not will nature's effects on their constitutions, such as hunger and the desire for food or cold and the desire for warmth. They are unavoidable and hence people never call them their own. People do cause spiritual activities. They know them to be their own because they are avoidable. They are the product of their elections and are not unavoidable coercions.
4. "One good man loves another and all good men love God" (p. 268). Each recognizes the righteous character of the other.
5. "Only in this capacity of will in liberty can the current of constitutional nature be resisted" (p. 268).
6. "When I bring my capacity of will within the light of consciousness ... I feel that my act of will [was not] without an alternative" (p. 272).
7. "All human language, all legislation, all the history of man speaks out what mankind in all ages have consciously felt, an alternative and avoidability to their inmost disposition" (p. 274).

Hickok's treatment of the will concludes with a distinction between acts of will that are an expression of a governing purpose that "prompts...and directs executive acts to its goals" (p. 286); and a desultory volition, that "carries out an executive act in gratification...against the direction of the governing purpose...while the governing purpose is not renounced" (p. 289). If a:

> bad man does a good deed ... all we can say in his favor is that his depraved disposition was not too strong for some transient traits of humanity; and when a good man does a bad deed he is a sinner...and should be debased and humbled by it and repent of it; but the real character of neither the bad man nor the good man was in this way at all changed. (p. 292)

THE COMPETENCY OF THE HUMAN MIND
TO ATTAIN THE END OF ITS BEING

Hickok began this fourth and final division of the text by identifying the end for which the human mind exists. It is to have "the intellect, susceptibility, and will... in complete conformity to...the highest good of [humanity]" (p. 294). "The highest good of the animal portion of our nature is [immediate] happiness." The spiritual in man "can see the relationship to the animal, and [what the animal wants] must be subservient" to the spiritual. The highest good of the spiritual man is spiritual self-approval: "To know myself to be worthy of my spiritual approbation is my highest good, and to remain so is my highest end" (p. 297).

Are there limits to the ability of the will to achieve this highest end? In a comment that is mindful of present-day discussions of the interaction of personality and environment in the control of human behavior, Hickok answered that there are and that they arise from two sources: outward nature too powerful for counteraction, thus excluding all moral accountability, and inner sources that, being wholly from within, stand wholly chargeable to its own account. The sources of this latter moral inability of the mind to attain the end of its being are several, including excessive motivation, or strong desire, and conflict, or balanced desires.

Hickok then completed this last section and the text as follows:

> Thus man is both able and unable to attain the end of his being, in holding all his activity wholly to the claims of his spiritual nature. But in this there is neither absurdity nor contradiction. He is able not in the same sense that he is unable. His ability is a freedom from all the coercions and necessities of nature, and his inability is a bondage of the spirit itself—self-imposed and self-perpetuated. His freedom from all the compulsion of nature leaves him wholly responsible, and utterly inexcusable. In his depravity: and his whole-souled subjection of his carnal appetites, and the fixed state of will on the end of animal gratification, render it utterly hopeless that the same spiritual will, left to its own way, is ever about to turn from that which it so loves, and fix anew upon that which it so hates. In such a condition, perpetuated depravity must have its perpetuated consciousness of degradation and guilt: and the recovery of the spirit to its original integrity awaits the gracious advent of One, who, by spiritual regeneration, may seek and save the lost. (p. 400)

CONCLUSION

In assessing the influence of early 19th century philosophy on the development of scientific psychology, Leary (1978) argued that Kant's pessimistic estimate of the probability that psychology could ever be a science was a challenge that was accepted by Jacob F. Fries (1773–1843), Johann F. Herbart (1776–1841), and Friedrich E. Beneke (1798–1854). The name of Laurens Perseus Hickok can be added to that list. Particularly in his textbook on empirical psychology, he responded to the challenge in ways that foreshadowed the thinking of psychologists in generations yet to come. He helped to make the point that psychological theorizing is possible, stressing, as many psychologists do today, that common sense has an important role to play in the science of psychology. He anticipated the psychological school of structuralism in his evaluation of the potential values and difficulties of the introspective method. He saw consciousness as a stream, as James would later put it. His theorizing included several of what are now called cognitive processes, including treatments of perception, imagery, prototypes, and organization of memory. He conceived the mind as an active and constructive processor of information and presented something like a modern psycholinguist's view that grammar provides a useful model of the mind. He discussed motivation and emotion in terms that are translatable into 20th-century ideas. His discussion of the relationship between animal and higher susceptibilities contained the germ of the essential ideas in Freud's concept of the pleasure principle and of the psychoanalytic treatment of the conflict between the id and the superego. All of these contributions identify Hickok as an important pioneer in the history of general psychology.

REFERENCES

Evans, R. B. (1983). The origins of American academic psychology. In J. Brozek (Ed.), *Explorations in the history of psychology in the United States* (pp. 17–60). Lewisburg, PA: Bucknell University Press.

Harms, E. (1972). America's first major psychologist: Laurens Perseus Hickok. *Journal of the History of the Behavioral Sciences, 8,* 120–123.

Hickok, L. P. (1854). *Empirical psychology. The human mind as given in consciousness.* Schenectady, NY: Debogert.

Hickok, L. P. (1973). *Rational psychology. A facsimile reproduction with an introduction by Ernest Harms.* Delmar, NY: Scholars' Facsimiles and Reprints. (Original work published 1849)

Hunt, M. (1993). *The story of psychology.* New York: Doubleday.

Kant, I. (1934). *Critique of pure reason. Introduction by A. D. Lindsay* (J. M. D. Meiklejohn, Trans.). London: J. M. Dent & Sons. (Original work published 1781)

Larrabee, H. A., Schneider, H. W., & Bixler, J. S. (1947). *Laurens Perseus Hickok, Class of 1820. Union worthies.* Schenectady, NY: Union College.

"Laurens Perseus Hickok" [Obituary]. (1888, May 8). *The New York Times, p. 2.*

Leary, D. E. (1978). The philosophical development of the conception of psychology in Germany, 1780–1850. *Journal of the History of the Behavioral Sciences, 14,* 113–121.

Leary, D. E. (1982). Immanuel Kant and the development of modern psychology. In W. R. Woodward & M. G. Ash (Eds.), *The problematic science: Psychology in the nineteenth century.* New York: Praeger.

Schneider, H. W. (1963). *A history of American philosophy,* (2nd ed.). New York: Columbia University Press.

Viney, W., Wertheimer, M., & Wertheimer, M. L. (1979). *History of psychology: A guide to information sources.* Detroit: Gale.

Watson, R. I. (1963). *The great psychologists: Aristotle to Freud.* New York: Doubleday.

Windelband, W. (1901). *A history of psychology, with special reference to the formation and development of its problems and conceptions* (2nd ed.). New York: Macmillan.

Chapter 2

Charles Darwin: Father of Evolutionary Psychology

R. Bruce Masterton

On February 12, 1809, the Western world had one of its better days. Within hours, Charles Darwin was born in Shrewsbury near Birmingham, England, and Abraham Lincoln was born in Hodgenville near Elizabethtown, Kentucky. Although the two men never met or corresponded, they are now associated with views of human nature that are diametrically opposed to one another. These two views—one biological, the other primarily political—have posed a dilemma with which psychology still struggles as it approaches the beginning of the 21st century.

Darwin has been the subject of at least 200 biographies of sharply differing value. Those written before 1990 were mostly based on limited materials—laundered to maintain standards of family propriety—by Darwin's daughter, Henrietta, and his son, Francis (1896), by his wife, Emma, and by Charles himself (Barlow, 1958). Since about 1990, however, a wealth of new materials has become available, including Darwin's notebooks and personal letters, both with his marginal notes and even notes about the notes. Taken together, these materials yield an entirely new view of his life both in science, in the tumultuous Victorian society of his time, and in the scientific politics of his day (see Browne, 1995).

CHRONOLOGY

The bare-boned facts of Darwin's life and contributions are summarized next, in chronological order. The quotations are from Barlow (1958).

---

*Photograph of Charles Darwin courtesy of the R. Bruce Masterson's collection.

Feb. 12, 1809: Darwin is born in Shrewsbury, England, son of wealthy Whig physician, Robert, and Emma Wedgwood Darwin, grandson of Erasmus Darwin, physician and outspoken social and religious critic who died before Charles was born.

1818–1825, Ages 9–16: Darwin boards at a local school. He is bored by standard classical education and hates repetitive exercises: "As I was doing no good at school, my father wisely took me away at a rather earlier age than usual" (p. 46).

1825–1827, Ages 16–18: Darwin goes to Edinburgh with his older brother, Erasmus, to study medicine. There, for the first time, he meets activists, true atheists, radicals, revolutionaries, and articulate anti-establishment intellectuals. He hates medicine, finds surgery and blood "gruesome," and pursues "independent studies in natural science." He cuts medical lectures to go collecting in the Firth of Forth with a true evolutionist, R. E. Grant, and quits medicine after 2 years.

1828–1831, Ages 18–22: Darwin attends Christ's College, Cambridge, to study for the clergy ["My time was wasted, as far as academical studies were concerned, as completely as at Edinburgh …" (p. 58)]. He still hates lectures and continues his outdoor life of hunting, hiking, and collecting. He meets botany Professor J. S. Henslow and joins Henslow's enthusiastic entourage of empirically oriented students. Darwin accompanies Adam Sedgwick (a Cambridge geologist) on a field trip through Wales and learns the basics of geology and their orthodox (biblical) interpretations.

1831, Age 22: Henslow recommends Darwin for the post of naturalist on the *Beagle*. After his appointment, Darwin begins a flurry of technical preparation.

1831–1836, Ages 22–27: Voyage on the *Beagle*, which Darwin calls "the most important event in my life [which] has determined my whole career" (p. 76). He sends an unprecedented number and variety of preserved plant and animal specimens to Henslow at every chance. Henslow distributes them to appreciative scientific authorities and publishes some of Darwin's notes.

1836–1839, Ages 27–30: Return of the *Beagle*. Darwin basks in the glory of his acceptance in scientific circles as a result of the specimens he made available to scientists and the notes published for him by Henslow. He prepares his *Beagle* journals for publication. In July, 1837, he "clearly conceives" his theory of natural selection and begins the first of several secret notebooks on transmutation of species with the deceptive title, ZOONOMIA, in bold letters on the title page. Darwin meets with Lyell. He begins to develop doubts about religion and (probably as a result) chronic illnesses emerge. Darwin begins a series of notebooks recording his opinions about the relevance of domestic breeding to his theories and his speculations on the wider consequences and the metaphysics of his theory. He reads Malthus' (1798/1914) *On Population* and then revises the concept of *natural selection* to *the struggle for survival*.

1839–1842, Ages 30–33: Darwin marries Emma Wedgwood. With financial support assured, he settles in London, finishes work on "Coral Reefs," and delivers papers to the Geological Society and the *Philosophical Magazine*. He meets and starts correspondences with Hooker, Huxley, Spencer, and others. He pumps botanist Hooker, just returned from his own voyage, about the world-wide distribution and variation in plants—without telling him why he is interested.

1842–1854, Ages 33–45: Darwin moves to Downe, in Kent, and involves himself in projects that seem calculated to postpone the publication of the theory of evolution: He organizes, outlines, reorganizes and re-outlines the sketch of his theory on the formation of new species; publishes observations on Volcanic Islands; and finally admits to Hooker (1844): "I am almost convinced...that species are not (it is like confessing a murder) immutable." He revises his "Journal of Researches" and his "Geological Observations on South America," and begins work on barnacles—ostensibly to establish his credibility with scientists.

1854–1856, Age 45–47: Procrastination continues. Darwin spends his time organizing and reorganizing his notes for *Origin of Species* yet again. "From September, 1854 onwards I devoted all my time to arranging my huge pile of notes, to observing, and experimenting, in relation to the transmutation of species." He refines his theory still another time. Lyell advises him to prepare the work for publication.

1856–1859, Age 47–50: Darwin receives Alfred Wallace's letter from Malaya "on the tendency of varieties to depart." Stunned, he panics over a threatened loss of personal priority for his evolutionary theory. He shares his agony with Lyell and Hooker, who persuade him to publish his own paper along with Wallace's. Surprised and flattered by Darwin's attention, Wallace agrees. The two papers are read back to back but neither receives a great deal of attention. Darwin quickly polishes and publishes *Origin of Species* (1858) without mention of Genesis, the descent of man, or other inflammatory implications he has thought of since its inception. Most scientists accept it; two printings sell out quickly. Soon, however, critics begin publicizing the (unmentioned by Darwin) objectionable implications of the theory for humankind, society, and religion. Criticism and public arguments begin slowly, then become heated. Some scorn and venom arise but not as much as he expected. Darwin secludes himself at Downe, "too ill to travel" to London or scientific meetings; he lets his scientific friends (Hooker, Lyell, and "my bulldog," Huxley) protect him from the popular furor he still fears.

1860–1871, Age 51–62: Darwin continues to stay away from public forums and answers only admiring or helpful letters. He begins several books on plants (*Variations of Animals and Plants under Domestications*, *Fertilizations of Orchids*, and *Dimorphic Condition of Primula*). He waits for furor to run its course.

1872, Age 63: In response to years of requests for his own view on implications of evolution and natural selection for humankind, Darwin finally writes *The Descent of Man* and *Expression of Emotions in Man and Animals*.

1875–1881, Ages 66–72: Darwin returns to work on plants. He publishes "Insectivorous Plants," "Effects of Cross and Self-Fertilization in the Vegetable Kingdom," "Power of Movement in Plants," "Formation of Vegetable Mould through the Action of Earthworms," and a second edition of his orchid book, *Different Forms of Flowers*.

April 19, 1882, Age 73: Darwin dies. After intensive lobbying of scientific societies and the government by Galton, Huxley, Hooker, and others, Darwin is buried in Westminster Abbey.

Perhaps the most interesting biographical question solved by the newly published materials concerns the reasons for the 20 years of procrastination that delayed the publication of *Origin of Species*. As it turns out, Darwin was frightened by the prospect of excoriation for his unorthodox theory by the closely intertwined Christians and Tories. Even more distressing was the prospect of ostracism from the same Whig society that he and his family held dear. His wife, a steadfast Christian and Victorian throughout, continuously warned him that his thoughts were unacceptable, although she continued to help edit his manuscripts throughout his life, appending "E.D." to her marginal notes to differentiate her remarks from those of others performing the same duty.

THE VOYAGE OF THE *BEAGLE*

Darwin's journey on the *Beagle* can be traced to the influence of Carl Linné (Linnaeus), who had made the systematic classification of plants both scientifically important and easy to do. The resulting enthusiasm for classifying every living thing in the world led the British Navy to include a naturalist on virtually every voyage with nonhostile intent (Boorstin, 1985). The fact that it was Darwin who filled that role on the *Beagle* was due most directly to the efforts of John S. Henslow, his mentor at Cambridge.

Quite contrary to past claims, Darwin did not depart on the voyage unprepared for the job he was about to undertake. After his appointment as the *Beagle's* naturalist, he threw himself into a near panic of preparation. He spent the last weeks before embarkation frantically criss-crossing the country learning firsthand the latest techniques of collecting, preserving, and shipping plants, animals, and minerals. He reread the important nature books of the time (including Humboldt's weighty "Personal Narrative" about his travels in South America). He avidly studied the first volume of Lyell's new book on geology, receiving the 2nd and 3rd volumes from Henslow during the voyage.

Throughout the voyage, Darwin kept a steady stream of specimens flowing to Henslow. Henslow, in turn, rerouted the materials to appropriate authorities—sea life to one, plants to another, reptiles to still another, birds to yet another, and so on. This dispersion of his specimens to the appropriate scientific authorities throughout England meant that, by the time Darwin returned to England 5 years later, he already had a good reputation as a naturalist. In his absence, many authorities had given him due credit for the materials on which they based their publications. He returned already well connected with the scientists he admired most. Darwin was delighted with his own success and proud that he succeeded on his own, without the benefit of his grandfather's (Erasmus Darwin's) reputation.

ELEMENTS OF EVOLUTIONARY THEORY

As Darwin described it in 1858, the theory of evolution is composed of three components: heredity, variation, and natural selection. *Heredity* simply means that offspring resemble their parents—cats give birth to kittens, not puppies. Although Darwin did not understand the mechanisms of heredity, we now know that it is the result of the self-replicating power of the genes. Similar genes construct similar bodies—again with the proviso, discovered later, that these bodies develop in similar environments.

Variation means that, although offspring resemble their parents, they are not identical to either parent or their average. If a 6-foot-tall father and a 5-foot-tall mother have children, the children will not necessarily be exactly 5-, or 6-, or 5.5-feet tall. Looking ahead once more, we now know that such variation occurs for three reasons. First, the environment can change genetic material through a process of mutation. Second, even identical genetic material will produce different bodies in different environments. For example, the average height of the American population has increased over the past centuries—something to which the sizes of beds and armor in museums will testify. Third, in bisexual reproduction, variation occurs because each parent contributes only one half of the genetic material in the offspring, who cannot be identical to either parent.

Selection means that not all offspring have the same chance of becoming parents and passing their traits along to future generations because some will be stronger, better looking, or more sexually capable than others. The greater the variation in offspring in the chance of becoming parents, the greater the selective pressure; that is, the greater the differences in the probabilities that some offspring will survive and reproduce while others perish. *Natural selection* means that the process of selection is imposed on species without any intent on the part of the selecting mechanism—not far from an assertion that selection occurs without divine intervention. Instead, natural selection occurs because variation results in unequal adaptation of individuals to the environment: Some individuals survive at least until sexual maturity. Some fraction of the survivors find mates and become parents. Thus, the process of natural selection has two components that are commonly called *survival of the fittest* and *sexual selection*.

DOUBTS ABOUT RELIGION

Victorian society quickly noted the implications of Darwinian theory of evolution and those who set human beings apart from other animals took offense at it. The general idea of the human mind acquired piece-meal—by undirected, virtually random, accretion over geological time and with no sharp evidence of distinctions among civilized human beings, savages, and apes—was an appalling idea to those who thought humankind deserved a special place in nature apart from and above all other living things. As one Victorian matron is said to have put it: "Evolution? Descended from monkeys? Let us pray that that it is not true; or if it is, let us trust that it will not become generally known!"

Throughout his voyage on the *Beagle*, and on his return, Darwin considered himself a geologist; he joined the Geological Society before any other, wrote first for their journal, and made specific efforts to wangle a formal introduction to Lyell, by then his (geological) idol. Although he credited Lyell's books for turning him into a geologist and historical naturalist, he received basic training in geology long before. On a walk through Wales with Adam Sedgwick, the geologist at Cambridge, he learned the significance of stratification, including the limestone versus sandstone distinction—the former being interpreted by the orthodox Sedgwick as evidence of the Flood. Thus, Darwin was surprised to see, but correctly interpreted, widely separated strata of limestone seen during the voyage. (Could there have been two Floods?)

As a result of many such experiences, Darwin's belief in Genesis slipped a notch and his fear of ostracism began. His Biblical faith continued to decline as he recorded more and more distinct species, living and fossilized, throughout the remainder of the voyage. Acutely aware of the cramped conditions on the *Beagle*, he must have wondered just how big an Ark Noah had built. The final blow came when, later in his life, his favorite daughter and his father died in quick succession. He abandoned Christianity, not just Genesis, forever. Henceforward, he would refer to himself as an *agnostic*, although the distinction between that designation and the more inflammatory *atheist* was more an accommodation to political and social preferences than it was a theological subtlety (Moore, 1994).

After realizing that his theory was so godless in its implications, Darwin experienced an intense approach–avoidance conflict (personal ambition vs. social fear). He suffered from frequent episodes of serious illness. These periodic bouts of illness, which persisted throughout Darwin's life, have been interpreted by Freudians as manifestations of a psychosomatic disorder. However, more sympathetic sources assign causes related to his travels (e.g., a bite by a particularly ugly beetle while hiking in the Andes). His severe personal conflict, extending at least 20 years, came to an abrupt end only after he received a friendly and modest letter from Malaya by Alfred Wallace, indicating that he, too, had discovered natural selection.

DARWIN'S CONTRIBUTIONS TO PSYCHOLOGY

Darwin's contributions to psychology were of two kinds: direct and indirect. The direct contributions are in his books, *The Expressions of Emotions in Man and Animals* (1872) and *The Descent of Man* (1871), and in the chapter on instinct in *The Origin of Species* (1858). In *The Descent of Man*, he takes up the evolution of the "higher faculties of human mental life" and traces them from animals through savage and barbarian stages inferred from his observations of the aborigines in Tierra del Fuego and the slaves, masters, and natives in South America. In both books, Darwin used the anecdotal method that was standard at his time, but only after he had recited the homologous anatomical structures among humans and animals. His underlying argument was that, given clearly homologous structures (facial muscles or brains), their use must be at least analogous.

It can be argued, however, that the most important contributions to psychology of the theory of natural selection were not those that can be found in Darwin's own writings or in those of his contemporaries. Instead, these lasting contributions were indirect. They came through the impact of the theory on Darwin's contemporaries: Spencer, Galton (chap. 1, *Pioneers I*), Romanes, and their intellectual progeny, who were pioneers in the functionalist and behavioristic schools of psychology, such as William James, Edward L. Thorndike, John B. Watson (chap. 2, 10, and 12, *Pioneers I*), Robert Yerkes (chap. 7, *Pioneers II*), and others.

Initially, (in his *Biology* [1866]), Herbert Spencer was a powerful critic of natural selection. He later reversed himself and became one of natural selection's most influential and vocal supporters. The idea that the human mind accumulated bit by bit over eons of time was a key insight to Spencer. His treatment of this idea in his later two-volume work, *Psychology* (1886), is in most respects more useful than Darwin's own version in *The Descent of Man*.

Francis Galton, Darwin's half-cousin (chap. 1, *Pioneers I*), also found the ideas of evolutionary theory exhilarating. He set out to demonstrate that heredity with variation existed among living people. Galton's contributions to psychology, in particular to the measurement of individual differences and heredity, were legion. (He also invented the now-disparaged term *eugenics*, by which he simply meant the improvement of humanity's condition through science.)

Darwin also made early indirect contributions to comparative psychology. George John Romanes (1896) contacted Darwin early and became a protégé. Together they discussed the types of evidence that would illustrate the gradual evolution of human intelligence. Unfortunately, they were unaware of the tortuous problems that confront the necessary demonstrations. Hence, they both made primary use of anecdotal data of a kind that is still quite common among nonscientists (Romanes, 1883, 1888). In this method, to gauge the intelligence of any animal, one compares that animal's behavior to that of human beings. The more similar the animal's behavior is to human action, the more intelligent the animal. The idea that intelligence is a one-dimensional talent—with animals, apes, savages, barbarians, and non-Europeans arrayed in an ascending line to Europeans at the top—was axiomatic in this outlook. Although the anecdotal method was to go out of fashion with the work of William James, E. L. Thorndike, and J. B. Watson, who, among others, studied the evolution of the human mind with the aid of direct experimentation on animals, it was more than a half-century more before animal psychology could produce useful comparative results (Masterton, Skeen, & Robards, 1974).

REACTIONS TO DARWINISM

Although the earliest and most persistent objections leveled at *The Origin of Species* were the more theological ones raised by orthodox Christians, others were based on valid scientific concerns. Many of these were anticipated and explained by Darwin. As one example, Darwin interpreted the apparently ill-adapted tail of a peacock as a sexual display designed to attract a mate. As a second example, Darwin responded to the criticism that the age of the earth was inadequate to accommodate the sluggish operation of evolution, with the argument that the earth was far older than was commonly believed. Even Darwin did not guess that its age might be measured in billions rather than just millions of years.

A more subtle problem anticipated by, and troubling to, Darwin was how a complex organ (such as a bird's wing) could develop gradually because its ultimate function (flying) would not be available to the selective process during evolutionary development. The geological record does contain fossils possessing wings that increase gradually in size, as evolutionary theory seems to require. Although this problem has not been completely solved, we now know some of the ingredients of the solution. (a) For example, wings may have developed out of membranes that cooled the body, which increased in size so as to serve this purpose better. Their usefulness for flying may have come as a serviceable by-product. (b) Some evolutionary changes are the results of mutations, which produce sudden and marked changes in biological structures and functions. Moreover (c), the majority of structures and their functions do develop on the gradual schedule that Darwin's theory demands.

Still another kind of objection was that the theory of natural selection was reckless in its range of application. One joker ridiculed this far-too-sweeping logic in a caricature that imagined how the process would operate in the world of inanimate objects: "The reason all rocks drop down is that all of those that once dropped up are now long gone." Staying within reason, does it really make any sense to think of human altruism, abstract thought, and patriotism as products of blind evolution? Recent developments in genetics have made the answer to such questions closer to "yes" than is comfortable for those who ask them.

Impact of the Science of Genetics

The one true scientific threat to natural selection came at the turn of the century with the rediscovery of Mendelian genetics. It was clear from the outset that genetics provided the mechanism of both heredity and variation as required by Darwin's theory. Although Darwin would have been delighted with this development, things were soon to take a turn that would have left him uncomfortable. Once it was shown that some of the variation among members of a species resulted from physical changes or mutations in the genotype, the question arose whether evolution might be explained by progressive mutation alone—without the necessity of any Darwinian process of selection at all. This scientific possibility was pounced on by many critics of evolution as well as the enemies of natural selection. The result was that the Darwinian view of evolution began to subside as an important idea. It reached its nadir in the 1920s.

This decline came to a sudden halt after Hardy, a mathematician, and Weinberg, a physician, both discovered what is now called the *Hardy–Weinberg Law*. They showed mathematically that, in a large random-breeding population, evolution based solely on the mutation of genetic material quickly leads to a stationary, albeit dynamic, equilibrium, rather than to progressive change of any kind. The direct implication of the Hardy–Weinberg discovery was that selection is indeed required for evolution to occur. Unselected mutation is not sufficient.

Within a decade, this discovery allowed Ronald Fisher (1930)—to most psychologists the inventor of modern experimental design and analysis of variance (ANOVA), but actually also a distinguished geneticist and experimental agronomist—to tie evolution to genetics and combine Darwin's principles of survival and sexual selection into a concept of *reproductive success*. With support from similar publications by Haldane (1932) and Wright (1931), the new science of population genetics, based on gene frequencies, allowed Darwinian evolution to be resurrected with even more assurance than it had enjoyed in the 19th century.

The Triumph of Materialism

Decades later, when molecular biology began to discover the physical arrangement of the key molecules of life (proteins, DNA, RNA), and still later, when it found that DNA can divide and reproduce itself while accumulating variation, it became possible to declare that evolution, and indeed life itself, is the passive result of the properties of a few peculiar, self-replicating molecules. No doubt it is obvious that this knowledge came as another severe blow to anthropocentrism, the view that considers humankind to be the highest form of life—the standard against which other species are to be compared. Worse was still to come before the anthropocentric view of life was finally defeated.

First came the radical opinion that life is nothing but the properties of these molecules. Even this view was not the last step in the systematic march of biological science toward strict materialism initially set in motion by Darwin's original insight. A related but equally startling idea, especially for psychology, was a revision in the scientific understanding of the locus of the evolutionary process. Darwin believed—and most educated people still believe—that selection operates at the level of individual organisms. The genetic interpretation changed the emphasis: from the evolution of individual organisms to the evolution first of genotypes, then of molecules of DNA. Such reasoning led to the view that bodies and brains are nothing more than contrivances built by DNA for no other reason than to further the reproduction of the DNA. Organisms are merely tools that thoughtless molecules use to exploit living things for their own good. George Gaylord Simpson (1949) expressed the sense of this idea in his note that "Hens are an egg's way of begetting another egg." This view of life, which has no visible scientific basis for rejection and much usefulness in its acceptance, means that even human beings and their precious minds are being exploited by their own DNA. This idea, perhaps the final triumph of materialism, is the topic of *The Selfish Gene* (Dawkins, 1976). Although that book is not correct in every detail—it is entire genotypes and not individual genes that are selected—it is a powerful and convincing argument for this modern insight into life.

CONCLUSION: IMPLICATIONS
FOR THE NATURE–NURTURE ISSUE
IN PSYCHOLOGY

Although the last vestige of anthropocentrism now seems to have been stamped out of biology, it is alive and well in several segments of psychology, where it dictates an ill-informed but widely held position in the dispute over the relative importance of heredity and environment in the determination of behavior.

Implications for Psychology's Environmental Bias

Potentially, positions on the nature–nurture issue may occupy any of an infinite number of locations on a dimension that extends from exclusive genetic determinism, on the one hand, to exclusive environmental determinism, on the other. Although it has been clear for generations that every characteristic of every individual depends on heredity and environment and interactions between the two, it is not difficult to demonstrate that many psychologists, particularly those who deal with human beings in clinical or educational settings, believe in something close to exclusive environmental determinism. The extreme version of this faith in environmental determinism was espoused unequivocally by J. B. Watson in his book, *Behavior* (1914), a reaction to the genetic determinism prevalent in previous centuries. Although Watson (1903, 1914, 1924) made a good case for rejecting genetic determinism, it is now clear that he went too far. Despite that obvious truth, however, many psychologists believe that human behavior is influenced much more by the environments to which people are exposed than by the genetic endowment which they received at their conception.

Paradoxically, the studies of the extreme environmentalists themselves provided some of the best support for the importance of genetic determinism. There now have been dozens of reasonably careful research projects that began with the hypothesis that behavioral differences are the result of differences in childhood environments rather than genetic variation. Many of these investigations were conceived with the explicit aim of contributing to the development of interventions that would rescue disadvantaged individuals from the consequences of their hostile or impoverished environments and upbringing. For example, during the 1960s, many clinical psychology students wrote dissertations on the thesis that schizophrenia is the result of a peculiar family lifestyle or a scolding, unforgiving, "refrigerator" ("schizophrenogenic") mother. Their hope was that the results of these investigations would point the way to effective therapeutic intervention. However, it is notable, that none of these projects was totally successful. In fact, the data from studies of many different types (including adoption studies and studies of identical twins reared apart) show that there is a strong genetic component in the determination of schizophrenia—and every other mental disorder that has been investigated.

The Concept of Environment

Are genetic factors, then, more important than the environment in the determination of behavior? As it turns out, the answer to this question is "no." An understanding of this answer hinges on a rejection of the usual conception that the environment is just the individual's immediate personal surround. Rather, the environment is everything beyond the individual's DNA. Even the material within the fertilized cell's nucleus is part of the environment, and the environments in which DNA exists stack up as successively broader environments are considered. These environments include the egg's nucleoplasm, cytoplasm, surrounding amniotic fluid, the egg's mother's body, her physical environment, and eventually her personality, society, and culture.

The original genotypic blueprint inherited by an individual is immutable for the entire life of that person, but each cell's copy of that blueprint is somewhat different from the original because it is modified by these several environments. For this reason alone, nongenetic variation should be expected to play a large part in the total variation within and among phenotypes. The accumulating evidence supports the notion that, although both nature and nurture are crucial determinants of adult behavioral characteristics (see Bouchard et al., 1990), their contributions to behavioral variation are usually not equal and, for traits of interest to psychology, environment is usually more important.

Implications for Social Policy

An argument that frightens many people away from any acceptance of the genetic side of the nature–nurture argument grows out of an implication for social and political policy. Here, there is a goblin awaiting. The goblin is the possibility that, if enough people believe in genetic rather than environmental determinism, political policies including mandatory eugenics might follow (Gould, 1981). The several trials of coerced eugenics, sometimes including genocide, that dot political history are appalling to most people, including most psychologists. As a result, they shy away from admitting even the possibility of a strong genetic component in human behavior. This is the arena where the ideals of a democratic republic diverge from those of science. It is the place where Darwin and Lincoln—whose philosophies were contrasted at the beginning of this chapter—would have had to have a long discussion to come to some agreement. Lincoln would have pointed out that the democratic ideal requires that everyone be treated equally—that every human being has the same privileges, responsibilities, and opportunities as every other. Responding to this argument, Darwin would have pointed out that the brute biological fact is that people are *not born equal* in the biological and behavioral traits required to make such equality a reality, despite all claims to the contrary (Rushton & Ankney, 1996). Thus, Myrdal's (1964) American dilemma remains an unresolved problem, instigated by Darwin and exacerbated by modern politics.

ACKNOWLEDGMENTS

Bruce Masterton mailed this chapter to the senior editor of this volume shortly before (probably the day before) his untimely death from a heart attack in December 1996. As presented here, the chapter is very much as he wrote it. The editors have made small changes to handle typographic problems and have added a small section, derived from another Masterton publication, to flesh out the description of Darwin's theory. We wish to thank Pauline Masterton, Bruce Masterton's widow, for help with the identification of the sources of many of the quotations; and Debra Brock, Bruce's assistant, for providing the photograph of Darwin.

REFERENCES

Barlow, N. (1958). *The autobiography of Charles Darwin, 1809–1882 with original omissions restored.* London: Collins.
Boorstin, D. J. (1985). *The discoverers.* New York: Vintage Books.

Bouchard, T. J., Jr., Lykken, D. T., McGue, M., Segal, N. L., & Tellegen, A. (1990). Sources of human psychological differences: The Minnesota study of twins reared apart. *Science, 250*, 223–228.

Browne, J. (1995). *Charles Darwin*. New York: Knopf.

Darwin, C. (1858). *The origin of species*. Reprinted New York: Modern Library.

Darwin, C. (1871). *The descent of man*. Reprinted New York: Modern Library.

Darwin, C. (1872). *The expression of the emotions in man and animals*. Reprinted Chicago: University of Chicago Press.

Darwin, F. (Ed.). (1896). *The life and letters of Charles Darwin*. New York: Appleton.

Dawkins, R. (1976). *The selfish gene*. New York: Oxford University Press.

Fisher, R. A. (1930). *The genetical theory of natural selection*. Oxford: Clarendon.

Gould, S. J. (1981). *The mismeasure of man*. New York: Norton.

Haldane, J. B. S. (1932). *The causes of evolution*. London: Longmans, Green.

Malthus, T. R. (1914). *An essay on the principle of population*. London: J. M. Dent & Sons. (Original work published 1798)

Masterton, R. B., Skeen, L. C., & Robards, M. J. (1974). Origins of anthropoid intelligence: II. Pulvinar-extrastriate system and visual reversal learning. *Brain, Behavior and Evolution, 10*, 322–353.

Moore, J. (1994). *The Darwin legend*. Grand Rapids, MI: Baker Books.

Myrdal, G. (1964). *An American dilemma*. New York: McGraw-Hill.

Romanes, E. (1896). *The life and letters of George John Romanes*. London: Longmans, Green.

Romanes, G. J. (1883). *Animal intelligence*. New York: Appleton.

Romanes, G. J. (1888). *Mental evolution in man*. London: Kegan Paul, Trench.

Rushton, J. P., & Ankney, C. D. (1996). Brain size and cognitive ability: Correlations with age, sex, social class, and race. *Psychonomic Bulletin and Review, 3*, 21–36.

Simpson, G. G. (1949). *The meaning of evolution*. New Haven, CT: Yale University Press.

Spencer, H. (1866). *The principles of biology*. New York: Appleton.

Spencer, H. (1886). *The principles of psychology*. New York: Appleton.

Watson, J. B. (1903). *Animal education*. Chicago: University of Chicago Press.

Watson, J. B. (1914). *Behavior*. New York: Holt.

Watson, J. B. (1924). *Behaviorism*. New York: Norton.

Wright, S. (1931). Evolution in Mendelian populations. *Genetics, 16*, 97–159.

Chapter 3

Leipzig, Wilhelm Wundt, and Psychology's Gilded Age

Arthur L. Blumenthal

As one can sense from the old travelogues, the air was likely heavy with smoke and dust on that day in 1875 when Wilhelm Maximilian Wundt stepped out of a train and into the crowded Leipzig *Bahnhof* ending a long journey from Zurich. His greater journey into the pages of the history of the new scientific psychology, which he was often credited with founding and sometimes accused of imperializing, was just then beginning. Although later generations would remember the image of an elderly Wundt—a stooped, gray-bearded, half-blind octogenarian—in 1875 he was a straight-standing, high-spirited individual with sharply focused eyes that seemed to sparkle with a defiant ambition. Ambitious he surely must have been; by the end of the century, he was not only a *Rektor* (i.e., president) of the University of Leipzig, but also what the historian Fritz Ringer (1969) described as a "German mandarin."

Ringer's book goes on to relate how the forces came together that doomed Wundt to suffer the precipitous decline of the German mandarin culture. Wundt's ascent to great heights was, in fact, followed by a breath-taking eclipse amid the flames and chaos that spanned the period from the outbreak of World War I to the end of World War II. No small part of that chaos was the radical shifts in intellectual trends that consigned Wundt to the dying and discredited old order of the 19th century. What then happened to his psychology was more devastating than the effects of the wars, the anti-German sentiments, or any defection of his students. The very subject matter of his science came to be widely denied, even forbidden, as inherently unscientific and unknowable. For Wundt's psychology was the science of consciousness.

---

*Sketch of Wilhem Wundt courtesy of the Wundt Family Archives.

A THEORY FROM THE GILDED AGE

Wundt's teachings about the nature of consciousness evolved as a set of explanatory principles that were heavily invested with notions of volition or purposivism and a radical form of what is now called *constructivism*. That latter orientation was stated in his first and foremost principle of *creative synthesis* (*schöpferische Synthese*)—the principle that configurations of immediate experience cannot be derived, bottom–up, by collating isolated elements. Wundt spelled out this principle in his earliest writings and emphasized it continually as his most important principle up to his deathbed dictation of his memoirs to his daughter, Eleonore, in 1920. Because his intellectual legacy went into such a steep decline after his death, little serious study was to be devoted to his system of thought until recently. In the intervening period the textbook writers promoted a pattern of myths about Wundtian psychology that came to be widely accepted. Most of these discussions were short, dismissive reviews that did not convey the creative synthesis notion or other core ideas of Wundt's psychology.

The creative synthesis doctrine concerns the emergent phenomena of consciousness—the products of cortical activity that yield the qualities and patterns of experience. From that beginning, Wundt's system developed as a set of explanatory principles concerning fluctuations of consciousness especially as they come under processes of self-control. The whole scheme leaned heavily on the argument that psychology, or specifically its subject matter, is fundamentally different from the physical sciences and therefore not understandable by means of any analogies with them. Here, Wundt seems to have had physics and chemistry in mind primarily.

THE PRIMACY OF PSYCHOLOGY

Psychology for Wundt was the basis of all the other sciences: It studies the processes with which they all begin and, thus, is prior to philosophy, logic, linguistics, and social analysis. During Wundt's later years this became known as *psychologism* and became a negative epithet among scholars and scientists who wished to expel all psychologistic explanations. Not long after Wundt's death, the spoils of his defeated academic and institutional legacy were divided between hostile Marxist-Leninist interpreters in the East and equally hostile American behaviorists and their satellites in the West. The history of this episode as it unfolded in Germany, with Wundt on center stage, has recently been well described by Kusch (1995).

At the time this chapter is being written—toward the end of the 20th century—the style of Wundtian research and theorizing has resurfaced in moves toward a more mentalistic cognitive psychology that have stirred up a flurry of historical comparisons with Wundt. This chapter says little about those discussions, but focuses instead on the historical contexts that produced Wundtian psychology and the core themes that ran consistently through Wundt's works.

THE VIBRANT HISTORICAL SETTING

Leipzig in 1875 was a scruffy old city, a wide-open place of international mer-chants—a crossroads for the arts, free thinkers, political subversion, and radicalism. When we go back to the older Leipzig depicted in 19th-century travelogues, city records, and demographic and cultural data, we find that Wilhelm and Sophie Wundt's newly adopted home, where they would remain for the rest of their lives, was a disorderly and tumultuous place. This Leipzig contrasted with pictures of it from the later Nazi period of the 1930s, which show a precision-polished, perfectly manicured place with everything appearing thoroughly bourgeois and orderly—un-nerving pictures when they are accompanied by the knowledge of the horrors that lay just beneath that shining surface.

Apparently Leipzig had a personality that separated it from other German cities. As the early American psychologist G. S. Hall (1881) remarked in his observations of the city, it had "a distinct type of character" that it "cultivated with no little complacency....No one is fonder or prouder of his city, dialect, folk-festivals, ancient customs, etc., than the average inhabitant of Leipzig."(p. 73). It was a city soon to be recognized as the birthplace of experimental psychology, sometimes of all of modern psychology—that the Wundt of Mannheim and Heidelberg by way of Zurich was destined to fit in quite well and eventually dominate as one of its leading citizens.

Hall also noted that in the streets and restaurants of old Leipzig every other man was a professor, author, or critic more or less known to fame. Wundt moved among them, taking a walk through those streets every afternoon and debating the issues of the day in those restaurants. It could not have been a more intellectually competitive and verbose atmosphere. The city was also the central European capital of book publishing, with 50 publishing houses and over 200 bookstores—certainly the perfect setting for so prolific a writer as Wundt. Leipzig was also a world capital for music—once the home of Bach and then the great *Gewandhaus* orchestra, which continues to this day. Just when Wundt arrived, Leipzig was becoming the artistic fortress of the maestro Richard Wagner who was then staging his operas in the magnificent Leipzig opera house. So, too, the maestro Wundt was on the eve of "staging" psychology in a truly imposing setting and before a large audience. Wundt's life in Leipzig was a rare blend of historical contexts, influences, oppor-tunity, ambition, resources, and timing.

The source city for the *new* psychology was an ancient place that was decorated with statues of the icons of German art, science, literature, and philosophy who had passed through its portals. It would not be long before other statues commemorating the greats of early psychology would take shape there. In looking at the pictures one might sense the pride-filled German chauvinism—the polemics of cultural superiority—that was to arise in the majority of the local intellectual community, including Wundt, at the outset of the first World War. Then all the philosophical and theoretical rivalries that had bitterly divided many leading names in the universities of that land seemed to disappear as they came together to speak with one voice in support of their nation, just before their national tragedy was to send many of them into oblivion.

A Carnival of Commerce

To the eyes of his many students, both German and foreign, including most of the first generation of American psychologists who gathered in Leipzig to study with Wundt, the city was even more a scene of noise and commotion than were Wundt's lectures or Wagner's operas. There was more to the scene that gave Leipzig the unique personality described by Hall. Ever since the 11th century, Leipzig had been the central European crossroads for trade, which led to the emergence of huge annual commercial fairs that dominated city life for much of each year. That is why its populace was known as stemming from diverse nationalities and ethnic groups—a rich cauldron for what Wundt was to write about at length under the title of *Völkerpsychologie*. Perhaps that scene of diversity is why the city was also a magnet for radical political movements. In the 19th century, it was a place of perpetual skirmishes between those forces and the opposing German conservatism. Fiery socialists harangued crowds of workers on street corners. In his younger days, Wundt had been a left-of-center politician; in later life, he continued to speak and write on political issues.

The great international commercial fairs brought hordes of merchants from as far as Africa and the Middle East to fill Leipzig's streets with tents and booths crammed with wares. Hangers-on bent on radicalism, thievery, spiritualism, or other avenues of opportunity followed the crowds. Leipzig was a festival and carnival. On one street you could find the best of china and pottery. In the old Jewish quarter were displayed the finest furs gathered from across the continent. On other streets were foods of all nationalities. Music and the cacophony of languages poured out of sidewalk cafes. At fair time one met iron mongers, wool merchants, rug sellers, book traders, and so on. For Wundt's interests there were also to be found more representatives of the best technical and scientific instrument makers than could be met in any other place in Europe—not an inconsiderable fact for the soon-to-emerge laboratory style of the new psychology.

Along with all this commercial and festive activity, the wealth of Leipzig grew and grew and, in tandem, the university blossomed to become evermore magnificent, as did Wundt's *Psychologische Institut* within it. Wundt's initial two-room quarters of the late 1870s eventually became a large, lavishly funded, multistoried center for psychological research reaching its greatest point of expansion on the eve of World War I. (For a description, see D. K. Robinson, 1987.) However, the American students who had once been so prevalent had by then largely disappeared because American graduate schools and PhD programs had begun to take shape and new definitions of psychology were arising in America that had greater appeal to the more pragmatic and physicalistic American temperament.

American Innocents Abroad

There was surely a clash of cultures when the American students were in Leipzig. The character of the American colleges of that time was quite different from that of the German universities. For instance, in Germany there was a widespread turning away from traditional religion that was so centrally rooted in American colleges. In Germany one met atheism, *Naturphilosophie*, various pantheisms, and Eastern mysticisms. At that same time, revivalist upheavals were arising in Puritan America and were preaching a simpler, plainer, more pragmatic, less intellectual lifestyle. Early American psychologists who were hostile toward religion had to be much more circumspect about this attitude were they to survive in American academia. Nor could they as easily employ new scientific instruments to tinker with the sacred soul. Thus, behaviorism would be more acceptable here because it did not attempt to meddle with the private domains that were the concerns of the church. From America there also came that especially practical-minded mentality that was so highly approved of by the Puritan ethic. It was the attitude of seeking fixes for everyday problems, of finding the value of science in its engineering applications—all quite foreign to the basic separation of science and technology as found in Germany. One can sense something of that German–American cultural clash in the following statement from G. Stanley Hall (1912): "We need a psychology that is usable, that is dietetic, efficient for thinking, living and working, and although Wundtian thoughts are now so successfully cultivated in academic gardens, they can never be acclimated here, as they are antipathetic to the American spirit and temper" (p. 421).

The Strict Prussians Versus the Gemütliche Bavarians

In Germany, too, there had long been a clash of cultural style between the Apollonian north and the Dionysian south. The more relaxed, gemütliche (easy-going/friendly) south contrasted with the formal, militaristic, Prussian north. The conflicts that were later to separate Wundt's orientation in psychology from those of several of his northern colleagues (e.g., Hermann Ebbinghaus, chap. 4, this volume; G. E. Müller) were to parallel that north–south rivalry, distrust, and ridicule. One sees this in Wundt's critical approach to his northern Prussian colleagues and in the way they were critical of him. In family backgrounds and personal leanings Wundt was of southern roots, which he seemed to be fond of displaying to the irritation of certain colleagues. This difference of style may also partly account for why Wundt had so many more students than Germany's great northern representative of experimental psychology, G. E. Müller. Müller was famous for having the strictest and severest of standards as to who would be allowed to study with him. However, Wundt let any students who were interested into his program regardless of background or theoretical leanings.

A ROAMING MIND

Wundt's youth was a period of daydreaming, distraction, and wandering thoughts. On reaching early adulthood, family pressures steered him into a medical career—decidedly a mistake because of his wandering mind. Wundt's thoughts had a strong theoretical flavor. He feared that his constant thoughts about philosophical questions could be endangering his patients' lives. For such reasons, he changed course and threw himself into the study of theoretical physiology, which inspired him on to psychology, cultural studies, and, eventually, to the professorship in philosophy at Leipzig, where he remained, in dramatic Wagnerian form, for the rest of his life.

Wundt was called to this professorship at a time when philosophy, which had always been very psychological in Germany, was widely viewed as suffering a prolonged lack of progress. A positivistic move developed in several universities there to bring methods of science into the service of philosophy. Wundt's role, as one of a new generation of scientific philosophers, was to contribute to a new science-based philosophy at Leipzig. The result was experimental psychology.

Although Wundt proclaimed experimental psychology to be a new science, he always saw it as a fundamental part of the philosophy department not a breakaway department, as was soon to be the pattern in American universities. In Germany it was the philosophers, threatened by the growing number of experimental psychologists in their midst, who eventually forced them out.

That development led to the institutional crisis for German psychology that Wundt (1913) discussed in his essay, "Psychology's Fight for Its Existence" (*Die Psychologie im Kampf ums Dasein*). In that work, Wundt was actually quite sympathetic to much of the philosophical opposition. He agreed that any limitation to one particular methodology for theory verification would be crippling for any discipline. With the movement toward experimentalism beginning to produce laboratory technical expertise to the degree that some experimental psychologists seemed more interested in apparatus than anything else, Wundt thought that these narrowly focused experimentalists, whom he was partly responsible for creating, would spend their time and talents better on improving the technology of sewing machines.

THE "VOLUNTARIST" SCHOOL OF PSYCHOLOGY

Shortly after Wundt arrived in Leipzig, his school of thought became widely known, at least in Europe if not America, as the voluntarist school because of its emphasis on volition and self-control. This emphasis conformed to a strong accent in the language of the German philosophy of that day, but it is absent in most American textbooks. Most of those texts mistakenly assigned Titchener's title for the Cornell school of thought—*structuralism*—to Wundt's psychology, although Wundt never used the term as the title for his school of thought.

In actuality, the school of structuralism—stemming from Titchener's British background—bears little resemblance to the Leipzig school of voluntarism. Throughout his career, Wundt championed a German Leibnizian tradition, which emphasized internal mental dynamics over and against the competing Lockean empiricistic tradition and, by implication, its American derivatives. This crusade created a barrier to the dispassionate examination of Wundt's work in the Anglo-American world. American psychology was evolving as a new-world, forward-looking, rebuilding of the discipline. It worked toward uniting psychology with the physical sciences. Wundt's historically focused and antiphysicalist orientation was its opposite.

Introspection? Overcoming a Powerful Myth

In much of the American-dominated 20th century, there surely was little concern with the niceties of precise and correct interpretation of the foreign Wundtian theoretical system. If anything, Wundt was the sporting target of polemics designed to show how misguided some of the prebehaviorist German ancestry of psychology had been. For many Americans at that time, there was no reason to approach Wundt with the same care that one would use in a systematic study of, say, Pavlovian psychology.

There is one interpretation that would most certainly have infuriated Wundt had he lived to see its development through mistranslations into English. Contrary to the impression conveyed by those translations—because the truth violates such a good story about why psychology took the particular turns it did in the early 20th century—Wundt was probably history's most vocal campaigner against the use of classical armchair introspection. Refutations of introspectionism run through his essays in the *Philosophische Studien* and the *Psychologische Studien,* as well as in those longer works that went into issues of methodology in detail (e.g., in his *Logik,* 1908; for a few of many examples, see Wundt, 1882, 1883, 1888, 1893, 1900, 1907).

A Plague of Textbook Writers

The fact of Wundt's refutations of introspection must be repeated many times over if psychology is ever to defeat the textbook writers' tradition that equates Wundt's name with introspection. As Danziger (1990) suggested, in his detailed analysis—the most complete to date in the efforts to correct this error—if any corpse can be made to turn over in its grave, then surely Wundt's body must have rotated many times with the descriptions of him as the father of an introspectionist school. In his earlier years, Wundt repeatedly unraveled the old *reflection psychology*, a term then used to designate inner examinations of private mental processes as a form of scientific data. Wundt initially offered his new psychology in opposition to that legacy, opposing the old introspection with a new method of self-observation (*Selbstbeobachtung*), which was to be scientific in that it would use objective procedures that were controllable and replicable.

If one does not know how these terms were used and what their users meant by them in the 19th century, it is easy to translate *Selbstbeobachtung* as *introspection*. Unfortunately, the few historians who have recognized this problem have been too timid in their efforts to correct it, perhaps because the correction contradicts a view that is deeply entrenched in popular textbook writing, where the Wundt-as-introspectionist story is used to justify for students some of the post-Wundtian movements in this field.

CONSCIOUSNESS

Wundt defined *psychology* as the study of consciousness. Just as astronomy is about stars and planets, so psychology is about consciousness. He based his research on consciousness on an actuality principle—the idea that consciousness is a natural process and an immediate reality, not some mystical or spiritual notion. We have naturalistic observations of consciousness in alternations between sleep and wakefulness, in lapses of attention, and in other fluctuations that, according to Wundt, could be manipulated and measured in laboratory settings. For Wundt, to deny psychology this subject matter would be like denying astronomers their stars and planets. To say that there is no phenomenon to be studied here, that consciousness is described only as the physics and chemistry of the brain, or that the language of psychology can refer only to behavioral movements and external environmental objects would mean, to him, that there can be no psychology—because there is then only physics, chemistry, biology, and zoology.

The first experimental question that Wundt investigated around 1860, in this new science, was the temporal characteristics of the fluctuations of consciousness that occur when one attempts to attend to two stimuli at once—the so-called *complication experiment*. It represented a tradition of research that continued into the 20th century as found in the dichotic listening experiments or in the modern work on mental chronometry, as seen, for instance, in Posner's (1978) *Chronometric Explorations of Mind* (1978).

Views about the reality of consciousness quite similar to Wundt's were expressed well by George Miller a century later in 1981 in his review of trends in American cognitive psychology. Miller and Wundt both argued that all moving creatures must be conscious because their motility reveals it especially in their patterns of safe navigation. Any number of behavioral indications, in the view of these theorists, reflect the existence of consciousness. If all moving life forms are conscious, then automatized processes or complex unconscious controls are the result of a progressive development that occurs as organisms become more complex. That is, all mental/behavioral capacities in the Wundt–Miller view had originally required awareness. What most characteristically distinguishes Wundt's theory, however, is its emphasis on one aspect that he held as the key aspect of consciousness—namely, *impulse, desire,* or *urge.* (The German word was *Trieb,* a term that became synonymous with Wundtian psychology, at least among many continental writers. In Wundt's usage, that term did not carry the connotation of *instinc*t—a more mechanistic, less emotionlike rendering.)

To Speak of Consciousness

Wundt argued that it is important never to let oneself think of consciousness in terms of some material substance. That would be a lapse into physicalistic mysticism. He also argued that consciousness can never be described as a stage on which certain events play for a while and then retire to some place off stage only to be called back for a later reappearance. This violates the principle made popular later by William James (chap. 2, *Pioneers I*)—that consciousness is a constant flow. The stream is always changing, never repeating. Memory is only a new construction that is attributed to the past, but logically never a revival of a bit of the past that no longer exists. When something is left behind subsequent to an image, emotion, or thought, the only thing we can logically speak of as being left behind is some hypothetical change in a conceptual nervous system. Wundt argued that, although we may discover and describe those changes in a science of neurology, we will never find consciousness in them. To say that eventually we will see the emotional quality of pain by looking through a microscope at a piece of nervous tissue was the sort of nonsense that Wundt could not abide. For him, it was also a violation of logic to speak of bits of consciousness floating around somewhere that are not within the set we define as *immediate consciousness.* In Wundtian psychology, consciousness was viewed as an *"Entwicklung"*—a constant construction, regeneration, or refreshing of experience. It never rests except to stop intermittently during sleep or attention lapses. However, the rate and capacity of that flow can be measured—the major thrust of the early Wundtian experimental laboratory.

Wundt's actuality principle also carries his strong opposition to classical faculty psychology because, in his view, we must regard consciousness as one basic process. References to perception, recognition, memory, thinking, or daydreaming only refer to different slants on one and the same process. The principles of consciousness operate in fundamentally the same way in all these spheres. They all involve the same bottleneck of central selective attention. They are all limited by the same central reaction times. They all exhibit the same limitations in capacity or spans. They are all equally under the same constraints of the same short-term memory. They are all influenced in the same way by affective-motivational states. They all reflect the same emergent phenomena associated with the holistic nature of mental events in which the whole is always more than the sum of the parts. Associative phenomena (which Wundt saw as affecting only peripheral aspects of consciousness) behave the same ways in all forms of consciousness. In the study of development, all forms of consciousness reflect the same patterns of growth.

AN ORNATE TECHNICAL LITERATURE

The scattered and profuse quality of Wundt's writings, along with the well-known awkwardness of translating German conceptual terms into English, served as a further barrier to the reception of Wundt in some areas outside Germany. One deterrent is found in the quality of his *Outlines of Psychology* (1896), translated by C. H. Judd—for the most part a dry and tedious book. Judd's translation has been criticized for its awkward English rendering of the German text (e.g., the loose and contradictory use of the word *introspection*).

The first half of the book surveys the quality dimensions of experience—the dimensional systems of sensation, perception, and emotion. In the second half, the typical and cardinal volitional-motivational theory emerges. The book does not give a good picture of experimental psychology; for that you must dig rather deeply into Wundt's three-volume *Grundzüge der Physiologischen Psychologie*, which is massive in technical detail and packed with philosophy and intellectual history.

When *Physiologischen* Did Not Mean *Physiological*

Translated literally, the full title of Wundt's *Grundzüge der physiologischen Psychologie* is *Principles of Physiological Psychology*. Something quite antiquated or parochial stands out in the use of the adjective *physiological* in that title, as Wundt pointed out. It is a usage, found briefly in Germany around the mid-19th century, that seems to have escaped many of the historians who wrote about Wundt a century later. The older parochial German vogue was to use *physiological* to indicate a style of research that adopted the methods of the then-new and successful experimental physiology of the mid-19th century created by such great experimenters as Wundt's mentor, Helmholtz. In the 1894 edition of his *Grundzüge*, Wundt was already noting that his usage of *physiological* to mean *experimental* was a local custom that had gone out of style, and therefore might cause some confusion because the newer usage of *physiological psychology* meant something quite different (see Wundt's 1894 edition, Vol. I, p. 9). Wundt noted that his book had attained a strong identity with that title and thus he felt he could not change it. Therefore, the odd way of indicating experimental continued in subsequent editions. The three-volume work was in part a continuing, constantly updated, summarization of the field. Wundt began writing it in the mid-1870s and continued rewriting it until his death in 1920. The momentary form of the summarizations were published at approximately 10-year intervals. He left an unfinished further edition on his deathbed.

Wundt's Students

When American histories of psychology have described Wundt's prominent students, they have focused on those who diverged from Wundt and were attracted to the later positivistic movements that opposed Wundt. Those who remained close to Wundt and who expanded his system of thought (Wirth, Krueger, Klemm, Meumann, Dittrich, Sander, Vokelt, Judd, to name a few) are rarely discussed or mentioned.

To say the least, Wundt's students were numerous and came in all varieties, representing any number of distinct, even conflicting, intellectual traditions. In the late 19th century, a large number of Americans in their early 20s armed with only a year or two of college German journeyed to Leipzig to spend the 2 years necessary to earn a German doctorate. That degree was about the equivalent of the modern American master's degree, or much easier than the doctorate degree that was soon to appear as the highest academic degree in American education. The reason was that, in Germany, there was another level of achievement beyond the doctorate, the *Habilitation*, which was required for teaching in a German university.

Wundt attracted students from most countries around the globe in which there was a strong interest in higher education. When they returned home they filtered what they had been exposed to in Leipzig through the categories of their home cultures. Today the historian might experience vexation in comparing the remembrances of Wundtian psychology published by his American students with the truly different remembrances in another commemorative volume authored, say, by Wundt's followers in India (e.g., the 1932 volume of the *Indian Journal of Psychology*) or even with those remembrances in the several commemorative volumes that appeared in Germany. What arose in the American accounts was a Westernized Wundt that overlooked large parts of his work and that dressed Wundt in the ill-fitting clothes of an associationistic and mechanistic theorist, often yielding something quite preposterous.

Hugo Münsterberg's "Three-Ring Circus"

Those of Wundt's students who followed the path of physicalism or early behaviorism offer instructive contrasts with the old master of Leipzig. One of the most informative was the illustrious Hugo Münsterberg, who had been wooed away from Germany by William James to develop Harvard's first large psychology laboratory in the early 1890s. A monumental disagreement over theory had previously erupted between the protobehaviorist Münsterberg and Wundt when Münsterberg presented Wundt with an 1888 doctoral dissertation opposing Wundt's voluntarist theory. Münsterberg argued for an anti-Wundtian theory in which all contents of consciousness were to be reduced to sensations. Wundt's volitional-affective dimension of mental processes was omitted. In Wundt's view, Münsterberg was arguing for an old and discredited peripheralist theory that acknowledged only sensori-motor processes. In disagreement with Münsterberg, Wundt taught that stimuli are not fixed pieces of information from the environment, but rather that experiential information is derived from environmental stimulation in terms of individual desires and needs. Goal orientations, as Wundt replied to Münsterberg, determine the form of stimulus information that is developed in immediate experience.

The strong-willed and brash Münsterberg, son of a prominent Prussian family of Danzig on the northern coast, reflected the image of something like a German version of the American president Teddy Roosevelt whom he came to admire so much after his arrival at Harvard. Hale (1980) wrote a useful history of the colorful Münsterberg who imported the gilded age of Leipzig psychology to Harvard in the form of ornate and polished brass instrumentation for measuring reaction times and controlling stimulus presentations.

In 1893, Münsterberg transported many of these instruments to the World's Fair exposition in Chicago as an elaborate exhibit that introduced the new experimental psychology to the American public for the first time and in a sensational way. However Münsterberg left the Wundtian theory behind, substituting his own increasingly mechanistic views that found fertile soil in the new American setting. He sensed the American temper well and, to his advantage, quickly conformed to the model of a technological pragmatist. Münsterberg's showy commercial style soon left Harvard's William James disillusioned, leading him to refer to Münsterberg's activities as a "three-ring circus."

In Münsterberg's hands, the Harvard psychology department was to be identified with prediction and control of behavior, with practical interests in manipulating behavior in what he called his *action psychology*. Dismissing Wundt's theories of consciousness, he advocated physicalism when teaching his Harvard students, who included Robert Yerkes (chap. 7, *Pioneers II*), Knight Dunlap, Floyd Allport (chap. 8, this volume), and Edward Holt. He knew how to read and respond to the culture of his new American society. In those years, Wundtian psychology was more faithfully taught at Yale by the team of C. H. Judd, E. W. Scripture, and G. T. Ladd. When adding up the personalities of those three, you could not get half the charisma of Münsterberg, nor even less of a match to the charisma and influence of the imposing and articulate Edward Titchener, the great British empiricist at Cornell, who had also spent the 2 years in Leipzig necessary for earning a doctorate in psychology because no psychology doctorate was offered in his native England. The Wundtian school at Yale quickly withered. Judd, Scripture, and Ladd all left academic psychology at a relatively early point in their careers (see Blumenthal, 1985, for a brief account of the ill-fated early Yale psychology department).

Münsterberg became so enthralled with wearing the mantel of the German mandarin professor that it eventually destroyed him when he became entangled with celebrities, politicians, and stars of the new Hollywood movie industry. He engineered grandiose receptions, even a parade, for German royalty visiting in the United States. He was an advisor to the leaders of society even reaching the president. He put forth Herculean efforts to influence the U. S. government against entering World War I. It all eventually fell into a pattern of scandal and public disgrace, the stress of which may have contributed to his sudden collapse and death in front of a lecture audience at Harvard. Although Münsterberg's name seems to have been removed from much of Harvard's history, one can still find a glass case in William James Hall housing ornate specimens of the brass and mahogany psychological apparatus that Münsterberg brought from Germany. One might say that, with him, psychology's gilded age had come to America for a brief time in the same polished style, if not the same theoretical system, that one would have found in Leipzig in those years.

ANTI-ELEMENTISM—MORE MYSTERIES IN HISTORICAL SCHOLARSHIP

Without a clear conception of Wundt's general theoretical position, and of the intellectual contexts of his time and place, attempts to comprehend specific areas of his work could easily lead to confusion. Certainly in Wundt's formative years, and through much of his career, Herbartian associationistic psychology was one strong psychological model in the German academic community. The Germans read Herbart rather than the parallel British associationists. Wundt's thinking developed in to a career-long rebellion against the Herbartian elementistic, associationistic, and mechanistic approach. Wundt upheld those very different traditions in German intellectual history that emphasized more organismic models.

Wundt's Opposition to Herbart

Only a fragment of Herbart's writings were ever translated into English. However knowing Herbart is extremely important for an understanding of the history of modern psychology because individuals as diverse as Fechner (chap. 1, *Pioneers II*), Freud (chap. 4, *Pioneers I*), G. E. Müller, and Piaget (chap. 9, this volume) all reflect basic elements of Herbart's system. The learning curve formula offered by the leading neobehaviorist, Clark Hull (chap. 14, *Pioneers I*), is identical to Herbart's earlier formula.

Herbart's psychology was mechanistic to the core—one of its most attractive features for many of its adherents. It may even have outdone the British associationists in the more developed forms of associationism that it conceived. Herbart's way of describing things according to mechanical models was carried into numerous other fields by his followers. Wundt's *Voluntarism* was the focus of opposition to the Herbartian tradition in Germany. Wundt's entry into such fields as cultural studies or linguistics often seems to have been inspired by his wish to refute those variations of Herbartian thought (see Blumenthal, 1970).

An Odd Footnote in Germany's Darkest Hour

By 1943, Germany was descending into the lowest levels of the Nazi hell. The grand gilded age of its past was now smoke and ash. On the night of December 4 of that year, the once resplendent Leipzig *Psychologische Institüt* was hit by a joint Anglo-American bombing raid. With bombs falling around him, Max Wundt, the wayward and troubled son of the Wundt family, wrote a short footnote in a book that was published in 1944. It was a note that expressed his astonishment about an historical misinterpretation concerning something critical for a correct telling of the history of psychology. It was an observation concerning an historical interpretation that is, in the context of many history-of-psychology texts, surely astonishing. In referring to his father's psychological system, Max Wundt (1944) wrote,

> One may follow the methodologically obvious principle of advancing from the simple to the complicated, indeed even employing the approach that would construct the mind from primitive mechanical elements (the so-called psychology of mental elements). In this case, however, method and phenomena can become grossly confused.... Whoever in particular ascribes to my father such a conception could not have read his books. In fact, he had formed his scientific views of mental processes in reaction against a true elementistic psychology, namely against that of Herbart, which was dominant in those days. (p. 15)

Indeed it is true. Wundt's attacks on mechanistic and atomistic psychology, a psychology that American textbooks later erroneously attribute to him, can be found in virtually all his works. For example, "There are absolutely no psychological structures that can be characterized in their meaning or in the value of their contents as the sum of their elemental factors or the mere mechanical results of their components" (Wundt, 1908, p. 276).

The temptation to adopt Newtonian physics as an analogue for psychological theory was not just a trait of the English. Herbart's theory conformed to that approach in many ways. Wundt showed no disrespect for the great achievements of physical science. However, with a vigor perhaps unmatched, he opposed all attempts to create explanations in psychology based on analogies with physics or chemistry. He disputed that analogy wherever it appeared—in psychology, linguistics, philosophy, sociology, and political science. The mechanistic character of some strains of British ethical theory brought forth Wundt's critical rebuttals in especially strong statements that were distributed in anti-British propaganda during World War I.

VOLITION

Putting it most simply, Wundt expounded endlessly in this antimechanist campaign because he believed that psychologies modeled after Newtonian physics would misrepresent desires, feelings, urges, strivings, motivations, and self-control. As early as 1858, when the young Wundt was involved in medical and physiological research, he was arguing that there are phenomena in biology and psychology that require explanations that are different in their fundamental form from the pattern of explanation found in physics and chemistry. These explanations, as he argued, had to involve notions of purposivism and goal-oriented actions.

Creative Synthesis Again

In his early years as a psychologist, when he was somewhat more concerned with perception than in his later years, what impressed Wundt most was the emergent nature of many psychological phenomena. There are no *psychological qualities* in physics. For example, there is no red, or green, or blue in that world. Redness, greeness, and blueness are phenomena that are created by the cortex of the experiencing individual. A musical quality, the flavor of a wine, or the familiarity of a face is a rapid creative synthesis that cannot, in principle, be explained as a mere *sum* of elemental physical features. However, those ephemeral qualities can be studied scientifically, through the methods of psychophysics. When Wundt used the phrase "psychological elements" in his chapter titles, it referred to these abstract qualities.

In Wundt's theory, these creative syntheses are under the control of a central process that channels the flow of the stream of consciousness. Unlike many of his contemporaries who speculated about consciousness as being a recent or highly evolved function, Wundt saw it as the primitive initial state of life, speculating that in primitive life forms volition must begin as elemental urges or impulses. The automatic processes are the ones that are highly evolved (i.e., later appearing). Automatization of function is, in this view, the result of great stretches of time filled with countless repetitions of mental and behavioral acts that lead those acts to develop into nonconscious automatic mechanisms. A core principle for Wundt is that all these processes are, in their evolution, expressions of initially goal-directed volitional processes.

Evolution of Mental Processes

The particular forms and qualities of consciousness, in Wundt's theory, are the repositories of a long evolutionary history. Every mental event, each emergent form or quality, is ultimately to be explained as evolving from a volitional central control process. Initially all mental events must be in the selectively controlled focus of attention (for which Wundt used the old Leibnizian term *apperception*). The syntheses of experience take their particular form because they have long had a particular value for the organism. Perceptual and other mental constructions are all originally motivated, only later becoming automatized or functionally autonomous. Reflexes too, in this theory, are explained as automatized volitions.

Affective-motivational processes are thus placed in a position of primacy in all psychological processes in this theory. However, volition, is not employed here in the sense of free will. It is under the control of a system of emotional tones, impulses, urges, and automatizations that determine the course of thought and behavior.

Wundt argued that the volition that occurs in human consciousness cannot be the same volition that occurs in primitive animal life. As the volitional process evolves in higher life forms, it obviously expands and differentiates. More complex forms of impulse emerge. It makes sense to conjecture that the impulses or urges at least become more numerous as life evolves. More complex organisms have an increasing variety of desires and urges, which means that there may be the simultaneous presence of several urges at once—so that this inner emotional control of behavior must be considerably complicated by multiple and often competing drive states. With the appearance of more highly evolved nervous systems, said Wundt, we can have conscious deliberation, decision, and choice as influencing the predominance of one volitional urge over another. Volitional states were seen as occurring in varied forms or levels—from primitive impulses (in which only one urge or desire is present) to volitional acts (in which more than one urge is present but one predominates) to selective acts (in which many urges are present and a conscious choice is made among them). For further theoretical details, see Danziger's (1980) summary.

GENERAL CHARACTERISTICS
OF THE STREAM OF CONSCIOUSNESS

Wundt's mature theory was often identified with his development of a set of principles that frequently appeared in a concluding summary in many of his later works. They are six related generalities about the characteristics of the flow of the stream of consciousness. The first three concerned the microgenetic processes of immediate consciousness. The second three principles concerned the longer developmental and historical processes.

The first principle is that of *creative synthesis*, which has already been introduced. It was the postulation of a central construction of emergent qualities.

Second is the principle of *psychological relativity*, which describes mental processes as having their existence and identity only as part of larger configurations of experience. The first principle has to do with emergent qualities in the synthesis of experience, whereas the second refers to the differentiations of experience through the analytical process of selective attention. Any item of mental focusing has meaning or identity only as it is related to some context. For example, words can have meaning only as a function of their membership in some present or implied sentence, and the uttered sentence is meaningful only as it relates to some larger mental context (see Blumenthal's, 1970, translations from Wundt's *Die Sprache*).

The third principle is that of *psychological contrasts*, which is an elaboration of the second principle. Simply stated, antithetical experiences intensify each other. After a period of pain, a slight pleasure will loom large. Similarly, a sweet substance tastes sweeter if eaten after a sour substance. Emotional elation may dispose one to a subsequent period of depression. The examples of such opponent processes were numerous in Wundt's discussions.

The fourth principle was the principle of the *heterogeneity of ends*. A change produced by a purposive volitional action is often different from the change intended, and that discrepancy results in further action. The changes that result here are often emergent social, intellectual, and cultural forms.

Fifth is the principle of *mental growth*. As cultural or mental forms evolve and become progressively differentiated, older and simpler forms emerge into more elaborate forms that must be understood through their relation to the earlier parent forms. The evolution of the world's languages was a popular example for Wundt because he had contributed heavily to the technical literature on linguistics. In the case of individual development, he cited at length the unfolding of language in the child. From this view, the child's language begins with impulses, urges, or desires that are reflected in global emotional gestures. The emergence of language then proceeds in accord with the unfolding and differentiation of those original germinal forms.

Sixth is the principle of *development toward opposites*, which is the long-term parallel of the principle of psychological contrasts. It is the statement that the development of attitudes and cultural forms fluctuates between opponent historical or developmental processes. A period of one type of activity or experience evokes a tendency to seek some opposite form of experience or action. These fluctuations, as Wundt observed, are found not only in the life and experience of the individual, but also in the cyclical patterns of history, economic cycles, and social customs.

CONCLUSION

The 1880s, 1890s, and first decade of the 20th century had indeed been a gilded age for Wundt, for psychology, and for Leipzig. Approximately 17,000 students (according to D. K.. Robinson's 1987 archival research) passed through Wundt's afternoon lectures on general psychology, which were popular partly because they were embellished with demonstrations of the strange, new gilded instruments for measuring the flow and control of consciousness. As the word *gilded* may imply, the whole enterprise was doomed to come crashing down from its own weight and from the shifting historical ground on which it rested. One of the key features of Wundt's final system concerned the cyclical nature of human mental activities (the principle of development toward opposites). If anything, the fate of his own intellectual enterprise and that of Leipzig reflected that principle only too well. However, the principle is about *cyclicality*. If true, it cuts both ways.

REFERENCES

Blumenthal, A. L. (1970). *Language and psychology: Historical aspects of psycholinguistics.* New York: Wiley.

Blumenthal, A. L. (1985). Shaping a tradition: Experimentalism begins. In C. Buxton (Ed.), *Points of view in the modern history of psychology* (pp. 51–83). San Diego: Academic Press.

Danziger, K. (1980). Wundt's theory of behavior and volition. In R. W. Rieber (Ed.), *Wilhelm Wundt and the making of a scientific psychology* (pp. 89–115). New York: Plenum.

Danziger, K. (1990). *Constructing the subject: Historical origins of psychological research.* England: Cambridge University Press.

Hale, M. (1980). *Human science and social order: Hugo Münsterberg and the origins of applied psychology.* Philadelphia: Temple University Press.

Hall, G. S. (1881). *Aspects of German culture.* Boston: Osgood.

Hall, G. S. (1912). *Founders of modern psychology.* New York: Appleton.

Kusch, M. (1995). *Psychologism: A case study in the sociology of philosophical knowledge.* London: Routledge.

Miller, G. A. (1981). Trends and debates in cognitive psychology. *Cognition, 10,* 215–225.

Posner, M. I. (1978). *Chronometric explorations of mind.* Hillsdale, NJ: Lawrence Erlbaum Associates.

Ringer, R. (1969). *The decline of the German mandarins,* Cambridge, MA: Harvard University Press.

Robinson, D. K. (1987). *Wilhelm Wundt and the establishment of experimental psychology, 1875–1914: The context of a new field of scientific research.* Unpublished doctoral dissertation, University of California, Berkeley.

Wundt, M. (1944). *Die Würzeln der deutschen Philosophie in Stamm und Rasse* [Roots of German philosophy in clan and race]. Berlin: Junker, Dunhaupt.

Wundt, W. (1882). Die Aufgaben der experimentellen Psychologie [The tasks of experimental psychology]. *Unsere Zeit.* (Reprinted in Wundt, W., *Essays,* 2nd ed., Leipzig: Engelmann, 1906.)

Wundt, W. (1883). Ueber psychologische Methoden [Concerning psychological methods]. *Philosophische Studien, 1,* 1–40.

Wundt, W. (1888). Selbstbeobachtung und innere Wahrnehmung [The examination of self-processes and the act of inner perception]. *Philosophische Studien, 4,* 292–309.

Wundt, W. (1893). *Logik* [Logic] (2nd ed.). Stuttgart: Enke.

Wundt, W. (1896). *Grundriss der Psychologie.* Leipzig: Englemann. (translated by C. H. Judd as *Outlines Of Psychology,* 1897.)

Wundt, W. (1900). Bemerkungen zur Theorie der Gefühle. [Observations on the theory of feelings]. *Philosophische Studien, 15,* 149–182.

Wundt, W. (1907). Ueber ausfrage Experimente und über die Methoden zur Psychologie des Denkens. [Concerning interrogation experiments and methods in the psychology of thinking]. *Psychologische Studien, 2,* 301–390.

Wundt, W. (1908). Logik [Logic] (3rd ed.). Stuttgart: Enke.

Wundt, W. (1913). *Die Psychologie im Kampf ums Dasein.* [Psychology's fight for its existence]. Leipzig: Engelmann.

Chapter 4

Hermann Ebbinghaus:
On the Road to Progress
or Down the Garden Path?

C. Alan Boneau

Many of the chapters in the original volumes of *Portraits of Pioneers in Psychology* were presentations at conventions, most of them organized by the Division of General Psychology of the American Psychological Association. In several of these presentations, the speaker played the role of a deceased pioneer in psychology and, in the language that that person used or might have used, discussed the pioneer's work and its relationship to modern developments. The following chapter on Ebbinghaus continues that tradition. The first and final sections are in the words of the chairperson at such a session [Eds.].

INTRODUCTION:
CHAIRPERSON'S OPENING REMARKS

Ladies and Gentlemen: We are gathered here today to honor a major pioneer in psychology, Hermann Ebbinghaus. Professor Ebbinghaus's small but immensely significant monograph, *On Memory,* was first published in 1885. It was an immediate sensation, and Professor Ebbinghaus was lauded by the great names of his time, including William James and E. B. Titchener among many others. I do not now discuss the contents of the book because we have present today the spirit of Professor Ebbinghaus to present his work and comment on these contributions in the light of later developments. By way of introduction, however, I will provide a brief biographical sketch of Professor Ebbinghaus and then I will turn over the

---

*Sketch of Hermann Ebbinghaus. From *Human Memory and Cognitive Capabilities* by F. Klix & H. Hagendorf (Eds.), 1986, North Holland: Elsevier.

podium to the spirit of our guest of honor. I will return at the end to make a few summary statements and provide a more objective assessment of the contributions of our guest than his modesty will permit.

Biographical Sketch

Hermann Ebbinghaus was born in 1850 in Barmen, Germany, near Düsseldorf, the son of a merchant. He mentions his early life in a short autobiographical statement contained in his doctoral dissertation of 1873. There he notes that his early education was in the local area and that later he attended the universities of Bonn, Halle, and Berlin, studying history and philology. In 1871, he switched to philosophy and received his doctorate at Bonn in 1873 on the basis of a dissertation entitled "On Hartmann's Philosophy of the Unconscious." We note here that he has come to see this early concern with unconscious thought processes as instrumental in developing his later thinking. After receiving his doctorate, he spent several years studying in England, France, and Germany and then supported himself in Berlin for some time by giving lectures at the university.

Ebbinghaus conducted the first of a series of experiments on memory, that he will describe today, in 1878–1879; he presented this research to the University of Berlin in 1880 as his "habilitation thesis," one of the credentials required at German universities to qualify a person to serve as a paid lecturer. He stayed in Berlin until 1893. While there, in 1883–1884, he conducted another series of memory experiments, which, combined with his earlier work, formed the basis for the 1885 book he discusses today. In 1893, he was passed over for promotion and then left Berlin to become full professor at the University of Breslau. Subsequently, he wrote a very successful textbook in psychology, developed a successful test for assessing intelligence in children in 1897, and conducted a variety of laboratory experiments in psychophysics.

In 1905, Ebbinghaus left Breslau for the University of Halle, where he died in 1909. Earlier, in 1890, he had turned down an offer to become professor of psychology at Cornell—the position that E. B. Titchener later accepted—for personal reasons (Bringmann & Bringmann, 1986). The history of psychology in America could have been much changed had Ebbinghaus' decision been different. Those in psychology who do not know Ebbinghaus' work, which must be a small minority, will at least recognize the aphorism that opens his text *Psychology: An Elementary Textbook* (1908, 1973): "Psychology has a long past, but a short history." I bring you now one of the most important figures in that short history, Professor Hermann Ebbinghaus.

EBBINGHAUS: INVITED LECTURE

Thank you, Mr. Chairman, for that kind introduction. Ladies and gentlemen, it gives me great pleasure to be permitted to discuss my work before a group of such distinguished guests. It has been suggested that I limit my remarks to the development of the ideas that went into my book, *On Memory*, and to second thoughts I might have from the perspective of a hundred years or so. This provides a long time for such later thoughts and, in many respects, my first thoughts are the most interesting and the ones of which I am most proud. This is because the first thoughts were the most difficult ones—the ones that represented breaks with tradition and a striking out into the unknown. I am fortunate that, as was the case with Columbus, there was something there to be discovered.

Important Figures in My Background

I have had time, of course, to ruminate on the influences that led me to develop my ideas, and I have recognized that, like Newton, I had been standing on the shoulders of giants. Historians of psychology make much of the fact that I ran across a used copy of Fechner's *Elements of Psychophysics* in a Paris bookstall. However, none of them seems to have recognized the profound effect that that book had on my thinking, nor did I make this point very clear before. Many say that Fechner's book provided me with the inspiration to take a mathematical approach to psychological material. It was more than an inspiration. In fact, it was the kernel of my whole understanding of what it was that I was doing and would do.

By that time, many of the pieces of the formulation were falling into place. I was already intrigued by problems of memory, particularly of forgetting. I knew by then that the second time one memorized a poem, the task was easier than it was the first time, although few or none of the actual words in it were recallable. My earlier experience in my dissertation with the work on the unconscious by Professor Hartmann and my exposure as a student to the theories of Professor Herbart about unconscious mental activities suggested that some residue of the poem might have a nonconscious presence in memory although it was not recallable. However, I had not put this together until I read Fechner, and there it was.

Professor Fechner, you will remember, was concerned with our ability to detect as sensations small physical values of, say, sound energy. In one of his procedures, he started from some energy level that was not detectable and increased step by step the energy level until it could be barely detected as a sound sensation. It stands to reason, as Professor Fechner believed on the basis of the principle of conservation of energy (Fechner, 1850/1966; Lowry, 1971), that the nondetectable levels of sound energy were nevertheless influencing the nervous system, but they were not conscious. Gradually changing the sound energy level must have also increased the energy level in the nervous system until it was sufficient for a conscious detection or, stated otherwise, reached the threshold for the sensation of sound.

Association Theory

How does that relate to forgetting? At that time, I was also steeped in the notion of learning by association. I believed that the strength of the association between two items is increased if they occur together—the principle of contiguity, which, of course, goes back at least to Aristotle. In learning a poem, then, one simply repeats it until the associations between successive words are sufficiently strong that every word successfully suggests the next. Relating this to Professor Fechner's formulation, it occurred to me that a repetition is analogous to increasing the energy level of a physical stimulus; it simply increases the strength of associations at an unconscious level until the associated words are pushed into consciousness. As I surmised, with time, association strength seems to fade or decay and the poem gradually sinks below threshold and is no longer recallable. According to this view, the poem is still present in memory, but the associations are too weak to produce a conscious recall.

Here again is where I was inspired by Fechner's work. Using his method of limits, Professor Fechner would successively increase his stimulus strength incrementally from a subthreshold level until it was detectable as a sensation. Then he would start with an above-threshold value and decrease incrementally until the stimulus was no longer detectable, and then back up again. Forgetting must be like the downward side of the Fechner procedure. All I had to do with a forgotten poem that had declined below threshold was start with its present subthreshold levels of association strength and increase them as before by repetitions until the poem was again recallable. If I assume that a repetition always produces the same increase in association strength, then the number of repetitions to relearn is a measure of how much was forgotten. The number of repetitions for original learning minus the number to relearn, the amount saved, must be a measure of the amount of association strength retained after forgetting. This was a kind of psychophysics, with repetitions playing the role of the physical dimension and recallability, or the appearance of the to-be-recalled word in consciousness, the role of the psychological. As you say today, I was now in business.

As an aside, I am reminded that in the book I make use of the metaphor *impressed in memory* when I discuss the development of strength of association. I felt at the time that it was like writing in wax and making the impressions deeper and deeper with each repetition. Later, Professor Thorndike used a similar metaphor, *stamping in*, to characterize the learning of his cats. I have now come to prefer a more abstract, more neutral way of discussing the process.

Experimental Studies

In 1878, I was excited enough about my insights into unconscious association strength to begin a well-controlled study of memory, but there was a problem of materials to learn. I loved poetry, but with poems there is a definite theoretical problem. I was interested in manipulating the strength of association between successive items by the process of repetition. With poems, or with any meaningful material, however, pairs of words have various strengths of association between them even before the learning begins. This seemed to create a confounding situation that might mask the results I was interested in. So I experimented with items made of digits, but found them unsatisfactory because of their limited numbers of combinations.

Nonsense Syllables.   So as everybody now seems to know, I thought of using nonsense syllables made of two consonants with a vowel in between. They were generally pronounceable, and the German alphabet provided me with some 2,300 items. Some of these, of course, were real German words, but for my purposes that did not matter. In a random sequence of these syllables, I thought, to start there would be virtually zero association strength between all pairs of items although some might be words. For reasons that were unclear to me at the time, some syllables were much easier to learn than others, producing what I described earlier as an "almost incomprehensible variation." Later investigators seem to have accounted for these differences. For example, Jenkins (1985), identified phonetic and orthographic variables of syllables that predict ease of learning. It turned out, however, that many of the things that I learned from nonsense syllables also seem to apply to poems, as a few later variations on my procedure demonstrated to me.

Method.   With these materials, I was ready to begin my studies. Let me describe the general procedure that was followed, with variations, in all of my experiments. I prepared a set of 2,300 cards, each with one of my syllables on it. For my experiments, I shuffled these cards and selected sequences of specific lengths from the top of this randomly ordered deck. In successive tests, I always used new cards from the top until the pile was exhausted. I then reshuffled and started the whole process over.

In all of my studies, which employed several conditions, I used one of two processes, always going through the set of cards in the same order. Sometimes I read aloud the set of cards over and over for a fixed set of repetitions and then tried to recall the syllables in order. Sometimes I read the sequence once and then attempted to predict the next items in the sequence before the cards were turned over one at a time and continued until, for the first time (sometimes for the second time), I was able to recall all the items without hesitation. This was my criterion for learning. My dependent variable was the number of repetitions before reaching that criterion. In all my studies, I read at the rate of 150 items per minute, usually with the aid of a metronome or clock tick. Between successive repetitions, there was a 15-second pause. Later investigators have noted that this procedure prevented me from focusing on what has come to be called the *serial position effect*. I apologize to these investigators for my lack of foresight.

I must reiterate that this procedure utilized only mere repetition as the basis for learning. There are, of course, other procedures for learning—the so-called *mnemonic techniques* that have been known since antiquity being a set of these. From the beginning of my studies, I was interested only in the effects of mere repetition on association strength. Today this procedure seems to be called *rote learning*. I believe that I was reasonably successful in utilizing only rote learning as a memory technique although I was guilty of what today would be called *chunking* (Miller, 1956), in that I tended to group syllables and emphasized the pronunciation of the syllable that began each group.

In retrospect, the magnitude of the task seems staggering to me. In one of my experiments, for example, I conducted two series of studies: one in 1879–1880, the other in 1883–1884. The test series were composed of sequences of various lengths, and I have analyzed extensively the data on sequences of 16 items. There were also 92 series of eight sequences each and 84 series of 6 sequences each. I replicated these sequences in this way to make use of statistical procedures for analyzing and minimizing error. Each of the sequences of 16 items required about 30 trials to reach criterion, or upward of 37,000 repetitions of these materials for the original learning alone. This is only a small part of the total. I shall not go into the agony that months on end of such study engendered in me. I attempted to keep conditions as similar as possible and so I tried to spend an hour or so at the same time every day on these studies. William James said of Fechner's psychophysical work that it could only take place in a country in which the natives refused to be bored. I tried to refuse to be bored, but I was not successful all the time.

The Forgetting Function

In the brief time I have here today, I go into detail about only a few of the studies that I undertook, and I summarize some of the others. Those interested in the details can find them in my book. Because most people seem to know about my forgetting curves, perhaps I should start with those. The studies involved 163 series of learning eight sequences of 13 syllables each and then relearning them to the same criterion after a delay of one of the following: 20 minutes, 1 hour, 9 hours, 1 day, 2 days, 6 days, or 31 days. I was somewhat surprised at the results, which showed a rapid initial decay that then became much smaller after a day. Figure 4.1 shows these results. From the graph, it can be seen that the savings—the percent of trials saved in relearning compared with the number for original learning—was less than 50% after only an hour and at 2 days the savings had declined almost to an the asymptotic level of about 20% that existed after a month. Thus, my method clearly demonstrated the existence of some residue of the prior learning of the sequences for long periods of time although they were utterly impossible to recall.

Learning to Learn

In another study, I investigated the effects of relearning sequences over and over again. I used sequences of various lengths: 9 sequences of 12 syllables, 3 of 24 syllables, 2 of 36 syllables, and six stanzas of Byron's "Don Juan," which were

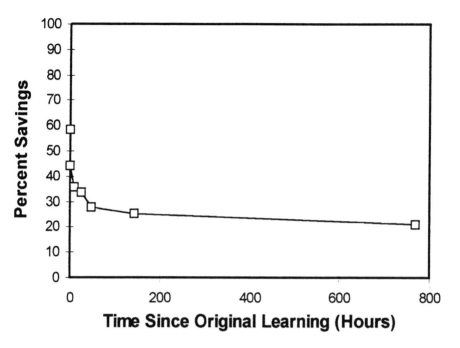

FIG. 4.1.   Forgetting over time. Showing percent of savings as a function of the time between original learning and the relearning session. Times are: 20 minutes, 1 hour, 9 hours, 24 hours, 2 days, 6 days, and 31 days.

roughly comparable to the others in length. I repeated this whole regimen seven times. The items were learned to a criterion of one perfect recitation for original learning as well as for the relearning trials, of which there were six that occurred and reoccurred after 24 hours. Figure 4.2 summarizes the results of this experiment, giving averages for the several conditions for original learning as well as for each of the relearning sessions. It was not surprising, I think, to find that relearning got easier and easier with each bout of relearning.

Distribution of Practice

In a somewhat similar experiment, I varied the number of repetitions spent each day in learning several sequences. I called this manipulation the *effect of number of repetitions*, but it later came to be called *massed and distributed practice*. I concluded that "with any considerable number of repetitions, a suitable distribution of them over a space of time is decidedly more advantageous than the massing of them in a single trial" (Ebbinghaus, 1885/1962, p. 89). To be able to recall without first prompting oneself by looking at the material, it appears to be necessary to make use of spaced practice. I hope that students in particular will be able to see the implications of this finding. In a separate set of studies, I also increased the number of repetitions in original learning far beyond that required to reach criterion. This maneuver provided only a small benefit for recall the next day.

Jost's Laws

A dozen years after I published my book, Professor Jost of Göttingen University made use of my results and methods in formulating what are now called *Jost's laws* (Jost, 1897). His first law states that, "Given two associations of equal strength, the older will benefit more from another repetition." This law is apparently an inference from my findings on the effect of massed versus distributed practice and is based on extensions of my work conducted in his laboratory by Professor Jost. Using my relearning procedure, Professor Jost showed that it requires more repetitions to recite to criterion items that have been read 30 times the day before than to learn items that have been read for 10 times on each of the last three days. Professor Jost interpreted this small but consistent advantage of the distributed practice as an indication that each repetition of the distributed and, hence, older materials must provide a greater increase in strength of association. The law as stated is an obvious generalization of that inference.

Professor Jost's second law states that, "Given two associations of equal strength, the older will decrease less with the passage of time." He seems to have

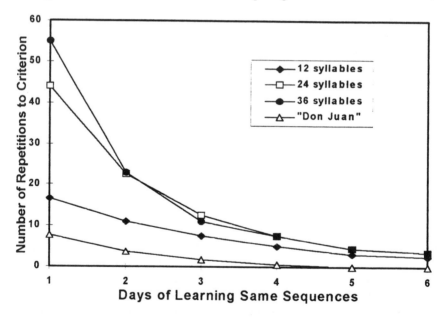

FIG. 4.2. Effects of relearning. Showing number of repetitions required to meet criterion of one perfect repetition each day of the same sequences.

gotten this idea from my relearning experiment. Professor Jost reasoned that if relearning to the same criterion takes fewer trials each day, the associations must lose strength at a slower rate as they become older with each relearning session. It follows that it would take longer for an older association to decay to the same strength as a younger association, but at that point, other things being equal, it should continue to decay more slowly. I see no a priori reason that either law should hold, but, of course, they are only empirical generalizations.

Remote Associations

The last study that I will report on is the one that I am most proud of and, for that reason, I have left it for last as I did in my book. Ever since Aristotle, people have believed that one of the conditions for the formation of associations is that the elements of the association must be in the mind at the same time. My last experiment tested this hypothesis and, I believe, demonstrated it to be false. My inspiration for this study was the philosopher-psychologist Herbart, who speculated that the associations between items in a sequence are not limited to successive pairs of items, but that associations are formed between the first and the second, the first and the third, the first and the fourth and, likewise, the second and the third, the second and the fourth, and so on. The strength of the union, Herbart expected, should be a decreasing function of the time or number of intervening members and should be stronger forward than backward. It occurred to me that my method of savings permitted me to measure the strength of these remote associations.

To do this, I first learned sequences of 16 items to a criterion of one perfect recall. I then composed derived lists consisting of new sequences of the same items but skipping over in-between items and replacing the skipped items later. For example, a sequence with one item skipped would consist of the following ordering of items, the numbers representing the order of the items in the original sequence: 1, 3, 5, 7, 9, 11, 13, 15, 2, 4, 6, 8, 10, 12, 14, 16. I could learn this sequence and compare the number of repetitions to learn this sequence with the number to learn the original sequence. Any savings would be attributed to the residual strength of associations existing between items that were not adjacent, but adjacent plus one. I also used sequences separated by 2, 3, and 7 items. For the last derived sequences, the positions were 1, 9, 2, 10, 3, 11,…, 8, 16. Because I could ordinarily maintain in consciousness only seven items at a time, it seemed to me that this last list prevented the items in the derived list from being in consciousness at the same time during the original learning. The results of this series of tests was enlightening. Figure 4.3 presents the data for the 4 degrees of separation, 1 through 7. Although the savings are small, there is a consistent decline from the smallest number of intervening items to the largest. My control group was a random rearrangement of the original list and this showed no savings, perhaps even a small amount of *negative savings*, an interference effect. Later I showed that associations were also made in a

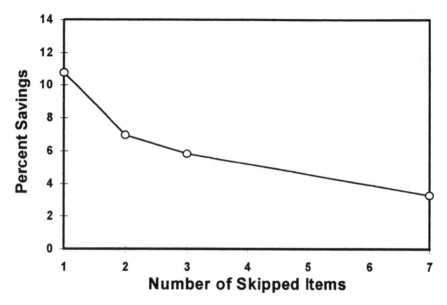

FIG 4.3.   Savings scores with derived lists. Showing percent savings as a function of the number of items from the original sequence that were skipped in constructing the derived lists.

backward fashion. For example there was savings between Items 3 and 1 and 4 and 1 in a similar kind of study.

I concluded from these findings that the learning process for a sequence of items is complex and involves association not just among pairs of items but among all of the items, both forward and backward. Professor Slamecka (1985) recently referred to this as the *bundle hypothesis*, signifying that learning is of a sequence as a unified, tied-together whole and that this kind of rote memorizing cannot be considered a learning of elements by themselves. Professor Estes (1985) amplified this notion of a bundle to include other aspects of the learning situation, such as the name of the bundle. I am told that you all have an identification number that you were required to memorize. So part of the bundle for you would be the fact that it is—what is it called?—your Social Security Number.

Unfortunately, I have come to the end of my allotted time with these final observations. However, I have just a few more things to say. Before me there was no experimental study of memory or other aspects of thinking. Professor Kant and Professor Herbart, giants in our history, had asserted that the recalcitrance of the problem of measurement applied to higher mental processes would prevent the development of a true science of mental life. You now appear to have one. Professor Kintsch (1985), however, has contended that my work set the study of cognition back several decades. Along with many other contemporary cognitive psychologists, he thinks that associationism should have been abandoned long before my time because the structure of cognition is semantic. The glue that holds ideas together is not simple associations but meaning. That kind of talk makes me irate. These critics argue that my program of research—focused on pure associative strength resulting from practice—interesting and fruitful although it may have been—tempted psychology to travel down a garden path.

That kind of talk bothers me because it slams shut the door to progress. The final answer to the question of my contribution's importance is not yet in. For example, Estes (1985), without discounting the importance of semantic processes, pointed out some areas in which associations play an important role and concluded that, "It may be that Ebbinghaus's contributions as a theorist will prove greater than [some of us] appreciate" (p. 454). One hundred years from now, let's see who is on some stage somewhere discussing these issues. Will it be Professor Kintsch or will it be me? I am quite willing to let history decide; it has been good to me so far. I now turn the microphone back over to our moderator for some final comments. Pardon me for my brief burst of—I hope uncharacteristic—splenetic passion, and thank you for your kind attention.

CONCLUSION:
CHAIRPERSON'S CLOSING REMARKS

Thank you, ladies and gentlemen. Professor Ebbinghaus certainly deserves that standing ovation. History has, indeed, been good to him and for good reasons. I would like to spend a few minutes enumerating several of those reasons in an outline of his contributions.

Advancing Psychology As a Science and Profession

In addition to his well-known memory research, Professor Ebbinghaus was also the author of a respected elementary textbook that was republished as recently as 1973; he was co-founder of the *Zeitschrift für Psychologie und Psychologie der Sinnesorgane*, which provided a publication outlet for those German psychologists who were not of the Wundtian school, which had its own journal. He also devised an intelligence test for assessing aptitudes of German schoolchildren.

Ebbinghaus' pioneering work on memory was, of course, a milestone in the progress of psychological science because it demonstrated that higher mental processes can be measured and studied experimentally. Professor Mandler (1985) pointed out that Professor Ebbinghaus' work demonstrated that human memory could be studied in the laboratory and that controlled experiments could provide valuable insights into complex problems. Mandler also asserted that Professor Ebbinghaus was a pioneer in using psychological variables such as association strength as theoretical explanations for empirical psychological phenomena. Professor Ebbinghaus, according to Mandler, was also one of the first to see that mental activity, the mind, extends far beyond mere consciousness when he posited sub-threshold association strength. Such unconscious processes were shown by Professor Ebbinghaus to influence conscious thought processes such as recall. This was, indeed, an insight and a monumental finding. Before this, said Mandler, "all the important mental events were conscious and...these processes represented both the data and the processes that gave rise to them" (p. 465). It was after this that Sigmund Freud hopped on this idea and rode it to international fame or, as some say, notoriety.

Theoretical Contributions

Professor Ebbinghaus also made a number of other theoretical, empirical, and methodological contributions to psychology that deserve mention. In the theoretical area, he made use of the concept of association strength between items in a sequence and showed that such strength could be increased by mere repetition of the sequence. Strength of association could also be present at an unconscious level, and this unconscious strength can be assessed by finding the effort required to bring it into consciousness. In his work with remote associations, he showed that strict mental contiguity is not a required condition for the formation of associations, and that each of the items in a sequence has associations with the other items. He also noted differences in the phenomenological characteristics of the material learned: With a small number of repetitions, he did not recognize sequences from the day before; with larger numbers of repetitions, the old sequences seemed like old friends that were remembered distinctly. These observations foreshadow distinctions made much later between episodic and semantic memory (Tulving, 1985a) and remembering versus knowing (Tulving, 1985b).

Empirical Contributions

On the more empirical side, Ebbinghaus provided a map of the course of forgetting that has not changed over time. He proved, not surprisingly, that meaningless material is more difficult to remember than meaningful material. He showed that, contrary to expectation, increasing the size of the amount to be learned does not inordinately increase the magnitude of the learning task. In fact, there may be an advantage to learning a greater amount (Slamecka, 1985). Memorizers also benefit from relearning material learned earlier, and each further relearning slows down the rate of later forgetting. As Professor Jost (1897) surmised from the work of Professor Ebbinghaus and later demonstrated in the laboratory, the process of relearning and spacing practice in this way is more effective than spending a like amount of effort all at one time in massed practice. Perhaps more important than all of these is his demonstration that research on mental processes does not need to depend on introspection for its data. What Ebbinghaus showed is how using behavioral measures makes it possible to be completely objective in our data collection. Without this step, modern cognitive science would not have been possible.

Methodological Contributions

Finally, Professor Ebbinghaus has enriched our bag of experimental tricks, by inventing a number of methodological innovations that have furthered later research. The nonsense syllable is probably the innovation of Professor Ebbinghaus that everyone recalls first. Of course, later research has attempted to relate learning more exactly to meaningfulness and other properties of the many kinds of materials that may be utilized in the laboratory, but Professor Ebbinghaus's work still stands as a baseline. Simply doing the first memory experiment in a laboratory setting required the invention of procedures such as the study–test method, which involved reading the sequence over and over again under fixed conditions or, under some conditions, attempting to anticipate the next item as he went through the sequence. He invented the method of relearning the items to a fixed criterion and devised the savings method for quantifying the amount retained from previous bouts of learning. He invented the method of derived lists for studying remote associations. Furthermore, as Wertheimer (1986) pointed out, the early decades following Ebbinghaus' original study generated a variety of investigations into aspects of memory that uncovered the superiority of recognition over recall, the efficacy of recitation as opposed to passive reading, the phenomenon of inhibition, and the development of other methods such as free recall and reconstruction. These advances are unlikely to have happened, at least when they did, without Professor Ebbinghaus' ground-breaking investigations.

In the methodological area, we must also mention Professor Ebbinghaus' utilization of statistical analysis, which was very sophisticated for his time. In conducting his research, he found results from trial to trial that were widely discrepant due to a large number of possible factors. He was concerned that these discrepancies implied a lack of lawfulness in his results. He knew about the law of errors and the reassuring conclusion that averages of results would tend to cluster more tightly about a central value if the number of measurements is increased. He examined the original data of prominent scientists such as Helmholtz and Joule and convinced himself that, even in physics and biology, at least in their early stages, individual measurements may be sloppy in the singular but when averaged provide the lawfulness required. The answer to the problem of measurement error is replication, and that he did. Even after Professor Ebbinghaus' time, the issue of experimental error and its control would forever pester psychological investigators. He also showed the field how to deal with this problem. This sort of compulsion about error and its control through statistics, however, was only another example of the exquisite care and precision that is evident in all of his work. Finally, the book *On Memory* represents an exercise in conceptualization and implementation in science that continues to serve as a model for scientific research.

We may ask, as did Professor Ebbinghaus in his remarks, Could the work we have just heard about possibly have set psychological science back several decades? The answer from all of us who heard him talk today is "No way!" We might just as well say that Columbus set back the development of Philadelphia because he landed in the Caribbean. Science always needs pioneers to point out new directions and show how to proceed toward new understanding. Professor Ebbinghaus, a true pioneer, we salute you and give you our profound thanks for starting us on an exciting voyage of discovery.

REFERENCES

Bringmann, W. G., & Bringmann, N. J. (1986). Ebbinghaus and the new world. In F. Klix & H. Hagendorf (Eds.), *Human memory and cognitive capabilities* (pp. 3–34). Amsterdam: New-Holland.

Ebbinghaus, H. (1962). *Memory: A contribution to experimental psychology.* New York: Dover. (Original work published 1885.

Ebbinghaus, H. (1908). *Psychology: An elementary textbook.* Boston: D. C. Heath. (Reprinted in 1973 by Arno Press.)

Estes, W. K. (1985). Levels of association theory. *Journal of Experimental Psychology: Learning, Memory, and Cognition, 11,* 450–454.

Fechner, G. (1966). *Elements of psychophysics* (H. Adler, Trans.). New York: Holt, Rinehart & Winston. (Original work published 1850.)

Jenkins, J. J. (1985). Comprehending the "almost incomprehensible variation." *Journal of Experimental Psychology: Learning, Memory, and Cognition, 11,* 455–460.

Jost, G. (1897). Die Associationsfestigkeit in ihrer Abhängigkeit von der Verteilung der Wiederholungen. *Zeitschrift für Psychologie, 14,* 436–472.

Kintsch, W. (1985). Reflections on Ebbinghaus. *Journal of Experimental Psychology: Learning, Memory, and Cognition, 11,* 461–463.

Lowry, R. (1971). *The evolution of psychological theory.* New York: Aldine.

Mandler, G. (1985). From association to structure. *Journal of Experimental Psychology: Learning, Memory, and Cognition, 11,* 464–468.

Miller, G. A. (1956). The magical number seven plus or minus two: Some limits on our capacity for processing information. *Psychological Review, 63,* 81–97.

Slamecka, N. J. (1985). Ebbinghaus: Some associations. *Journal of Experimental Psychology: Learning, Memory, and Cognition, 11,* 414–435.

Tulving, E. (1985a). How many memory systems are there? *American Psychologist, 49,* 385'398.

Tulving, E. (1985b). Memory and consciousness. *Canadian Psychologist, 26,* 1–12.

Wertheimer, M. (1986). The annals of the house that Ebbinghaus built. In F. Klix & H. Hagendorf (Eds.), *Human memory and cognitive capabilities* (pp. 35–44). Amsterdam: New Holland.

Chapter 5

Alfred Binet, General Psychologist

Raymond E. Fancher

Ask a psychologist to associate to the name *Binet*, and the chances are overwhelming that the response will make some reference to the intelligence tests pioneered in the early 1900s by the French psychologist Alfred Binet (1857–1911). Although understandable enough, given the high profile of intelligence testing, this powerful but narrow association does scant justice to Binet. Historical scholars such as Cunningham (1988, 1995), Nicolas (1994a), Siegler (1992) and especially Wolf (1973, 1976) have shown that intelligence testing was just a small and, in some ways, unrepresentative part of Binet's total psychological contribution. He published prolifically on a broad array of topics, including psychophysics, associationistic psychology, hypnosis, abnormal psychology, sexual deviation, developmental psychology, craniometry, suggestibility, memory, eyewitness testimony, imageless thought, creativity, and personality assessment. Thus it is highly appropriate that Binet's biography should be included in this series sponsored by the APA Division of General Psychology, because few individuals have ever held better claim to the title, *general psychologist*.

A SELF-EDUCATION IN PSYCHOLOGY

For all the breadth of his interests and accomplishments in psychology, Binet received no formal training in the field. The first and only child of a wealthy physician father and an artistically inclined mother, he experienced a materially privileged but not particularly happy childhood. "Timid to excess" (as he later remembered himself), he was once forced by his stern father to touch a cadaver—a

*Photograph of Alfred Binet courtesy of Archives of the History of American Psychology, Akron, Ohio.

horrendous experience that haunted Binet throughout his life. His parents did not get along and separated when he was young, leaving him—probably to his relief—in the custody of his mother. He did well at schools in his birthplace of Nice and in Paris, winning prizes in the literary subjects of Latin translation and French composition. Then Binet took a preliminary degree in law but found the subject uninspiring—"the career of men who have not chosen a vocation"—and did not continue. Medical school followed, but proved even worse. Probably as an after effect of his childhood trauma with the cadaver, he became overstrained, suffered from cerebral anemia, and had to take 6 months of complete rest to recover. Toward the end of his convalescence, he obtained a reader's ticket for Paris' great Bibliothèque Nationale and, following some vague intuition, began reading about recent developments in psychology (Wolf, 1973).

At that time, psychology as a discipline was relatively undeveloped in France. Philosopher Théodule Ribot (1839–1916) had recently published French language accounts of German and English advances in the field and had founded a journal that published articles on psychological topics, the *Revue Philosophique*. From these starting points, Binet moved into the primary psychological literature and, with mounting excitement, began to suspect that at last he had found his vocation.

Fascinated by some accounts of sensory psychology, he conducted some simple experiments of his own on the two-point threshold. Then another passion took hold. "One of my greatest pleasures," he later reported, "is to have a piece of white paper to fill up" (Wolf, 1973, p. 34). He quickly filled a few sheets with an account of his sensory experiments and submitted them to the *Revue Philosophique*. Ribot accepted them, but did their young author no real favor by doing so because this maiden publication elicited a scathing critique in the next issue by the respected Belgian physiologist Joseph L. R. Delboeuf (1831–1921). Binet's procedures had been imprecise; he had overlooked much relevant previous literature on the subject (Binet, 1880; Delboeuf, 1880).

Undiscouraged, Binet next became enthusiastic about strongly associationistic psychology, such as that propounded by John Stuart Mill. In his second venture into print, an article on reasoning in perception, Binet boldly declared: "The operations of the intelligence are *nothing but* diverse forms of the laws of association.... Explanation in psychology, in its most scientific form, consists in showing that each mental fact is only a particular case of these general laws" (Binet, 1883, p. 412, emphasis added). Binet would always retain a healthy respect for the explanatory power of association and experience, but soon realized that he overstated the case and was lucky not to have attracted a second public criticism. Newly emerging dynamic psychologies were just then demonstrating the powerful effects of disassociated ideas and unconscious and variable motivational factors that were not easily reducible to the classical laws of association. Moreover, one of the world's great centers for the new dynamic psychology existed virtually beneath Binet's nose at Paris' Salpêtrière Hospital, under the eminent neurologist Jean Martin Charcot (1825–1893). Seeking some practical experience in this new field, in 1884 Binet arranged to go to the Salpêtrière as an unpaid research assistant.

LESSONS AT THE SALPÊTRIÈRE

Binet remained at the Salpêtrière for 6 years and learned a great many lessons there, both positive and negative. Charcot was famous for his intensive clinical studies of individual cases, and Binet now learned something of this art, developing in the process a keen appreciation for the complexity and individuality of all real people. Binet's wish to broaden and deepen his naive associationistic psychology was also amply fulfilled, along with his passion for filling up sheets of paper. Between 1884 and 1890, he published three books and 20 articles on a variety of the new dynamic topics, including hypnosis, illusions of movement, sexual *fetishism* (a term Binet himself coined), alterations of personality, and the importance of attention. Binet's first book, the 1886 *La Psychologie du Raisonnement* (*The Psychology of Reasoning*), explicitly modified his earlier associationism by conceptualizing mental images not as static elements, but as organismic, flowing, and dynamic states of consciousness somewhat similar to those postulated by William James (Cunningham, 1995, p. 958). An article the year after noted that unadorned associationistic psychology "tends to reduce the mind to a sort of passive automatism, that is, to a *spectator*-me rather than to an *actor*-me" (cited in Wolf, 1973, p. 67). Binet now saw that any adequate psychology would have to acknowledge that the effects of association by similarity or contiguity are constantly modified and directed by acts of motivated *attention*—a subject that would assume prominence in his subsequent psychological thought.

While becoming a much more complete psychologist through these positive lessons at the Salpêtrière, Binet also learned to be a more careful one as the result of a humiliating negative lesson. Together with Charles Féré (1852–1907), another young assistant, Binet became a major investigator and proponent of Charcot's controversial theory of *grand hypnotisme*. Noting the apparent similarity between common hypnotic effects and the typical symptoms of hysteria (amnesias, paralyses, anaesthesias, etc.), Charcot had argued that the susceptibility to hysteria and the responsiveness to hypnotic suggestion were one and the same thing—the result of a generalized undercapacity of the nervous system for processing excitation. Charcot further proposed that hypnotizability and hysteria both had a pure form or type—*grand hypnotisme* and *grande hystérie*—that occurred only in a minority of cases, but that reflected the most significant and purest aspects of the conditions. The more common minor (petit) cases presumably represented incomplete or blurred forms of the same conditions. Conditions of *grand hypnotisme* were believed by Charcot to follow an invariable sequence, beginning with a state of muscular relaxation or *catalepsy*, followed by a distinctive *lethargy*, and concluding with a *somnambulistic stage*, where all manner of complex activities are performed on the suggestion of the hypnotist. Salpêtrière research focused almost exclusively on a small number of patients who could be relied on to produce these regular sequences of effects.

Binet and Féré worked intensively with one of these, a young woman named Blanche Wittmann who produced Charcot's stages with such striking effect and had such a haughty attitude toward the other patients that she was locally known as "Queen of the Hysterics." For some reason—perhaps thinking back to Mesmer's early theory of hypnotism as animal magnetism—the young investigators introduced a magnet into their experiments. To their purported surprise, *Wit* (as they named their subject in published reports) responded readily and dramatically to their magnetic manipulations. In response to a flick of the magnet, her paralyses or anaesthesias shifted from one side of the body to the other or her expressions of happiness transformed into the "complementary emotion" of sobbing and grief. Binet and Féré admitted the implausibility of these magnetic effects, but assured their readers that they had been "entirely unexpected, and issued therefore from nature herself, thus showing an inflexible logic" (Binet & Féré, 1885, p. 375).

However, not all readers were reassured. Indeed, Charcot's entire theory of *grand hypnotisme* had already been questioned by Henry Beaunis (1830–1921), Hippolyte Bernheim (1840–1919), and others from the provincial city of Nancy. These members of the "Nancy School" argued that their own experiments with a much larger subject base than Charcot's showed hypnotizability to be a normal characteristic, uncorrelated with susceptibility to hysteria or any other pathological condition.

The magnetic reports also caught the skeptical eye of Binet's old nemesis, Delboeuf, who had a side interest in hypnosis and who, in December 1885, came to the Salpêtrière to see things for himself. He later reported, "I will never forget those delicious hours." Of the two young investigators, Féré was "more reflective … and more open to objections raised; M. Binet more adventurous and more affirmative … with fine features and a mischievous expression." The placid Wit sat beside them, "not only wearing a complacent look, but finding visible pleasure in getting ready to do anything asked of her,…a veritable human guinea pig." Delboeuf observed that the hypnotists manipulated Wit "as if playing upon a piano …a light touch on any muscle—or even pointing to it without touching—made Wit contract any muscle, even in her ear" (cited in Wolf, 1973, p. 50). As for the celebrated magnetic effects, these occurred only when Féré conspicuously manipulated a large horseshoe magnet in front of Wit and spoke openly about her expected reactions. When asked why they did not take elementary precautions to hide their expectations, such as using an electromagnet whose polarity could be reversed covertly, the experimenters blithely responded that such were unnecessary because Wit was unable to understand things in the usual way while in the somnambulistic stage of Charcot's *grand hypnotisme*.

After Delboeuf published a description of his visit and added that he had been unable to reproduce the magnetic effects in subjects after taking proper safeguards against experimenter suggestion, Binet and Féré retorted at first that Delboeuf, practicing in the provinces, had been unable to find any of the relatively rare cases of *grand hypnotisme* with which to work. Gradually, however, the terrible truth dawned on Binet that he had been naive. *Grand hypnotisme* was not a condition "issued from nature herself," but rather the result of a few skilled performers following an implicit script created by the experimenters' expectations. Binet publicly conceded in 1891 that his hypnotic studies had presented "a host of causes of error," and that "one of the principal causes of unceasing error...is suggestion, that is, the influence of the operator by his words, gestures, attitudes, and even silences" (cited in Wolf, 1973, p. 63).

From this painful experience, Binet learned that unintended suggestion—which he later called the *cholera of psychology*—was something to be avoided at all costs in psychological experiments. More positively, he also learned that intended suggestion might be a powerful and interesting psychological phenomenon in its own right—one that in due course he would study systematically and innovatively in the laboratory.

RESEARCH WITH THE BINET DAUGHTERS

After the hypnosis fiasco, Binet became understandably eager to leave the Salpêtrière. Just as understandably, prospective alternative employers did not flock to his door, even though his various positive and negative lessons at the hospital had made him an excellent psychologist. Thus, for a while, he conducted his most important research at home—a small series of studies on his young daughters, Madeleine and Alice, who had been born in 1885 and 1887 respectively. This led to three short, but provocative *Revue Philosophiqe* papers published in 1890 (translated and reprinted in Pollack & Brenner, 1969).

Binet gave his daughters some tests of reaction time and sensory acuity, similar to those advocated by Francis Galton and James McKeen Cattell for use in adult populations as measures of neurophysiological efficiency, and hence (so they argued) of natural ability or intelligence. Binet found that, in judging the relative lengths of parallel lines and acuteness of pairs of angles, 5-year-old Madeleine performed slightly better than an average adult and 3-year-old Alice nearly as well. Although while the girls had slower average reaction times than adults, they also showed much greater variability because of lapses in attention; when they paid full attention to the task, they were just as fast as adults. On a color naming test children were slower than adults, but on color matching they were just as accurate.

From these results, Binet surmised that children do not differ significantly from adults in their sensory and neurophysiological abilities per se, but rather in other qualities. Attention, whose theoretical importance he had learned to appreciate at the Salpêtrière as a modifier of pure associationism, was one obvious factor. The children's relative deficiency at naming—as opposed to matching or differentiating—colors pointed to another verbal factor, which Binet specified further by asking them to define everyday objects. In response to questions such as, What is a knife?...or a box?...or a snail?, the children simply described the immediate and concrete actions associated with the objects. A knife was "to cut meat," a box "means put candies inside it," and a snail was simply "Squash it!" Binet concluded that his young subjects were incapable of *defining* in the adult sense: "When you say 'definition' you imply a certain work of reflection, of comparison, of elimination, etc. The little children that we studied responded immediately without thinking, and their replies express very simply the first images which were evoked by the [questions]" (Pollack & Brenner, 1969, p. 120). Needless to say, this finding has been reconfirmed countless times since.

In another experiment that anticipated later developments, Binet tested the ability of 4-year-old Madeleine, who could only count to three, to differentiate larger from smaller collections of counters or tokens. When all the tokens were the same size (2.5 cm in diameter), she could accurately identify a collection of 18 tokens as larger than one of 17, even though both numbers were much higher than she could count. When the numerically smaller collection was made up of larger (4-cm) tokens, however, Madeleine made many mistakes; for example, she judged that a set of 10 large ones contained more than the set of 18 small ones. Siegler (1992) called this experiment a *first cousin* of Piaget's famous later investigations of number conservation, although Piaget (chap. 9, this volume) did not cite it when he first published his own findings.

Throughout these studies, Binet was repeatedly struck by the distinctly different and characteristic styles of his two girls as they approached the same tasks, with Madeleine being generally serious, deliberate, and reflective and Alice more emotional and impulsive. In an article entitled "Movements in Children," Binet told how these differences had been obvious even as the infant girls had learned to walk. Madeleine,

> standing on her feet, holding on to a solid object...risked abandoning that support only when she had visually selected another object a short distance away which would offer new support; she directed herself very slowly towards the second object, paying great attention to the movements of her leg...[which] were executed with great seriousness in perfect silence. (Pollack & Brenner, 1969, p. 157)

As for Alice:

> When put on her legs she remained immobile for some moments and then was pushed forward by a desire to progress....She advanced without hesitation to the middle part of an empty room. She cried out, she gestured, she was very amusing to watch; she advanced staggering like a drunken man. (Pollack & Brenner, 1969, p. 157)

At this point in his career, Binet was not concerned with measuring individual differences in intelligence. Nonetheless, these small home studies helped establish some attitudes that would later prove important. Because tests of sensory or neurological efficiency per se did not effectively differentiate young children from adults, Binet became skeptical about their usefulness as indicators of meaningful differences in general intellectual ability. Tests directly involving verbal and other more complex mental abilities seemed much more promising. And further, the qualitative issue of *how* individuals go about solving problems would always seem just as important to Binet as the measurement of *how well*.

THE SORBONNE PSYCHOLOGIST

In 1891, the year after Binet published his home experiments, a surprising encounter finally led him to a real psychology laboratory. While awaiting a train at the station in Rouen, he saw an older man whom he recognized as Henry Beaunis, a leader of the Nancy School with whom he had so ingloriously debated about the nature of hypnotism. Knowing that Beaunis was also the part-time director of France's only laboratory for experimental psychology, just established at the Sorbonne, Binet put misgivings aside and approached Beaunis—whom he had not met before—to ask for a position. Beaunis later recalled that, despite their prior disagreements, he immediately appreciated "the depth of [Binet's] intelligence, that vivacity of a mind always on the alert" (Nicolas, 1995, p. 281). No doubt it also helped that Binet offered to work without pay at a laboratory that was seriously underfunded and understaffed. In any event, Beaunis offered Binet a position as unpaid assistant (*"préparateur"*) and Binet accepted.

Beaunis made no mistake, because Binet immediately became the small laboratory's most productive member, and within a year, was named its (still unpaid) associate director. The laboratory lacked the authority to grant degrees, but occasional students arrived for extracurricular training and, thanks largely to Binet's efforts, a substantial amount of research got conducted. In 1894, Binet concluded that the laboratory's output justified a publication outlet of its own, similar to Wundt's *Philosophische Studien* for his famous Leipzig laboratory. Thus, Binet proposed an annual publication to report each year's original research at the laboratory, along with summary accounts of psychological developments in the rest of the world. Beaunis approved the project with misgivings, but these proved unfounded because the first issue, published in 1895 and covering the year 1894, paid for itself in subscriptions (Nicolas, 1995, pp. 281–284). More than a century later, *L'Année Psychologique* continues as one of France's leading psychology journals and stands as Binet's most important institutional contribution to psychology. Its quick success may have improved Beaunis' ease of mind when ill health forced him to resign as director in 1895 and the still unsalaried Binet was named his successor.

Much of Binet's research during those early years at the laboratory applied the same case study methods he had learned at the Salpêtrière, only to people with unusual talents rather than disabilities. His early subjects included *lightning calculators* who could solve complicated arithmetic problems rapidly and completely in their heads and chess prodigies who could play and win several simultaneous games while blindfolded. In several articles and a summarizing book (Binet & Henneguy, 1894), Binet reported two important and then-surprising findings. First, these subjects' prodigious memory skills were specialized rather than general. The calculators showed extraordinarily keen retention of numbers and the chess players of imaginary lines of force surrounding the visualized pieces on the board. In other situations, their memories were not unusual. Second, the mnemonists went about their tasks in individually distinctive ways (e.g., one calculator used exclusively auditory imagery whereas computing, while another always visualized the numerals).

A second series of case studies directed toward understanding the creative imagination, reinforced this finding of qualitative differences. Binet and his friend, Jaques Passy, used interviews and questionnaires to investigate the working habits of several of France's best-known creative writers, including François de Curel, Alphonse Daudet, Alexander Dumas, and Edmond de Goncourt (Binet, 1895; Binet & Passy, 1895). Here again diversity reigned. For example, some authors reported that they worked effectively only while in intense and intermittent states of spontaneous inspiration, whereas others wrote methodically and every day.

At the same time that he was conducting these case studies, Binet also investigated some larger groups of subjects, usually school children. In much of this work, he was assisted by one of the laboratory's first students, a cosmopolitan young man named Victor Henri (1872–1940). A French orphan adopted by Russian parents, Henri grew up in both France and Russia and was educated partly in German. In Paris for university study in mathematics and the physical sciences, he happened to take Ribot's psychology course at the Collège de France and subsequently gravitated to the Sorbonne laboratory for further hands-on training (Nicolas, 1994b). With energy to rival Binet's, Henri joined him in a brief but highly productive partnership.

Their first collaboration, partly intended to complement Binet's case studies of memory in extraordinary adults, investigated visual memory in children (Binet & Henri, 1894a). Children of differing ages were briefly shown a straight-line stimulus and later asked to choose the one of the same length from a group of possibilities presented to them. On the average, older children proved to have more accurate memories than younger ones. These rather unsurprising results provided a baseline for a second, much more innovative study (Binet & Henri, 1894b), which concerns the effect of suggestion on reported verbal memory. Using the same memory task, the investigators assessed the effect of various suggestive influences such as leading questions (e.g., "Are you sure? Isn't it the next line?") and group pressure, where student leaders publicly announced incorrect choices. Suggestive effects were strongest for younger children, but extended to all age groups. Remarkably, even the line-estimating task in this research closely resembles that used by Asch in his much later, classic studies of group pressure and conformity (e.g., Asch, 1952, 1951/1963). Asch did not cite Binet and Henri.

In 1895, Binet and Henri co-authored the first two articles in the very first volume of *L'Année Psychologique*—studies of children's memory for lists of unrelated words and for sentences from meaningful paragraphs of varying length (Binet & Henri, 1895a, 1895b). In sheerly quantitative terms, the children remembered much more material from the paragraphs. They did not do so literally, however, but instead translated the sentences into their own words: "They impose on the passage...the mark of their personality, they make it their own, they give it their perspective of thinking" (Binet and Henri, 1895b, p. 52). Here again Binet and Henri anticipated important developments far in the future; it would be the 1970s before cognitive psychologists began to seriously explore contextual effects on memory. Here again Binet and Henri were seldom credited in the primary literature, although a few historically oriented articles have attempted to redress this injustice (Cunningham, 1995; Nicolas, 1994a; Siegler, 1992; Thieman & Brewer, 1978; Wolf, 1976).

INDIVIDUAL PSYCHOLOGY

In 1896, Binet and Henri published a fifth important article together, in which they proposed an ambitious new program to be called Individual Psychology. Whereas general psychology focused on processes common to all individuals, individual psychology would study "those properties of psychological processes which vary from one individual to another. It must determine those variable processes, and then study to what degree and how they vary" (Binet & Henri, 1896, p. 411). More concretely, the authors proposed to develop a series of short tests that (a) could be given in less than 2 hours and (b) would yield a personality profile equal in richness and complexity to that obtainable from many more hours of intense interviews and individual case history taking. What should those tests be? Here was (and indeed remains today) a crucial question facing psychologists who wish to investigate individual personalities. Already suspicious about the sensory and physiologically based "mental tests" then in general vogue, the authors surmised that "if one wishes to study the differences existing between two individuals it is necessary to begin with the most intellectual and complicated processes" (Binet & Henri, 1896, p. 417). As a provisional starting point, they suggested a battery of 10 tests measuring individual differences in memory, imagery, imagination, attention, comprehension, suggestibility, aesthetic sentiments, moral sentiments, muscular strength, and motor coordination. Binet and Henri had already developed a few such tests, and they gave hints as to how the others might emerge.

Unfortunately, by the time "Individual Psychology" appeared in print, Binet and the Sorbonne had already lost the energetic Henri to other laboratories where he could get academic credit for his work. He went first to Wundt in Leipzig and then completed a dissertation on tactile sensation under G. E. Müller in Göttingen. During his German sojourn, he published nine articles on his own and was available only as an occasional and long-distance partner for Binet (Nicolas, 1994b). His successor, a Romanian student named Nicholas Vaschide who came to work at the Sorbonne with his own funding, worked out much less well. Vaschide and Binet collected a large amount of data involving the correlations between psychological and physiological variables, such as blood pressure, physical strength, physique, and head measurements. Detailed technical reports of these findings dominated the 1897 and 1898 volumes of *L'Année Psychologique*, but these were immediately criticized for carelessness and numerous calculating errors, mostly in the direction of the experimenters' preferred hypotheses. Vaschide was apparently responsible for most of the errors, and a mortified Binet terminated their relationship (Wolf, 1973).

Perhaps an unintended but positive side effect of this distressing experience was a re-awakening of Binet's concern about that "cholera of psychology"—suggestibility. In any event, his 1900 book *La Suggestibilité* significantly elaborated on his earlier work with Henri. In one major new study, children were given a brief look at a poster with various stimulus objects attached (e.g., coin, stamp, picture of a crowd scene, photograph of a man) and then were asked various kinds of suggestive questions about what they had observed. Direct suggestions, such as "Wasn't the [actually uncancelled] stamp canceled?", produced the most erroneous replies, but even more neutral wording, such as "Was the stamp canceled?", produced a number of mistaken, affirmative recollections. Mistakes were fewest when the children were simply asked to write an open-ended description of what they had seen. Binet advised those concerned about the accuracy of children's testimony: "If you want to achieve maximum verity...do not pose questions to them, even questions devoid of precise suggestions, but simply ask them to describe everything they recall and leave them with paper and pencil" (Binet, 1900, p. 294). Once again, Binet had closely anticipated both a research topic and findings that would assume great visibility and importance many years after his death: the reliability of eyewitness testimony in children.

La Suggestibilité also contained an incidental passage that one cannot read today without a sense of irony. Although in the course of his research he had calculated various numerical suggestibility scores for individual subjects, he cautioned that these quantified results had to be interpreted with extreme caution because "mere numbers cannot bring out the intimate essence of the experiment." No experimenter can hope to express

all the oscillations of a thought in a simple, brutal number, which can have only a deceptive precision. How, in fact, *could* it summarize what would need several pages of description!...It is necessary to complete this number by a description of all the little facts that complete the physiognomy of the experiment." (Binet, 1900, pp. 119–120)

Binet maintained this attitude toward quantified data of any sort, including results from the intelligence tests that he invented, for the rest of his life.

Immediately following *La Suggestibilité*, Binet focused on two different research enterprises. First, he conducted several systematic studies of tactile sensation and the two-point threshold, which filled more than 200 pages of *L'Année Psychologique* and more than compensated for the deficiencies Delboeuf had detected in his first published article. Second, he pursued the search for usable tests in Individual Psychology largely by continuing to experiment with his daughters, Madeleine and Alice, who had now developed into bright teenagers. In doing so, he devised several techniques that today would be called *projective tests*. He asked his daughters to write down the first 10 words, sentences, or memories that came into their heads without further specification. He also asked them to complete partially begun sentences and to write open-ended themes about stimulus objects, such as an old coin or a chestnut tree leaf, or imaginary situations, such as the death of a dog. He even asked them to respond to inkblots a full decade before Rorschach. Throughout, he continued to be struck by the stylistic differences between the two young women as they went about these tasks. Madeleine, much as she had learned to walk as a young child, continued to be deliberate, matter-of-fact, and down to earth in her responses. Her father characterized her as *"l'observateur*. Alice, much more dramatic, emotional, and fanciful in her typical responses, was *l'imaginitif*.

Binet presented a detailed account of these experiments in *L'Étude Expérimentale de l'Intelligence* (*The Experimental Study of Intelligence*; Binet, 1903). Although highlighting *intelligence* in its title, the book is more accurately described as a pioneering project in the assessment of *personality*. Here, Madeleine and Alice came vibrantly alive as distinct personalities in what were arguably the best of the many case studies ever published by Binet. Florence Goodenough (1886–1959), herself a pioneering and influential projective tester in the 1920s, praised Binet's book as "perhaps the earliest and certainly one of the best studies of projective methods that has appeared in the literature" (cited in Wolf, 1973, p. 117).

In the course of his testing, Binet sometimes quizzed his daughters about the particular imagery that passed through their minds as they performed tasks. He noticed that often their reported imagery was substantially sparser than the elaborated thoughts involved. For example, the content-laden thought of "a planned visit to the country" was accompanied by a single, bare image of a green field. This seemed to contradict the widely held belief that thoughts could not be expressed without specific underlying images. Thus, Binet included a section of *L'Étude Expérimentale*, and wrote a separate article for the 1903 volume of *L'Année Psychologique*, on the subject of *imageless thought* (la pensée sans images). He did not know that a similar idea had already been implicit in work by the Würzburg psychologists A. Mayer and J. Orth published in 1901. In fact, neither their paper nor Binet's attracted much immediate attention. In 1907, however, the concept of imageless thought was given prominence in a major synthesizing treatise on thinking by the Würzburger Karl Bühler—a work that cited Mayer and Orth, but not Binet. Subsequently, "imageless thought" became inextricably and almost exclusively associated with the "Würzburg School" of psychology. Binet believed that his own work had actually been a major stimulus for Bühler, and thus he expressed bitterness at what he saw as a deliberate snubbing of "the school of Paris" (Wolf, 1973).

In the meantime, Binet was losing confidence in the general project of Individual Psychology, at least in the form in which he and Henri had proposed it in 1896. Despite the interest of extensive case studies like those in *L'Étude Expérimentale*, or of a report on the dramatist Paul Hervieu published by Binet in 1904, no universally applicable and short set of tests had materialized. The Hervieu study had required many hours of detailed observation and interviewing, and Binet reluctantly concluded that that seemed to be the only way to arrive at a sufficiently rich understanding of any individual personality. Henri joined Binet for one last paper, presented by Henri at a 1904 psychology congress in Germany, in which they conceded that now they "could only recommend long systematic investigations of each person studied" (Wolf, 1973, p. 140).

THE INTELLIGENCE TESTS
AND BINET'S REPUTATION

Binet could hardly have known that his most famous achievement would quickly follow the collapse of Individual Psychology, but its seeds had been germinating since 1899. That year he joined La Societé Libre pour l'Étude Psychologique de l'Enfant (The Free Society for the Psychological Study of the Child), a new organization dedicated to educational research. He quickly became the group's leader and founded a *Bulletin* to publish articles geared to the practical interests of teachers and educational administrators. Like *L'Année Psychologique*, the *Bulletin* proved to be a lasting success, and a major celebration was held in 1968 to mark its 500th issue. In 1917, six years after Binet's death, the group renamed itself "La Société Alfred Binet" to honor his many contributions.

At about the same time Binet joined La Société, a young physician named Theodore Simon (1873–1961) came to work at the Sorbonne laboratory, with professional connections at an institution for mentally subnormal children. Fortuitously, the problem of mental subnormality was particularly pressing for members of La Société at that time—in the wake of recently enacted universal education laws. Now and for the first time, mentally handicapped children were legally required to be provided with schooling. Binet, following his appointment to a government commission charged with investigating the issue, came to believe that accurate diagnosis was a key to the problem of dealing with mental subnormality: Children with genuine deficiencies that required special education would have to be identified and graded in terms of their maximum potential and differentiated from those at the lower end of the normal intelligence range, who could benefit from a normal school curriculum.

Binet and Simon set out to develop such a diagnostic instrument. The story of how they created their famous test of intelligence has been detailed before (e.g., Fancher, 1985, Tuddenham, 1962; Wolf, 1969, 1973), and needs only to be sketched here. Crucial to their success was the recognition that the age at which children learn new tasks can reflect their intelligence levels, and that mental deficiency can therefore be understood as a retardation in the development of normal or average intellectual capability. This idea seemed a surprising insight to Binet when it occurred, but of course his earlier studies of age differences in reaction time, memory, suggestibility, attention, and language use had well prepared him to make that discovery.

Thus, Binet and Simon came to see *intelligence* as a capacity that grows with children's ages but at varying individual rates. By testing samples of average children at various ages, it was possible to identify items to serve as standards for each particular age. For example, typical 3-year-olds (but not 2-year-olds) could give their last names and correctly point to their eyes and noses when requested; 6-year-olds could count 13 coins and draw a diamond-shaped design from memory. Such items then could be assembled into a scale capable of estimating the "mental level" of any particular child in age-graded terms (e.g., a particular 5-year-old might be tested as having the mental level of a typical 4-year-old). Binet and Simon's first test, published in the 1905 volume of *L'Année Psychologique*, was composed of 30 items establishing norms for ages between infancy and 11 years. Expanded and revised versions appeared in 1908 and 1911, with the latter containing five items pegged to each age between 3 and 15 years, as well as a generalized adult category of the five most difficult items.

Binet consistently emphasized that the "intelligence" measured by his tests is both complex and constantly developing throughout childhood: Any child's intelligence at age 6 is a very different thing from what it was at age 3. Partly for this reason, Binet never quantified his test results beyond giving a mental level (*niveau mental*), which is not fixed but is assumed naturally to increase at some rate, along with the chronological age of a child. For diagnostic purposes, Binet suggested that children who appeared healthy and well motivated on taking the test, came from a reasonably ordinary French background, and whose mental levels trailed their actual ages by more than 2 years should be seriously considered as cases requiring special education. That was as close as he ever came to reducing his test results to numbers. Consistent with his appreciation for individuality, Binet expressed reservations about even this limited degree of quantification. He emphasized, for example, that the same mental levels can be achieved in different ways by different children, who correctly respond to different combinations of items and in entirely different stylistic ways.

Binet also believed that the "intelligence" measured by his tests could be improved by training. In his book *Idées Modernes sur les Enfants* (*Modern Ideas about Children*), he criticized the "deplorable verdicts" and "brutal pessimism" of those who hold relative individual intelligence levels to be fixed at birth (Binet, 1909/1973, p. 101). He went on to describe a program of "mental orthopedics," providing retarded children with exercises designed to improve such elementary components of intelligence as attention, memory, or simply sitting still. After practicing these exercises, many children showed genuine intellectual gains. Binet did not deny that every person has an inborn upper limit for intellectual development; he did not argue that mental orthopedics could elevate retarded children's intelligence indefinitely, but he believed that, as a practical matter, few individuals come close to achieving their upper limits. Thus, in most cases, and especially with retarded children, there is considerable room for the enhancement of intelligence by training.

Unfortunately, Binet did not live long enough to elaborate on these views or even to enjoy the success of his new approach to testing. The years from 1905 to 1911 brought personal difficulties: His wife suffered from an ill-defined malady that inhibited social life, and his own health declined as well. Perhaps partly as a reflection of his own gloomy thoughts, he collaborated with the dramatist André de Lorde—known popularly as "The Prince of Terror"—in writing and producing a series of psychiatrically oriented plays. In these plays, homicidal maniacs murder their brothers or infant sons, and a grief-stricken father makes a Frankensteinlike effort to revivify his daughter's dead body (see Wolf, 1982, for details). In 1911, the ultimate tragedy occurred: Binet died of a stroke on October 18, only 54 years old and at the height of his psychological powers.

Had he lived for another decade, Binet would undoubtedly have protested against three major developments that followed in the theory and practice of intelligence testing. One was the promotion of the Englishman Charles Spearman's (1863–1945) concept of *general intelligence*,— the notion that every person is born with a fixed source of general intellectual energy or "mental horsepower," which is employed to drive the specific neurological "engines" responsible for diverse intellectual tasks. Second was the American Henry H. Goddard's (1866–1957) widely publicized use of Binet's tests to detect *moronity* (a term coined by Goddard), a condition he believed to be completely hereditary, and determined by a single recessive gene. Goddard did much to make Binet's tests widely known, but his basic conception of the "intelligence" they measured was, like Spearman's, fundamentally different from Binet's. In a third controversial development, the German William Stern (1871–1938) proposed in 1912 to calculate "intelligence quotients" by dividing children's tested "mental ages" by their actual or chronological ages (chap. 6, *Pioneers II*). Unlike Binet's *niveau mental*, an intelligence quotient was assumed to remain relatively stable over the years of development. In the minds of many psychologists, these three ideas combined to establish the very un-Binetian notion that Binet's tests measure an "intelligence" that is unitary in essence, primarily determined by heredity, and specifiable as a single numerical quotient that remains relatively fixed throughout life.

These developments occurred outside France, and perhaps one might have expected Binet's own views to have been defended in his native land. Ironically, however, Binet's tests received little attention at all from his successors in France. Indeed, had the tests not been discovered almost accidentally by Goddard and promoted in the English-speaking world, they might well have slipped into the same near oblivion that was the fate of many of Binet's other contributions. During his relatively short psychological career, Binet published 13 books and nearly 200 articles on topics more diverse than could be covered in this short account. Many of these were highly original and anticipated important future developments in several fields of psychology. Yet for all of their virtues, they received surprisingly little direct recognition and the question arises as to why.

Wolf (1973) and Siegler (1992) suggested that Binet's lack of official recognition by French psychologists was at least partly attributable to his self-trained status. He had no benevolent mentor to caution him and tone down his youthful naiveté and excess of enthusiasm. He probably never completely shed his early reputation for making overly hasty claims. Later in his career, when he applied for three major professorships in psychology, he lacked not only official credentials but also personal support from teachers who could have helped him climb the normal rungs of career advancement. Thus, although his concrete accomplishments gave him claim to be the premier experimental psychologist in France, he was bitterly disappointed at the negative outcome of all three applications.

To the end of his life, Binet remained the unpaid *Directeur* of the small Sorbonne laboratory, lacking the authority to confer even token academic credit on the handful of students who came. He never had a real opportunity to create a strong institutionally based group or enough assistants to carry out large-scale programmatic research (even the famous test of 1905 was standardized on a small sample of just 10 children in each of five age groups). When Binet complained that the "Würzburg school"—a genuine community of scholars—had unfairly denied credit for imageless thought to the "school of Paris," he was surely aware of the irony in the latter designation. "Woe betide him who is alone," he wrote when describing children subject to group pressure in his suggestibility research (cited in Cunningham, 1988, p. 275). He well knew the pain of that situation from personal experience.

In part, however, Binet's isolation seems to have been self-inflicted. He was never a highly sociable or outgoing person. Although he was warmly remembered by those who knew him well, such intimates were relatively few. For all his propensity to express himself on paper, he avoided speaking at or even attending psychological conferences. Thus, he seldom made the kinds of personal contacts, either within France or internationally, that could have enhanced his reputation and influence.

Thus, a question arises as to whether Binet has been underappreciated out of willful neglect or simple lack of awareness of his contributions. As we have seen, Binet believed that Bühler had known about his work on imageless thought and deliberately denied him credit. Siegler (1992) argued that Piaget probably owed a greater direct intellectual debt to Binet than he acknowledged in his major works. It should be noted, however, that Piaget contributed an appreciative introduction to the 1973 re-issue of Binet's *Les Idées Modernes sur les Enfants*, partially compensating for any earlier injustice. Whatever the truth in these cases, it seems that in many instances Binet is better characterized as an *anticipator* than as a *founder* of new research traditions. As defined by Sarup (1978), anticipators promote "ideas that are historically anterior and substantively similar to, but effectively discontinuous with, subsequent formulations" (p. 478). The work of founders, by contrast, has direct and demonstrable developmental ties to the later ideas.

Even if Binet is classified (outside the domain of intelligence testing) as more an anticipator than a founder, he was an anticipator of extraordinary versatility and prescience. Slowly but surely, workers in fields such as memory, eyewitness testimony, suggestibility, child development, cognition, and abnormal psychology are recognizing that Binet can still be read with interest and profit today. He correctly foresaw many of the important psychological developments that would occur throughout the 20th century. It is appropriate to recognize and admire this fact as we stand on the eve of the 21st century.

ACKNOWLEDGMENT

Theta Wolf, whose biographical research is foundational for all Binet scholars today and who usefully commented on an earlier version of this chapter, died in April of 1997. This chapter is dedicated to her memory.

REFERENCES

Asch, S. E. (1952). *Social psychology*. Englewood Cliffs, NJ: Prentice-Hall.

Asch, S. E. (1963). Effects of group pressure upon the modification and distortion of judgments. In H. Guetzkow, (Ed.), Groups, leadership and men (pp. 177–190). New York: Russell & Russell. (Original work published 1951)

Binet, A. (1880). De la fusion des sensations semblables [On the fusion of similar sensations]. *Revue Philosophique, 10*, 284–294.

Binet, A. (1883). Du raisonnement dans les perceptions [Reasoning in perception]. *Revue Philosophique, 15*, 406–432.

Binet, A. (1886). *La psychologie du raisonnement* [The psychology of reasoning]. Paris: Alcan.

Binet, A. (1895). M. François de Curel (Notes psychologiques). *L'Année Psychologique, 1*, 119–173.

Binet, A. (1900). *La suggestibilité* [Suggestibility]. Paris: Schleicher.

Binet, A. (1903). *L'Étude expérimentale de l'intelligence* The experimental study of intelligence]. Paris: Schleicher.

Binet, A. (1973). *Les idées modernes sur les enfants* [Modern ideas about children]. Paris: Flammarion (Original work published 1909).

Binet, A., & Féré, C. (1885). La polarisation psychique [Psychic Polarization]. *Revue Philosophique, 19*, 369–402.

Binet, A. & Henneguy, L. (1894). *La psychologie des grands calculateurs et jouers d'échecs* [The psychology of great calculators and chess players]. Paris: Hachette.

Binet, A., & Henri, V. (1894a). Recherches sur le développement de la mémoire visuelle des enfants [Studies of the development of visual memory]. *Revue Philosophique, 37*, 348–350.

Binet, A., & Henri, V. (1894b). De la suggestibilité naturelle chez les enfants [On the natural suggestibility of children]. *Revue Philosophique, 38*, 337–347.

Binet, A., & Henri, V. (1895a). La mémoire des mots [Memory for words]. *L'Année Psychologique, 1*, 1–23.

Binet, A., & Henri, V. (1895b). La mémoire des phrases [Memory for sentences]. *L'Année Psychologique, 1*, 24–59.

Binet, A., & Henri, V. (1896). La psychologie individuelle [Individula psychology]. *L'Année Psychologique, 2*, 411–465.

Binet, A. & Passy, J. (1895). Notes psychologiques sur les auteurs dramatiques [Psychological notes on dramatic authors]. *L'Année Psychologique, 1*, 60–118.

Cunningham, J. L. (1988). Contributions to the history of psychology: XLVI. The pioneer work of Alfred Binet on children as eyewitnesses. *Psychological Reports, 62*, 271–277.

Cunningham, J. L. (1995). Binet's contextual study of memory. *Psychological Reports, 77*, 955–961.

Delboeuf, J. (1880). Note. *Revue Philosophique, 10*, 644–648.

Fancher, R. E. (1985). *The intelligence men: Makers of the IQ controversy*. New York: Norton.

Nicolas, S. (1994a). La mémoire dans l'oeuvre d'Alfred Binet (1857–1911) [Memory in the work of Alfred Binet (1857–1911)]. *L'Année Psychologique, 94*, 257–282.

Nicolas, S. (1994b). Qui était Victor Henri (1872–1940)? [Who was Victor Henri?]. *L'Année Psychologique, 94*, 385–402.

Nicolas, S. (1995). Henry Beaunis (1830–1921), Directeur-fondateur du Laboratoire de Psychologie Physiologique de la Sorbonne [Director-founder of the Sorbonne Laboratory of physiological psychology. *L'Année Psychologique, 95*, 267–291.

Pollack, R. H., & Brenner, M. W. (Eds.). (1969). *The experimental psychology of Alfred Binet: Selected papers*. New York: Springer.

Sarup, G. (1978). Historical antecedents of psychology: The recurrent issue of old wine in new bottles. *American Psychologist, 33*, 478–485.

Siegler, R. S. (1992). The other Alfred Binet. *Developmental Psychology, 28*, 179–190.

Thieman, T. J., & Brewer, W. F. (1978). Alfred Binet on memory for ideas. *Genetic PsychologyMonographs, 97*, 243–264.

Tuddenham, R. D. (1962). The nature and measurement of intelligence. In L. Postman (Ed.), *Psychology in the making: Histories of selected research problems* (pp. 469–525). New York: Knopf.

Wolf, T. (1969). The emergence of Binet's conception and measurement of intelligence: A case history of the creative process. *Journal of the History of the Behavioral Sciences, 5*, 113–134.

Wolf, T. (1973). *Alfred Binet*. Chicago: University of Chicago Press.

Wolf, T. (1976). Memory in the work of Alfred Binet. In D. Bastable (Ed.), *Philosophical studies* (pp. 186–196). Dublin: L. Leader.

Wolf, T. (1982). A new perspective on Alfred Binet: Dramatist of Le Théâtre de l'Horreur. *Psychological Record, 32*, 397–407.

Chapter 6

L. L. Thurstone's Vision of Psychology As a Quantitative Rational Science[1]

Lyle V. Jones

The biography of an individual scientist cannot be expected to be of general interest except when there has been a spectacular achievement or a colorful personality or both. The present case has no claim to either. Some students may find encouragement in knowing that something can be accomplished in spite of much floundering with objectives that do not seem as clear as they will in retrospect.

—Thurstone, 1952, p. 295

Although L. L. Thurstone's autobiography begins with these words, in actuality Thurstone's achievements were spectacular. His personality, if not colorful, certainly was strong and memorable. His career goals eluded him until his mid-thirties, but by that time he was aware that he had become a creative, productive, world-renowned research psychologist.

GROWING UP

Thurstone was born Louis Leon Thunström in Chicago on May 29, 1887. His father had been an instructor of mathematics and fortifications in the Swedish army, and

---

*Photograph of L. L. Thurstone, 1951, courtesy of Carl Davis.
[1]Thurstone's autobiography (Thurstone, 1952) provided useful information for this chapter. Details of his life that are not otherwise referenced are taken from this source. Biographies about Thurstone by Adkins Wood (1962) and by Guilford (1957) both include complete bibliographies of Thurstone's work. A short obituary was also published (Gulliksen, 1956).

later became, in turn, a Lutheran minister, a newspaper editor, and a newspaper publisher. His mother, Sophie Sträth Thunström, also Swedish, expressed her intense interest in music in part by insuring that both Louis and his younger sister received piano instruction at early ages. The piano provided much satisfaction to L. L. Thurstone throughout his life.

Thurstone started school in Berwyn, Illinois. Following a brief stay in Centerville, Mississippi, he moved at 8 years old with his parents to Stockholm, Sweden, where he first attended a public school and then a private boys' school. To dispel the image of being a foreigner among his classmates, he diligently studied to master the Swedish language. Throughout his life, he retained good command of Swedish, which served him well on return trips to Sweden.

In 1901, at 14 years old, Thurstone returned with his family to Jamestown, New York. To reduce the costs of travel, his parents brought only essential personal belongings with them. Thurstone announced, however, that he would not move with his family without his three favorite books—a world atlas, Euclid's Geometry, and an encyclopedic selection of philosophic essays. Although refusing to have these heavy books moved at family expense, his mother permitted him to carry them on shipboard in his arms (Thurstone, 1974).

In Jamestown, Thurstone experienced problems not unlike those he had encountered in Stockholm. Now, the mastery of English became his central goal. His grade-school principal volunteered to be his English tutor. With him, Thurstone spent countless hours of practice speaking sentences in English; on occasion, he would repeat a single word over and over, striving to pronounce it without a Swedish accent (Adkins Wood, 1962).

When he won a geometry contest in high school, Thurstone was awarded a prize of $30, with which he purchased a second-hand bicycle and a Kodak box camera. This acquisition marked the start of his life-long hobby of photography. While still a sophomore in high school, he enjoyed his first publication, a short letter to *Scientific American,* in which he proposed a solution to an emerging conflict between power companies and tourist interests regarding the possible diversion of water to power plants from Niagara Falls:

How to Save Niagara

To the Editor of the Scientific American:

There has lately been much discussion on how to save Niagara Falls. I take here the liberty to describe a method of utilizing the greater part of the energy in the falls without injuring in the least the beauty of the falls and without necessitating any engineering structures in the vicinity of the falls.

Suppose a dam, constructed across Niagara River, a few miles above the falls or at the beginning of the river. Let the gates of the dam be closed half of the time and opened half of the time, making the river flow, say, twelve hours in daytime. There would be no danger of overflow when the gates are shut, with the large area of Lake Erie above the dam. It is evident that twice the regular flow of the river could be extracted from Lake Erie in the daytime. Let the regular flow pass over the falls and take a quantity equal to half the regular flow continually for power purposes. This would give about 3,500,000 horsepower without injuring in the least the beauty of the falls. The gates of the dam could be open, say nine hours in the day and three hours in the night, in order to make it possible to see the falls also at night. It seems to be that if these arrangements were possible, it would give a great amount of power and at the same time save the destruction of the falls.

Louis L. Thunström
Jamestown, N. Y., June 20, 1905 (Thunström, 1905)

At about this time, his parents changed the family name to Thurstone, making it easier both to spell and pronounce. Later, L. L. Thurstone decided that he preferred to be called Leon (pronounced "LAYon"). In correspondence, however, he used neither first nor middle name, but signed typed letters either L. L. Thurstone or Thurstone, typically at a buoyant $45°$ left-to-right upward slant.[2]

BECOMING AN ENGINEER AT CORNELL

After graduation from high school, Thurstone entered Cornell to major in engineering. As one of his projects, he developed a motion picture camera and projector that eliminated flicker, which constituted a serious problem in early motion pictures. Thurstone's machine allowed a continuous movement of film and used two rotating mirrors to keep constant the distance from the film to the objective. The machine was actually built and patented. Thurstone demonstrated it a few years later for Thomas A. Edison in his New Jersey laboratories.

While at Cornell, Thurstone became interested in psychological aspects of machine design, especially on how an operator learns the visual-motor coordination needed to use a particular machine, an interest that anticipated, by many decades, the field of human engineering. To help him study the learning function as a scientific problem, he visited lectures in psychology of Professors Madison Bentley and E. B. Titchener (chap. 7, *Pioneers I*). Of the latter, he reported having been "curious about his extremely formal and pompous manner" (Thurstone, 1952, p. 298).

Thurstone was greatly impressed by one of his engineering professors at Cornell—Dexter Kimball. Kimball was dedicated to teaching, as exemplified by the near perfection of his classes that resulted from his extensive preparation for each. Later, as a professor, Thurstone typically spent 4 or 5 hours preparing for each 1-hour class, quite consciously aiming to teach as well as he remembered Kimball to have taught (Thurstone, 1974).

---

[2]In the 1950s, Thurstone developed a battery of objective tests to measure temperament. Among the tests was one for which items were short movie segments of forms in apparent movement. Thurstone hypothesized that a subject who perceived movement upward rather than downward and left-to-right in preference to right-to-left movement might be a person with optimistic tendencies. Under that hypothesis, his characteristic signature certainly did signify a positive outlook.

THOMAS EDISON'S ASSISTANT

Edison and his staff viewed Thurstone's motion picture machine and applauded its design, but they chose not to modify their plant to accommodate its manufacture. However, Edison offered Thurstone an assistantship in his laboratory. On graduation from Cornell with a Master of Engineering (ME) degree in 1912, Thurstone became Edison's assistant in the Edison laboratory in West Orange, New Jersey. In 1912, to include "Assistant to Thomas A. Edison" on one's résumé must have made a favorable impression on most potential employers. By that time, Edison had been issued many of his 1,093 patents. He was recognized as the "Father of Invention," and was as well known and widely respected as any public figure.

Thurstone later recalled that Edison had "a startling fluency of ideas, which often ranged far from the immediate problem. He seemed to have an absolutely endless array of stories; very few of them were fit for publication. If problem-solving ability is to be studied scientifically and experimentally, it will be advisable to include studies of different kinds of fluency" (Thurstone, 1952, p. 299). Thurstone was impressed by Edison's habit of discarding ideas that had been tried and found not to work. With no hesitation, Edison simply tried something else. It is said of Edison that after 10,000 unsuccessful efforts to develop a storage battery, a friend expressed sympathy for his failure. "I have not failed," replied Edison. "I have just discovered 10,000 ways that don't work." To a degree, Thurstone developed similar habits. When he became dissatisfied with a draft manuscript, he typically would not attempt to repair it through revision, but would discard it and start again (Thurstone, 1974).

ENGINEERING AND PSYCHOLOGY AT MINNESOTA, CHICAGO, AND CARNEGIE TECH

In the fall of 1912, Thurstone accepted a position as instructor at the Engineering College of the University of Minnesota, where he taught descriptive geometry and drafting. He also enrolled in courses in experimental psychology taught by Herbert Woodrow and J. B. Miner, reflecting his continuing attention to the experimental study of the learning function. Then, in 1914, he began graduate study at the University of Chicago. Motivated by his interest in learning, he enrolled initially in the Department of Education, where Professor C. H. Judd served as Head. Soon, he transferred to the Department of Psychology, under the tutelage of James Rowland Angell. About his classroom experiences at Chicago, Thurstone later wrote the following:

> I recall one of my first impressions of graduate students of psychology. When they were asked a question, they would start to talk fluently, even when they obviously knew nothing about the subject. I was sure that engineers had higher standards of

intellectual honesty. One of my first courses was called advanced educational psychology and it was taught by Professor Judd. I used to wonder what the elementary course could be like if the course that I was taking was called advanced. I soon became accustomed to the fact that prerequisites did not mean anything and that there was no real sequence of courses in psychology, even though they were listed by number and title to give the appearance of a sequence, in which one course was supposed to build on another. I never had an elementary course in psychology or in statistics. My first degree was M.E., and I was never flattered when it was interpreted at Chicago as a master's degree in Education! (Thurstone, 1952, p. 300).

Walter Bingham interviewed psychology graduate students at the University of Chicago in 1915 to select an assistant in the new Division of Applied Psychology at the Carnegie Institute of Technology. Thurstone was chosen and was offered a stipend of $1,000 for the year. He was elated. He accepted that appointment and then a reappointment for a second year, by the end of which, in 1917, he was awarded the PhD from the University of Chicago. His dissertation on the learning-curve equation appeared as a monograph (Thurstone, 1919), and he published several other papers on learning (Thurstone, 1918, 1930a, 1930b, 1933). Thurstone remained at the Carnegie Institute of Technology, but now as a faculty member. By 1920, he had become a full professor and chairman of the psychology department.

A YEAR IN THE NATION'S CAPITAL AND MARRIAGE

In 1923, the university administration at the Carnegie Institute of Technology disbanded the program in applied psychology and Thurstone left that institution. In January 1923, he accepted a position in the foundation-supported Institute for Government Research, in Washington, DC, where he was to prepare manuals and other materials to stimulate the improvement of civil-service examinations. His work at the Institute had a lasting impact on the quality of civil service tests (Guilford, 1957).

Thurstone's office happened to be in the building that also was occupied by the American Council on Education (ACE). After becoming acquainted with ACE staff members, he discussed with them the creation of examinations to guide college admission decisions. One year later, the ACE provided financial support to Thurstone, then at the University of Chicago, to develop such examinations (Thurstone, 1974).

Thelma Gwinn earned a master's degree in psychology at the Carnegie Institute of Technology in 1923. At Thurstone's invitation, she joined him at the Institute for Government Research. The following year, the two were married in Washington, DC. Both then moved to the University of Chicago, he as an associate professor of psychology, she as a PhD student in the psychology department. The Thurstones' three sons were all born in Chicago. Robert, born in 1927, became a professor of engineering at the University of Alabama, Huntsville; Conrad, born in 1930, became a professor of surgery at Stanford University; and Fritz, born in 1932, was professor of biomedical engineering at Duke University.

RESEARCH AND TEACHING AT CHICAGO

On arrival at The University of Chicago, Thurstone taught a course in descriptive statistics for psychology, but he also developed a unique course in mental test theory—unique in that he created the theory that was the content of the course. Prior to that time, courses in mental testing had been largely confined to the study of the Stanford–Binet intelligence scales.

In his first paper on psychological testing (Thurstone, 1925), which he considered one of his best, Thurstone developed a scaling method for psychological tests based on a normality assumption within age groups and simply requiring the estimation of a mean and a variance at each age. His interest in test theory soon developed into a more general interest in psychological measurement, and led to a burst of major publications between 1926 and 1928 in the *Psychological Review* and other journals of the American Psychological Association (APA).

One of Thurstone's major original contributions was the creation of a basis for psychological measurement that, in contrast to the traditional psychophysics of Fechner (chap. 1, *Pioneers II*), Müller, and Titchener, is completely independent of physical measurement. Traditional psychophysics can develop psychological scales for perceived length, or loudness, intensity of scent, or touch. Thurstone's theory accommodates the measurement of intelligence, ability or achievement, and attitude or opinion—psychological constructs that lack any direct physical correlates. Thurstone's interests in and contributions to psychological measurement continued throughout his career. Notable among later publications are Thurstone (1945, 1954) and Thurstone and Jones (1957).

Attitude Scaling

Thurstone's use of his psychological scaling theory for measuring attitudes (Thurstone, 1928) is of special interest because it led to many later applications in a variety of contexts. These scales were adaptations of the psychophysical method of equal-appearing intervals. In this method of scale construction, the individual constructing the scale presents to a group of judges a large number of statements about some issue, concept, or institution. These judges do not say whether they agree or disagree with the statements. Instead, they sort them into a number of categories, often 11, that range from *very favorable* to *very unfavorable*, with respect to the target of the judgments. The instructions are to let the middle category—6 on an 11-point scale—represent neutrality and let the differences separating adjacent, other categories represent equal steps along a scale of favorability. When the results of 50 or so judges are available, items for the final scale are selected on the basis of two statistical criteria: The statements finally chosen must form a series of roughly equal steps, ranging from *very unfavorable* to *very favorable*; the measure of favorability is the median category value that the judges assign to the statement. The statements must be unambiguous, as evidenced by most judges assigning them nearly the same rank; the measure employed to determine ambiguity is the sem-interquartile range—half the distance between the 25th and 75th percentiles of these ratings. Only items with low variability are retained for the final scale of attitude.

The three items following (with scale values at the left) taken from Thurstone and Chave's (1929) scale of attitude toward the church (high numbers represent negative attitudes) serve as examples of those that appear on such scales.

(0.2) I believe that the church is the greatest institution in America today.
(5.9) I do not believe in any brand of religion or in any particular church, but I have never given the matter much thought.
(11.0) I think that the church is a parasite on society.

The actual Thurstone scales contain many such items (scale values omitted) covering the range of attitudes in smaller steps. Respondents simply check those with which they agree. The measure of their attitudes is the median scale value of the items that they check.

Establishing a Psychometric Laboratory

Thurstone was invited by Charles Merriam, Chairman of the Department of Political Science at the University of Chicago, to occupy a suite of offices in the Social Science Research Building, which was shared by faculty in anthropology, economics, and sociology, but not psychology. Thurstone accepted the invitation and, sometime around 1930, he told his wife that he intended to tack on the door of his workroom a sign that identified it as the "Psychometric Laboratory." She cautioned that such an action would require approval by the Department of Psychology and the University administration. "Oh, they wouldn't approve," said Leon—and he attached the sign that remained there until his retirement from Chicago in 1952 (Thurstone, 1974).

Beginning in 1938, Thurstone produced a series of *Psychometric Laboratory Reports*, which were among the earliest of such institutional research reports in psychology. They served as progress reports of work in the laboratory. The cover of each report featured an attractive photograph, taken by Thurstone, of the entryway to the laboratory. By 1952, 81 of these reports had been produced; all but a few of them were authored by L. L. Thurstone.

Factor Analysis

During World War I, Thurstone authored vocational tests for use in classifying military personnel. Then, from 1919 to 1923, he authored tests of intelligence, clerical skills, engineering aptitude, and ingenuity. (See Adkins Wood, 1962 or Guilford, 1957, for complete bibliographic citations of Thurstone's tests.) Beginning in 1924 and continuing through 1947, Thurstone authored or co-authored with Thelma G. Thurstone annual editions of the ACE Psychological Examination for High School Graduates and College Freshmen. These were later converted to the Scholastic Aptitude Tests, administered by the Educational Testing Service, an organization that was founded primarily for that purpose.

Thurstone's involvement with psychological testing, in the context of his engineering training and his scientific curiosity, led him to seek methods with which to determine the structure of performance on psychological tests, that is, the dimensionality of latent variables that might produce observed patterns of relations among test items. This directly led to his work on multiple-factor analysis, contributions for which he probably is best known. He developed a centroid method for the extraction of factors from an intertest (or interitem) correlation matrix, he proposed and supported the use of "communalities"—estimates of common rather than total test variances—in the analysis, and he invented the construct of simple structure to transform arbitrary dimensions from a centroid solution into more psychologically meaningful dimensions. Among his major publications on these methods are Thurstone (1931, 1935, 1947).

In the mid-1930s, Thurstone sought to employ his new multiple-factor methods to produce concrete empirical results. As he and Thelma Gwinn Thurstone continued to publish new editions of the ACE examinations, he was approached by representatives of the Community Work Education Service, the higher education branch of the Works Progress Administration that provided funds to employ college-educated personnel. Thurstone was asked if he could employ 100 workers. "No," he said, "but I might usefully employ about 20" (Thurstone, 1980). Suddenly, the Thurstones had a score of assistants.[3] With their help, the Thurstones then constructed a set of 57 psychological tests that required about 15 hours of time for each person tested. During a vacation week, this test battery was administered to about 300 volunteers from the freshman class at the University of Chicago. Results were scored by hand and then were factor analyzed. Results led to the conceptualization of a set of primary mental abilities (PMA) as defined in Thurstone (1938a) and the development of tests for each (Thurstone, 1938b).

Thelma Gwinn Thurstone became Instructor in Psychology at Chicago Teachers College in 1938. Her employment provided access to the Chicago Public Schools and

---

[3]One of these was Ledyard R Tucker. Among Tucker's many accomplishments was his conversion of an IBM optical reader into a test-scoring machine, which subsequently was heavily used to score answer sheets from the Thurstones' testing programs. Tucker received his PhD with Thurstone as his sponsor and is well-known for his many seminal contributions to quantitative psychology while a research scientist at ETS, and later a faculty member at the University of Illinois–Urbana.

led to the administration of PMA tests to students in Chicago's public grade schools and high schools. Analysis of test data from these students supported the earlier findings from the more select sample of freshmen at the University of Chicago (Thurstone & Thurstone, 1941) and resulted in the publication of tests for a broader range of ages (Thurstone & Thurstone, 1942, 1943). With the active support of the Thurstones, Science Research Associates (SRA) was founded by Lyle Spencer and Robert Burns to make the PMA test batteries available to a wide audience.

In 1929, at 29 years old, Robert Hutchins became President of the University of Chicago. Among the innovative programs he initiated in the 1930s was one that provided course credit to students by examination. L. L. Thurstone agreed to serve as Chief Examiner, accepting responsibility for creating the exams and for supervising their administration and scoring. Examiners under Thurstone included Dorothy Adkins, Harold Gulliksen, Paul Horst, Marion Richardson, John Stalnaker, and Dael Wolfle, among others whose later distinguished career achievements became well-known.

Honors and Recognition

By the early 1930s, Thurstone's contributions to psychology were widely recognized. He served as President of the Midwestern Psychological Association from 1930 to 1931, and as President of APA from 1932 to 1933. From 1936 to 1937, he was Charter President of the Psychometric Society, an organization dedicated to "the development of psychology as a quantitative rational science." In 1938, he was elected to membership in the National Academy of Sciences, 1 of only 18 psychologists to be Academy members at that time. According to Daniel Barbiero, Assistant Archivist, National Academy of Sciences (personal communication, July 31, 1996), the other 17 psychologists who were members in 1938 were James Rowland Angell, E.G. Boring, James McKeen Cattell, John Dewey (chap. 4, *Pioneers II*), Clark L. Hull (chap. 14, *Pioneers I*), Walter S. Hunter (chap. 18, *Pioneers I*), Karl Lashley (chap. 20, *Pioneers I*), Walter M. Miles, W. B. Pilsbury, Carl E. Seashore, George M. Stratton, Lewis M. Terman, Edward L. Thorndike (chap. 10, *Pioneers I*), E. C. Tolman (chap. 15, *Pioneers I*), and Clark Wissler, Robert S. Woodworth, and Robert M. Yerkes (chap. 7, *Pioneers II*). Thurstone also was elected as a Fellow of the American Academy of Arts and Sciences, a Fellow and member of the Board of Directors of the American Statistical Association, President of APA's Division on Evaluation and Measurement, and an Honorary Fellow of the British Psychological Society.

WORLD WAR II AND AFTER

During World War II, Thurstone served as a member of the Committee on Classification of Military Personnel of the U.S. Adjutant General's Office and he authored several psychological tests that were then used for military selection and classification.

Later, in the 1940s, before external research support for academicians had become common, Thurstone was awarded a number of grants and contracts from both corporate and governmental sources. Prominent were contracts with Sears, Roebuck, & Co. to develop employment tests, with the U.S. Army Quartermaster Corps, to develop "hedonic scales" for assessing soldiers' preferences for items of food and clothing, and grants from the Air Force Office of Scientific Research (OSR), to create and experimentally evaluate objective tests for the measurement of human temperament.

Academic Life at Chicago

During 1948 and 1949, while on leave from the University of Chicago, Thurstone was Visiting Professor of Psychology at the University of Frankfort. On his return, he continued teaching and also attracted many postdoctoral fellows who enrolled in his courses. In the academic year of 1950–1951, postdoctoral visitors from the United States included James E. Birren, Allen L. Edwards, Lyle V. Jones, and Edward Lawlor. At the same time, foreign visitors included Melanie Baehr and Carol Pemberton from South Africa, Rolf Bargman from Germany, Jean Cardinet from Switzerland, Sten Henrysson from Sweden, Horace Rimoldi from Argentina, and Per Saugstad from Norway.

Thurstone enjoyed being an active participant in the Quadrangle Club, the Faculty Club of The University of Chicago. Most weekdays, he would lunch at the Club, usually eating with friends from disciplines other than psychology. He often commented on the value he placed on his lunchtime conversations. He found especially useful his contacts with faculty in mathematics, who directed his education in matrix algebra, and faculty in economics, with whom he discussed mutual interests in the measurement of consumer behavior.

When I joined the faculty at the University of Chicago, Thurstone encouraged me to select a sample of Quadrangle Club members to serve as participants in a study using scaled preferences for menu entrees and their prices to predict the popularities of alternative lunch entrees at the Club dining room. We had planned to be joint authors of the resulting publication, but complications arose regarding the technique for determining scale values for the menu items and their prices, which delayed the completion of the project and of its publication until several years after Thurstone's death (Jones, 1959).

Home Seminars

The Thurstones maintained in their home a seminar room, complete with blackboard, that seated about 30 guests. For many years, they hosted Wednesday evening seminars—sometimes weekly during the academic year—whose speakers were visiting scholars or faculty members at the University of Chicago or nearby institutions. Attendance was strictly by Thurstone's invitation. Lively discussion typically followed each presentation. The emphasis was on work in progress rather than on completed research. The intent was that discussion should provide aid for the project's successful completion. Attendees felt honored to be invited to these sessions, came away intellectually stimulated, and also enjoyed the coffee and cake that followed, hospitably served by Mrs. T., as Thelma Thurstone was affectionately known.

THE MOVE TO NORTH CAROLINA

As he approached the mandatory retirement age of 65 in 1952, Thurstone sought a new academic home. He and Thelma considered offers from the University of California-Berkeley, the University of North Carolina and the University of Washington. The University of North Carolina (UNC) offer was the only one to include a professorial appointment for Thelma (in the School of Education) as well as for Leon (in the Department of Psychology). The offer of a faculty appointment for Thelma proved to be the decisive factor in the Thurstones' decision to settle in Chapel Hill. The Thurstones rented a house for their first year there, while they built an attractive one-story ranch-style home near campus that included a large study with built-in blackboard to accommodate evening seminars that were reminiscent of those at Chicago. Figure 6.1 is from 1952, as Dorothy Adkins, Mr. and Mrs. Thurstone, and Guy B. Phillips (Dean, School of Education) agree to the Thurstone's faculty appointments at UNC.

It was understood that Thurstone's salary, together with that of other laboratory staff members, and graduate research assistants, would be paid from other than University sources. His research grants, particularly from the Air Force Office of Sceintific Research, generously provided sufficient funding to meet that expectation, supporting two other faculty members and several graduate student research assistants. A new Psychometric Laboratory was established in a two-story brick building—Nash Hall. Thurstone's photograph of the building, with a large dogwood tree blooming in the foreground, became the frontispiece for a new series of *Psychometric Laboratory Reports* (currently numbering 183 and counting).

Thurstone took leave in the spring of 1954 to be Visiting Professor at the University of Stockholm. He lectured also at other Swedish universities, and at universities in Helsinki and Oslo. Accompanying him on that adventure was not only his wife, but also Dorothy Adkins, Chair of the Psychology Department, the person who had engineered the faculty appointments for the Thurstones at UNC and who had become a close friend.

Thurstone also had intended to visit Europe again in the summer of 1955, but in a letter to me dated June 25, 1955, he wrote: "Medical advice in Chapel Hill was that I should not venture a trip to Europe this summer so I had to cancel the trip. I was sorry

FIG. 6.1. Dorothy Adkins, Mr. and Mrs. Thurstone, and Guy B. Phillips in 1952.

because I looked forward to the Paris Conference of about 50 to 60 including eight of our former students in Europe and an evening lecture I was supposed to give in London at the XII International Congress of Psychotechnology." Thurstone spent the summer of 1955 with his family at their summer home on Elk Lake near Rapid City in Upper Michigan, where he died on September 19, 1955, at 68 years old.

SOME PERSONAL MEMORIES

For my master's thesis in 1948 at the University of Washington, I was fortunate to be advised by Lloyd Humphreys, my faculty sponsor, to employ factor analysis to study the structure of the Stanford–Binet intelligence test (Jones, 1949). At Washington, I had also been influenced by other faculty members—Allen L. Edwards, Paul Horst, Tommy Hermans, and Louise Heathers in the Psychology Department and Z. William Birnbaum in the Mathematics Department—to learn statistics as a tool for research in psychology.

Moving to Stanford as E. R. Hilgard's research assistant in the fall of 1948, while committed to study learning, I also enrolled in Quinn McNemar's statistics course and chose a formal minor with Albert Bowker, the young chairman of Stanford's brand new Department of Statistics. In addition, 18 hours of coursework in advanced mathematics substituted for the requirement of a second foreign language, especially important to me because I had failed to master a first one.

In the interest of still further quantitative training, I wrote to L. L. Thurstone in the fall of 1949, asking if he would sponsor me as a postdoctoral fellow if I earned a PhD and if my application for a National Research Council (NRC) Fellowship was approved. He replied that he would do so. A few months later, in the early spring of 1950, while completing a dissertation about learning sets in pigeons (Jones, 1950), I was considering job opportunities. Choices narrowed to an instructorship at Harvard or assistant professorships at the Universities of Hawaii or Kansas. Before I made one of those choices, however, I learned that I had been awarded an NRC Fellowship. The stipend of $3,500 was comparable to the academic salaries offered at the three universities (which ranged from $3,100 to $3,600), so I promptly accepted the NRC Fellowship and so informed Professor Thurstone.

I recall the 1950 to 1951 postdoctoral year with great satisfaction. Together with other postdoctoral visitors, I enrolled in Thurstone's courses and in others. I will always remember my short interview with Thurstone when I told him that I would like to sit in on a course in factor analysis taught in the School of Education by Professor Holzinger. He stared at me in disbelief. "Of course, Jones," he said, "if you want to, but you'll find it a complete waste of time."

I regularly attended the Wednesday evening seminars at the Thurstones' home and also engaged in independent research, having chosen to re-analyze data from my master's thesis without the constraint that factors be orthogonal. As a research mentor, Thurstone was generous with his time and his advice. Every few days, I would complete the manual construction of graphs of projections on each of seven newly rotated factors with the other six. Thurstone and I would then scrutinize all 21 graphs, laid out on a large table, and agree on a next set of adjustments for the axes. I came to appreciate the skill with which Thurstone could visualize multidimensional space and could anticipate the degree of fitness in some dimensions that would result from transformations imposed in other dimensions. This project was successfully completed, thanks to Thurstone's help and support (Jones, 1954).

In the spring of 1951, anticipating the end of the postdoctoral year, I considered offers of faculty appointment from Cornell, Johns Hopkins, and the University of Michigan. While trying to decide among these attractive opportunities, I was startled when Thurstone informed me that I was welcome to join the psychology faculty at the University of Chicago. There had been no intimation that that might be a viable opportunity. Thurstone quietly arranged the appointment. Happily, I accepted. A further surprise awaited when Thurstone invited me to join him in developing psychological scaling procedures for a research grant from the U.S. Army Quartermaster Corps. Then, as my first year on the faculty progressed, I learned that Thurstone had reached retirement age and that I would become the acting director of his Psychometric Laboratory.

From the fall of 1952, when Thurstone moved to Chapel Hill, until the fall of 1955, he and I continued to engage in joint research on psychological scaling. We maintained an active correspondence. Typical is this exchange. I wrote:

January 6, 1953

Professor L. L. Thurstone, Director
Psychometric Laboratory
University of North Carolina
Chapel Hill, North Carolina

Dear Mr. Thurstone:

. . . My activities on the Quartermaster Research during the past two months have been almost wholly restricted to the word meaning study and the optimal questionnaire study, both of which I hope to have completed by the end of this month. Enclosed is a draft of the phase report entitled "Investigation of Descriptive Adjectives for use with Successive Interval Preference Schedules." I would be most appreciative if you had an opportunity to look at this, suggesting changes if such are appropriate. I have written this from a practical viewpoint, so as to be most readable and useful to the Food and Container Institute. I propose that any publication stemming from this study be modified, made more succinct and be more clearly psychological in outlook. Would a good title for such publication be "The Psychophysics of Semantics: An Experimental Investigation"? If I prepare the first draft for such a publication, may I request that you join me in authorship? [That title was adopted and the paper appeared under joint authorship (Jones & Thurstone, 1955)] . . .

As soon as the termination report is completed, for this year's contract, I shall spend more time with the Quadrangle Club Study. We have scaled all of the items, using Allen Edwards' method, modified so as to get estimates of the dispersion associated with each item. The distributions of preferences upon the psychological continuum are amazingly close to Gaussian distributions. This is also true of the data in the optimal scale study. I continue to be surprised.

Cordially yours,
Lyle V. Jones
LVJ:bhs

Thurstone replied:

January 12, 1953
Dr. Lyle V. Jones
Department of Psychology
The University of Chicago
Chicago 37, Illinois

Dear Lyle:

I have just received your letter of January 6 in which you enclosed a copy of your manuscript on "Investigation of Descriptive Adjectives for use with Successive Interval Preference Schedules." For publication purposes such a title is rather long. As you probably know, I try to reduce the length of titles for journal articles, but in this case the title is appropriate for the quartermaster corps.

Before reading your manuscript I can answer several questions that you have raised in your letter. . . .

I am interested in your proposed title for a more psychological publication of your present manuscript, namely, "The Psychophysics of Semantics: An Experimental Investigation." That is a good title. It is attention commanding, and it gives the reader immediately an idea of what the paper is about. Although in a sense I initiated this study by proposing it some time ago, the fact remains that you have carried out this study not only as far as the detailed work is concerned but also largely in the formulation of methodology. If I am a co-author of that paper, I would certainly be the second author. The case is a little different with the other papers on methodology for determining the zero point of the scale of utility and prediction of choice, where I did perhaps relatively more than setting up the papers, but I am willing to join you as second author on this paper that you have now sent me or in its revision as a psychological publication. . . .

I am, of course, interested also in your finding that our preference studies seem to yield normal distributions so generally that the assumption works out satisfactorily. Perhaps we can proceed with the simple method that Allen Edwards worked out and which we had considered before but discarded in our belief that the distribution would not be normal often enough for this to be used as a general method. Perhaps we should use this simple method on survey studies of this kind and accept the results when there is a good fit. We should always be on the lookout for the occasional stimulus that misbehaves as regards the normality of the distribution. . . .

I hope that the Psychometric Laboratory in Chicago is getting under way and that you will find it a challenging and interesting undertaking. Your success so far with the Quartermaster Corps projects on food preferences certainly ought to give you a good chance for new research contracts with the Quartermaster Corps, and with other agencies. . . .

Cordially yours,
L. L. Thurstone
LLT:ec

Figure 6.2 is a 1954 memo from Thurstone to me, uncharacteristically messy, (he was on vacation), but otherwise reflecting the character of the man.

Later in 1954 and 1955, Thurstone and I continued to correspond by letter and to exchange drafts of research reports. In a note to me on July 17, 1955, from Elk Lake, Michigan, he wrote to say that "Thelma and I would be glad to see you here for a few days whenever you can get air reservation to Traverse City. It is Capital Air Lines. The flight takes less than two hours on DC3. We shall meet you at the airport in Traverse City....PS: Bring your swimming suit and old informal clothes. This is not a dress up resort."

L. L. THURSTONE
The Psychometric Laboratory
University of North Carolina

MEMO

August 28, 1954

Professor Lyle Jones

Dear Lyle:

Thanks for your note of August 19.
We do not have duplicates of the papers and
monographs which the people in Poland want
and I do not have the references available
for the papers they inquire about.

<u>The Zero Point in Scaling</u> is the
title that I am using for a paper that is
partly written. The results look very good
and I believe you will like it. I shall send
you a draft for your approval as co-author.
A least squares solution gives good results
with the Chapel Hill data. I am satisfied
with the method of analysis that we have
now but you may have some new interesting tricks
on the problem. I believe the study will be
well received. At least I hope so.

Your name occurred to me as a possibility when I was asked in Washington to nominate
some people who could represent our subject
adequately in foreign countries. I have found
that a lot of incompetents are being sent abroad
who are certainly spotted quickly in the Scandi-
navian countries and in Germany. They say
nothing until you get to know them fairly well
as I have in being there for five months.

Best of luck with the new baby. I hope
that yours will be medically an ordinary and
uninteresting case. I hope you will not need to
call in the experts.

Cordially,

Thurstone

This is written at our summer cottage in
Michigan.

We had a conference here like last year of a group of officials/
from General Motors in Flint and Detroit. It was on the creativity
problem on which we are working. They flew here in an amphibian
plane and landed in front of our cottage on Elk Lake. They did
the same stunt last year. I don't quite comprehend their way of doing business

FIG. 6.2.   1954 memo from L. L. Thurstone.

100

I visited for several days in early August 1955. Thurstone and I discussed progress on several joint research projects. Swimming was also on the agenda, and the Thurstone boys tried their best (without success) to teach me to water ski. I was puzzled during that visit by the tone of some of Thurstone's conversation. For example, he commented about the role of Principal Investigator on research funds, noting that I should jealously guard the authority for expending money, especially against department chairs and deans. He wondered aloud if he had chosen correctly at UNC to affiliate with the Psychology Department rather than with the Institute of Statistics. Only later did I recognize that, from his perspective, this may have resembled a deathbed discussion. I wrote Thurstone letters on August 22 and August 29, 1955, but received no reply. When I learned that he died on September 19, I was stunned and saddened.

Thelma Gwinn Thurstone, when asked by the University administration at UNC to succeed L. L. Thurstone as Director of the Psychometric Laboratory, agreed to be Acting Director for a short term, to fulfill commitments under terms of unexpired research grants and contracts; she firmly declined to continue for a longer term. Thus, one other surprise awaited me in 1957, when I was asked to join the faculty and become Director of the Psychometric Laboratory at UNC. I have never regretted doing so, in large part because it provided the opportunity to maintain a program of education and research that was so firmly and competently established by L. L. Thurstone.

REFERENCES

Adkins Wood, D. (1962), *Louis Leon Thurstone*. Princeton, NJ: Educational Testing Service.

Guilford, J. P. (1957). Louis Leon Thurstone, 1987–1955. *National Academy of Sciences Biographical Memoirs, 30*, 349–382.

Gulliksen, H. (1956). A tribute to L. L. Thurstone. *Psychometrika, 21*, 309–312.

Jones, L. V. (1949). A factor analysis of the Stanford–Binet at four age levels. *Psychometrika, 14*, 299–331.

Jones, L. V. (1950). *Analysis of visual discrimination learning by pigeons*. Unpublished doctoral dissertation. Stanford University.

Jones, L. V. (1954). Primary abilities in the Stanford–Binet, age 13. *Journal of Genetic Psychology, 84*, 125–147.

Jones, L. V. (1959). Prediction of consumer purchase and the utility of money. *Journal of Applied Psychology, 43*, 334–337.

Jones, L. V., & Thurstone, L. L. (1955). The psychophysics of semantics: An experimental investigation. *Journal of Applied Psychology, 39*, 31–36.

Thunström, L. L. (1905). How to save Niagara. *Scientific American, 93*, 27.

Thurstone, L. L. (1919). The learning curve equation. *Psychological Monographs, 26* (no. 114).

Thurstone, L. L. (1925). A method of scaling psychological and educational tests. *Journal of Educational Psychology, 16*, 433–451.

Thurstone, L. L. (1928). Attitudes can be measured. *American Journal of Sociology, 33* , 529–554.

Thurstone, L. L. (1931). Multiple factor analysis. *Psychological Review, 38*, 406–427.

Thurstone, L. L. (1935). *The vectors of mind: Multiple factor analysis for the isolation of primary traits.* Chicago: The University of Chicago Press.

Thurstone, L. L. (1938a). Primary mental abilities. *Psychometric Monograph* (no. 1).

Thurstone, L. L. (1938b). *Tests for primary mental abilities, experimental edition.* Washington, DC: American Council on Education.

Thurstone, L. L. (1945). The prediction of choice. *Psychometrika, 10,* 237–253.

Thurstone, L. L. (1947). *Multiple-factor analysis.* Chicago: The University of Chicago Press.

Thurstone, L. L. (1952). L. L. Thurstone. In E. G. Boring, H. S. Langfeld, H. Werner, & R. M. Yerkes, Eds. *A history of psychology in autobiography, Vol. IV* (pp. 295–321). Worcester, MA: Clark University Press.

Thurstone, L. L. (1954). The measurement of values. *Psychological Review, 61,* 47–58.

Thurstone, L. L., & Chave, E. J. (1929). *The measurement of attitude.* Chicago: University of Chicago Press.

Thurstone, L. L. & Jones, L. V. (1957). The rational origin for measuring subjective values. *Journal of American Statistical Association, 52,* 458–471.

Thurstone, L. L. & Thurstone, T. G. (1941). Factorial studies of intelligence. *Psychometric Monograph* (no. 2).

Thurstone, L. L. & Thurstone, T. G. (1942). *The Chicago tests of primary mental abilities.* Washington, DC: American Council on Education.

Thurstone, L. L. & Thurstone, T. G. (1943). *The Chicago tests of primary mental abilities, single booklet edition.* Chicago: Science Research Associates.

Thurstone, T. G. (1974). Remembering the founding of psychometrics (Cassette recording). Chapel Hill, NC: L. L. Thurstone Psychometric Laboratory.

Thurstone, T. G. (1980). The Psychometric Laboratories at Chicago and North Carolina (Cassette recording). Chapel Hill, NC: L. L. Thurstone Psychometric Laboratory.

Chapter 7

Kurt Lewin: His Psychology and a Daughter's Recollections

Miriam A. Lewin

Kurt Lewin, my father, was a significant contributor to psychological theory and research for more than 30 years. During that time, he focused on a variety of topics ranging from the cognitive and motivational processes of individuals, to the dynamics of intra- and intergroup relationships, to the relevance of psychology for social programs. The common threads that tied these interests together were a theoretical orientation that Lewin called *field theory* and a concern for application—two themes that he saw as intimately connected. Lewin liked to say that there is nothing so practical as a good theory and that the best way to obtain theoretical understanding of a phenomenon is to try to change it. This chapter begins with a description of Lewin's position as it applied to individual behavior. A later section tells the story of Lewin's life and provides an account of some of his other contributions.

FIELD THEORY AND INDIVIDUAL BEHAVIOR

The most fundamental idea in Lewin's field theory (e.g., Lewin, 1936, 1938) was that behavior (B) is a function (F) of an interaction between a person (P) and that person's environment (E). As he often wrote it,

$$B = F(P,E)$$

The Environment

The environment in Lewin's equation is a perceptual or psychological environment. It includes only those aspects of the environment that are perceived by the

---

* Photograph of Kurt Lewin courtesy of Miriam Lewin.

individual—at some level, conscious or unconscious. Factors without such a representation are specifically excluded; they are assigned to what Lewin sometimes called an *alien* [or foreign] *hull*. The environment, as Lewin conceived it, had certain structural and dynamic properties.

Structure.   The Lewinian environment is made up of regions that roughly correspond to physical areas and objects (home, its rooms and furnishings), social entities (family, religious group, professional colleagues), or even concepts (abstract art, etiquette, and happiness). Regions are defined by boundaries that may separate them sharply—religious membership may have nothing to do with abstract art. However, regions may also overlap—happiness may involve home, family, and professional colleagues. Some regions contain goals that have positive or negative valences (attracting or repelling features). People are pushed toward positive and away from negative valences. The environment also contains paths connecting regions in the environment. Some of the important ones are paths to goals. Sometimes barriers block these paths and prevent the individual's progress. In such cases, the individual may find detour paths that circumvent the barrier and allow movement toward or away from the goal.

Dynamics.   The most important dynamic concept in Lewinian theory was that of driving and restraining forces, which are a result of the positive and negative valences of goals. With respect to any given goal, these forces have direction, distance, strength, and point of application: the person. The person's reaction to these forces is physical or psychological movement toward or away from the valenced region—an effect that Lewin called *locomotion*.

To make these concepts more concrete, imagine a little boy, age 2 or 3, who is trying to reach (driven by force established by) a piece of chocolate candy (a goal with positive valence) that is located in another part (region) of a room. The direct path to that goal is blocked by (a barrier) furniture in the way. To get the candy, the child must change his perception of the situation—something that Lewin called restructuring the environment. He must see that a path that includes a detour around a chair will get him to the goal. This perception is difficult because it requires an initial move in a direction away from that in which the operating force is urging him. The difficulty of the solution to such problems increases as the attractiveness of the goal increases.

Another type of difficulty occurs in conflict situations when objects with similar valences occupy different locations in the environment or when the same object or state of affairs has opposing valences or elicits opposed locomotions for some other reason. Lewin's analysis identifies four types of conflict.

Approach–approach conflicts are those in which the individual must choose between two alternatives, both of which have positive valences. Such conflicts may be divergent or convergent. The divergent form requires a choice between two different goals, as in the case of the proverbial ass who starved to death between two stacks of hay. The convergent form occurs when a person feels incompatible positive actions toward the same object. The little boy who wants to hug and hit his new baby brother simultaneously (incompatible approach reactions) is an example. Usually approach–approach conflicts are easily resolved in favor of one alternative or the other.

Avoidance–avoidance conflicts are those where the individual must choose between alternatives with negative valences—go to the dentist or continue to suffer with your toothache. Again the solution to these conflicts is usually the quick choice of one alternative.

Approach–avoidance conflicts occur in situations where the same object has both positive and negative valences so that the corresponding forces drive the person simultaneously toward and away from it. The classical Lewinian example is that of a little girl who wants to go wading in the ocean but is afraid of the water. The normal reaction to these conflicts is indecision and compromise—the child approaches but does not quite go into the water, or she hesitantly goes in, or reluctantly goes away, after a period of vacillation.

Multiple approach–avoidance conflicts occur in situations where there are alternative possibilities, both of which have several positive and negative features: College A or College B? This major or that one? Marriage or career? A home in the city or the suburbs? These conflicts can be difficult.

The Person

In Lewin's theory, the person is inseparable from the environment and the two together define the concept called the *life space*. Thus, the equation for behavior [B = f(P,E) may be rewritten to become:

$$B = F(\text{Life Space})$$

Structure.   The person, like the environment, is divided into regions that are separated by more or less permeable boundaries. These regions correspond to the individual's needs, capabilities, and perceptions of the environment (e.g., the psychological distances that separate the person from home, from another individual, or from the solution to a problem). The number of regions determines the complexity of the person. The permeability of boundaries reflects the degree to which the different regions communicate with one another.

Dynamics.   The activation of a region (e.g., when a person tries to solve a problem) puts that region under tension. This tension, which persists until the activity that established it is completed, spreads to other regions to a degree that depends on the permeability of the boundaries that separate them. In effect, as tension spreads to other regions, the inter-region boundaries are weakened and the person becomes a simpler individual.

The makeup of both the person and environment are ever-changing. As the individual matures, the person becomes more differentiated: The regions become more numerous and the boundaries between them become less permeable. That is, people become more complicated but also more set in their ways.

In the case of the environment, the changes are in two dimensions. Some of them are horizontal. The goals, paths, detours, barriers, valences, and forces in a restructured environment may be perceived differently and take on different values, as in the prior hypothetical example of the little boy who wanted candy. When a person is under stress, there also may be vertical changes in the environment: The person may move to a higher level of unreality where forces are weaker, conflicts are less intense, barriers are more easily overcome, and goals can be attained with less effort. Of course, this is the world of daydreams and wishful thinking.

Experimental Tests

The theory sketched here gave rise to a considerable amount of research, of which two examples serve as illustrations.

Memory for Unfinished Tasks.   As mentioned earlier, activation of a region puts that region under a tension that persists until the activation disappears. One implication of this idea is that a person should remember activities that correspond to regions under tension better than activities corresponding to regions in which tension has dissipated. Zeigarnik (1927) put this idea to a test in an experiment in which 138 participants in several experiments performed as many as 20 different tasks, such as naming 12 cities that begin with the letter K, stringing beads, solving puzzles, and molding animals from clay. They were permitted to finish half the tasks, but were interrupted before they had completed the other half. Zeigarnik's idea was that leaving a task unfinished would leave its corresponding region under tension, which would lead to better recall of that activity.

To test this hypothesis, when the experiment was ostensibly over, the experimenter asked the participants to recall the tasks on which they had been working. The results provide impressive support for the theory. Of the 138 subjects, 110 remembered more of the unfinished than of the completed tasks, 11 remembered the same number of each, and 17 remembered more of the completed tasks.

Frustration and Regression.   Two other ideas from Lewinian theory presented earlier are these: (a) With maturity the number of regions in the makeup of an individual increases: The individual becomes more differentiated and increasingly complex. (B) Tensions in one of these regions may spread to other regions and weaken interregion boundaries, thus simplifying the individual—a process Lewin called *dedifferentiation.* In an elaborate experiment carried out with Barker and Dembo (1941), Lewin tested the hypothesis that frustration has this effect on children's play.

The experiment began with observations of the free play of nursery-school children in a situation where standard toys (e.g., a teddy bear, a doll, a telephone, crayons, writing paper, boats, and a toy duck) were available. These observations allowed the experimenters to assign scores that reflected the constructiveness of the children's play in this standard situation. These measures correlated highly with mental age.

Following the initial observations, the children were allowed to play in much more attractive situations where they had access to a doll house that was big enough for them to enter. Inside the doll house was a bed with a doll on it, a kitchen complete with utensils, an iron and ironing board, and a telephone with a light and bell. Outside the house was a clothesline with doll's clothing on it, a small truck and trailer, and a table set for a party. In another corner of the room was a toy lake with real water that contained an island with a lighthouse, a wharf, a ferry boat, and toy fishes, ducks, and frogs.

After the children had become involved in playing with these elaborate toys, they were required to return to playing with the standard toys—a maneuver that was intended to frustrate them—and the experimenters observed the constructive-ness of their play again. The important finding was that the constructiveness of the children's play decreased considerably. In terms of mental age, the decrease was an average of 17.3 months. Lewin treated the phenomenon of regression as a reflecting the dedifferentiation produced by a breakdown of the boundaries between regions, rather than as a return to old but repressed habits, as psychoanalysis and learning theory suggested.

BIOGRAPHY

Kurt Lewin was born in 1890 in Mogilno, a village of around 5,000 people, in what was then Prussia in east Germany but now is Poland. Kurt had an older sister and two younger brothers. The family lived modestly in an apartment above their dry goods store. Kurt's father, Leopold Lewin, probably attended a boy's secondary school until he was 16. Leopold read Hebrew and both spoke and read German, Polish, and possibly Yiddish.

In those days, Germany was a hierarchical society in which the *right* sort of people enjoyed great esteem and the *wrong* sort of people were looked down on. The right sort of people were Christians and, especially, the aristocratic landed gentry whose names began with *von* (from). The wrong sort included the working poor and the members of minority groups, especially the Jews.

There were only about 35 Jewish families in Mogilno, of which the Lewins were one. Within this tiny Jewish community, relations were much less hierarchical—a difference that young Kurt noticed. He once described the Christians of Mogilno as follows: "100% anti-Semitism of the coarsest sort was taken for granted and constituted the basic stance, not only of the landed aristocracy, but also of the peasants" (Lewin, 1933). No Jew could become an officer in the military; obtain a position in the civil service, which included university faculty; or even own a farm. Leopold and his brother did own a much-beloved farm, but legally the title had to be held by a Christian. This was also the era of the emancipation of the Jews. Gradually they were beginning to enjoy the same legal rights as the Christians.

Education

When Kurt was 15, the family moved to Berlin so that the three boys could get a better education—there was no such thing as higher education for girls at that time. By 1909, Kurt had graduated from the Gymnasium, the university preparatory school, with a solid background in mathematics, science, history, Latin, Greek, and French. Kurt began his further education at the University of Berlin, with the intention of becoming a country doctor. However, at the university he discovered that he disliked the medical curriculum and, by 1911, shifted to philosophy and psychology. In Germany, as elsewhere, psychology was still a part of the philosophy department and the two disciplines were closely linked.

In addition to the traditional courses in philosophy, which covered Aristotle, Leibnitz, Kant, Locke, and Spinoza, Lewin had three courses with Professor Ernst Cassirer, the distinguished phenomenological philosopher, that had an enduring impact on his thinking. In part because he started at the university as a medical student, Lewin also acquired a grounding in physics, chemistry, neurology, and physiology.

In psychology, Lewin's chief professor was Carl Stumpf, the head of the department. Stumpf was a strong supporter of the new experimental approach to psychology; eventually he lured the three stars of Gestalt psychology—Max Wertheimer, Karl Koffka, and Wolfgang Köhler—to Berlin, but only after Lewin had finished his studies. Lewin took 14 courses with Stumpf and hoped that Stumpf would be his doctoral dissertation advisor. Under the hierarchical norms that were in place at that time, however, it would have been improper for him to speak to the professor directly about his dissertation plans. Instead Lewin asked the professor's assistant to ask Herr Professor Doctor Stumpf (the proper way to refer to faculty in those days in Germany) whether Lewin's dissertation proposal was acceptable. Over the next 4 years—until the day of Lewin's doctoral examination—he and Stumpf never spoke of his dissertation research. In his own life, Lewin rejected this hierarchical relationship to his students and colleagues. Later on, the easy acceptance of democratic interactions became one of the things he loved most about America.

During his second year at the University of Berlin, Kurt decided to aim for a career as a professor. Although it was virtually impossible for a Jew to become a full professor, and he might well remain at the untenured and ill-paid lowest academic rank forever, Lewin was willing to take that risk. He had become passionately committed to the goal of a career of research in social science. Lewin's family was initially puzzled at this strange and economically unwise choice, but finally came around and even agreed to assist him financially if need be.

Fascination with and enthusiasm for the social sciences remained with Lewin for all his life. In a 1920 paper on humanizing factory work, he wrote, "The worker wants his work to be rich, wide, and Protean, not crippling and narrow. Work should not limit personal potential but develop it. Work can involve love, beauty, and the soaring joys of creating" (p. 13). Many years later, on rereading this passage, his wife Gertrud remarked, "This was how he felt about his own work and how he lived" (G. Lewin, personal communication, 1970s). No doubt one of the reasons that, throughout his life, Lewin's ideas attracted the interest of so many colleagues and students was his deep conviction that psychological theorizing and research are such exciting and valuable things to do.

Military Service

As Lewin completed his PhD studies in 1914, World War I broke out. He and his two brothers and his brother-in-law all joined the armed services. Despite a strong revulsion to militarism, they had an intense love of their homeland, and the German Jews felt an especially strong pressure to prove their patriotism. Lewin's brother, Fritz, qualified for admission to the air force but was rejected and assigned ground combat duty because he was a Jew. A few months later Fritz was killed in combat while defending the rear as his unit moved on.

Kurt enlisted in a field artillery unit, serving in France and Russia. While in the service, he married Maria Landsberg, whom he had met at the university. Following the war, Kurt and Maria had two children—a daughter, Esther, and a son, Reuven—but, after much turmoil, they were divorced in 1927. Both Maria and Esther suffered from episodes of schizophrenia in later life.

Academic Career

During his second year in the army, Lewin was severely wounded and spent 8 months recuperating in a hospital. While in the hospital, he tried to continue with his studies and writing as best he could. After the war ended, he returned to the University of Berlin as a young faculty member. At that time, most psychologists believed that topics such as needs, will, hopes, fears, aspirations, and feelings of reality and unreality were inherently impossible to study in a scientific manner. Influenced by the Gestalt school and Professor Cassirer, however, Lewin began to violate these methodological taboos and continued to challenge them all his life.

In Germany in the 1920s and '30s Lewin and his students—from Germany, Finland, Russia, the United States, and elsewhere—did experimental research on will, hope, anger, and levels of aspiration. These years were exciting and productive. Among Lewin's students were several of the first German women who were allowed to attend the university, as well as Tamara Dembo and Bluma Zeigarnik, both of whom came to Germany from Russia. Lewin spent many hours happily debating scholarly questions with his students—often in their favorite coffee house, a practice he continued all his life. Lewin frequently found creative insights in other people's ideas—sometimes insights that the other person failed to recognize.

Transfer to the United States

In 1929, Lewin married his second wife, Gertrud ("Gerti") Weiss. They had two children: the author of this chapter and a son, Daniel, born in 1931 and 1933, respectively. In 1933, leaving his pregnant wife with her parents, Lewin was a visiting professor in California. While he was traveling home by way of Japan and Russia, Adolf Hitler became Chancellor of Germany and the Nazis took over the government of the country. Still in Russia when that news came, Lewin realized that he and Gerti had to leave Germany because life there had become intolerable for Jews. A Jewish doctor in Gerti's home town had just been beaten to death by a local Nazi. Gerti had been expelled from her professional association of kindergarten teachers because she was a Jew. When she became pregnant with her second child, the obstretrician who had delivered her first child agreed to accept her as a patient only with great reluctance, again only because she was Jewish.

Thus, with good reason, Lewin looked for a job abroad. One of his preferences grew out of his strong belief that the Jews should have a national home in Israel. As citizen of such a nation, they would have more control over their own destinies if only because they no longer could be expelled from one country after another, as they had been for centuries. Lewin communicated with the administration at the Hebrew University in Jerusalem about a position there, but it could not be worked out.

As it happened, largely because of the efforts of Dr. Ethel Waring, who had studied with Lewin in Berlin, an opening became available at Cornell University in the school of home economics. Waring obtained a grant from a charitable foundation to pay the salary at Cornell for a refugee scholar fleeing from the Nazis. Elated, Lewin, now 44 years old, accepted the position and the family of four emigrated to the United States. One condition was attached to the appointment: Lewin agreed to accept any other academic job that became available to free the Cornell job for another refugee. Two years later such an opening appeared at the Child Welfare Research Station at the State University of Iowa and, in 1935, the Lewin family moved to Iowa City.

EXPANDED AND REDIRECTED
RESEARCH INTERESTS

After he emigrated to the United States, Lewin continued many of the lines of research that he had initiated in Germany. He also began publishing articles that described his conception of the appropriate philosophy of science for psychology and elaborated an approach he called *topological psychology* (Lewin, 1936). He also developed broader research interests. These shifts were a direct result of his move to America and the circumstances that led to it.

Changing cultures is no small matter, even when the cultures, superficially, are as similar as those of Germany and America. There are always changes in group memberships and there can be massive alterations in a person's self-concept. When the change involves rejection in one's homeland because of prejudice, insults, and the threat of death, as in Lewin's case, the impact is even greater. Although Lewin's devotion to research in psychology remained as firm as it had been before, spurred on by the momentous events that he had experienced, he turned his attention to social psychology, group processes, and the psychological issues associated with minority—especially Jewish—identity.

Styles of Leadership

One of these topics had to do with the nature of democracy: Could it really be as bad a system as much of the world believed? The Fascists, of course, despised it. Not only did they view democracy as a form of society for weak and lazy sissies, but they also considered it hopelessly ineffective. Even today, however, sensible discussion of the value of democracy is difficult because, except for the recognition that such practices as open elections happen in democracies, those who feel more positive have no clear idea of what a definition of *democracy* might be. Lewin believed that the definition of democracy had to be in terms of behavior (e.g., the behavior that defined a style of leadership).

Soon after he arrived at the University of Iowa, Lewin decided to make this image of democracy the object of an empirical investigation of social climates and styles of leadership, including democratic leadership. Working with two graduate students, Ralph White and Ronald Lippitt (an experienced Boy Scout leader), he did a study of this topic using several groups of 10-year-old boys who came together for after-school club meetings.

Initially, Lewin, Lippitt, and White (1939) worked out careful operational definitions of two different styles of leadership: *democratic* and *autocratic*. These definitions identified precisely a set of behaviors that democratic and autocratic leaders employ and do not employ. For example, a democratic leader explains the reasons for instructions to the group, whereas the autocratic leader insists on obedience without giving reasons.

Such definitions may raise an important question in the minds of thoughtful readers: How could Lewin, Lippitt, and White (or anyone) know that these are the correct definitions of democratic and autocratic leadership. Other investigators might offer different definitions. In that case, who (if either) would be right? The answer to this question is that the adjectives, correct and incorrect, do not initially apply to definitions. The only criterion that definitions have to meet is that of specifying operations. Gradually, over time, research suggested by the different definitions may lead to agreement on a single definition or, conceivably, to the recognition that there is more than one type of (say) democratic leadership. That is the way that psychology as a science is supposed to work—a point to which the outcome of Lewin's research on styles of leadership testifies.

In the actual experiment, Lippitt and White played the roles of both autocratic and democratic leaders at different times, so that the outcomes of the study could be attributed to style of leadership rather than personalities of the leader. Thus, when the groups were making masks out of papier maché, and either Lippitt or White were behaving as autocratic leaders, they were supposed to tell the boys to tear newspaper into strips and nothing more. When they were democratic leaders, they were supposed to tell the group why this chore was necessary and what the further steps in the whole project would be.

As it turned out, however, this plan was not so easy to follow as it sounds. One of the leaders (White) did not behave as the definition of a democratic leader demanded when it was his turn to play that role. Specifically, this leader left the boys too much to their own devices. Once he realized that this error had occurred, in his characteristic manner, Lewin suggested that they carry out a serious exploration of the consequences of this wrong style of leadership, which they called *laissez-faire*. They ran additional groups and discovered that the boys' behavior under laissez-faire leadership was not the same as it was with a democratic leader.

The results of the experiment, which now involved three styles of leadership, were impressive. Children in the groups with autocratic leaders tended to be submissive and docile in the presence of the leader, often behaving in an apathetic fashion. When the leader left the room, however, there was a great deal of aggression. Some members of the group became scapegoats and were made objects of derision. By contrast, the children in the democratic group were convivial and playful. The little aggression that existed was largely lacking in hostility. Those in the laissez-faire condition tended to be disorganized and nonconstructive. Group members frequently interfered with one another, creating self-imposed frustrations that led to aggression within the group.

Thus, this study showed that the three styles of leadership, as they had been defined, produced important consequences in behavior. The difference between democratic and laissez-faire leadership is particularly worth noting because, as mentioned earlier, people are not clear about the difference. Sometimes they reject what they think of as democracy in favor of autocratic leadership without realizing that what they are rejecting is actually a laissez-faire arrangement.

One thing that these studies did not prove is that democratic, or any other form of leadership, is always the best. Lewinian field theory anticipates this actuality in its basic assumption that behavior is the result of an interaction between the characteristics of the individual and the perceived environment. For example, people brought up in an autocratic culture (e.g., Nazi Germany) might reject a democratic supervisor and work better under an autocratic leader, whereas in a democratic culture the results might be the opposite.

Reactions in the Psychological Community

Although the results of this research on leadership had important implications, some traditional American psychologists found Lewin's treatments of such topics irritating. From the 1920s to the present day, many psychologists—of whom the unreconstructed Watsonian behaviorists were the most vocal—have argued that research in psychology should be modeled after research in the more mature sciences like physics, chemistry, and biology. The extremists in that camp insist that such intangibles as thoughts, goals, choices, consciousness, insight, and styles of leadership are beyond the pale. Those who try to study them are relegated to the camp of mushy, fuzzy, soft-headed pseudoscientists.

As Lewin's work in this and many other areas implies, however, this belief is false. One of Lewin's great strengths was his ability to take vague and general ideas that had not been investigated by psychologists before and turn them into issues that could be studied objectively in experiments. To accomplish this, the fundamental requirement was to obey the standard rules of research: define concepts operationally, use standard experimental designs, and assess outcomes with appropriate measures. The application of such an approach enhances the relevance of psychology to the realities of the world in which we live. The promotion of this goal was Lewin's most general contribution.

Group Decision Making

The initial report of the studies of leadership came out in 1939, not long before the beginning of World War II. During that war, Lewin contributed his skills to the American war effort. Exercising his belief in practical theorizing—the notion that theory must be married to practice and that each strengthens the other—he tried to find ways to make food shortages and food rationing less negative in their impact. The U.S. government was encouraging people to eat healthy utility meats, such as sweetbreads and kidney (this was before the era of nervousness about cholesterol), which were not normally a part of the American diet. Lewin and his students did a number of studies (Lewin, 1943, 1947a, 1947b) on the question of how best to change American attitudes about these foods.

Out of these studies came the concept of *channels of social influence*, which incorporated the typical Lewinian belief that understanding any case of social change requires an identification of the steps that make up the whole process. Important figures in these channels of social influence are the gatekeepers, located at important junctions, who can promote changes or resist them. In the 1940s families, whose attitudes toward certain foods Lewin sought to change, the gate-keepers were the wives, who did the grocery shopping and decided what to cook—although husbands had veto power if they did not like the way the food tasted.

In Lewin's studies aimed at altering attitudes toward foods, housewives met in small experimental and control groups. Both groups received identical information about the nutritional value of utility meats and identical recipes. Members of the experimental groups engaged in group discussions about how housewives like themselves might be encouraged to try these meats. Members of the control groups only heard a lecture from an expert. At the end of the session, members were asked to raise their hands to indicate a willingness to try such a meat within the next week. A follow-up showed that the women who had participated in the session with group discussion with public decision were significantly more likely actually to serve the utility meats.

Research Center for Group Dynamics

In 1944–1945, Lewin was thinking about a new academic discipline. He had developed the ambition to found a center for the study of group dynamics that would investigate such topics as group cohesion and the forces that lead social groups to change or to resist change, social power and social conflict, and differences between individual and group tension. At the same time, however, Lewin wanted to be doing more action research, by which he meant applied research conducted from the beginning with the active participation of clients. This research would apply advanced and theoretically sophisticated academic thinking to the alleviation of social problems as these clients understood them.

The Massachusetts Institute of Technology agreed to sponsor this new Research Center for Group Dynamics, and so the Lewin family moved to Boston in 1945. At about the same time, Lewin founded the Commission on Community Interrelations (CCI), which was funded by the American Jewish Congress. CCI's objective was to do action research on how to reduce prejudice and bigotry against minority groups. Its first project was a workshop held to teach prejudice-reduction skills to a group of Connecticut government employees. It was in that context that Lewin discovered the effectiveness of giving feedback to group members by reviewing with group members what had happened in each session. To everyone's surprise, such feedback led to powerful changes in attitudes.

SOME PERSONAL RECOLLECTIONS

My fondest recollections are of the Iowa City days. During his 9 years there, Lewin was able to create an exciting milieu for research in psychology. There was much informal contact among Lewin, his graduate students, visiting colleagues, and all their families. I remember the informal cookouts and picnics that we had in Iowa City. People dressed in old clothing, ran after their toddlers, told jokes, and had potluck suppers. Conversations about psychological research might occur at any time. Although as a child I could not follow these discussions, I could easily enjoy the general good feeling. What I liked best of all was when the whole group sang songs together, mostly American songs but some European songs as well. Although I have been a part of many academic settings, I have never found one in which good-natured socializing, including families, was combined with such enthusiasm for psychology and for designing and doing the research that would decide among its theories. The fact that Iowa City was a small town, where people lived near to one another, no doubt helped to make this lifestyle possible.

Like any *real American*, my father loved his old second-hand Ford automobile. One day when he was driving, the car radio was playing Mozart. Delighted, he began to sing along and conduct the orchestra with both hands. Fortunately a graduate student in the front seat grabbed the wheel and steered the car so that it did not go into the ditch.

Father respected children as young human beings who had their own thoughts and understandings. He saw them as trying to comprehend the world around them, and he tried to understand their perceptions of that world. When he fixed something around the house, he showed us children how the gadget worked, using simple language. In fact, both of my parents tried to explain things in a vocabulary that we could understand.

DEATH COMES

In 1945, after World War II ended, the Lewin family received the terrible news that Lewin's mother, as well as her sister (his aunt), had been murdered by the Nazis. They had been taken first to Camp Westerbork, in the Netherlands, and then sent off in a cattle car to a death camp in Poland. Although he rarely spoke about it, the death of his mother weighed on Lewin very heavily.

Despite this personal tragedy, Lewin worked very hard and put in long hours at that time. His efforts to raise funds and administer two organizations required huge amounts of time and constant travel. He squeezed his scholarly work into what was left of his already-too-full days. On the evening of February 11, 1947, he suddenly felt ill and died of a heart attack. He was 57 years old and had lived in the United States for only 12 years.

CONCLUSION

Some of the next generation's most outstanding American social psychologists had either studied with Lewin directly or were students of his students. His influence reached into several disciplines, different countries, and many areas of psychology—a point made with the aid of a personal example. Some years ago, I had the opportunity to take a trip to China with a group of women in psychology and related fields. Near the end of the trip, we were, for the first time, introduced to a Chinese social psychologist. Four of us received permission to visit her at her university. The young woman explained that she had recently received her MA in social psychology—the first advanced degree in that subject to be granted since World War II within a radius of 1,000 miles surrounding her university. She told us that the topic of her thesis had been the work of Kurt Lewin, although she had only been able to obtain a copy of one of his books. As I sat speechless, my colleagues shouted excitedly, "This is his daughter." The young woman stared at us for a minute and then burst into happy tears. It seemed amazing to all of us that ideas that began to develop in the mind of a man born in Mogilno, Germany/Poland in 1890 had caught the attention of a young, isolated graduate student in China a century later.

REFERENCES

Barker, R. G., Dembo, T., & Lewin (1941). Frustration and regression: An experiment with young children. *University of Iowa Studies in Child Welfare, 18*, 32–96.

Lewin, K. (1920). Die Sozialiserung des Taylorsystems [The humanization of Taylor systems]. *Prakischer Sozialismus*, Berlin, no. 4.

Lewin, K. (1986). Letter to Wolfgang Köhler. *Journal of Social Issues, 42*, 39–47. (Original work written 1933)

Lewin, K. (1936). *Principles of topological psychology*. New York: McGraw-Hill.

Lewin, K. (1938). *The conceptual representation and measurement of psychological forces*. Durham, NC: Duke University Press.

Lewin, K. (1943). Forces behind food habits and methods of change. *Bulletin of the National Research Council, 108*, 35–65.

Lewin, K. (1947a). Group decision and social change. In T. M. Newcomb & E. L. Hartley (Eds.), *Readings in social psychology* (pp. 330–344). New York: Holt, Rinehart & Winston.

Lewin, K. (1947b). Frontiers in group dynamics: Concept, method and reality in social science; social equilibria and social change. *Human Relations, 1*, 5–42.

Lewin, K., Lippitt, R., & White, R. K. (1939). Patterns of aggressive behavior in experimentally created social climates. *Journal of Social Psychology, 10*, 271–299.

Zeigarnik, B. (1927). Ueber das Behalten von erledigten und unerledigten Handlungen [On the memory for completed and uncompleted tasks]. *Psychologische Forschung, 9*, 1–85.

Chapter 8

Floyd Henry Allport:
Founder of Social Psychology
As a Behavioral Science

Daniel Katz, with the assistance of Blair T. Johnson
and Diana R. Nichols

As a topic of theory and speculation, social psychology has a history that goes back to Plato, Aristotle, and other ancient philosophers. As a research-based discipline, however, it is a creature of the 20th century. The transformation of social psychology from philosophical conjecture to empirical science was due in large part to the work of Floyd H. Allport, who is widely regarded as the father of experimental social psychology.

ANTICIPATIONS OF EXPERIMENTAL
SOCIAL PSYCHOLOGY

The actual origins of the empirical investigation of social psychological phenomena date to 1897—to Émile Durkheim, who used statistics to support his sociological research on suicide—but most accounts of social psychology's history trace its beginnings to 1908. That year witnessed the appearance of two volumes, one by the sociologist Edward A. Ross and the other by the psychologist William McDougall, each taking a different scientific approach to the study of human social behavior. As the field of social psychology developed, it turned out that the two themes implicit in the writings of Ross and McDougall would intertwine with two others in Allport's social psychology.

---

* Photograph of Floyd Henry Allport courtesy of Marian Allport.

The book by Ross (1908) was grounded in French thinking on such topics as suggestibility, imitation, and crowd behavior (e.g., Gabriel Tarde's, 1898/1903, *The Laws of Imitation* and Gustave Le Bon's, 1894/1930, *The Psychology of the People*). It opened the door to behavioral interpretations of social behavior. The McDougall (1908) text, with its reliance on instincts, sentiments, and the group mind, represented a biological approach. Neither book was research oriented or based on scientific evidence. Allport, in concert with other American psychologists, attacked that weakness of the Ross and McDougall doctrines, but the themes implicit in those books still had an impact. Allport's own text was strongly behavioristic, with an emphasis on environmental influences, and strongly biological, although it replaced McDougall's instincts with a concept of prepotent reflexes. Finally, as shown later, despite his strong behaviorism, Allport's social psychology incorporated many cognitive ideas.

The two other general themes in Allport's social psychology were those of laboratory experimentation and survey research. Laboratory experimentation, which became the hallmark of scientific social psychology, came from Germany in the person of Hugo Münsterberg, who emigrated to the United States and became a professor at Harvard University, where Floyd Allport was to be a student. Survey research began with the use of questionnaires that sought information about the public attitude toward such practical problems as the demographics of health and deprivation. By the end of the 19th century, they had become quite common and, in 1890, William James worried that these questionnaires would soon invade every area of life: "Messrs. Darwin and Galton have set the example of circulars of questionnaires sent out by the hundreds to those supposed able to reply. The custom has spread, and it will be well for us in the next generation if such circulars be not ranked among the common pests of life" (Vol. 1, p. 194). Despite James' complaints, however, these early antecedents of opinion polling and field research defined an important component of the science of social psychology—one that Allport helped make more acceptable.

In his expression of these several influences, Floyd Allport made fundamental contributions to social psychology in many areas. Along with Kurt Lewin (chap. 7, this volume), he saw the need for using a variety of methods to find valid answers to scientific questions. Most social psychologists then, as now, however, were narrower. They tended to limit their research either to laboratory studies or field methods. Later on, as this division hardened, House (1977) called it "the two faces of social psychology" (p. 165) in recognition of a reality that Floyd Allport would have despised.

BIOGRAPHICAL NOTES

Before presenting an account of Allport's major contributions and continuing influence, a few words on his life, his teachers, and his career—with an occasional side glance at features of his personality—may be in order.

Family Background

Floyd Henry Allport was born in Milwaukee, Wisconsin, in 1890. He was the second of four sons, the youngest being Gordon W. Allport, who also became a prominent psychologist. Floyd and Gordon Allport grew up in a community where family values and personal relations were important. Their father was a physician who made house calls and often took one of the boys with him. The Allport family required its members to develop independence, responsibility, integrity, and sensitivity to the needs of others. These values were so deeply ingrained in Floyd that they colored his way of thinking as a person as well as a scientist. They motivated his assault on then-standard concepts in psychology and sociology, which he saw as institutionalized fictions (to be discussed later in this chapter), and convinced him that solutions to the problems of society would never come from the creation of bureaucratic agencies but would require a revolution of people's thinking.

Floyd's younger brother, Gordon, was also influenced by the values of the Allport family and the community, but his expression of these values took a different turn. Gordon was at the forefront of humanism in psychology, an enthusiastic follower of William Stern's (chap. 6, *Pioneers II*) personalism, but Floyd had a strong leaning toward behaviorism. Gordon made peace with bureaucracy with the aid of his highly polished political skills, but Floyd never could. Although the brothers collaborated on some of the first tests of personality traits (Allport & Allport, 1921, 1928) and discussed many of their ideas, they seldom saw eye to eye on theoretical issues. Both reflected the values of their family in backing social causes, but for Floyd scientific understanding came first and for Gordon the need for active involvements had a higher priority.

Education

Floyd received his AB and PhD degrees from Harvard in 1913 and 1919, respectively. The flavor of his later work on social psychology owed much to Edwin B. Holt and Hugo Münsterberg, with whom he studied as a student at Harvard. Holt had been a student of William James, so this Harvard tradition of scholarship and creativity directly influenced Floyd's background. From Holt, Floyd also acquired epistemological sophistication, an understanding of the logic of science, and the makings of a behavioristic interpretation of social phenomena. From Münsterberg, Allport received the heritage of German work on group influence, as well as the conception that the operationalization of the concepts to be studied in research is an essential skill of a true experimentalist. Although Allport's dissertation, which was a systematic exploration of the influence of the group on the individual, was directed by Herbert S. Langfeld, an experimental psychologist, the dissertation's penetrating analysis of data, its systematic and thorough character, derived from the work of Hugo Münsterberg.

At Harvard, Allport was Langfeld's teaching assistant and the two men collaborated on a laboratory manual for the introductory course. Langfeld's emphasis on scientific rigor reinforced Münsterberg's message of the importance of sound experimental methods and contributed to Allport's scientific outlook. Although Langfeld had little interest in social psychology, he and Allport became and remained friends for the rest of their lives. One basis for their relationship might have been their mutual affinity for art. Langfeld had an abiding affection for aesthetics—his APA presidential address took the position that art is the communication of emotion—and Allport's hobbies included music and painting.

In 1928, the personal relationship between Allport and Langfeld netted benefits for me as well. By then, Langfeld had moved to Princeton University and had a faculty position available, so Langfeld asked Allport if he had a student to recommend. (In those days, new faculty appointments usually began with such recommendations, there being no standard way of advertising positions, as is the practice today.) On Allport's recommendation, I became an instructor in the Princeton department of psychology in 1928, stayed on during the depression years, and was promoted to associate professor with tenure in 1940. Langfeld was a supportive friend and surrogate father during my entire 15 years at Princeton.

Employment

After Allport received the PhD, he remained at Harvard for 3 years as an instructor. In 1922, he accepted an associate professorship at the University of North Carolina, where his primary colleague was John F. Dashiell. Then in 1924, he left North Carolina to become professor of social and political psychology in the Maxwell School of Citizenship and Public Affairs at Syracuse University, where he remained until his retirement in 1957.

The Maxwell School was founded in 1924, the year of Allport's appointment. Its primary goal—the achievement of theoretical integration of the behavioral sciences—was the vision of the statesman Elihu Root and other educational revolutionists. The Maxwell School had considerable independence from other organizational units at Syracuse University. It recruited its own staff, introduced new courses, admitted its own graduate students, and had its own degree programs. Nonetheless, the programs of the school were also tied into the structure of the university. Its graduate students could take courses in other departments, and professors from these other departments could serve on doctoral committees at the Maxwell School. In the interest of strengthening its integration of the social scientists, the school recruited Floyd Allport away from North Carolina, appointed him to a new chair, professor of political and social psychology, and supported his efforts to start the first doctoral program in social psychology.

After Allport's appointment, and in no small part due to his accomplishments, the Maxwell School quickly became a prestigious institution, attracting excellent graduate students and a distinguished faculty who were successful in writing and receiving research grants. Although funding of research projects in those days was extremely meager, these grants still enabled the school to award a few fellowships. I was fortunate to receive one of them and to become a research assistant to Allport. When I graduated from the University of Buffalo, there were very few openings in top-flight graduate schools for first-year graduate students from the provinces. Coming from a poor family and having few resources of my own, I was over-whelmed by, and accepted without hesitation, the offer of a full assistantship at the Maxwell School.

When I began my studies at the Maxwell School in 1925, I was first assigned as a research assistant to a professor of political science but, when Floyd Allport lost an assistant and I had a chance to work with him, I jumped at the opportunity. Many people get an important lucky break sometime in their lives, and this was mine. Not only was Floyd an intellect of the first order, but also his relationships with students were exemplary and he was much admired by them. One of Allport's first actions was to give me a copy of the article describing his research with Dale Hartman on the motivation of atypical opinion (Allport & Hartman, 1925). Naive though I was, I found it a fascinating paper and was delighted to have such a researcher as a mentor. Unfortunately, that paper has been all but forgotten. In addition to being one the earliest scientific studies of attitudes, it demonstrated that the extremists of the political left and right have similar personalities, anticipating later work on the authoritarian personality.

Allport's Personality and Relationships With Students

Allport's mother and his brother, Gordon, described Floyd as stubborn. Indeed, he was stubborn in his convictions about science: He could not be swayed from reliance on his own way of thinking. Moreover, he had no patience or respect for those whose values ran counter to his faith in science, no matter what their rank or status. Allport was also introverted, shy, and modest. Today we would call him a very private person. This was the aspect of his personality that struck people most forcibly.

To illustrate, Allport's graduate studies at Harvard were interrupted by military service in World War I. As a second lieutenant in the U.S. Army, one of his initial duties was to serve as a balloon observer and courier in France—a role that ended very dramatically. During his first flight in a balloon, carrying a dispatch case of important papers, the German artillery shot down the balloon; in a narrow escape, Allport parachuted to safety, still clutching his dispatch case of papers. The French recognized this deed of heroism by awarding him the Croix de Guerre and a citation from the French Corps d'Armée. We students were naturally interested in the details of this war experience and his awards so we questioned him about it. Allport explained that, when the Germans shot him down, he had no recourse but to jump and involuntarily held onto the case of documents. Despite this example of his characteristic modesty, we suspected that he actually had performed heroically.

Floyd's students held him in reverence not only because of his profound mind and wisdom but also because he was kind, generous, understanding of their needs, and astute in recognizing their different abilities and bringing out the best in them. Floyd treated his students as an extended family. He fought for them within the university and helped greatly in placing them when they were in the job market, just as he helped me get my position at Princeton. After completing our degrees and leaving Syracuse, many of us returned to visit Floyd and, on occasion, he would visit us in our homes.

Like other major professors of the day, Allport had his doctoral students work on his own projects—a practice that is still widely followed today. When students had original ideas, they were usually within the framework of Allport's research program. My dissertation work under his direction was no exception to this rule: As a logical extension of the Allport and Hartman (1925) attitude paper mentioned earlier, Allport had a Syracuse University grant to take a census of its students' reactions to their college experiences. These data, which resulted in my dissertation, were based on a 2-hour interview that we conducted with the students. Allport did not squelch his students' independence. Instead, he made them justify their views in the few instances that they ran counter to his own. In my 3 years as his assistant, there were only two occasions when he and I had any important kind of conflict.

The first of these occurred when I told Floyd that I believed that his characterization of radicals as personality misfits was incorrect and reactionary. I came from a socialist home and I thought I knew more about radicalism than Floyd did with his elitist background. His response to that challenge was to turn his advanced social psychology course over to me for two sessions to document my opinions. This turned out to be an easy assignment because the students were on my side and I was knowledgeable on the subject. In the end, Floyd graciously admitted he might have been wrong.

The second incident was one when I was wrong. It involved issues related to values, strategy, and scholarship. Floyd thought my dissertation on student attitudes should be prepared for publication as a book-length monograph. He extended my assistantship to a full summer so that I could put the results of the study into publishable form. I worked alone for 3 months while Floyd was away from the university, intent on making our work understandable and useful. When Floyd returned and read the manuscript, he was shocked because I had ignored the scientific implications of the investigation and written the report in the style of an adolescent journalist. It was as if I had learned nothing from the great man. My version might have created a stir for a few weeks (at least at Syracuse) by its vulgarization of the study. In contrast, Floyd thought of my dissertation as a scientific project that made a lasting contribution to the field. We scrapped that manuscript and then Floyd helped me work on a complete revision. Although the work and the ideas in the work were mostly his, Floyd generously made me senior author (Katz & Allport, 1931) and the experience sealed our friendship. We remained fast friends until Allport's death on October 15, 1978.

Public Service

Although Allport's main commitment was to the advancement of social psychology as a science through his theory and research, his talent for organizational leadership did not go unnoticed by his colleagues. Allport served editorial roles with several journals. Notably, he was the first cooperative editor of the *Journal of Abnormal Psychology and Social Psychology*, beginning in 1921. Morton Prince had founded this publication as the *Journal of Abnormal Psychology* and later broadened its scope to include social psychology, with Floyd Allport as fellow editor; in 1925, Prince shortened the title to the *Journal of Abnormal and Social Psychology*. From 1925 to 1938, his title changed to *associate editor*. Allport continued as consulting editor until 1949. The journal quickly became the leader in the field of social psychology. In 1926, it became an official periodical of the American Psychological Association; in 1965, the journal again split, with the abnormal portion going into *Journal of Abnormal Psychology*, its original title, and the social psychology portion resulting in the *Journal of Personality and Social* Psychology. It continues as the best journal in its field today. As its inaugural editor, I was proud to serve in the same capacity as Floyd had so many years earlier.

Allport's colleagues also recognized his statesman's qualities and began assigning him administrative duties and responsibilities for policy formation in the profession early in his career. Allport was a member of the Board of Directors of the American Psychological Association from 1928 to 1930 and a member of the Social Science Research Council from 1925 to 1927 and 1929 to 1931. Based in part on his popular *Social Psychology* (1924) text and from a series of articles he wrote for the prominent national publication, *Harpers Magazine* (e.g., 1929, 1934), Floyd's national prominence brought him an appointment by President Hoover to serve on the research subcommittee of a Conference on Home Building and Home Ownership (1931). He also was active in the Society for the Psychological Study of Social Issues, serving on its Council of Directors from 1938 to 1940 and as its president from 1940 to 1941. On the basis of these contributions, as well as those to social psychological research and theory, Floyd received numerous honorary citations and awards, including fellow status in the American Association for the Advancement of Science, the Distinguished Scientific Contribution Award of the American Psychological Association (1966), the Gold Medal Award of the American Psychological Foundation (1968), and an Honorary Doctorate from Syracuse University (1974).

ALLPORT'S *SOCIAL PSYCHOLOGY*

Allport's (1924) textbook *Social Psychology*, the first to view that discipline as an experimental science, had a major impact on psychology in part because it was much stronger on the psychological side than on the sociological side, emphasizing individuals rather than groups as the agents of social behavior. It presented the results of Allport's own studies of social influence, including those obtained in his Harvard dissertation (also published as Allport, 1920), as well as research findings from other studies that he and others had conducted. In the colleges and universities, Allport's *Social Psychology* defined a field of study and courses in social psychology sprang up all over the land. Despite the seminal nature of this book, however, there were no major changes in the traditional social science departments. Other than the program Floyd founded at Syracuse University, no programs in social psychology appeared. Instead, most universities assigned a lone professor to the chore of teaching the subject. Indeed, even Syracuse University had only one faculty member dedicated to social psychology—Floyd Allport—until the 1950s. As the new kid on the block, social psychology generally had a lonely existence in the academic community until the field blossomed following World War II. Despite the slow initial spread of social psychology, both Allport's text and the topics he studied throughout his career helped to define and advance the field of social psychology.

Social Influence

The phenomena of social influence are familiar to everyone. The presence of an audience may bring out the best in human performance (social increment) or destroy it (social decrement). Judgments of whether someone's behavior is moral or immoral, whether a certain painting is beautiful or ugly, and whether the decision of a jury is just or unjust tend to converge on the reactions of the individuals around one. Even when people are alone, their behavior is greatly affected by the attitudes and values (social norms) of the reference groups of which they happen to be members. Among the most important of Allport's contributions were his studies of such influences. Although there had been earlier experiments on that topic (e.g., Triplett, 1897), Allport (1920, 1924) was the first to explore group effects on individual performance systematically.

Social Increment and Decrement.   In his studies of social influence, Allport (1920, 1924) gave participants different types of tasks and measured the quality and quantity of their performance when they worked alone or in the presence of "co-groups"—groups of people who worked in parallel without interacting with one another. In these experiments, the effects obtained were produced by nothing more than the sight and sounds of other people doing the same things as the participants. In a series of three studies on attention and mental work, the tasks employed were the following: (a) in a vowel cancellation test, crossing out the vowels in columns of newsprint as rapidly as possible; (b) in a reversible perspective test, reversing that perspective as quickly and as often as possible in a certain amount of time; and (c) in a multiplication task, finding the solutions to a set of problems as quickly and correctly as possible. In all three of these experiments involving simple tasks, Allport found that the quantity and speed of work were enhanced (social increment) for a majority of the participants when they worked together, but the performances of a small minority were better when they worked alone (social decrement).

Allport believed that the facilitating effects of social groups are circular and mutual. As he described in his social psychology text, just as the presence of other people enhances the performance of the individual, the improved performance of the individual raises the level of performance of the other group members. The underlying notion in this interpretation was a generalization to social groups of a reflex-circle hypothesis of self-stimulation, according to which the stimuli produced by one's own responses are the stimuli for the continuation of the response that made them. For example, the stimuli provided by babies' hearing their own utterances lead to the verbal repetitions that we call *babbling*. This work foreshadowed Allport's event-structure theory, which he formally developed late in his career.

Following these studies, Allport went on to explore group effects on the performance of more complex tasks. In one experiment, participants wrote as many valid arguments as they could, in a given amount of time, about passages taken from the writings of ancient philosophers. When the participants worked together, they produced a greater number of arguments than when they worked alone, but the quality of the arguments was poorer.

Other investigators followed Allport's example and confirmed his finding of social facilitation with respect to quantity but not quality of performance, depending on the difficulty of the task. On the basis of his own investigations and a survey of the literature, Zajonc (1965) offered a more specific interpretation of this relationship. He suggested that social influence improves performance on tasks that subjects had mastered previously, but hinders performance on new tasks. His interpretation was similar to that offered by Spence (chap. 17, this volume) for the effects of anxiety on performance: Like anxiety, social stimulation energizes dominant reactions—an effect that leads to the social facilitation of well-established habits but, with some frequency, to social decrement in new learning because it can energize wrong responses. Social psychologists continue to pursue the implications of these ideas yet today, with the result that hundreds of studies have been performed (for a review, see Bond & Titus, 1983).

Convergence and Conformity. Another of Allport's important contributions was on the convergence of individual judgments in group settings. In one set of experiments, participants judged the heaviness of weights or the pleasantness of odors when they were alone or in a co-group situation. The results were similar in both cases. Although they did not know the judgments of the other participants in these studies, they avoided what seemed to be extreme opinions. Allport attributed this tendency to an unconscious attitude of submissiveness or social conformity that people assume when they are in groups. In his own words, "To think and to judge with others is to submit one's self unconsciously to their standards. We may call this the *attitude of social conformity*" (Allport, 1924, p. 278). Allport believed that this attitude could be attributed to various sources, such as the dependence of children on their parents, the authority of leaders, and the influence of large numbers of observers.

Allport singled out sheer numbers of observers as a factor of prime importance in the creation of conforming behavior. He believed that people bring their behavior into line with what they believe others think and feel. The fact that large numbers of people seem to share the same opinions may create an impression of universality, which facilitates this tendency. Thus, people tend to conform to their unconfirmed and potentially incorrect impressions of what others believe. Allport asserted that the impression of universality is a powerful illusion that political leaders and advertisers both capitalize on when they use a *bandwagon appeal* to promote a candidate or product—"Everyone else is voting our way (buying our product).Why not you?"

Another manipulation of opinion involving the impression of universality occurs when propagandists attempt to create the impression that people who do not hold a particular opinion are a powerless minority and might as well do nothing—for example, not bother to vote. Allport called such unfounded beliefs *pluralistic ignorance*. This phenomenon is distinct from other types of cognitive error in that the mistaken belief is shared by a number of people. Although the term first appeared in our work on student attitudes (Katz & Allport, 1931), Allport developed the concept as a special case of the impression of universality. He claimed that the fact that these unfounded beliefs were shared simply represented a tendency to make mistaken judgments about one's social environment (O'Gorman, 1986). Research on this phenomenon was recently revived by Prentice and Miller (1996). Allport's (1924) broader term *social projection* captured the attitudes and beliefs involved in the impression of universality and pluralistic ignorance by applying one's own reactions to others. Similarly, other researchers have documented a false consensus effect, in which a person engaging in a behavior overestimates the number of other people engaging in the same behavior (e.g., Mullen & Hu, 1988). Thus, it can be claimed with more than a little validity that Allport presaged social psychology's subfield of social cognition, with its emphasis on discovering and explaining errors and biases (e.g., Fiske & Taylor, 1991).

The J-Curve Expression of Conforming Behavior.   Another of Floyd Allport's important contributions was a refinement of the methods of naturalistic observation and field study—a contribution that may well have grown out of classroom exercises. Allport often assigned students the task of observing group behavior in some natural setting and recording data that revealed the extent to which that behavior matched group expectations. No doubt Allport and his students, at first, anticipated results that would fit the ubiquitous normal distribution. To their surprise, however, frequency distributions of responses looked more like a reversed J than a bell-shaped distribution (Allport, 1934). He and his students found that the great majority of people conform to the normative behavior of the group in any situation, and the number of nonconformers decreases as the nonconforming behavior departs increasingly from the expected norm. At an intersection with a stop sign, the majority of motorists come to a complete stop, only a few just slow down, and even fewer maintain their speed or go faster. Most workers and students come to work or class on time or they arrive a little early. In churches, most people observe the rituals with few deviations. Allport hypothesized that conforming behavior in these cases would only occur if there were a distinct purpose for the behavior, a rule or law clearly defining proper behavior, and a large proportion of people following the rule.

Allport believed that individual personality tendencies (e.g., intelligence), biological tendencies (e.g., appetites), and conformity-producing agencies (e.g., institutional rules) affect the conformity distribution, forcing it from a normal bell shape into the non-normal J shape. For example, institutional sanctions force the replacement of the normal variability of personality, as shown in a study conducted by Allport's student, Richard Schanck (1932). As Fig. 8.1 shows, the vast majority of Methodists thought that their Bishop had expended real effort in helping to select preachers to send to their community. Yet this conformity, as evidenced by the slight variations in the curve, was not absolute. Social influence was a powerful force acting on individuals, but not powerful enough to induce complete conformity. Moreover, the influence of institutional norms affected only those in the ingroup. For example, another of Allport's students, Basia Zambrowsky (cited in Allport, 1934), conducted a study in which she recorded how many of the people entering a Catholic cathedral performed the complete ritual of dipping their finger in holy water and making the sign of the cross, compared with the numbers who performed other acts of varying compliance with the ritual. As Fig. 8.2 shows, a large majority completely complied with the ritual, with small fractions performing acts of partial conformity and a substantial minority performing no ceremony at all. This last group upset the J-shaped character of the distribution and probably reflected the behaviors of non-Catholic visitors to the cathedral—members of the outgroup (Allport, 1934).

Scholars at the time regarded the J-curve nature of conformity as a fascinating phenomenon reflecting the growing maturity of the field (e.g., Newcomb & Hartley, 1947). In the *Social Psychology* text that I co-wrote with Schanck (Katz & Schanck, 1938), we noted that the existence of such characteristic distributions boded well for the field of social psychology in comparison to the more mature physical sciences. "The discovery of the J-curve distribution," we wrote, "suggests a stability in social relationships . . . capable of quantitative analysis into dependent factors" (p. 51). Allport regarded his development of the J-curve hypothesis of conforming behavior as one of his most significant contributions to psychology.

Reference Groups.   A modification of Allport's concept, impression of universality, is at the heart of the more nearly contemporary concept of reference group (e.g., Hyman, 1942)—any of the groups with which an individual identifies. The

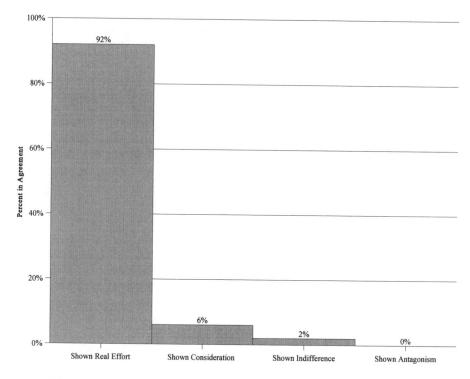

FIG. 8.1. J-curve pattern of parishioners' opinions about the role of the bishop in selecting preachers for the parish. From "A Study of a Community and its Groups and Institutions Conceived of As Behaviors of Individuals," by R. Schanck, 1932, *Psychological Monographs*, *43*, p. 39.

modification adds the notion that the majority (which is not necessarily universal) views of the members of these reference groups have greater influence than the views of other groups. Thus, farmers are more influenced by the majority opinion of other farmers than by the opinions of nonfarmers, labor union members are more influenced by the views of other labor union members, and the members of the general public are more influenced by the majority opinions obtained in polls of opinion than by minority opinions.

Frames of Reference and Group Norms.   Allport's concepts of (a) the attitude of social conformity based on his observation that people avoid making extreme judgments, (b) the J-curve hypothesis of conformity, and (c) his studies on the influence of the group on performance found a later expression in Sherif's (1936) experiments, which used the autokinetic phenomenon to demonstrate the importance of group norms. Although a dim light in a totally darkened room, without a frame of reference does not actually move, it appears to do so. When participants are tested alone, the distance and direction of this illusory movement varies from person to person and from time to time in the same individual. Sherif tested subjects when they were alone and when they were together. He found that there was a reduction in the variation of the participant's estimates (convergence) in both conditions, but that the effect was greater when they were together. Sherif saw this phenomenon—the establishment of a social norm that persisted in the individual—as a basic model of societal functioning. However, his emphases differed from those of Allport. He gave less importance to the coercive force of numbers and perceived authority than Allport and more to the power of frames of reference, group standards, and social norms. Of course, this emphasis on social influence remains an important area of social psychology to this day.

Personality Theory

Although best known for his work in social psychology, Allport made significant contributions to personality theory, not the least of which was urging his brother, Gordon, to pursue research in this area. As mentioned earlier, Gordon became a

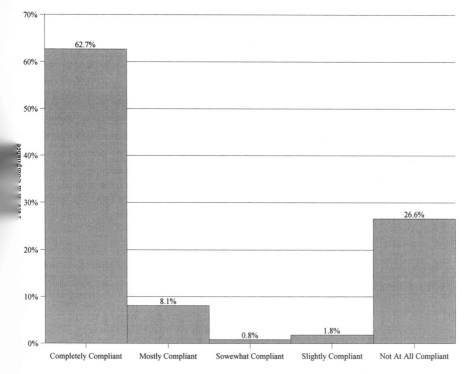

FIG. 8.2. J-curve pattern obtained in Zambrowsky's study of conformity to church ritual. *Journal of Social Psychology, 5*, p. 146. Reprinted with permission of the Helen Dwight Reid Educational Foundation. Published by Heldref Publications, 1319 Eighteenth St., NW, Washington DC 20036-1802. Copyright © 1934.

leader in the field of personality, writing a pioneering book on the subject (G. W. Allport, 1937). Prior to this book, however, the two Allports collaborated on two papers regarding the measurement and classification of personality traits (F. H. Allport & Allport, 1921, 1928). They examined personality in four major trait clusters: intelligence, temperament, self-expression, and sociality. They were particularly interested in the trait they termed *ascendancy-submission*, developing a scale to measure it by examining how active or passive a person was in interactions with others. For example, the Allports asked people to imagine themselves in specific scenarios in which they would be humiliated and then write down what they would do or say. These responses were then rated according to their dominance or passivity and provided a fairly reliable measure across the different situations.

In response to questions raised during the 1920s regarding the lack of cross-situational consistency with these types of trait measures, however, Allport (1937) proposed examining behaviors in view of their purpose in reaching some end that the individual habitually attempts to achieve. He argued that, in understanding an individual, a trait measure may quantify the trait, but would not allow for prediction of future behavior based on past tendencies. For example, one person might display honesty with the intention of helping others, whereas another may be honest to maintain self-esteem. Allport argued that these underlying motivations that he termed *telenomic trends* had greater predictive value for other behaviors than did the trait label *honesty*. Further, he pointed out that different and apparently contradictory behavior patterns of an individual were best described not by some underlying trait, but by the fact that the same individual, with fairly consistent goals, performed them all. In emphasizing that behaviors should depend more on traits that are important to the individual, Allport foreshadowed his brother Gordon's work on cardinal traits (G. W. Allport, 1937) and modern work on person-by-trait interactions (e.g., Bem & Funder, 1978) and self-schemas (Markus, 1977), which refer to trait dimensions that are subjectively important to the individual.

Measurement of Attitudes

As mentioned earlier, quite early in his career, Allport began to carry out extensive surveys of attitudes (Allport & Hartman, 1925; Katz & Allport, 1931). However, he soon became dissatisfied with the measuring techniques that were then available. A common procedure at the time was to have respondents rate their degrees of approval or disapproval of some issue on scales from 1 to 10—a method that Allport found fraught with ambiguity. A judgment of 2 by one person might really be the equivalent of a judgment of 3 or 4 by others. Moreover, the distances between ratings at one point on these scales might be different from the same distance at another: The difference between ratings of 2 and 4 might not be the same as the difference between 6 and 8. In his work with Hartman on atypical political opinion (Allport & Hartman, 1925), Allport created a forerunner of techniques that his friend L. L. Thurstone (chap. 6, this volume) developed later. Allport created lists of items generated by his students consisting of different positions one might hold regarding a political issue such as prohibition. The items on these lists were ranked from one extreme to the opposite by independent judges. The final rank of each position in the completed scale consisted of the average rank assigned by the judges. For example, his prohibition scale consisted of items ranging between the extremes of advocating more severe enforcement of prohibition laws and of universal permission of an "open saloon system" (Allport & Hartman, 1925, p. 753). In use, students checked the one position that best represented their own views and also rated the certainty and intensity with which they held that position. Because he was troubled by the psychometrics of his scale, Allport enlisted the services of Thurstone to attack problems of scaling. The result was Thurstone's (1928) pronouncement that "attitudes can be measured."

Although Allport's early work in scaling has largely been forgotten, his methods were later found to be reliable and valid. For example, Sherif re-invented aspects of Allport's scale when he and his colleagues studied "ego-involvement" and attitudes using latitudes of rejection, acceptance, and noncommitment (Sherif & Sherif, 1967). Like Allport's early scale, position statements regarding an issue were ranked from one extreme to another. Latitudes of rejection were assessed as people indicated a position that they most disagreed with, along with several other positions that they found objectionable. Similarly, one's latitude of acceptance on an issue consisted of the position one most agreed with, as well as several other acceptable statements. The latitude of noncommitment consisted of any remaining, neutrally rated positions. Scaling procedures like this, although created long after Allport's work in the area, clearly demonstrate the impact he had on the development of attitude measurement. Finally, modern researchers have returned to the simple kinds of scales that Allport originally used, asking respondents to rate their degrees of approval or disapproval of some issue on numbered scales. It turns out that the original formulation has sufficient validity (see Eagly & Chaiken, 1993).

ATTACKS ON FALLACIES AND FICTIONS

Allport was considerably ahead of his era in his insistence that the metaphors of the social sciences—often thinly disguised common sense—should not be confused with knowledge. He frequently questioned popular beliefs in an effort to identify the realities that such clichés might obscure, distort, confuse, and cloak. He was a model of objectivity in a field of study in which the scientific attitude did not always prevail in either research or application. Allport maintained that too much theorizing in the social sciences uses the language of the streets and popular analogies in place of factual and controlled observations. He noted that, too often, widely accepted concepts came from a specific culture or from temporary fads and fashion of the day. Sometimes they are little more than the acceptance of established authority and power. Often they are imperfectly hidden slogans of a special interest group and a means to conceal the actual interests. They can be euphemisms that gloss over the complexity required to produce more truthful and useful accounts. For example, many treatments of social causality personify the group, giving it a group mind with such personal characteristics as the ability to learn and vulnerability to psychosis. Such theorizing has little to recommend it over the popular fiction that gives Wall Street a quasimental identity that determines the Dow-Jones Industrial Average, thereby ignoring the complexity of the interacting causes that determine the behavior of the stock market. At its worst, this usage gave invalid descriptions; at its best, it was a form of intellectual stammering.

Allport's criticisms of the group mind began early in his career. His major objection to such ideas was that, although the group-mind approach could provide an adequate description of the phenomenon under study, the description was too often and too easily regarded as an explanation. He argued that only by studying the individual could a behavior be understood. This position was in direct opposition to much of the sociological thought of the day. For example, Herbert Spencer, the great sociologist, nurtured the metaphorical type of thinking in which social relationships constitute an entity external to the individual. Sometimes the entity is a nation, other times a university or church, and still others a political party or the family. In this way of thinking, individuals are the cells of a social-group entity that has all the features of an individual: mind, purpose, welfare, needs, desire, and even soul. Similarly, Émile Durkheim held that an individual has no existence except as a member of society. Allport countered that if these social entities are organisms, obviously some people are muscle and other people brains; but in the human organism, the parts do not change places. Similarly, Allport was fond of saying that "only an individual has a nervous system."

These attacks on the most treasured assumptions and ideas of sociological perspectives earned Allport the ridicule of sociologists. In his autobiography (Allport, 1974), Floyd described an episode at an annual meeting of the American Sociological Society. At the podium was its president, who described how, in the Middle Ages, people in vigorous arguments often angrily recited lengthy quotations from Aristotle's philosophy. Finally, someone would stop the debate with the exclamation that "there's no truth in Aristotle." "So now," the speaker continued, "I say there is no truth in Floyd Allport!" As the speaker completed this dramatic line, he made a sweeping gesture and accidentally struck a glass chandelier, sending its pieces flying.

In the face of such opposition, it is a testimony to Allport's great pride and fortitude that he continued to develop his views on the subject of group fictions. His *Institutional Behavior* (1933) was the capstone of these attacks. This collection of essays, several of which had been published previously in the highly regarded *Harpers Magazine*, traces the consequences of fallacious thinking on human relationships and society within political, economic, familial, educational, and religious institutions. In the book, he developed the view that institutions are falsely viewed as independent of the individuals who create and maintain them. He further argued that individuals were expected to work through their institution to better society, but without regard for the effect that the institutions had on the individuals. For example, Allport claimed that our economic institutions, based on mechanization and similarity of production, draw attention away from the individual and toward the patterns of behaviors that make the machines operate. People are seen not as individuals, but as "units in the super-organism of economic society" (p. 202). Because the institution has become more important than the individual, people are subject to the institutions they created.

In Allport's view, these forces were perhaps most at work in the case of gender—a theme that he developed early in his career. In contrast to the popular view that these "basic, inborn, mental differences between the sexes *must exist*" (Allport, 1929, p. 397), Allport asserted that the only significant differences between the sexes were that "women are more personal and emotional in their interests than men" (Allport, 1924, p. 345). He saw little evidence for any other of the supposed differences, such as that women are less intelligent, less well suited for work, and so on. His essay on "Seeing Women as They Are" (Allport, 1929) took these popular stereotypes to task. He cogently argued that because men and women

> are descended from the same parents and the same ancestors, their mental traits are probably inherited without distinction from both father and mother. On the whole, therefore, the hypothesis of fundamental psychological similarity is quite as reasonable as that of basic difference. (p. 398)

Thus, Allport was an early proponent of a view that became popular in intellectual circles in the 1960s and 1970s—that of minimizing gender differences (see Eagly, 1995). In Allport's view, any gender differences that do exist owe more to "the heavy influence of family and social pressure" (p. 399) than to innate traits. Put starkly, these social forces meant that "she must react to people rather than things....Human feeling rather than natural law becomes her guiding principle in life" (1924, p. 345).

Put in the modern terms of Bakan (1966) and Eagly (1987), Allport saw a socialized difference whereby women are more communal (interpersonally oriented) and men more agentic (task oriented). Moreover, the institutionalized nature of the socialization processes—reflected in the fact that educators, policymakers, and religious leaders also believe in the stereotypes about women—serves to perpetuate gender differences and keep men superior to women in society. The differences between men and women reflect "the effects of the masculine stereotypes upon women rather than the nature of women themselves" (Allport, 1929, p. 401). A vivid example of this process appears in Allport's (1924) social psychology text: "The girl who has lost her reputation for chastity finds the downward path an easy one, because the community shows that it expects further lapses in her conduct" (p. 327). Similarly, "stereotypes, though they may be false as a picture of fact, are real enough as psychological forces. Men may fail to see women as they are; but women tend to become as men see them" (Allport, 1929, p. 406). In short, in institutionalized views about women, Allport saw what we would today call a *self-fulfilling prophecy*—a view that became a major emphasis within social psychology. Expectations of one person for another can cause that other person to confirm the expectations (e.g., Rosenthal, 1966; Snyder, Tanke, & Berscheid, 1977).

Finally, Allport's (1929) analysis of gender keenly identified two other critical aspects of stereotyping processes. First, Allport recognized that one aspect of gender stereotypes is "that one sex *varies* more than the other in its physical and mental traits" (p. 399). In short, he called into question the popular conception that women are more alike than men are, pointing out that actual comparisons between men and women showed no differences in variability whatsoever. This emphasis on perceived and actual group variability as a component of stereotyping remains important in contemporary social psychology (e.g., Mullen & Hu, 1989; Mullen, Rozell, & Johnson, 1996). Second, Allport (1929) recognized that stereotyped views of women assumed that *normal* meant male. In assuming that men are the superior and more perfect sex, they became the measuring instrument against which to compare others. "Practically nothing is said or written about the psychology of men as a group, for that would be equivalent, in popular thinking, to a treatise on human nature" (p. 398). In short, it is women who differ from men, not men from women. This assumption—that the ingroup defines normality—finds its contemporary expression in popular treatises such as *The Mismeasure of Man* (Gould, 1981), which discussed how Caucasian norms are often misapplied to other races, and *The Mismeasure of Woman* (Tavris, 1992), which discussed how male norms are often misapplied to women. Finally, this sort of ingroup norming has been extensively studied—and often confirmed—in modern social cognitive theories of racial and gender stereotypes (e.g., Zárate & Sandoval, 1995). Thus, Allport's views on gender and other issues were remarkably progressive for their time and have remained fresh even to this day.

In the years after the publication of his volume on *Institutional Behavior*, Allport moved beyond his negative critique of conventional popular and sociological wisdom to propose specific new directions that the social sciences should take, and to offer positive proposals related to the criteria that must attend the treatment of phenomena and the gathering of data. His two main criteria were explicit denotation and observable measurement. *Explicit denotation* took the empiricist position that science and, therefore, social psychology must begin with phenomena that are observable, at least with the aid of instrumentation. The criterion of *observable measurement* was Allport's equivalent of an insistence on operational definition: Explicitly denoted concepts derive from acts that can be measured and furnish the variables in a given study. Thus, because institutions and groups, in and of themselves, are not explicitly denotable, they cannot be examined apart from individuals. Allport's struggles with this issue led to his event-structure theory, in which he attempted to explain how individuals constitute social reality.

EVENT-STRUCTURE THEORY

As Allport became more involved in studies of social behavior outside the laboratory, he also became increasingly dissatisfied with his earlier behavioristic theory, which neglected the problems inherent in the fact that social behavior occurs in social structures. He felt the need for concepts that deal with social relationships and social constraints, but he rejected sociological classics in the Weber or Durkheim tradition and the economic doctrines of Marx and Marxian revisionists. For Allport, these positions lacked objectivity and scientific precision and missed the actual social processes at work. For similar reasons, he found Lewinian field theory uncongenial to his way of thinking; it was too mentalistic in its acceptance of the individual's own perceptions and cognitions and too far from objective reality. Allport's search for a more satisfactory account of social behavior resulted in his event-structure theory.

Following a general statement of his model (Allport, 1954), Allport comprehensively tackled the topic of perception. In *Theories of Perception and the Concept of Structure* (Allport, 1955), he analyzed then-current theories of perception and gave an initial formal statement of his own theory of individual and social behavior; he later elaborated the theory in two other statements (Allport, 1962, 1967). In Allport's structural view, "Causation ... is not historical nor linear, but continuous, time independent, and reciprocally cyclical. One looks for it neither in society nor in the individual, [which are] traditionally seen as separate levels or agencies, but in compounded patterns of structuring" (Allport, 1962, p. 19). Individuals are seen as occupying a matrix of involvements in many different structures, the influences of which may not be the same. For example, in one study, Morse and Allport (1952) showed that feelings of aversion characterize the personalities of racially prejudiced people, whereas overt hostility toward minority groups depends primarily on environmental factors. The self-fulfilling prophecy and social conformity effects discussed earlier also fit neatly within Allport's event-structure theory—the behavior of individuals to some extent depends on the presence and expectations of other individuals. Although Allport never fully completed his theory, his ideas find modern expression in dynamical systems, which explain complex human social behavior using the concept of nonlinear, evolving, and interacting systems (e.g., Vallacher & Nowak, 1994).

CONCLUSION:
FLOYD H. ALLPORT'S INFLUENCE

As mentioned at the beginning of this chapter, Floyd H. Allport is rightly regarded as the founder of social psychology as a scientific discipline. This is a recognition that came to him more because of his promotion of the search for objective truth than for a program of research on any particular set of problems. For the science of social psychology, Allport brought theory and research together in a systematic fashion. His work gave identity and respectability to a new field of scientific endeavor. It connected social psychology to other branches of the discipline, including biological, educational, developmental, and personality psychology. It offered a behavioristic translation of the Freudian concepts of conflict and applied Freudian mechanisms to social problems. It opened the way for basic and applied researchers to come together on standards, methods, and concepts.

A large part of Allport's impact came from an influence on social psychology's perception of itself, an influence that had two somewhat different parts:

1. Through his research and writings, Allport defined *social psychology* as a science in which the measurement of *individuals* is the primary focus. Although, as in sociology, such measurement should be guided by theories of social process, in contrast to sociology, the data of social psychology should always be at the individual level.
2. Allport challenged the conventional thinking of his day. His insistence on defining concepts in terms of their behavioral symptoms and his refusal to let social scientists fall back on nonoperational higher level constructs furnished the rationale and set the example for a behavioristic interpretation of social phenomena.

This latter contribution was what made a science of social psychology possible. The crux of Allport's argument was that the progress of a science depends, first, on the development of the methods that produce reliable and valid observations and, second, on the development of interpretations that are more than the fallacies and fictions of common sense. In 1924, Floyd Allport's voice was crying in the wilderness. Now, three quarters of a century later, some of the foolishness that Allport criticized is still with us (see Kimble, 1996) and that voice still deserves to be heard.

REFERENCES

Allport, F. H. (1920). The influence of the group upon association and thought. *Journal of Experimental Psychology, 3*, 159–182.
Allport, F. H. (1924). *Social psychology*. Boston: Houghton Mifflin.
Allport, F. H. (1929). Seeing women as they are. *Harpers Magazine, 158*, 397–408.
Allport, F. H. (1933). *Institutional behavior: Essays toward a reinterpreting of contemporary social organization*. Chapel Hill: University of North Carolina Press.
Allport, F. H. (1934). The J–curve hypothesis of conforming behavior. *Journal of Social Psychology, 5*, 141–183.
Allport, F. H. (1937). Teleonomic description in the study of personality. *Character and Personality, 5*, 202–214.

Allport, F. H. (1954). The structuring of events: Outline of a general theory with applications to psychology. *Psychological Review, 61*, 281–303.

Allport, F. H. (1955). *Theories of perception and the concept of structure: A review and critical analysis with an introduction to a dynamic–structural theory of behavior*. New York: Wiley.

Allport, F. H. (1962). A structuronomic conception of behavior: Individual and collective. *Journal of Abnormal and Social Psychology, 64*, 3–30.

Allport, F. H. (1967). A theory of enestruence (event–structure theory): Report of progress. *American Psychologist, 22*, 1–24.

Allport, F. H. (1974). Floyd H. Allport. In E. G. Boring & G. Lindzey (Eds.), *History of psychology in autobiography* (Vol. 6, pp. 189–193). Englewood Cliffs, NJ: Prentice-Hall.

Allport, F. H., & Allport, G. W. (1921). Personality traits: Their classification and measurement. *Journal of Abnormal Psychology, 16*, 6–40.

Allport, F. H. & Allport, G. W. (1928). *A-S reaction study: A test for measuring ascendance–submission in personality*. Boston: Houghton Mifflin.

Allport, F. H., & Hartman, D. A. (1925). The measurement and motivation of atypical opinion in a certain group. *American Political Science Review, 19*, 735–760.

Allport, G. W. (1937). *Personality, a psychological interpretation*. New York: Holt, Rinehart & Winston.

Bakan, D. (1966). *The duality of human existence: An essay on psychology and religion*. Chicago: Rand McNally.

Bem, D. J., & Funder, D. C. (1978). Predicting more of the people more of the time: Assessing the personality of situations. *Psychological Review, 85*, 485–501.

Bond, C. F., Jr., & Titus, L. J. (1983). Social facilitation: A meta-analysis of 241 studies. *Psychological Bulletin, 94*, 265–292.

Durkheim, E. (1897). *Le suicide*. Paris: F. Alcan.

Eagly, A. H. (1987). *Sex differences in social behavior: A social-role interpretation*. Hillsdale, NJ: Lawrence Erlbaum Associates.

Eagly, A. H. (1995). The science and politics of comparing women and men. *American Psychologist, 50*, 145–158.

Eagly, A. H., & Chaiken, S. (1993). *The psychology of attitudes*. New York: Harcourt Brace.

Fiske, S. T., & Taylor, S. E. (1991). *Social cognition* (2nd ed.). New York: McGraw-Hill.

Gould, S. J. (1981). *The mismeasure of man*. New York: Norton.

House, J. (1977). The three faces of social psychology. *Sociometry, 40*, 161–177.

Hyman, H. H. (1942). The psychology of status. *Archives of Psychology* (whole no. 269).

James, W. (1890). *The principles of psychology*. New York: Holt, Rinehart & Winston.

Katz, D., & Allport, F. H. (1931). *Student attitudes: A report of the Syracuse University reaction study*. Syracuse, NY: Craftsman.

Katz, D., & Schank R. (1938). *Social psychology*. New York: Wiley.

Kimble, G. A. (1996). *Psychology: The hope of a science*. Cambridge, MA: MIT Press.

Le Bon, G. (1894/1930). *Psychologie des foules* [*The psychology of the people*]. London: E. Benn.

Markus, H. R. (1977). Self-schemata and processing information about the self. *Journal of Personality and Social Psychology, 35*, 63–78.

McDougall, W. (1908). *Introduction to social psychology*. London: Methuen.

Morse, N., & Allport, F. H. (1952). The causation of anti-Semitism: An investigation of seven hypotheses. *Journal of Psychology, 34*, 197–233.

Mullen, B., & Hu, L. (1988). Social projection as a function of cognitive mechanisms: Two meta-analytic integrations. *British Journal of Social Psychology, 27*, 333–356.

Mullen, B., & Hu, L. (1989). Perceptions of ingroup and outgroup variability: A meta-analytic integration. *Basic and Applied Social Psychology, 10*, 233–252.

Mullen, B., Rozell, D., & Johnson, C. (1996). The phenomenology of being in a group: Complexity approaches to operationalizing cognitive representation. In J. L. Nye & A. M. Brower (Eds.), *What's social about social cognition?* (pp. 205–229). Thousand Oaks, CA: Sage.

Newcomb, T. M., & Hartley, E. L. (Eds.). (1947). *Readings in social psychology*. New York: Holt, Rinehart & Winston.

O'Gorman, H. J. (1986). The discovery of pluralistic ignorance: An ironic lesson. *Journal of the History of the Behavioral Sciences, 22*, 333–347.

Prentice, D. A., & Miller, D. T. (1996). Pluralistic ignorance and the perpetuation of social norms by unwitting actors. In M. P. Zanna (Ed.), *Advances in experimental social psychology*, (Vol. 28, pp. 161–209). San Diego: Academic Press.

Rosenthal, R. (1966). *Experimenter effects in behavioral research.* New York: Appleton-Century-Crofts.

Ross, E. A. (1908). *Social psychology.* New York: Macmillan.

Schanck, R. (1932). A study of a community and its groups and institutions conceived of as behaviors of individuals. *Psychological Monographs, 43* (whole no. 195).

Sherif, M. (1936). *The psychology of social norms.* New York: Harper.

Sherif, M., & Sherif, C. W. (1967). Attitude as the individual's own categories: The social judgment-involvement approach to attitude and attitude change. In C. W. Sherif & M. Sherif (Eds.), *Attitudes, ego-involvement, and change* (pp. 105–139). New York: Wiley.

Snyder, M., Tanke, E. D., & Berscheid, E. (1977). Social perception and interpersonal behavior: On the self-fulfilling nature of social stereotypes. *Journal of Personality and Social Psychology, 35,* 656–666.

Tarde, G. (1898/1903). *The laws of imitation.* New York: Holt, Rinehart & Winston.

Tavris, C. (1992). *The mismeasure of woman.* New York: Simon & Schuster.

Thurstone, L. L. (1928). Attitudes can be measured. *American Journal of Sociology, 33,* 529–544.

Triplett, N. (1897). The dynamogenic factors in peacemaking and competition. *American Journal of Psychology, 9,* 507–533.

Vallacher, R. R., & Nowak, A. (1994). *Dynamical systems in social psychology.* New York: Academic Press.

Zajonc, R. (1965). *Social psychology: An experimental approach.* Belmont, CA:Wadsworth.

Zárate, M. A., & Sandoval, P. (1995). The effects of contextual cues on making occupational and gender categorizations. *British Journal of Social Psychology, 34,* 353–362.

Chapter 9

The Legacy of Jean Piaget

Edward Zigler
Elizabeth Gilman

It has frequently been asserted that no theoretical framework has had a greater impact on developmental psychology than that of Jean Piaget (Beilin & Pufall, 1992; Flavell, 1996). Using concepts from biology, psychology, philosophy, and mathematics to examine the manner in which children learn about the world, Piaget gave us a remarkably well-articulated and integrated theory of cognitive development. A highly productive worker, he published some 70 books and over 100 articles in psychology. Despite criticisms of the limitations and the lack of objectivity of Piaget's methods (see e.g., Gopnik, 1996; Lourenco & Machado, 1996), our understanding of children's intellectual development would never have evolved as it has without his pioneering efforts. Piaget's theoretical formulations have stimulated a vast amount of research. This chapter, written in the year that marks the 100th anniversary of Piaget's birth, provides an appropriate occasion for the celebration of his achievements and the deep and continuing influence of his work.

PIAGET'S EARLY LIFE AND WORK

Jean Piaget was born in the Swiss university community of Neuchatel in 1896. His mother was intelligent and religious and his father was a historian with a special interest in medieval literature. Piaget took up serious scientific pursuits at a youthful age. He showed an early passion for observing nature and a precocious interest in biology and psychology (Brainerd, 1996; Evans, 1973). His interest in biology resulted in a publication when he was only 10 years old—an article describing a rare albino sparrow that he had seen in a local park. Shortly thereafter, he began

---

* Photograph of Jean Piaget courtesy of Archives of the History of American Psychology, Akron, Ohio.

assisting in the local natural history museum, where he helped classify its zoology collection. He began studying molluscs and published articles on them when he was still in his teens. As a result of these articles, Piaget was offered a curator's position at the Geneva museum of natural history—one that he was forced to decline in order to finish school. He was 14 years old at the time.

During adolescence, Piaget combined his interest in biology with a fascination for epistemology. He began to study logic, philosophy, and religion. As these investigations continued, however, he never abandoned his biological orientation. Subsequently, in his research, Piaget would attempt to bridge the intellectual gap between the two disciplines.

Piaget completed his undergraduate work in the natural sciences in 1915, at the University of Neuchatel, when he was 18 years old. At this point he suffered a nervous collapse, which he later attributed to overexposure to the study of philosophy, particularly that of Henri Bergson. During this difficult period, he withdrew to the mountains for over a year (Brainerd, 1996). From this bit of history, it comes as no surprise that Piaget became a lifelong critic of speculative philosophy that is untempered by empirical data (Brainerd, 1996). Finally, 2 years after his recovery from the breakdown, he submitted a thesis on molluscs and was granted his doctorate. His later studies of the nature and theory of knowledge were to be cast solidly within the framework of biology.

Piaget then turned his attention to psychology. He studied the ideas of Freud and Jung (chaps. 4 & 11, *Pioneers I*) and worked in Zurich in Bleuler's clinic and in two psychological laboratories. In 1920, he published an article on child psychology and psychoanalysis and spent the following 2 years studying logic, abnormal psychology, and epistemology at the Sorbonne.

As a young investigator, Piaget took a position as an assistant to Theophile Simon in Alfred Binet's (chap. 5, this volume) laboratory in Paris. His first assignment was to standardize a French version of Cyril Burt's reasoning tests by giving them to Parisian school children. Standardizing a test involves tedious repetition, posing identical questions to subjects to elicit their individual responses. Piaget apparently disliked the process. As seen from his own account:

> From the very first questioning I noticed that though Burt's tests certainly had their diagnostic merits, based on the number of successes and failures, it was much more interesting to try to find the reasons for the failures. Thus I engaged my subjects in conversations patterned after psychiatric questioning, with the aim of discovering something about the reasoning process underlying their right, but especially their wrong answers. I noticed with amazement that the simplest reasoning task...presented for normal children up to the age of eleven or twelve difficulties unsuspected by the adult. (Piaget, 1952, p. 244)

Piaget proposed that complete information about the nature of the evolving mind could not be gleaned from correct or incorrect test responses alone. He noted qualitative differences in the responses given by children of different ages. The incorrect answers of children of the same age tended to be wrong in the same way. When he questioned children of various ages about their answers, there were distinct differences in the types of mistakes they were apt to make. Thus, Piaget concluded that the more fruitful question was not how many correct answers a child could give at a certain age, but what modes of thinking were used by children as they developed. His technique of verbal probing has come to be known as the *methode clinique*. Reasoning that standardized questioning would not reveal the thinking processes of children, Piaget encouraged a free-form style of questioning, similar to a psychiatric interview. With the development of this method, Piaget was launched on his life's work.

Impressed by Piaget's early articles on children, the Director of the Rousseau Institute in Geneva offered Piaget the position of director of research. Piaget took this opportunity to continue his study of children's thinking. From this experience flowed a series of articles and his first five books, published from 1923 to 1932.

From 1921 until his death, Piaget was engaged in studying child psychology: the development of logic, causal reasoning, and thought; the growth of moral development; the child's conception of the world; and the emergence of intelligence during infancy and early childhood. This work led to the evolution of his theory of intelligence and its development. During the 1920s and 1930s, this work was highly regarded in the United States. However, during the 1940s and 1950s, the period when psychology was dominated by the philosophy of logical positivism, it met with criticism. Subsequently, as Piaget's later work appeared in English translation, interest in his work grew once again.

Piaget remained an active scientist well into his 80s, revising his theoretical formulations throughout his entire career. He noted that he had provided only a rough sketch of human cognitive development and that later research would provide the parts that were lacking or that needed to be modified or abandoned. Today psychologists debate the merits of Piaget's work even as they continue to respect his contributions to methodology and to an overarching theory of intellectual development. After a brief overview of the principle components of Piaget's theory, this chapter discusses some of the controversial elements of his conceptual framework.

MAJOR PRINCIPLES OF PIAGET'S THEORY

Perhaps Piaget's most significant contribution was to demonstrate the fundamental differences between the intellectual functioning of children and that of adults. At birth, infants are not conscious of themselves or objects as independent structures. From this primitive level, children's cognitive systems change to become more adaptive and to provide a more realistic understanding of the world. Central to Piaget's theory is the view that knowledge of the world is not simply an internalized replica of what is external to the self. Rather, acquisition of knowledge is a creative event that depends on and is limited by the cognitive processes that the child has developed. For example, a 2-month-old baby has only a few ways of knowing—by sucking, by touching, and by focusing on round, facelike objects. The infant's understanding of the world cannot go beyond what is provided by these first cognitive resources.

Schemes and Operations

To consider sucking and touching as cognitive activities may seem odd, but Piaget believed that physical actions are the initial basis for all knowledge and cognitive growth. He believed that actions are so essential that he devised a special terminology for describing them: He spoke of *schemes* to refer to organized patterns of physical action, such as sucking and grasping. A scheme does not refer to discrete motor actions, but to a generalization based on different instances of specific motor actions and their common characteristics. For example, a child's scheme of grasping is made up of the features that are common to all the child's many acts of grasping. Schemes carried out mentally are *operations*. Both schemes and operations are children's ways of knowing.

Assimilation and Accommodation

Cognitive growth takes place as schemes and operations develop and become more complex. The process by which this is accomplished consists of two complementary components: assimilation and accommodation. When a child encounters an operation or event for the first time, that object or event is assimilated into the child's existing cognitive framework. The child may then reorganize the cognitive structure to accommodate the new experience. Thus, *assimilation* becomes the process of taking in new information and interpreting it—sometimes even distorting it—to make it agree with the available mental organization. *Accommodation* involves a modification of the cognitive system to provide a more precise match with external information.For example, newborn infants reflexively suck the breast. They literally assimilate the breast into one of their existing schemes for behavior. If a finger or the corner of a blanket is placed on their lips, they also suck the finger or blanket. For a time they continue to assimilate objects into one of the few organized responses they possess. To continue treating the finger or blanket as if it were a breast is maladaptive, however. Therefore, in the process of sucking the blanket, they must reorganize their responses and cognitive representation—their scheme—of the blanket. They must shape their lips differently and, in so doing, change their schemes of sucking. This reorganization in response to the demands presented by an alien object is an example of accommodation.

The child's explanation of dreams is another example of cognitive growth through assimilation and accommodation. A little boy who asserts that dreams come from balloons sent from God has assimilated the experience of dreaming into his existing cognitive framework. Because dreams have certain visual qualities similar to those of external events, he has associated them with balloons—external objects with which he is familiar. If the child then says that the balloons "burst into pictures inside your head," he has begun to show some degree of accommodation; he has made a distinction between inside and outside. Later, as he is forced to come to grips with certain unacceptable aspects of his explanation, he will have to make further accommodations. For instance, after having many dreams, he will realize that dreams are unreal and without substance and that they consequently differ from objects like balloons and events taking place outside the head. The differences he notices between dreams and nondreams, as well as the greater differentiation within his cognitive system, will lead the boy to the next cognitive level of understanding dreams. Each instance of assimilation and accommodation stretches the mind to some extent; this stretching enables the individual to make new and somewhat altered assimilations and accommodations in the future. These, in turn, bring additional small increments in mental growth. Thus, by repeated assimilations and accommodations, the cognitive system gradually evolves and provides the child with an increasingly accurate view of the nature of things. When children make a startling leap in understanding phenomena, they move onto the next stage of cognitive development.

Stages of Cognitive Development

Piaget argued for a basic continuity between biological and psychological function (Piaget, 1975). He emphasized the adaptive significance of intelligence and traced its growth through a series of four stages. Each of these stages is part of a continuous adaptational process, yet is distinct in important respects from those preceding and following it. The four major stages are: sensorimotor, preoperational, concrete operations, and formal operations. During each stage, certain critical cognitive abilities are achieved—abilities that make it possible for the child to process information in ways that were previously impossible. The age ranges cited for the stages are only rough approximations; they vary considerably from child to child and from task to task.

Piaget's stage theory has been criticized for its failure to include the total range of competence of young children (see e.g, Gopnik, 1996). For example, more recent researchers have been able to identify cognitive competencies that appear earlier than Piaget recognized (see e.g., Baillargeon, 1987, 1991). However, it is important to understand that the essential concept in Piaget's framework is not the precise chronological moment of passage from one stage to the next, but the sequence of transformation (Smith, 1991). The fact that ongoing research may reveal previously unnoticed complexities in the cognitive development of children does not negate the conceptual basis of Piagetian theory. Rather, such investigations serve to underscore the lasting value of his concepts, in that they have sparked a rich line of inquiry that continues to the present day.

The Sensorimotor Stage—Birth to 2 Years.   The sensorimotor stage of development is the one in which the most fundamental and rapid changes in cognitive structure take place. Piaget called it the *sensorimotor* stage to reflect his belief that knowledge is built up from sensory perceptions and motor actions. At birth, the infant has no sense of an individual self that can act on the world as a separate entity. The infant is the center of the universe—a universe that consists of ever-changing perceptions but no permanent objects. Piaget (1973) compared development during this stage to the Copernican revolution. Cognitively, the child is unseated as the axis of the universe and reduced to the status of one object among other objects. In this stage, children also learn that they and other objects exist in space and that objects can cause things to happen to other objects. Infants acquire the concept of an object as a permanent structure whose existence is independent of their perceptions. Children gain all this knowledge before they acquire language.

At birth, infants make only isolated movements and have only isolated schemes. As they repeat and coordinate their movements, the schemes are elaborated by new assimilations and accommodations. The sensorimotor intelligence typical of this stage allows the child to pull a blanket that has a toy resting on its far end to obtain the toy. This task may appear simple, but Piaget has shown what a cognitive feat it really is. Before children can perform this task, they must have constructed and mastered several relationships—in particular, "resting on" and "moving an object from one place to another"—and coordinated them for their purposes.

Perhaps the most significant achievement during this period is the development of the object concept or a sense of object permanence. As noted earlier, infants do not at first realize that objects, including people, exist independently of their perceptions. They may gaze at a toy held within their view, but when the toy is removed they do not reach for it. The object simply ceases to exist for them once it leaves their visual field. This lack of the concept of object explains the delight infants derive from playing peekaboo. If a mother removes her face from her infant daughter's view and then reappears, she is surprised and pleased by her re-creation. Later in the sensorimotor stage, children will gaze at the point where an object disappeared; by the end of the sensorimotor period, they will actively seek to find an object after it has vanished. By this time, children have a sense that objects exist even when they cannot see or find them—a sense of object permanence.

Their inadequate concept of objects explains why infants less than a year old cannot successfully play the "guess which hand" game. When they watch you hide a coin in your hand, place your hands behind your back, and return an empty hand, they will begin to search where they believe the coin disappeared. Early in the sensorimotor stage children will think it disappeared when you first hid it in your hand and they will begin to search among your fingers. By the end of the sensorimotor period, they look behind your back because that is where they first lost track of the coin. At this time, intelligence is restricted primarily to the level of physical actions. Next comes the preoperational stage, when children begin to use symbols, imagery, and language and come to understand identity constancy.

Preoperational Stage—2 to 7 Years. During the preoperational stage, children engage in symbolic activities that draw on mental imagery and language. For example, they can now mentally represent an object to themselves when it is not visually present. Their intellectual functions are no longer restricted to physical actions. By the end of this period, children are able to talk about objects, draw them, tell stories, and assemble three-dimensional constructions. They also learn to use language to direct their behavior. The stage is called *preoperational* because children are unable to engage in certain basic mental operations. They cannot focus on two dimensions, such as height and width, at the same time; they cannot reverse or change actions mentally. They can repeat old actions in their minds, but they cannot think of actions that they have not yet engaged in or seen. Their thinking is egocentric: They cannot see another person's point of view or put themselves in another's place.

When Piaget first developed his theory, he believed that young children's thinking, initially prelogical and egocentric, is gradually tempered by the influence of social interaction. Recent research, however, suggests that children may not be as wholly egocentric or limited in their thinking as Piaget first thought. In their excellent review of Piagetian thought in light of contemporary criticisms of his concepts, Lourenco and Machado (1996) noted that Piaget's formulation of young children's thinking is often presented as a deficit model: The very young child is seen in terms of operations he or she cannot perform. However, they carefully pointed out that the stages posited by Piaget do not present themselves suddenly with rigid boundaries; they occur gradually, as a progressive transformation, differentiation, and integration over time (Smith, 1993). Thus, to characterize Piaget's model as a *negative* one is to misconstrue the essential developmental and process-oriented nature of his concept. Children do not abruptly leave one stage behind as they move to the next; they integrate their previous capacities with the new ones as they are acquired.

For example, the use of language by preoperational children is different from that of adults. When children first learn that objects have names, they believe that the names are an essential part of the objects. For instance, the word *ball* is just as much a property of a ball as its physical shape and color. This mode of thinking about the names of things is called *nominal realism*. In the earliest stages of nominal realism, the child finds it nonsensical to question why certain objects have the names they do. Because the name is part of the object, the child reasons, the object could have no other name. Further, children may also believe that an object could not have existed before it had its name. In later stages, children will abandon this view and realize that names are assigned to objects. It is not until the age of 11 or 12, however, that they fully comprehend the arbitrary nature of the naming process.

Another characteristic of preoperational thinking is *animism*—a belief that inanimate objects have mental processes. Preoperational children ascribe thoughts, feelings, and motives to clouds, streams, trees, and bicycles. Plants may hurt when they are picked; clouds may chase each other. In accordance with the child's egocentric thought, the motives of external objects are based on the child's activities—the sun and the moon "follow" as the child walks.

One of the important achievements of the preoperational period is the development of identity constancy. The child comes to realize that an object remains qualitatively the same despite alterations in form, size, or general appearance. DeVries (1969) devised an interesting way to study the development of identity constancy in 3- to 6-year-old children. The children were individually shown a docile cat. After they had identified it as a cat and petted it, the experimenter told them that soon the animal would look different. She asked the children to look only at the tail end of the cat. Then, while screening the cat's head from their view, she placed a mask of a ferocious-looking dog over the cat's head. The cat was turned around and the children were asked what animal it was now. DeVries found that the older children understood that the cat has retained its identity. Many of the younger children, however, thought that the cat had become a dog—a real dog that could bark.

Stage of Concrete Operations—7 to 12 Years.   In the stage of concrete operations, children organize into structural wholes many of the scattered schemes and conceptualizations developed during the earlier stages. They form mental representations that accurately reflect possible actions and transactions in the physical world. As indicated earlier, operations are mental acts—schemes carried out in the mind. During the stage of concrete operations, the child is able to act on objects and transform situations mentally. However, the operations are termed *concrete* because the child can only reason about physical things like blocks or lumps of clay. Reasoning about abstractions such as words and mathematical symbols is not possible until the next stage of development. In the concrete operations period, children acquire the ability to conserve number, length, quantity, weight, volume, space, and time. In the final stage, formal operations, children become capable of considering a problem in the abstract without requiring a concrete representation of it.

Stage of Formal Operations—12 Years and Above.   During the final stage of development, children become able to consider a problem in the abstract without needing a concrete representation. They search for alternatives in trying to solve problems, rejecting inappropriate solutions without physically testing their adequacy. Children are now free to manipulate all sorts of conceptual hypotheses about the world, thinking not only about what is, but also about what could be. When younger children are confronted with the phrase, " If coal is white, snow is _____," they will respond by insisting that coal is black. Through formal operations, children free themselves from such physical givens and now have the cognitive ability to consider a totally hypothetical realm of possibilities, which nevertheless retains some order. This new ability of the person to deal in hypothetical terms is described by Flavell (1963):

> No longer exclusively preoccupied with the sober business of trying to stabilize and organize just what comes directly to the senses, the adolescent has, through this new orientation, the potentiality of imagining all that might be there—both the very obvious and the very subtle—and thereby much better insuring the findings of all that is there. (p. 205)

The questions that older children ask when playing the game, *Twenty Questions*, indicates the higher level of abstraction in their formal operational thought. In guessing what object the experimenter has in mind, 11-year-olds, like adults, will begin with general questions to narrow the range of their alternatives: "Is it alive?" "Is it a tool?" Six-year-olds, however, immediately guess at specific objects: "Is it a dog?"

Eight-year-olds often combine these strategies. They begin with a general question but move straight to specific guesses. Thus, they might follow "Is it a tool?" with "Is it a hammer?", whereas the 11-year-old's next question might be, "Can you cut with it?" This use of questions that progressively restrict the alternatives demonstrates a broad conception of the range of potential answers, which is not evident in the questions of younger children (Mosher & Hornsby, 1966).

Formal operations are the basis of adult thought. In addition to abstract, logical reasoning, they make possible the creative reasoning that brings about some of humanity's most impressive achievements: a grasp of truth, beauty, and other ideals; being able to think about thinking; the ability to delve into probabilities and improbabilities; and imagining other worlds. Not all adolescents or even adults ever attain the stage of formal operations. The ability to deal logically with abstractions becomes possible in this stage, but whether it is exercised depends in part on cultural and educational factors. Further, individuals who are somewhat below average in intelligence may never attain formal operational thought (Inhelder, 1966) and very bright children may perform as well as or better than some adults (Neimark, 1975). In any case, by late adolescence, individuals have developed all the cognitive processes that they will ever possess. New knowledge can be acquired and individuals may thus accumulate more contents in their intellectual system with the passage of time, but the processes underlying cognitive interchange with the world are established, for the most part, by the age of 20.

CROSS-CULTURAL PIAGETIAN STUDIES

Cross-cultural studies of Piagetian theory have addressed the basic question of whether human cognition follows the same course of development in children throughout the world. Piaget's notions have sometimes been criticized as being a theory of cognitive development solely for Western scientists (Greenfield, 1976)—a theory that may be no more than an ethnocentric description of mental development in the urban, technological cultures of Europe and North America. It is argued that members of other societies may develop cognitive processes more adaptive to their own surroundings and of greater cultural value within their social realm.

Cross-cultural studies conducted in countries as far afield as Thailand, Rwanda, Papua, Iraq, Ghana, Australia, and Mexico yielded two important findings (Dasen, 1977). The first is that the developmental stages observed by Piaget in Switzerland also occur in children of these very different societies. The sequence of cognitive development—from sensorimotor to formal operations—seems to be universal. The second finding is that the rate of cognitive development may vary from one civilization to another. Children may pass from one stage to another at different ages.

Because intelligence reflects adaptation to the environment, it is not surprising to discover that concepts important to a culture are gained relatively early (Dasen, 1975, 1977). For example, Mexican children who grow up in pottery-making families are accelerated in their development of conservation of substance. Children living in rural Baoule on the Ivory Coast of Africa have greater sensorimotor skills than their contemporaries in other countries. Apparently the particular experiences of children as well as their ways of life and the values of their culture can affect the rate of cognitive development.

Within a given cultural group, cognitive development may also be affected by education and whether a child's residence is urban or rural. In Rwanda, a country in central Africa where mandatory education was instituted relatively recently, schooling was found to help children master tasks requiring concrete operations (Laurendeau-Bendavid, 1977). In a review of research comparing the cognitive skills of schooled and nonschooled individuals, Rogoff (1981) concluded that clear relationships exist between school activities and specific cognitive skills. As for the skills of urban versus nonurban children, another investigator found that rural Thai children lagged behind urban children in mastering several concepts requiring concrete operations (Opper, 1977). Urban children acquired the concepts over 5 years, beginning at age 6. The rural children did not begin to acquire the concepts until age 9, but then mastered them rapidly in only 3 years.

Clearly the exploration of these cultural differences in cognitive development is a rich and valuable area of inquiry. Over the last 20 years, a great deal of cross-cultural investigation has taken place. The focus of this research in cognition has shifted gradually from the comparative study of performance on particular tasks to research on the transformation of thinking as individuals engage in various sociocultural activities. (For a recent comprehensive review of cultural variation in cognitive development, see Rogoff & Chavajay, 1995.)

ACCELERATED PROGRESS
THROUGH THE STAGES

Whether special training can accelerate children's progression through Piaget's cognitive stages is a subject of continuing interest. Many investigators have attempted to help children develop certain aspects of cognition by providing specific training. A number of these efforts have apparently succeeded. One of these demonstrations was carried out by Gelman (1969), who trained 5-year-old children in conservation of number and length. Gelman's study appears to be a powerful demonstration that training and experience may help children acquire the principle of conservation. However, Gardner (1978) pointed out that Gelman only studied 5-year-old children. It is possible that they were about to acquire principles of conservation on their own and Gelman's procedures simply nudged them a bit prematurely into operational thinking. Additional research will no doubt reveal the extent to which mental growth can be accelerated and the conditions that foster such growth. At this time, the best conclusion appears to be that children will attain the cognitive abilities described by Piaget provided they have the requisite experiences in the world and have reached the cognitive maturational level of the stage in question.

It is conceivable that hurrying a child from one stage to the next might interfere with normal cognitive development and that such acceleration might lessen the child's cognitive achievements. Interestingly, Piaget referred to these efforts to accelerate as *the American disease*. Wohlwill (1970) noted that the modes of early childhood reasoning, although generally superceded in later cognitive stages, may be useful to the individual later in life, especially as a foundation for their imaginative and creative acts. If children are hurried through early stages, the early processes may not be properly incorporated in the overall cognitive apparatus and certain valuable ways of thinking may be lost to them as adults.

SOCIAL COGNITION

Although happenings in the physical world are relatively predictable, those in the social world are complex and more unpredictable. The responses of human beings to one another are more complexly determined by motives, mutual intentions, shared perspectives, and coordinated actions that are elusively subjective. Given the complexity of its determination, perhaps it is surprising to discover that social cognition seems to develop more rapidly than physical cognition (Hoffman, 1981). In fact, some of the research findings on social cognition challenge Piaget's statements about the cognitive capacities of young children. These findings have led to the contemporary view that Piaget underestimated the importance of social interaction in cognitive development (Gopnik, 1996; Rogoff, 1990).

For example, children develop the concept of person permanence before they develop the concept of object permanence. There are several possible explanations for this developmental difference. The people with whom a child interacts are apt to be more familiar than physical objects. Children are likely to have a greater emotional investment in people than in physical objects. Hoffman (1981) suggested that this involvement intensifies children's motivation for learning and cognitive development. Furthermore, such interactions provide children with a constant source of feedback—other people's reactions—and this feedback may promote cognitive development by showing children when their hypotheses about the appropriate social interactions are correct or incorrect.

There is some evidence that social interaction can promote cognitive development as well as social development, as this line of reasoning suggests. William Doise and his colleagues demonstrated that children working together were able to master a spatial task—copying a model village when the model was rotated to change the child's perspective—that children of the same age working alone could not (Mugny & Doise, 1976). In related studies, children who were initially unable to conserve acquired this operation after working on conservation tasks with peers or with an experimenter who challenged their assessments by offering either correct or incorrect alternatives. Discussing these results, Damon (1981) suggested that social interactions require children to restructure their cognitive processes and that this may influence their modes of thinking in lasting ways. The existence of such a relationship between social interaction and physical cognition makes good sense when we consider that children often explore the physical world, as well as the social one, in the context of interacting with other people.

Role Taking and Empathy

If children never outgrew the egocentricity of their early years, adult human social interaction would be different and difficult. There would be no cooperation, sharing, or selflessness. The capacity to put oneself in another's place—to take another's role—is vital to social interactions. Children are not born with this capacity. Empathy, the recognition and sharing of the emotions of others, depends on being able to see things from another's perspective. According to Piaget, the capacity for role taking develops gradually as a result of social interactions. A good example of egocentric thought comes from a study in which children heard a story while their mothers were out of the room and were asked whether their mothers knew what happened in the story. Two-year-olds demonstrated their egocentricity by assuming that their mothers knew what had happened. Most 4-year-olds recognized that their mothers could not possibly know (Mossler, Marvin, & Greenberg, 1976).

As noted earlier, however, other research suggests that young children are not as egocentric as Piaget initially considered them and that egocentricity declines gradually during the preoperational period. For example, adults use simpler terms, speak more slowly, and repeat themselves more often when talking to young children than when talking to other adults. In one study, 4-year-olds were also found to modify their speech patterns when they talked with 2-year-olds (Shatz & Gelman, 1973). The 4-year-olds seemed to recognize and respond to the needs of the younger children. In short, by the age of 4, children in our culture can engage in role taking. They have developed levels of social cognition that seem more advanced than their cognition of physical properties.

Scripts

One hypothesis of how children learn about their own and other people's social roles holds that they develop scripts for what happens in familiar situations. They develop scripts for what one does at lunch time, when meeting a stranger, and when eating in a restaurant (Abelson, 1981). These scripts reflect the regularities in a child's experience and can act as cognitive mediators of the child's behavior.

Children acquire some scripts, such as eating dinner, by participating directly in the activity. This dinnertime script, learned through direct participation, is sure to be limited because children typically do not participate in the planning or preparation of a meal. Other scripts are learned through observation. Children reveal some knowledge of other people's roles in their fantasy and role playing. For example, Nelson (1981) cited a dialogue in which two 4-year-olds indicated some understanding of a dinner-planning script: They carried on a make-believe telephone conversation in which they played mother and father planning dinner.

Scripts are important guides for activities because, once learned, they allow people to attend to new features of the environment. For example, on the first day of school, when every aspect of experience is new, children must attend to everything—to the teacher, peers, desk, snack, and lesson. If the routine aspects of the school day did not become familiar, there would simply be too much to attend to for a child to learn much beyond these routines. By the second week of school, however, the child's classroom script has made the routines almost second nature and the child can focus on each day's special activities, undistracted by the need to pay attention to routine details.

Scripts foster cognitive development because children are capable of more advanced cognitive functioning in familiar situations than in novel situations. For example, although 4-year-olds are egocentric in their discussions with peers, recent evidence shows that they can in fact communicate cooperatively, sticking to a given topic while they take appropriate turns in speaking. Nelson (1981) suggested that two young children can communicate competently when both of them know the script for the event they are discussing. When there is no shared script, their speech may revert to egocentric speech. Thus, scripts have a meaningful place in development, although blind adherence to childhood scripts may prevent adults from adopting more suitable behavior in later life.

Perceptions of Others

For an adult, the perception of another person includes a host of inferences about the attributes of that other individual. Research has shown that such perceptions develop gradually. In studies in which children and adolescents were asked to describe people they know (Peevers & Secord, 1973), young children tended to refer to concrete aspects of behavior—"She give me candy"—and use undifferentiated adjectives such as *nice* or *kind*. Older children and adolescents tended to use more informative, differentiated, and other-oriented descriptions—"She is always ready to help people who are in trouble"—and draw abstract and general inferences from concrete events. These inferences about psychological states become more common with increasing age.

Similar trends are evident in children's descriptions of people they do not know. In one study, children and adolescents of different social classes were asked to describe rich and poor people and how they were similar to and different from each other (Leahy, 1981). Younger children emphasized peripheral characteristics—possessions, appearances, behavior—in their descriptions, but adolescents emphasized traits, thoughts, and sociocentric factors such as life chances and class consciousness.

According to Piaget, young children evaluate others' behavior by its consequences and older children consider the actors' motives and intentions. For example, children might be told one story about a boy who accidentally trips and breaks several cups while helping to clear the table and another about a boy who breaks a single cup while trying to steal from the cookie jar. Most children under age 6 or 7 consider the first child naughtier because of the greater damage done. Older children and adults usually consider the second child naughtier because the accident occurred during a forbidden activity. It appears, however, that even younger children can clearly recognize specific intentions and that this capacity develops before the ability to infer others' motives (Irwin & Ambron, 1973). Piaget's ground-breaking work in the area of perception of others' actions and the growth of moral judgment has inspired the work of subsequent researchers, notably that of Lawrence Kohlberg, who has contributed significantly to our knowledge through his stage theory of moral development (Kohlberg, 1984).

CONCLUSION

Jean Piaget has given developmental psychology a rich and complex body of work—work that has provided, and continues to provide, valuable material that sparks our thinking and has formed the basis of many fruitful careers in the field. Surely many researchers would concur with Lourenco and Machado's (1996) paraphrase of Einstein on Euclid: "If Piaget failed to kindle your youthful enthusiasm, you were not born to be a developmental psychologist" (p. 157). In a field sometimes criticized for its preoccupation with minutiae, we are still grappling with the major conceptual issues Piaget taught us to investigate: the nature of thinking, the relation between knowledge and values, and the meaning of logic and necessary knowledge. Were he still with us, we are confident he would continue to address these questions and explore further the issues raised by his critics as well as those he himself perceived. One hundred years after his birth, we continue to refine and expand on Piaget's splendid body of work. Surely this is the mark of a great theoretician whose efforts remain a major milestone in our understanding of human cognitive development.

REFERENCES

Abelson, R. P. (1981). Scripts: The psychological status of the script concept. *American Psychologist, 36*, 715–729.

Baillargeon, R. (1987). Object permanence in 3 1/2- and 4 1/2-month-old infants. *Developmental Psychology, 23*, 655–664.

Baillargeon, R. (1991). Reasoning about the height and location of a hidden object in 4.5- and 6.5-month-old infants. *Cognition, 38*, 13–42.

Beilin, H., & Pufall, P. (Eds.). (1992). *Piaget's theory*. Hillsdale, NJ: Lawrence Erlbaum Associates.

Brainerd, C. J. (1996). Piaget: A centennial celebration. *Psychological Science, 7*, 191–195.

Damon, W. (1981). Exploring children's social cognition on two fronts. In J. H. Flavell & L. Ross (Eds.). *Social cognitive development*. Cambridge, England: Cambridge University Press.

Dasen, P. R. (1975). Concrete operational development in three cultures. *Journal of Cross-Cultural Psychology, 6*, 156–172.

Dasen, P. R. (1977). Introduction. In P. R. Dasen (Ed.), *Piagetian psychology: Cross-cultural contributions*. New York: Gardner.

DeVries, R. (1969). Constancy of generic identity in the years three to six. *Monographs of the Society for Research in Child Development, 34* (Serial 127).

Evans, R. L. (1973). *Jean Piaget: The man and his ideas*. New York: Dutton.

Flavell, J. (1963). *The developmental psychology of Jean Piaget*. Princeton, NJ: Van Nostrand.

Flavell, J. (1996). Piaget's legacy. *Psychological Science, 7*, 200–209.

Gardner, H. (1978). *Developmental psychology*. Boston: Little, Brown.

Gelman, R. (1969). Conservation acquisition: A problem in learning to attend to relevant attributes. *Journal of Experimental Child Psychology, 7*, 167–187.

Gopnik, A. (1996). The post-Piaget era. *Psychological Science, 7*, 221–225.

Greenfield, P. M. (1976). Cross-cultural research and Piagetian theory: Paradox and progress. In K. Riegel & J. Meacham (Eds.), *The developing individual in a changing world*. The Hague, Netherlands: Mouton.

Hoffman, M. L. (1981). Perspectives on the difference between understanding people and understanding things: The role of affect. In J. Flavell & L. Ross (Eds.), *Social cognitive development*. Cambridge, England: Cambridge University Press.

Inhelder, B. (1966). Cognitive development and its contribution to the diagnosis of some phenomena of mental deficiency. *Merrill-Palmer Quarterly, 12*, 299–319.

Irwin, D. M., & Ambron, S. R. (1973). *Moral judgment and role-taking in children aged three to seven*. Paper presented to the Society for Research in Child Development.

Kohlberg, L. (1984). *Essays in moral development: Vol. 2*. New York: Harper & Row.

Laurendeau-Bendavid, M. (1977). Culture, schooling, and cognitive development: A comparative study of children in French Canada and Rwanda. In P. R. Dasen (Ed.), *Piagetian psychology: Cross-cultural contributions*. New York: Gardner.

Leahy, R. L. (1981). The development of the conception of economic inequality: I. Descriptions and comparisons of rich and poor people. *Child Development, 52*, 523–532.

Lourenco, O., & Machado, A. (1996). In defense of Piaget's theory: A reply to 10 common criticisms. *Psychological Review, 103*, 143–164.

Mosher, F. A. & Hornsby, J. R. (1966). On asking questions. In J. S. Bruner, R. R. Olver, & P. M. Greenfield (Eds.), *Studies in cognitive growth*. New York: Wiley.

Mossler, D. G., Marvin, R. S., & Greenberg, M. T. (1976). Conceptual perspective taking in two-to six-year-old children. *Developmental Psychology , 12*, 85–86.

Mugny, G., & Doise, W. (1976). Socio-cognitive conflict and structuration of individual and collective performances. *European Journal of Social Psychology, 17*, 181–192.

Neimark, E. D. (1975). Intellectual development during adolescence. In F. D. Horowitz (Ed.), *Review of research in child development* (Vol. 4). Chicago: University of Chicago Press.

Nelson, K. (1981). Social cognition in a script framework. In J. H. Flavell & L. Ross (Eds.), *Social cognitive development*. Cambridge, England: Cambridge University Press.

Opper, S. (1977). Concept development in Thai urban and rural children. In P. R. Dasen (Ed.), *Piagetian psychology: Cross-cultural contributions*. New York: Gardner.

Peevers, B. H., & Secord, P. F. (1973). Developmental changes in attribution of descriptive concepts to persons. *Journal of Personality and Social Psychology, 27*, 120–128.

Piaget, J. (1952). Autobiography. In E. G. Boring (Ed.), *A history of psychology in autobiography* (Vol. 4). Worcester, MA: Clark University Press.

Piaget, J. (1973). States of cognitive development. In R. I. Evans (Ed.), *Jean Piaget: The man and his ideas*. New York: Dutton.

Piaget, J. (1975). *L'equilibration des structures cognitives [The equilibrium of cognitive structures]*. Paris: Presses Universitaires de France.

Rogoff, B. (1981). Schooling and the development of cognitive skills. In H. C. Triandis & A. Heron (Eds.), *Handbook of cross-cultural psychology* (Vol. 4, pp. 233–294). Rockleigh, NJ: Allyn & Bacon.

Rogoff, B. (1990). *Apprenticeship in thinking: Cognitive development in social context*. Oxford, England: Oxford University Press.

Rogoff, B., & Chavajay, P. (1995). What's become of research on the cultural basis of cognitive development? *American Psychologist, 50*, 859–877.

Shatz, M., & Gelman, R. (1973). The development of communication skills: Modifications in the speech of young children as a function of listener. *Monographs of the Society for Research in Child Development, 38* (Serial 152).

Smith, L. (1991). Age, ability, and intellectual development in Piagetian theory. In M. Chandler & M. Chapman (Eds.), *Criteria for competence* (pp. 69–91). Hillsdale, NJ: Lawrence Erlbaum Associates.

Smith, L. (1993). *Necessary knowledge: Piagetian perspectives on constructivism*. Hillsdale, NJ: Lawrence Erlbaum Associates.

Wohlwill, J. F. (1970). The place of structured experience in early cognitive development. *Interchange, 1*, 13–27.

Chapter 10

Karl Duncker: Productive Problems With Beautiful Solutions

D. Brett King
Michaella Cox
Michael Wertheimer

The work of Karl Duncker has recently been rediscovered. In particular, cognitive psychologists have praised Duncker's 1945 monograph on problem solving and thinking, viewing it as a seminal contribution that is directly relevant to current work in the field. Little attention has been devoted to other aspects of Duncker's brief yet productive career; and no biography of him has yet been published, although Duncker was an intense, brilliant, innovative research psychologist who led an interesting but troubled personal life. He made lasting contributions to the psychology of productive thinking and to the perception of apparent movement, in particular induced motion. One of Duncker's mentors described Duncker's work as "concentrated on productive problems—with beautiful solutions" (Wertheimer, 1937b).

THE LIFE OF KARL DUNCKER

Karl Duncker was born February 2, 1903, in Leipzig, Germany, the son of a prominent Marxist educator and theorist. Little information is available about his childhood, upbringing, and early schooling.

Education

As a student at the University of Berlin, the most prestigious institution of higher education in German-speaking Europe, Duncker worked with Max Wertheimer and

---

* Photograph of Karl Duncker courtesy of Michael Wertheimer's collection.

Wolfgang Köhler (chaps. 13 & 17, *Pioneers I*), two of the founders of the Gestalt school of psychology. Probably because of this experience, he became an ardent and able disciple of Gestalt theory and was recognized as a worthy successor to these giants in the history of Gestalt psychology and as the most promising leader of the second generation of psychologists in that tradition.

In 1925 and 1926, Wolfgang Köhler, who then was professor of philosophy and director of the Psychological Institute at the University of Berlin, spent a year as a visiting professor at Clark University in Worcester, Massachusetts. One of the perquisites of this appointment was the opportunity to award a Clark University Fellowship to anyone Köhler selected; he chose Karl Duncker. As a consequence, Duncker's first advanced degree was not from a German university but from Clark—a master's degree that was awarded in 1926. Duncker's thesis, "A Qualitative Experimental and Theoretical Study of Productive Thinking," was approved by John Paul Nafe, who had obtained his doctoral degree from the leader of the structuralist school of psychology, Edward Bradford Titchener (chap. 7, *Pioneers I*), and had joined the Clark faculty in 1924. Because Nafe was strongly identified with the structuralist position—and because that position was fundamentally incompatible with Gestalt theory—it is unlikely that Nafe made major substantive contributions to Duncker's research. The content of the thesis was closely related to issues that Duncker had heard discussed by Wertheimer and Köhler during his studies at Berlin, and Duncker (1926, p. 645) noted that he was indebted to Köhler's (1917/1925) observations on intelligent behavior in apes and to an article by Wertheimer (1920) on productive thinking "Über Schlussprocesse im produktiven Denken" ("On Deductive Processes in Productive Thinking").

Duncker and Köhler were at Clark during an illustrious time in the history of the psychology department there. Although efforts were made to keep the atmosphere eclectic, the department was dominated by Walter S. Hunter's (chap. 18, *Pioneers I*) behavioristic orientation and Nafe's structuralist leanings. Apparently Duncker was not overly impressed by these then-prominent systems of American psychology. He was particularly critical of behaviorism. For example, in his thesis, Duncker wrote, "There is undoubtedly a high correlation between the stupidity of a problem solution and the possibility of explanation by behaviorist principles" (cited in Koelsch, 1990, p. 160). Although Duncker had the diplomatic sense to exclude this sentence when he published his thesis, two later articles (Duncker, 1927, 1932) contained blistering attacks on behaviorism.

After his year at Clark, Duncker returned to the Psychological Institute at the University of Berlin in 1926 and resumed research on issues central to Gestalt theory. His doctoral dissertation (Duncker, 1929) on induced motion made a brilliant contribution to the experimental psychology of apparent motion, which began with Wertheimer's (1912b) pioneer work on the phi phenomenon. We return to this point later in the chapter.

Early Career

After receiving his doctorate, Duncker continued as a research assistant to Köhler at the Psychological Institute at the University of Berlin. His studies, all conducted within the framework of Gestalt theory, focused primarily on learning and problem solving. They led to the publication of an article on "learning and insight in the service of goal attainment" (Duncker, 1935a). In that same year, Duncker (1935b) produced his classic book on problem solving, *Psychology of Productive Thought*. It was dedicated jointly to Köhler and Wertheimer, with whom Duncker worked closely until Wertheimer left Berlin for Frankfurt in 1929. Wertheimer's collaboration with, and respect for, Duncker continued despite the move to Frankfurt, as is evidenced in a letter Wertheimer wrote to Christian von Ehrenfels in 1929. Ehrenfels (1929) told Wertheimer that he was planning to write an essay on Gestalt theory after he turned age 70 (which would occur that June) and requested the fresh perspective of a scholar identified with the Gestalt school so that he would be better informed about its current perspectives and concerns. Wertheimer had just taken over the Frankfurt chair and felt that he could not serve in person as von Ehrenfels' tutor. Instead, he recommended two men whom he called two of the most promising of Köhler's assistants: Duncker and Wolfgang Metzger. However, both Duncker and Metzger were married and reluctant to leave home for the extended periods that would have been required to fulfill von Ehrenfels' request (Wertheimer, 1929). Thus, the contact between von Ehrenfels and one of the younger Gestalt scholars never did occur and von Ehrenfels died in 1932.

Wertheimer continued to correspond with and hold Duncker in high esteem. In an undated draft of a letter of recommendation that he wrote for Duncker, Wertheimer (n.d.-a) called Duncker's work on problem solving "fruitful, serious, and important." He wrote that Duncker "is not only talented and productive in science, but also with a wide knowledge of culture. Duncker is Köhler's and my favorite student and is the best among the younger psychologists." Köhler also expressed his high opinion of Duncker. When Duncker was contemplating going to America in 1930, he wrote to Wertheimer that Duncker was a good assistant and that he would "hate to see him go."

In the German system, aspiring academics were required to produce a second major work after the doctoral dissertation, the *habilitation thesis*. By 1930, Duncker had begun to prepare this thesis—it was to be on problem solving—but progress on it was slow. It was still unfinished in the summer of 1933, and Wertheimer (1933) wrote Duncker a strong letter urging him to complete it. Köhler too was concerned about the thesis; he wrote (Köhler, 1933) to Wertheimer that the current draft of the thesis was

a little incomprehensible. He undertook things for which he is not adequate in mathematics. His enormous intelligence leads him in all sorts of directions. He seems to have lost the main theme. It's unfortunate, because he is such a capable man (p. 1).

By April 1934, Köhler reported to Wertheimer that Duncker was making good progress on the habilitation thesis, was in fine health, and wanted to remain in Berlin.

Problems in the Political Climate

Duncker's career began at a time when the German academic system was undergoing a major upheaval because of the rising power of the Nazis. In response to that development, Wertheimer left Frankfurt for Czechoslovakia early in 1933 and moved to America late that summer, just before he was forced into retirement by the Nazis. Köhler also encountered threats from the Nazis beginning late in 1933. In March 1934 Köhler wrote to the American philosopher Ralph Barton Perry that good work is being done in Berlin, but "unfortunately my assistants have been in serious danger several times because of political denunciations—a denunciation a month is more or less our current rate; as yet, however, it has always been possible to save them" (cited in Henle, 1978, p. 941).

Köhler secured approval from the Rector of the University of Berlin, Eugen Fischer, to prevent the Institute from being searched. However, on April 24, 1934, Nazi storm troopers arrived with papers authorizing them to search the Psychological Institute. According to Henle (1978), the search produced evidence that was largely "suspicions, innuendoes, and accusations," and Duncker and two other assistants (Otto von Lauenstein and Hedwig von Restorff) were summarily dismissed—Duncker because two foreign newspapers were found on his desk (Koseleff, 1934). Köhler protested the action. In February 1935, he demanded that all three be reinstated because only they have the expert knowledge in the relevant special fields to make it possible for him as Director of the Institute to fulfill his responsibilities. His petition was denied. Duncker and von Lauenstein were accused of participating in anti-Nazi protests, and Duncker was characterized as acting in a "communistic manner," doubtless because of his father's communist connections (Ash, 1979). In September 1934, Köhler had lamented in a letter, "it is terrible how the Institute is so sad and collapsing." In a letter to Donald K. Adams, an American psychologist, Köhler had reported (cited in Henle, 1978, p. 944) that:

> The government has decided in May to dismiss all the assistants who were trained by me and in June, during the term, they were suddenly forbidden to continue their work and their teaching: Duncker, von Lauenstein and von Restorff.... I could not possibly remain as director without the help of my young friends.... My deepest anxiety refers to the assistants. I am not yet sure whether I shall be able to place them somewhere.

With his future threatened and his fate unclear, Duncker realized that he had to leave Germany (Duncker, 1934). Fully aware of Duncker's dire circumstances, Wertheimer, soon after his arrival in New York, tried to obtain a Rockefeller

Scholarship for Duncker at the New School for Social Research (Lederer, 1933) where he was teaching, but the effort did not come to fruition.

Duncker's Later Years

By February 1936, Duncker was working in the psychological laboratory of the University of Cambridge, England. The director of the laboratory was Sir Frederick Bartlett, Cambridge's first professor of experimental psychology and, at the time of Duncker's arrival, the editor of the influential *British Journal of Psychology*. Under Bartlett's supervision Duncker performed some research on pain, published in 1937. Late in 1936, Köhler wrote to Wertheimer that Duncker was not happy and expressed the wish that they could find him a position perhaps something like the chair that David Katz had managed to obtain at the University of Stockholm. Wertheimer (1936) had, in fact, tried to place Duncker in a post in Turkey, but the attempt had failed probably because Duncker had not yet completed his habilitation thesis.

Still later in 1936, Duncker spent time at an elegant 14th-century estate with gardens, trees, shrubs, and terraces, Dartington Hall. This establishment was owned and operated by Leonard Elmhirst, who had created an academic community there devoted to nature, the arts, "the individual as a whole" and research in such areas as farming, orchards, textiles, and quarrying. While he was there, Duncker (1938a) wrote on the social modification of British school children's food preferences.

By the summer of 1937, Duncker was suffering from severe bouts of depression. He was admitted for treatment to the clinic of the prominent psychiatrist Ludwig Binswanger at Kreuzlingen in Switzerland in August (Duncker, 1937b), although his English physicians did not favor this move (Wertheimer, 1937a). A friend of Duncker's and Wertheimer's, Lene Frank, arranged for Duncker's admission to Binswanger's clinic and warned that Duncker should not return to Germany because of stringent laws there requiring sterilization of patients with psychopathology. A letter from Köhler to Wertheimer (1937b) indicated that the physicians at Binswanger's clinic believed that Duncker's disorder was endogenous depression—a diagnosis supported by Binswanger (1937). Wertheimer (1937b) corresponded with Binswanger about the case and expressed guarded optimism about its prognosis.

During the 2 months that Duncker stayed with Binswanger in Switzerland, Wertheimer and Köhler (who had come to the United States in 1936) continued to struggle to find a post for him in America. A letter from Köhler (1937a) to Wertheimer mentioned the possibility of a position in Kentucky that would require Duncker to lecture for 12 to 14 hours a week, but understandably expressed concern that this would place Duncker under too much strain. Wertheimer (n.d., b) also drafted a letter to Köhler about a possible assistant professorship for Duncker at the New School for Social Research, but the prospects did not look promising. Late in October 1937, Köhler (1937b) wrote Wertheimer that Duncker had written him, informing him that Binswanger had released him from the clinic earlier that month, but Köhler was troubled by Duncker's letter: "I am not happy with the letter—there is an artificiality and correctness." He also reported that "Duncker would like to come to America right away but may not leave until December."

Köhler finally managed to arrange for Duncker's appointment as an instructor at the institution where he was teaching, Swarthmore College, for the fall semester of 1938. In December 1937, Köhler (1937c) wrote Wertheimer that Duncker would be arriving in New York by ship, but in the spring of 1938 was cautious about Duncker's status. In another letter to Wertheimer, he commented that, "I'm not sure whether Duncker is in order or well. This sharply thinking man occasionally makes errors in his discussion of things but remains effective in his investigations" (Köhler, 1938, p. 1). Köhler doubted that a major production can be expected soon. Duncker did continue to publish, although he was no longer as prolific as he had been earlier in his career. In 1939, he produced a paper on ethics, another on the influence of past experience on perception, and yet a third, co-authored with I. Krechevsky (later David Krech), on problem solving. Duncker and Krechevsky (1939) collaborated while the former was an instructor and the latter a research associate of Köhler at Swarthmore. Ironically, their joint publication appeared during Krech's brief and stormy appointment at the University of Colorado at Boulder, from which, like Duncker from Berlin, he was dismissed for political reasons (Krech, 1974). While he was at Swarthmore, Duncker (1938b) was also working on some larger issues of problem solving and hedonism.

Final Days

Back in 1928, long before her divorce from Duncker, Duncker's wife Gerda Naef (1928) wrote to Wertheimer with an ominous question: "Would you condemn a person who is unemployed and is in a hopeless business situation and who therefore takes his own life?" Clearly, depression and suicidal thoughts had been plaguing Duncker for at least a decade before he sought help from Binswanger at Kreuzlingen. In 1937, for example, Duncker (1937b) described his depression as a "veil of unreality over everything, especially the future." Köhler and Wertheimer had long been deeply worried about Duncker's mental health. Duncker did suffer from a series of what were then called *nervous breakdowns*, and in 1938 and 1939 the Köhlers took him into their home to keep an eye on him and care for him. His colleagues' concerns were indeed justified; he killed himself on February 23, 1940, less than a month after his 37th birthday. Köhler (1940) broke the news to Wertheimer in a letter:

> I have sad news—he is dead.... I had hoped to have him come live with us to get through this difficult time.... [I]n Baltimore he bought himself a weapon and was found Friday morning dead in his car. If he had stayed here I believe we could have

rescued him. What would his future have been like then? He was a superb person and a moving child. (p. 1)

Duncker's colleagues, although dismayed by Duncker's suicide, did what they could to save some of his unfinished work. Mary Henle and Herbert Spiegelberg edited Duncker's notes for a chapter on motivation into an article that was published in 1941 in *Philosophy and Phenomenological Research* (Duncker, 1941). Köhler oversaw the completion and publication of the English version of Duncker's 1935 book on problem solving in 1945 in *Psychological Monographs*. Köhler also arranged for the translation into English and the publication in *Philosophy and Phenomenological Research* of a paper by Duncker (1947) on the phenomenology and epistemology of consciousness of objects.

DUNCKER'S CONTRIBUTIONS TO PSYCHOLOGY

Karl Duncker tackled problems in a varied range of areas in psychology, sometimes spilling over into issues in philosophy. As his mentors had written, his was an exceedingly intelligent mind, well versed in a rich range of culture; he was also thoroughly fluent in several languages. His studies of problem solving and apparent motion are still widely cited today, more than a half century after his much too early death. He also did productive work on pain, an effect of past experience on taste perception, on motivation, and systematic psychology. These contributions are no longer well known, but deserve to be recognized as well. Consider first the work for which Duncker is currently receiving extensive acclaim among cognitive psychologists—his studies of problem solving.

The Psychology of Productive Thinking

Duncker's first publication—when he was only 23 years old—was his 1926 master's thesis, completed at Clark University, entitled "A Qualitative Experimental and Theoretical Study of Productive Thinking (Solving of Comprehensible Problems)." It already contains, in preliminary form, many of the ideas that were to receive a fuller treatment in his later works in the field. In the research for his master's thesis, Duncker had five students at Clark University work through a series of 20 different tasks. No doubt the most famous of these problems is the *radiation problem*. Suppose that a patient is suffering from an inoperable stomach tumor but that a physician has access to a type of ray machine that destroys organic tissue when the rays are of sufficient intensity. How could the physician destroy the tumor without at the same time damaging the healthy tissue around the tumor? One possible solution is to use a broad beam of weak rays that are brought to a focus with adequate intensity at the site of the tumor. Duncker's methodology included what is now called *verbal protocols*; during the experiment, he (1926) encouraged the participants to *"Try to think aloud.* I guess you often do so when you are alone and working on a problem. And draw as much as possible" (p. 664).

The more mature 1935 monograph, the now classic *Psychology of Productive Thinking* (the English version of which was published in 1945), was dedicated to his mentors Köhler and Wertheimer. In it, Duncker reported on an extensive series of experiments with a variety of mathematical and practical problems and methods similar to those in his 1926 thesis. Newell (1985) designated the 1926 and 1935 (1945) works as landmarks in the history of the study of problem solving and the history of cognitive psychology.

The 1935 (1945) book was divided into three main sections: (a) the structure and dynamics of problem-solving processes; (b) insight, learning, and simple finding (what might today be called *retrieval*); and (c) the fixedness of thought material. Newell observed that the third section, on *functional fixedness,* has generated the most attention among psychologists. Once one realizes that a particular item in a problem context can be used to solve a particular problem in a certain way, it is hard to see how that item could be used productively in another way in the context of a different problem. Newell (1985) wrote that this section

> is the smallest part of the monograph—twenty-six pages vs. forty-five and thirty-four, respectively, for the first two parts. Yet it had by far the largest impact. Functional fixity generated one of the major streams of research in problem solving until the shift in the mid-1950's to information processing. (p. 413)

The content and nature of Duncker's work can be viewed as a close outgrowth of Wertheimer's approach. Although Wertheimer's major book, *Productive Thinking*, was not published until 1945, Wertheimer had been conducting research on problem solving even before Duncker came to Berlin in the 1920s. Wertheimer (1945) explicitly mentioned "an investigation of the blinding effects of mechanical repetition in sequences of assigned tasks" (p. 131) that Duncker and Karl Zener conducted under Wertheimer's supervision at the Berlin Institute in 1924.

From the early 1920s, Wertheimer had distinguished between what he called *reproductive* and *productive thinking.* The former involved blind, rote memorization of the solutions to problems, whereas the latter involved insight and understanding. Duncker made the same distinction in his contrast between two types of problem solving: mechanical (analysis from below) and organic (analysis from above). He wrote (1945) that those who merely search their

> memory for a "solution of that such-and-such problem" may remain just as blind to the inner nature of the problem-situation before [them] as [persons] who, instead of thinking [themselves, refer] the problem to an intelligent acquaintance or to an encyclopedia. Truly, these methods are not to be despised; for they have a certain heuristic value, and one can arrive at solutions in that fashion. But such problem solving has little to do with thinking. (p. 20)

Duncker published two other articles on thinking that appear to have been neglected by contemporary psychologists. One, published in 1935 in German entitled "Learning and Insight in the Service of Goal Attainment," follows along the lines of Wertheimer's attempts to establish a Gestalt logic, as in his article on reasoning in productive thinking. A second article, co-authored by Krechevsky (chap. 18, this volume), was published in 1939 in English in the *Psychological Review*. Entitled simply "On Solution-Achievement," it attempted to bridge some theoretical gaps and elucidate the similarities and differences between Edward C. Tolman's (chap. 15, *Pioneers* I) and the Gestalt approaches to learning and thinking. Drawing on Krechevsky's work with Tolman on acquisition and on Duncker's work on thinking, Duncker and Krechevsky concluded that some unifying themes characterize both approaches. They wrote (1939) that:

> Where Krechevsky and Tolman speak of means-end-readiness at its most generalized level, Duncker speaks of range; where in the formal analysis, the term hypothesis is used, Duncker has the somewhat corresponding concept of specific solution. Both analyses describe the process of solution-achievement as involving an hierarchical succession of reductions or specifications.... Finally, both analyses consider the phenomenon of fixation and its inhibiting influence on problem solving. (p. 182)

In addition to proposing a synthesis of the psychologies of learning and thinking, the article clarifies certain specific parallels between Tolman's influential theory and Gestalt theory. All in all, Duncker's publications on thinking provide creative extensions of Köhler's and Wertheimer's—as well as Tolman's—work in the field and are now recognized for their seminal quality. Many of the concepts and methods of modern cognitive psychology have their counterparts a half century or more earlier in the writings of Karl Duncker.

The Perception of Motion

A number of Duncker's experiments done at Berlin during the 1920s were devoted to the perception of movement, especially of apparent motion, following on and complementing Wertheimer's (1912b) article on the apparent motion of two actually stationary but successively exposed stimuli. Among the most brilliant of these studies was Duncker's dissertation, published in 1929 in the "house organ" of the Gestalt school, *Psychologische Forschung*. Entitled "Concerning Induced Movement (A Contribution to the Theory of Visually Perceived Movement)," it contained reports on numerous experiments devoted to the common theme that when there is relative displacement between an object and its framework, the framework is typically perceived as relatively stationary while the object contained in the framework is perceived as moving. A common example of this phenomenon is the impression one gets—when looking through a stationary train's window while "sitting in a railway coach and a nearby train moves—that one's own train is moving in the opposite direction" (Duncker 1929/1950, p. 161). Another instance of the same phenomenon is the apparent motion of the moon when it is seen through moving broken clouds at night. A standard experimental procedure that Duncker used in his investigations was to project a small spot of light onto a large piece of cardboard suspended vertically a meter or so in front of the observer, who was asked to keep the gaze fixed on the spot. Duncker (1929/1950) found that:

> When the cardboard was moved back and forth [from the observer's left to right or right to left], the fixated spot appeared to move also but in the opposite direction. If the light point itself is occasionally set in motion also (either with or against the cardboard), it is impossible to tell at any given moment whether the point *is* objectively moving or not. It is only when two light points are used—one objectively moving and the other at rest—that the difference can be detected. (p. 161)

Yet another striking demonstration of the *frame of reference* effect in induced apparent motion involves suspending a bicycle wheel horizontally above an observer and hanging a cloth sheet from the rim of the wheel in such a way that the observer is, in effect, encased inside a vertical cylinder; some vertical black stripes are attached to the inside of the otherwise white cylinder. If the bicycle wheel is now rotated slowly in one direction, observers soon obtain the eerie but compelling impression that the cylinder is stationary but that they are rotating in the opposite direction. This illusion of apparent induced motion is so strong that it readily overcomes the contradictory information provided by the observer's inner ear mechanisms to the effect that the observer's body is actually stationary. These convincing demonstrations of the effects of context on perceived motion are still frequently referred to in technical discussions of perception and even in introductory psychology textbooks.

Studies of Pain

At the instigation of the director of the Cambridge psychology laboratory, Sir Frederick Bartlett, Duncker performed some preliminary studies there on the mutual influence of pain. Duncker again chose the premier Gestalt journal, *Psychologische Forschung*, as his publication outlet for a report on the experiments. Although the preliminary nature of the studies was acknowledged in the title of the article, which appeared in 1937, the article is still cited fairly often in the medical literature. In the introduction, Duncker observed that (1937a) that:

> In the dentist's chair many people pinch themselves when pain arises in the tooth operated upon, and in olden days when modern anesthetics were not yet discovered it was one of the critical functions of the dentist's assistant to pinch the patient at the critical moment. Other patients get themselves, or one of their limbs, into a state of high muscular tension, convulsively clenching their fists, pressing against some available resistance. ...A similar role seems to be played by screaming. (p. 311)

Thus, perhaps somewhat paradoxically, some relief from one pain may be obtained by intentional exposure to a second pain. For one experiment, Duncker constructed two levers. A blunt nail facing downward was attached to the end of each one. He pressed hard on an observer's forearm with one nail and, after a certain time interval, pressed hard with the second nail at a spot on the participant's forearm near where the first nail was continuing to be pressed down. Many participants reported a substantial decrement in the pain produced by the first nail following the application of the second nail. Duncker also reported a related experiment (1937a) that he performed on himself:

> Applying a nail on one of my arms and intermittently pinching the skin with a pair of pincers some 10 cm. away on the same arm I obtained the following striking experience: by applying the pincers the pain was "drained away" from the nail to which it "flowed back" as soon as the pincers released their grip. (pp. 318–319)

Effect of Past Experience on Perception

An article on the role of past experience in perception was published in 1939, this time in the prestigious *American Journal of Psychology* rather than in his customary outlet, *Psychologische Forschung*, which had suspended publication because of the dire international political situation at the time. The studies reported in the article concerned the interaction of perceived color and taste as mediated by past experience. In one experiment, blindfolded participants first tasted a piece of brown milk chocolate and then a piece of white chocolate, and then were asked to describe their experience. The blindfolds were removed and all participants again tasted the brown and then the white chocolate. When the participants were able to see the white chocolate, they reported that it tasted milkier than the brown, although during the blindfolded tasting they had rated the white chocolate as less flavorful than the brown. Duncker concluded that the findings were doubtless the result of the past experience that whiteness is associated with milkiness. He cautioned (1939b) that:

> There is a great variety of cases in which past experience comes in but does no more than supply conditions for other factors to work upon. It sets, as it were, the stage for the dynamics of forces which in themselves have nothing to do with past experience or learning (at least not with the learning that set the stage). (p. 265)

This passage succinctly states the Gestalt position on the role of past experience in perception. It could have been written as readily by any of the major Gestalt theorists—by Kurt Koffka, by Wolfgang Köhler, by Max Wertheimer, or by the field theorist Kurt Lewin (chap. 7, this volume)—as by Karl Duncker.

Writings on Systematic Psychology

A side of Duncker that is unfamiliar to many psychologists is his interest in and involvement with the systematic psychology of his time. Duncker's career flourished during a time when systematic psychology was a salient concern of almost all psychologists. It was a time of vigorous controversy among the major schools of psychology: structuralism, behaviorism, functionalism, Gestalt theory, and psychoanalysis. The Gestalt school, with which Duncker was closely identified, was widely viewed at that time as the arch enemy of behaviorism. Indeed the behaviorists (and several psychologists affiliated with other schools such as structuralism) frequently accused the Gestalt psychologists of vagueness and mysticism, arguing that their phenomenological and holistic approach lacked any experimental support or scientific value. Duncker's experimental work can be viewed as an elegant response to such accusations—as a demonstration of the feasibility of experimental phenomenology, the experimental investigation of naive subjective experience. For example, Duncker's work on pain, the effect of past experience on the apparent taste of chocolate, and apparent motion are not instances of muddy speculation or mystical vagueness. They are convincing demonstrations of concrete, experimentally induced phenomena.

Although these contributions to the systematic psychology of the time were only implicit, Duncker did not hesitate to enter the fray explicitly, and he was among the more effective advocates of Gestalt theory in these battles. As early as in his master's thesis, mentioned earlier in this chapter, he had speculated about the "high correlation between the stupidity of a problem solution and the possibility of explanation by behavioristic principles." Elsewhere in that document (1926), he criticized the behaviorist John B. Watson's proposals for how to go about solving problems—by bringing to bear one's previous manual or verbal organization upon the present problem, or by manipulating words as a poet does, shifting them about until a new pattern is hit upon—as not worth serious consideration. He was especially critical of the conditioned reflex as an explanation for problem solving (1926): "In view of the theory of probability, how could a number of isolated elements which necessarily have an enormous variety of associated traces in common lead to one of the few definite arrangements of traits, constituting appropriate solutions?" (p. 663) In a 1927 article in German, in which Duncker identified behaviorism as *the* American psychology and tried to present the major tenets of that school, he found that he could not avoid making comments that were sharply critical. In another German article published in 1932, he presented a critical analysis of Rudolf Carnap's work on "psychology in physicalistic [behavioristic] language." Although he congratulated Carnap for having written the best apology yet available for behaviorism, he took Carnap to task for ignoring subjective experience as well as the then-salient Gestalt concept of *isomorphism*: the structural identity between what is experienced and the brain correlate of that experience. Rather than accepting the reductionism and mechanism of behaviorism, Duncker argued, one must recognize the heuristic value of self-observation (phenomenology) in psychology.

Duncker co-authored two somewhat obscure books with an American industrialist, Donald Bates Watt, with Duncker as the senior author (Duncker & Watts,

1929, 1930). Both volumes were intended to help Americans read scientific psychology in German. The first contained interlinear translations of difficult German words into English. The second, clearly a supplement to the first, was an ambitious German–English dictionary that contained some 7,000 psychological terms. The 1929 book was a fairly accurate portrayal of Gestalt psychology—both theory and experiment—which was available to American students some 6 years before Koffka's (1935) more systematic and thorough volume. It summarized the then-extant Gestalt research on such topics as learning, sensation, perception, and memory in a reasonably succinct and comprehensible manner. Duncker and Watt probably based the book on lectures that Duncker had heard Köhler and Wertheimer give in Berlin and on reading done under their direction. However, Duncker showed more openness than his teachers. The last section of the book presents a relatively positive discussion of the psychoanalysts Sigmund Freud and Alfred Adler, to whom Köhler and Wertheimer were vehemently opposed.

Work on Motivation

Duncker's contributions to the psychology of motivation were both experimental and theoretical. Results of studies on the influence of social suggestion and prestige on English children's food preferences were published in 1938 in the *Journal of Abnormal and Social Psychology*. In one experiment, British school children listened to a story featuring a protagonist who was fond of one type of food (actually objectively a rather aversive one) but hated another kind. Although the hero's preferred food was inherently less attractive, children turned out to be more likely to modify their food preferences to match those of the hero. In another experiment, Duncker found that if a respected peer showed a strong liking for an unpleasant food, children were likely to change their preferences to match the peer's preference. Such findings led Duncker to conclude that social suggestion and the prestige of an actual or symbolic model can produce a genuine reevaluation of food preferences. Duncker's experimental investigations of the effects of social suggestion and prestige on preferences or opinions were, incidentally, among the earliest in what was to become an immense literature on this topic during the 1940s and 1950s.

A book about motivation on which Duncker was working was never completed. Fellow Gestalt psychologist Mary Henle edited a draft of a chapter for this book after Duncker died, and had it published in the journal *Philosophy and Phenomenological Research* under the title "On Pleasure, Emotion, and Striving" (Duncker, 1941). The article analyzed the hedonist and hormist (or purposivist) positions on the nature of pleasure, emotion, striving, and desire, and it discussed the component parts of pleasure, desire, and joy. Duncker found some positive features and some deficiencies in both the hedonist and hormist orientations, but offered no resolution or synthesis of the issues.

Duncker did finish an article on ethical relativity and the psychology of ethics, which was published in 1939 in *Mind.* In that article, Duncker (1939a) offered difficult but intriguing criticisms of the standard arguments for ethical relativism and, like his mentors Köhler and Wertheimer, opted for a position of ethical invariance that "does not apply to any given historical content of morality, but exclusively to the relationship between ethical variation and situational meanings" (p. 51). Duncker's discussion ranges across a variety of examples, including the practice of collecting interest on debts, clothing styles, and infanticide, all of which have different ethical interpretations in different cultures. The style of the entire article, one of Duncker's last publications, is hauntingly reminiscent of the style of the exercise in psychological anthropology in Wertheimer's (1912a) account of quantitative reasoning in indigenous people, which was among the first publications of Gestalt psychology.

CLOSING COMMENT

Despite a time of political and social upheaval that ended in World War II, an unsuccessful marriage that ended in divorce, consuming self-doubt, and severe psychopathology that ended in suicide, Karl Duncker—in his brief life of only 37 years—made substantial contributions in an astonishingly broad array of psychology's subfields. In a now-classic study of eminent contributors to psychology (Annin, Boring, & Watson, 1968), he received a high rating as one of the more eminent among 500 deceased psychologists. He is recognized today for his creative work in problem solving, cognitive psychology, and the psychology of the perception of apparent movement, and deserves to be recognized as well for his work on pain, the role of past experience in perception, systematic psychology, phenomenology, and motivation. Although much younger than his teachers Kurt Koffka, Wolfgang Köhler, and Max Wertheimer, he died before any of them. More than a half century after his death, Karl Duncker's work remains an inspiring example of responsible, creative, and dedicated psychological scholarship at its best. As Köhler (cited in Duncker, 1945) wrote in the preface to the posthumous publication of the English translation of Duncker's monograph on problem solving, "In Duncker this was the greatest intellectual virtue: He was forever impatient of little things and happy only when he found a way that led to fundamentals. The best we can do in remembering our friend is to give his work as an example which others may follow" (p. iv).

ACKNOWLEDGMENTS

Earlier versions of some of the material in this chapter were presented at conventions in 1991 of the Rocky Mountain Psychological Association and the American Psychological Association.

REFERENCES

Annin, E. L., Boring, E. G., & Watson, R. I. (1968). Important psychologists: 1600–1967. *Journal of the History of the Behavioral Sciences, 4*, 303–315.

Ash, M. G. (1979). The struggle against the Nazis. *American Psychologist, 34*, 363–364.

Binswanger, L. (1937, September 27). *Letter to Max Wertheimer.* Max Wertheimer Archives, University of Colorado, Boulder, CO.

Duncker, K. (1926). A qualitative experimental and theoretical study of productive thinking (solving of comprehensible problems). *Pedagogical Seminary, 33*, 642–708.

Duncker, K. (1927). Der Behaviorismus—die amerikanische psychologie [Behaviorism—The American psychology]. *Pädagogisches Zentralblatt, 7*, 690–702.

Duncker, K. (1929). Über induzierte Bewegung (Ein Beitrag zur Theorie optisch wahrgenommener Bewegung) [Concerning induced movement (A contribution to the theory of visually perceived movement)]. *Psychologische Forschung, 12*, 180–259.

Duncker, K. (1932). Behaviorismus und Gestaltpsychologie. Kritische Bemerkungen zu Carnaps Psychologie in physikalischer Sprache [Behaviorism and Gestalt psychology. Critical comments on Carnap's psychology in physicalistic language]. *Erkenntnis, 3*, 162–176.

Duncker, K. (1934, September 30). *Letter to Max Wertheimer.* Max Wertheimer Archives, University of Colorado, Boulder, CO.

Duncker, K. (1935a). Lernen und Einsicht im Dienst der Zielerreichungen [Learning and insight in the service of goal attainment]. *Acta Psychologica, Hague, 1*, 77–82.

Duncker, K. (1935b). Zur Psychologie des produktiven Denkens [Psychology of productive thought]. Berlin: Springer.

Duncker, K. (1937a). Some preliminary experiments on the mutual influence of pain. *Psychologische Forschung, 21*, 311–326.

Duncker, K. (1937b, August 20). *Letter to Max Wertheimer.* Max Wertheimer Archives, University of Colorado, Boulder, CO.

Duncker, K. (1938a). Experimental modification of children's food preferences through social suggestion. *Journal of Abnormal and Social Psychology, 33*, 489–507.

Duncker, K. (1938b, March 22). *Letter to Max Wertheimer.* Max Wertheimer Archives, University of Colorado, Boulder, CO.

Duncker, K. (1939a). Ethical relativity? (An enquiry into the psychology of ethics). *Mind, 48*, 39–57.

Duncker, K. (1939b). The influence of past experience upon perceptual properties. *American Journal of Psychology, 52*, 255–265.

Duncker, K. (1941). On pleasure, emotion, and striving. *Philosophy and Phenomenological Research, 1*, 391–430.

Duncker, K. (1945). On problem solving (L. S. Lees, Trans.). *Psychological Monographs, 58 (Whole No. 270)*. (Original work published 1935)

Duncker, K. (1947). Phenomenology and epistemology of consciousness of objects. (L. Haessler, Trans.). *Philosophy and Phenomenological Research, 7*, 505–542.

Duncker, K. (1950). Induced motion. In W. D. Ellis (Ed.), *A source book of Gestalt psychology*, (pp. 161–172). New York: Humanities Press. (Original work published 1929)

Duncker, K., & Krechevsky, I. (1939). On solution-achievement. *Psychological Review, 46*, 176–185.

Duncker, K., & Watt, D. B. (1929). *Exercises for the rapid reading of scientific German psychological text (with interlinear translation of difficult words)*. Ann Arbor, MI: Edwards Brothers.

Duncker, K., & Watt, D. B. (1930). *A German-English dictionary of psychological terms*. Ann Arbor, MI: Edwards Brothers.

Ehrenfels, C. von. (1929, April 29). *Letter to Max Wertheimer.* Max Wertheimer Archives, University of Colorado, Boulder, CO.

Henle, M. (1978). One man against the Nazis: Wolfgang Köhler. *American Psychologist, 33*, 939–944.

Koelsch, W. A. (1990). The "magic decade" revisited: Clark psychology in the twenties and thirties. *Journal of the History of the Behavioral Sciences, 26*, 151–175.

Koffka, K. (1935). *Principles of Gestalt psychology.* New York: Harcourt, Brace.

Köhler, W. (1925). *The mentality of apes* (E. Winter, Trans.). New York: Harcourt, Brace. (Original work published 1917)

Köhler, W. (1933, May 14). *Letter to Max Wertheimer.* Max Wertheimer Archives, University of Colorado, Boulder, CO.

Köhler, W. (1936, December 24). *Letter to Max Wertheimer.* Max Wertheimer Archives, University of Colorado, Boulder, CO.

Köhler, W. (1937a, August 6). *Letter to Max Wertheimer.* Max Wertheimer Archives, University of Colorado, Boulder, CO.

Köhler, W. (1937b, October 27). *Letter to Max Wertheimer.* Max Wertheimer Archives, University of Colorado, Boulder, CO.

Köhler, W. (1937c, December 11). *Letter to Max Wertheimer.* Max Wertheimer Archives, University of Colorado, Boulder, CO.

Köhler, W. (1938, May 8). *Letter to Max Wertheimer.* Max Wertheimer Archives, University of Colorado, Boulder, CO.

Köhler, W. (1940, February 25). *Letter to Max Wertheimer.* Max Wertheimer Archives, University of Colorado, Boulder, CO.

Koseleff, P. (1934, May 13). *Letter to Max Wertheimer.* Max Wertheimer Archives, University of Colorado, Boulder, CO.

Krech, D. (1974). David Krech. In G. Lindzey (Ed.), *A history of psychology in autobiography* (Vol. 6, pp. 219–250). New York: Appleton-Century-Crofts.

Lederer, E. (1933, November 16). *Letter to Max Wertheimer.* Max Wertheimer Archives, University of Colorado, Boulder, CO.

Naef, G. (1928, July 14). *Letter to Max Wertheimer.* Max Wertheimer Archives, University of Colorado, Boulder, CO.

Newell, A. (1985). Duncker on thinking: An inquiry into progress in cognition. In S. Koch & D. Leary (Eds.), *A century of psychology as science* (pp. 392–419). New York: McGraw-Hill.

Wertheimer, M. (1912a). Über das Denken der Naturvölker: I. Zahlen und Zahlgebilde [On the thinking of indigenous people: I. Numbers and number patterns]. *Zeitschrift für Psychologie, 60*, 321–378.

Wertheimer, M. (1912b). Experimentelle Studien über das Sehen von Bewegung [Experimental studies of the seeing of movement]. *Zeitschrift für Psychologie, 61*, 161–265.

Wertheimer, M. (1920). *Über Schlussprocesse im produktiven Denken* [On deductive processes in productive thinking]. Berlin: De Gruyter.

Wertheimer, M. (1929, May 31). *Letter to Christian von Ehrenfels.* Max Wertheimer Archives, University of Colorado, Boulder, CO.

Wertheimer, M. (1933, August 30). *Letter to Karl Duncker.* Max Wertheimer Archives, University of Colorado, Boulder, CO.

Wertheimer, M. (1936, September 13). *Letter to Alexander Rüstow.* Max Wertheimer Archives, University of Colorado, Boulder, CO.

Wertheimer, M. (1937a). *Letter to Wolfgang Köhler.* Max Wertheimer Archives, University of Colorado, Boulder, CO.

Wertheimer, M. (1937b, September 1). *Letter to Ludwig Binswanger.* Max Wertheimer Archives, University of Colorado, Boulder, CO.

Wertheimer, M. (1945). *Productive thinking.* New York: Harper.

Wertheimer, M. (n.d., a). *Letter of recommendation for Karl Duncker.* Max Wertheimer Archives, University of Colorado, Boulder, CO.

Wertheimer, M. (n.d., b). *Letter to Wolfgang Köhler.* Max Wertheimer Archives, University of Colorado, Boulder, CO.

Chapter 11

Milton Erickson: Scientist, Hypnotist, Healer

Harold Schiffman

Throughout history, the study of hypnosis has been a perilous career choice for a scientist to make. Mesmer's reputation was shattered by the conclusions of a blue ribbon committee, commissioned by the King of France in 1784, to examine Mesmer's claims. Many of Charcot's admirers deserted him when he shifted to the study of hypnotism. The reputation of John Elliotson (1843), a noted English surgeon, was ruined by his use of hypnotically induced anesthesia. James Esdaile (1847), a physician with impeccable credentials, was denied a scientific career because of his use of hypnosis in surgery. In addition to its negative effects on careers, this unfavorable attitude about this phenomenon impeded research on hypnosis. Sigmund Freud gave it up because of skepticism within the medical community and his difficulties with hypnotic induction. Freud's one-time disciple C. G. Jung abandoned hypnosis because he could not control or understand its power. Although some early work in this area was done by James, Prince, Janet, and others, hypnosis had no credibility in any of the major paradigms of clinical science and practice. It is therefore ironic that, in the 1920s, the major serious investigator of hypnosis was a man who was to become an influential learning theorist, Clark L. Hull (1933).

Milton Erickson's study of hypnosis began when, as a sophomore at the University of Wisconsin, Madison, he witnessed a demonstration of hypnosis by Hull. Erickson began hypnotizing friends, relatives, and almost anyone he encountered and became an expert in this discipline. In the fall of 1923, Hull offered a graduate seminar on hypnosis at Wisconsin and Erickson, now a junior at that institution, was invited to participate and demonstrate his findings on hypnotic phenomena. Although Hull appreciated his student's extraordinary gifts, there were

---

* Photograph of Milton Erickson courtesy of The Milton Erickson Foundation.

major differences in their conceptions of the process. These differences, of which perhaps the most important was that Hull wanted to standardize hypnotic methods and Erickson did not, inhibited further collaboration. Hull went on to Yale, where his interests turned in other directions (see chap. 14, *Pioneers I*, for Hull's own interpretation of the reasons). At roughly that same time, Erickson began a meteoric rise in his career as a master in the field of hypnosis.

BIOGRAPHICAL INFORMATION

Milton Erickson was born on December 5, 1901, in the small farm town of Aurum, Nevada. Soon after his birth, the family moved to a rural area in Wisconsin. Erickson's early childhood was physically difficult. He was almost completely color blind and had serious hearing difficulties. He was so completely tone deaf that he perceived singing as yelling. In addition to these sensory problems, he suffered from dyslexia, which produced confusions in meaning and affected his speech pattern. At the age of 17, Erickson contracted poliomyelitis, which left him severely paralyzed. He lost all bodily sensations to the extent that he did not even know where his legs were. Although the prognosis was that Erickson would be bedridden for life, after 10 years of effort he recovered sufficiently to walk with a limp. As a result of these experiences, Erickson developed keen observational powers and became an expert at interpreting gestures, facial dynamics, and other nonverbal stimuli. This talent, along with formal training in medicine, gave him an uncanny ability to diagnose and swiftly initiate unique therapeutic plans for his patients. In 1953, at the age of 52, Erickson had a second bout with polio that confined him to a wheelchair, restricted the use of his hands and mouth, affected his lungs, and left him with continuous pain for the remainder of his life. Despite these immense challenges, Erickson's passion for the study of hypnosis continued unabated. By the end of his junior year as a psychology major at Wisconsin, he had already hypnotized many hundreds of people and carried out large numbers of experiments. Knowledge of his expertise spread and he was invited to demonstrate hypnosis at Mendota State Hospital for the medical staff and psychologists.

Advanced Education and Career

After graduating from the University of Wisconsin, Erickson attended medical school at the University of Colorado and received the MD degree in 1928. After an internship at the Colorado Psychopathic Hospital, he first took positions at the Rhode Island State Hospital and, soon thereafter, at the Worcester (Massachusetts) State Hospital. At Worcester, Erickson continued his experimental and clinical work and published a number of significant papers dealing with various psychiatric problems. After 4 years at Worcester, he took a position as Director of Psychiatric

Research and Training at Wayne County General Hospital and Infirmary in Eloise, Michigan, in 1934. He also had joint appointments at Wayne State University College of Medicine and Michigan State University.

In July 1948, at the age of 46, after many years of illness and severe allergies, he left his university career and began a private practice in Phoenix, Arizona. For a time, he served as a Clinical Director and Assistant Superintendent of the Arizona State Hospital, and he spent the remainder of his life in Phoenix. For the last 28 years until his death on March 25, 1980, Erickson remained active, effective, and creative, giving lectures and demonstrations, consulting, and doing therapy. Initially his work had consisted primarily of experimental studies, but in the latter part of his career it became more applied to psychotherapy (Haley, 1985).

HYPNOTIC ALTERATION
OF SENSORY PROCESSES

Erickson (Erickson & Erickson, 1938) knew that hypnosis could effect transformations in cognitive and perceptual processes, but whether it could produce hallucinations of genuine color perceptions was problematic. He demonstrated that his hypnotized research participants did hallucinate colors and validated the authenticity of these effects by showing that the induced colors of red, blue, yellow, and green produced appropriate negative afterimages. Erickson's (1939b) further research on visual perception included a series of demonstrations that color blindness could be induced hypnotically. In these studies, his measuring device was the well-known Ishihara Color Blindness Test. This test presents participants with a series of plates with colored dots arranged to form different numerals. The correct identification of these numerals requires normal color vision.

Erickson believed that for people who are color blind for physiological reasons, colors are truly nonexistent; they elicit no associations and have no meaning. To demonstrate that the same is true of hypnotically induced color blindness, he designed a procedure that provided participants with amnesia for a chosen color and for its associations and connotations. This procedure led to an amusing finding on a subject to whom red blindness had been suggested. Because in the standard Ishihara test red is displayed as the number 3, when this individual was asked to count the number of fingers on both of his hands he was unable to do so unless he counted them by 2s. The number 3 was simply unavailable to him for his counting. As this participant put it, "The number 3 is red to me. I can't see a 3 or even think of it without thinking or feeling or seeing red" (Erickson, 1939b).

Erickson (e.g., 1928, 1938) also did pioneer experimental and clinical studies in other sensory modalities and demonstrated that partial, selective, and total deafness could all be induced. One set of experiments explored hypnotically induced deafness with a classical conditioning technique. The unconditioned response in these experiments was a contraction of the flexor muscle of the forearm elicited by electric shock (the unconditioned stimulus). The conditioned stimulus, which preceded the shock, was the sound of a loud buzzer. The conditioned response was a contraction of the flexor muscle induced by the buzzer prior to the delivery of the shock. With the aid of this procedure, Erickson showed that, when subjects were in a state of hypnotically induced deafness, the conditioned reaction was inhibited—the buzzer failed to elicit the flexor contraction. When normal hearing was reinstated, however, conditioning was disinhibited and the conditioned response reappeared.

HYPNOTIC ALTERATIONS
OF PHYSIOLOGICAL PROCESSES

In dealing with modifications of physiological processes by hypnotic means, Erickson activated physiological responses by suggesting appropriate stimuli, and he believed that these hallucinations had the status of reality. For example, he was able to increase the salivary response by the hypnotic hallucination of fudge (Erickson, 1943). He induced increases and decreases in the temperature of a subject's hand by creating the hallucination of immersing it in hot or cold water (Erickson, 1977).

Because Erickson spent most of his own life in extreme pain, it is not surprising that he gave serious attention to the analysis and hypnotherapy of pain (Erickson, 1959a, 1966). He viewed pain as a joint function of past-remembered pain, presently experienced pain, and pain anticipated in the future. In Erickson's view, present pain is intensified both by remembered pain and by the threat of future pain. He developed numerous procedures for handling pain, including hypnotic suggestion for total abolishment of pain and (with the aid of time distortion and amnesia), shortening the duration of present pain, and extending pain-free time when the pain is interrupted.

The following illustrates the latter method. In one case, Erickson used time distortion to ease the agony of a patient with chronic cycles of intractable pain whose frame of mind between attacks of pain was fearful dread of the next episode. Employing hypnosis, Erickson made the patient amnesic for every pain occurrence so that subsequent attacks came as a surprise. In addition, he used time distortion to shorten the perceived duration of the pain period to about 10 seconds. This treatment transformed the patient's affective state of chronic terror to one of relative peace.

On another occasion, a young man reported that his migraine headaches were invariably preceded by nausea and severe vomiting. Once started, the pain of the migraine could not be reduced and it would incapacitate the patient for days. In this situation, Erickson did not deal directly with the pain, but rather interrupted the process that led to the pain. He hypnotized this patient and suggested that he would now find it impossible to vomit. Aroused from the trance, the patient tried to vomit but reported that, "I always vomit when I am about to have a migraine and I am sure I had all the warnings signs this morning. But if I can't vomit, perhaps I won't have [the migraine]" (Erickson, 1936).

TIME DISTORTION

Later on, Erickson applied his work on the hypnotic expansion and compression of time to learning, memory, acquisition of a skill, and other complex functions. Hypnotized subjects received instructions to perform some task—in one case, the task of counting the number of jelly beans in a bag for 10 minutes. The normal rate of counting is approximately 59 beans per minute. However, one hypnotized individual reported counting 401 beans in only 10-seconds. This person reported that during the 10 second interval:

> he counted 401 candies, made piles of individually colored beans, noting that some fell on the floor, that they were predominantly yellow, and he had counted them one by one without hurrying, counting for what seemed to be about eight minutes. (Cooper & Erickson, 1950, pp. 51–52)

Erickson was also interested in whether time distortion could be used to aid the learning of a skill (e.g., playing a musical instrument). In one case (Cooper & Erickson, 1950), a participant who imagined practicing the violin for just 10 seconds while in a trance state, reported that: (a) she practiced in several different ways, (b) she marked and practiced spots that needed work and extra practice, (c) she played the whole composition for continuity, and (d) her memory for the piece and her skill in playing it increased dramatically.

THE PSYCHOPATHOLOGY OF EVERYDAY LIFE

Erickson demonstrated that trance behavior mimics everyday experiences, especially in connection with remembering and forgetting. His work on amnesia (Erickson & Rossi, 1974) anticipated the idea of state-dependent memory. In one study, he hypnotized a patient and suggested that what went on in the office could be recalled, but only there in the office. On leaving the office, the patient was amnesic for the events that took place in the office but, when the patient reentered the office, the memory returned. Erickson reported that trance-induced amnesia for certain events may remain in effect for years and is usually impenetrable to psychoanalysis and deep psychotherapy.

In 1933, in a seminar sponsored by the eminent anthropologist Edward Sapir, Erickson (1939a) used hypnosis to give a particularly dramatic set of demonstrations of the psychopathology of everyday life. In these demonstrations, participants were placed in a trance state and given suggestions, the effects of which were to be observed during the posthypnotic period. For example, a male subject who smoked Camel cigarettes was hypnotized and told that after awakening he would have a strong desire to smoke but would be without cigarettes and would be too courteous to ask for one. On arousal, the subject's obsessive need to smoke was very evident although thinly disguised. He told stories about how "the dromedary got one hump and the camel two," about the antics of dancers of a circus when "one would see elephants, hippopotami and camels," and about how the sight of water on the bay of New Haven always makes him thirsty," as did smoking." There was no topic of conversation that did not come back to the topic of smoking.

In another demonstration, Erickson gave a hypnotized male subject the false belief that "All German men marry women who are two inches taller than they are." When aroused from the hypnotic trance, this individual brought up the curious cultural fact that German men marry taller women. When challenged, he expressed surprise that anyone would doubt it. Counterexamples merely led him to suggest that, "every rule has its exceptions." Attempts to modify this belief by example and argument had little effect. While not in a trance he held onto the false, trance-implanted belief persistently, defending it with rationalization, denial, and contempt. The subject was placed back in the trance and the false belief was removed. On his awakening, it had disappeared.

In yet another demonstration, Erickson hypnotized a subject and put him into the conflict that was created by suggesting that he had stolen something of value from Professor D., who was present at the session. On arousal, the participant revealed an obsessive and defensive preoccupation with stealing. In conversation with Dr. D., he talked about "how everybody stole, how he himself had stolen things." The subject furtively kept trying to determine whether Dr. D. was a merciful, forgiving person who would forgive bad actions, especially stealing, but assurance that Dr. D. was a forgiving person had no effect. Reentering the trance and removing the conflict in that state, however, left the subject completely free of defensive behavior.

THE ROLE OF THE OPERATOR
IN TRANCE INDUCTION

Erickson believed that the induction of hypnosis and its subsequent altered state are different processes. The central tenet in the usual understanding of hypnosis is that hypnotic phenomena are due to suggestions by the hypnotist and that the role of the operator is central. In a series of insightful studies, however, Erickson (1964c) demonstrated that a trance could be instated without the use of the standard procedure of induction—indeed, without any activity on the part of the operator. The method was simply to have participants image, with the utmost concentration, the fine muscular sequence of the carrying out of a simple task. He found that when they detailed imaged attention to their kinesthetic experiences, many of them entered a hypnotically altered cognitive state automatically. These studies were significant because they indicated that although the role of the hypnotist is important, it is processes interior to the individual that produce the trance state.

Erickson maintained that the person is the key to success in induction of the trance state. In what he called the utilization theory of trance induction (1959b), he advocated nonformal methods of induction that involved little more than establishing rapport and using the subject's power and personality to induce the trance. In these methods, the operator follows the behavior of the participant in great detail and anticipates the direction of the subject's thoughts and behavior to guide the subject progressively toward the trance state.

In one instance, a patient was so anxious that he needed to pace back and forth in Erickson's office. Instead of reacting negatively to this behavior (e.g., by complaining about the patient's resistance to hypnotic induction), Erickson began by asking, "Are you willing to cooperate with me by continuing to pace the floor, even as you are doing now?" (Erickson, 1959b). Agreement with this small request allowed Erickson to redirect the pacing from criss-cross walking, changing the tempo of the walk, and interspersing the walk with sitting and relaxing. This technique provided a seamless entry into the altered state and utilized the resistance of the patient to *throw* him into a trance.

Erickson's formulation of the hypnotic process requires the deactivation of consciousness because the critical ability of consciousness prevents entry into the hypnotic state. To accomplish this, Erickson developed a *confusion technique* (1964a). Thoughts are stopped and interrupted by non-sequitors and irrelevancies. Given that the major motives of consciousness are understanding and awareness, when these goals are frustrated the subject becomes bewildered, uncritical, and confused. At this time, the subject becomes ready to accept and carry out the easily apprehended instruction necessary for the development of a trance. For example, Erickson (1964a) might say:

> I am so very glad you volunteered to be a subject. You probably enjoyed eating today. Most people do, though sometimes they skip a meal. You probably ate breakfast this morning. Maybe you will want tomorrow, something you had today. You have eaten it before, perhaps on Friday, like today. Maybe you will next week, but whether last week, this week or next week makes no difference. Because Thursday always comes before Friday. (p. 188).

This oblique and subtle method was developed from experience with patients who were desperate for therapy but, because of fear, disbelief, or hostility, had uncontrollable resistance to treatment. The method was even applicable to patients with sensory disabilities or language handicaps. For example, in dealing with deaf patients or patients who did not speak English, he transposed this method into a pantomime method (1964b), in which he used nonverbal behavior, intricate hand shakes, eye contact, and impeccable timing.

MECHANISMS OF POSTHYPNOTIC SUGGESTION

In the early 1940s, Milton Erickson and his wife, Elizabeth M. Erickson, turned their attention to the nature and character of trance-suggested posthypnotic acts,

> which are performed by a subject after awakening from a trance in response to suggestions given during the trance, the execution of the act being marked by the absence of any demonstrable conscious awareness in the subject of his causal motive for his act. (Erickson & Erickson, 1941, p. 104)

Pursuing this phenomenon, the Ericksons carried out some extremely fascinating demonstrations that indicated that, at the moment of execution of the posthypnotic suggestion, the person spontaneously reenters the trance state and remains in that state until the conclusion of the act. Consider the following account given by one participant after completion of a posthypnotic act:

> We were talking about something, just what I've forgotten now, when I suddenly saw that book and I simply had to go over and pick it up and look at it—I don't know why— I just felt I had to—a sudden impulse, I suppose. Then I came back to my chair. It just happened that way. But you must have seen me because I must have had to walk around you to get it—I don't see any other way I could have reached it. Then when I laid it down again, I must have put those other books on top of it. At least, I don't think anybody else did, since I don't remember anybody else being on that side of the room—but I wasn't paying much attention to anything, I guess, because, although I know I looked carefully at that book and opened it, I don't even know the author or the title—probably fiction from the looks of it. Anyway, it was a funny thing to do—probably an impulse of the moment and doesn't mean a thing. What was it we were discussing? (Erickson & Erickson, 1941, pp. 106–107)

This example illustrates that when a posthypnotic suggestion is initiated, participants (a) are unconsciously motivated to carry out that act, (b) enter the trance state during the execution of the act, and (c) after the completion of the act, return to normal functioning. Thus, posthypnotic suggestions have the characteristics of a need, which remains in a state of tension until the suggested act is carried out. According to this analysis, the subjects do not know why they perform the posthypnotic act, only that they have a need to execute it. After the necessary performance, there is a release of tension and a return to normal functioning.

In Erickson's analysis, because participants reenter a trance state during the execution of a posthypnotic act, it is possible to reestablish hypnotic rapport at that time, thereby eliminating the need for what might be a difficult induction procedure.

The following discussion clearly illustrates that, during the execution of posthypnotic suggestions, the trance state of the subject is reactivated and the rapport with the hypnotist is retained.

Shortly after his awakening, a subject was told that a certain topic of conversation would be introduced, whereupon he was to leave his chair immediately, cross the room, pick up a small statuette with his left hand, and place it on top of a certain bookcase. As the subject stepped in front of the hypnotist to cross the room, his left arm was gently raised above his head, where it remained in a cataleptic state. The subject continued on his way without hesitation. On approaching the statuette, he found himself unable to lower his left arm and turned to the hypnotist as if awaiting further instruction. Thus, he was used to demonstrate a variety of the usual phenomena of the ordinary induced trance. On the completion of this demonstration, he was instructed simply, "All right, you may go ahead now." In response to this vague suggestion, the subject returned to the interrupted posthypnotic performance, completed it, and resumed his original seat, awakening spontaneously with a complete amnesia for all of the events intervening between the giving of the cue and his awakening, without even an awareness that he had altered his position in the chair (Erickson, 1944).

The implications of this analysis are far reaching: Posthypnotic acts reassert the trance state as well as the relationship between the hypnotist and subject. That relationship is not exhausted at the conclusion of the hypnotic session, but may be revived at a later time.

THERAPY

In the 1940s and 1950s, other therapists were exploring specialized hypnotic techniques such as age regression, age progression, posthypnotic suggestions, positive and negative hallucinations, hypnotic dreams, and so on. However, in their book *Hypnotherapy*, Brenman and Gill (1947) reported:

> the most extensive therapeutic applications of [hypnotic techniques] have been made by Erickson. Combining a unique inventiveness with a shrewd and intuitive grasp of the patient's psychological status, he uses these methods as the essential levers of his therapy. (p. 77)

The "February Man"

Erickson was radically unorthodox in his approach to therapy. His published articles span an impressive range of topics, including studies on obsessional phobias, depression, traumatic neurosis, multiple personality, dental hypnosis, stuttering, epilepsy, drug addiction, migraines, and a myriad of other disorders that encompass a lifetime of problem solving in the unique Ericksonian way. As is evidenced by his many case studies, Erickson devised a therapeutic tactic for each individual case. His methods and the rationale for those methods were often unpredictable. The central core of his strategy was to effect a change that transforms the meaning of the situation.

On one occasion, a female patient approached Erickson because she was extremely fearful that her unhappy childhood would affect her handling of motherhood. She explained that she was an unwanted child, her mother never had time for her, and all of her early memories were colored by deep sadness and a sense of rejection. Erickson (cited in Rossi, 1980b) undertook to go beyond mere organizing and reorganizing the memorial, affective, and cognitive processes of the patient in a trance state. Instead, he placed the patient into a trance and regressed her to an earlier age. While she was in this trance, he entered into her life space as a kindly, grand-uncle type of a friend of her father, named "The February Man"—a confidant and power figure for her. With amnesia for the trance states, Erickson continued to regress the patient to different ages, interspersing new and benign life experiences, weaving them together with the original mental structures. In effect, he altered her beliefs about the past and the values she placed on it. This treatment was effective. The patient lost her fear of not being a good parent, went on to have children, and, in her own estimation, became a good mother. This dramatic change in behavior and attitude marks it as one of the boldest uses of age regression in the history of modern hypnosis.

Psychotherapy Without Hypnosis

Erickson's therapeutic methods did not always involve hypnosis. He found that many times merely modifying the context of a problem was effective. For example, in one interesting case (Haley, 1973), a 16-year-old high school student whose most obvious problem was chronic thumbsucking was unwillingly, brought to see Erickson. After discussing the situation with her parents, he told them that under no conditions were they to mention the thumb sucking to the girl for the next month, nor were they to interfere with the therapy. He then met with the young woman:

> She removed her thumb sufficiently to declare she didn't like "nut doctors."
>
> I replied, "And I don't like the way your parents ordered me to cure your thumb sucking. Ordering me, huh! It's your thumb and your mouth, and why in hell can't you suck if you want to? Ordering me to cure you! The only thing I'm interested in is why, when you want to be aggressive about thumb sucking, you don't really get aggressive instead of piddling around like a baby that doesn't know how to suck a thumb aggressively."

Erickson then proceeded to tell her to sit by her father when he read the paper at night, and really:

> nurse your thumb good and loud, and irk the hell out of him for the longest twenty minutes he has ever experienced. Then go in the sewing room, where your mother

sews for one hour every night before she washes dishes. Sit down beside her and nurse your thumb good and loud and irk the hell out of the old lady for the longest twenty minutes she ever knew. Do this every night and do it good. And on the way to school, figure out carefully just which crummy jerk you dislike most, and every time you meet him, pop your thumb in your mouth and watch him turn his head away. And be ready to pop your thumb back if he turns to look at you again. And think over all your teachers and pick out the one you really dislike and treat your teacher to a thumb pop every time he or she looks at you. I just hope you can be really aggressive.

At the conclusion of the session, Erickson met with the girl's parents and once again told them that if they kept their promise to be quiet, the girl's thumb sucking would end. The girl did not suck her thumb on the way home and the parents telephoned Erickson with the good news. However, that evening the girl followed through with Erickson's strategy and the parents also obeyed their promise to Erickson and said nothing. For a few nights, the girl followed through with her plan; however, after a while she started to shorten the duration of thumb sucking, she began late and quit early, and even skipped a night. After some time she even forgot! It took less than 4 weeks for the girl to stop sucking her thumb at home as well as other places. This was accomplished in one therapeutic session as a result of transforming the neurotic problem or obsession into a requirement or a duty.

Strategic Therapy

One of Erickson's important contributions to psychotherapy was a set of ideas that has been termed *strategic therapy*. In this form of treatment, the therapist is extremely active and directive, dealing with problems head on. The method involved a number of counterintuitive maneuvers. In the course of therapy, Erickson frequently created paradoxical situations in which the patient was forced to choose to get better because other alternatives were worse.

Consider this illustrative case (Erickson, 1965): George had been a patient in a mental hospital for 5 years. He was approximately 25 years old and his identity was unknown. His only spoken words during those 5 years were, "My name is George," "Good morning," and "Good night." He spoke only a *word salad*, which was completely without meaning to anyone.

For the first 3 years he sat on a bench at the front door of the ward and eagerly leaped up and poured forth his word salad most urgently to everyone who entered the ward. Otherwise, he merely sat quietly mumbling his word salad to himself. Innumerable patient efforts had been made by psychiatrists, psychologists, nurses, social service workers, other personnel, and even fellow patients to secure intelligible remarks from him, all in vain. George talked only one way—the word salad way.

Erickson joined the hospital staff during George's sixth year. He created a therapeutic plan to cure George. Erickson had a secretary transcribe George's word salad in shorthand. After much study, Erickson devised his own vocabulary of a word salad with the same intonations but a different vocabulary. Erickson then began entering the ward and sitting beside George on the bench, gradually increasing the time span to 1 hour, without saying a word. At the next sitting, Erickson identified himself verbally, addressing the air. The next day, he addressed George. George responded with an angry outburst of word salad, to which Erickson calmly produced his own word salad back. At this, George looked puzzled and spoke back and then Erickson replied with still further word salad. This happened about six times, at which point Erickson went on with other matters.

The next morning, appropriate greetings were exchanged employing proper names by both. Then George launched into a long word salad speech to which the author (Erickson) courteously replied in kind. There then followed brief interchanges of long and short utterances of word salad until George fell silent and the author went on to other duties.

The next day, George made his meaningless utterances for 4 hours without stopping. Erickson sat by his side, responding in kind, right through the lunch period. George answered back for another 2 hours, to which Erickson responded for another 2 hours. The whole time, George was watching the clock.

The next morning, George returned the usual greeting properly but added about two sentences of nonsense. The author replied with a similar length of nonsense. George replied, "Talk sense, Doctor."

"Certainly, I'll be glad to. What is your last name?"

"O'Donovan, and it's about time somebody who knows how to talk asked. Over five years in this lousy joint" (to which was added a sentence or two of word salad).

The author replied, "I'm glad to get your name, George. Five years is too long a time" (and about two sentences of word salad were added).

As may be expected, George completed his history and, as always, the conversations with him contained a few lines of the word salad. His subsequent outlook and treatment was excellent. Although he was never completely free of his word salad, it was reduced to an occasional mumble. Within the year, he was able to leave the hospital and gain employment. He kept in touch and reported doing fine.

He could, as he frequently did on these visits, comment wryly, "nothing like a little nonsense in life is there, Doctor?", to which he obviously expected and received a sensible expression of agreement to which was added a brief utterance of nonsense. After he had been out of the hospital continuously for 3 years of fully satisfactory adjustment, contact was lost with him except for a cheerful postcard from another city. Erickson had limited George's alternatives by producing his own word salad. It got to the point where George was forced to listen to the noxious word salad of Erickson, or give it up.

The Exploitation of Resistance

Erickson also encouraged, accepted, and utilized resistance by creating paradoxical situations such that the choice to resist became a step in the therapeutic direction.

Hence, if a patient says, "I can't,...", Erickson might agree and even urge the patient to be careful not to do that thing, thereby forming a collaborative situation. In one such case (Haley, 1973),a seventh-grade boy was brought to Erickson because he could not read. On speaking with the boy, Erickson learned that the boy wanted to go fishing with his father in the summer instead of working with tutors. In typical Ericksonian fashion, he encouraged the boy to forget about learning to read. Instead, he concentrated on the father's fishing. Erickson took out a map, and the two of them started to explore the different places the boy's father had fished. Together they tried to locate the names of the towns on the map. It is important to note that they were not reading the names, just locating them:

> I would confuse the location of certain cities, and he would have to correct me. I would try to locate a town named Colorado Springs and be looking for it in California, and he had to correct me. But he wasn't reading, he was correcting me. He rapidly learned to locate all the towns we were interested in. He didn't know he was reading the names. We had such a good time looking at the map and finding good fishing spots. He liked to come and discuss fish and the various kinds of fish in the encyclopedia.

> Near the end of August, I said, "Let's play a joke on your teachers and on your parents. You've been told you'll be given a reading test when school starts. Your parents are going to be anxious about how you'll do, and so will your teacher. So you take the first grade reader and you carefully stumble through it. Botch it up thoroughly. Do a better job on the second grade reader, and a somewhat better one on the third grade reader. Then do a beautiful job on the eighth grade reader."

> He thought that was a wonderful joke. He did it just that way. Later he played truant and came over to tell me about the appalled look on his parents' faces and his teacher's face. If he had read the first grade reader correctly, it would have been an acknowledgment of failure on his part. But when he misread that and then went beyond the seventh grade to do the eighth grade reading well, that made him the winner. He could confound his teacher, bewilder his parents, and be the acknowledged winner. (pp. 174–175)

In this case, Erickson encouraged the boy's resistance to gain rapport and form a collaborative relationship with the boy. By giving the boy permission not to read, it enabled the boy to choose, ultimately, to read.

CONCLUSION

As a master hypnotist and psychotherapist, Erickson set a high standard of excellence in a field known for its mystery, vagueness, controversy, and tendency toward charlatanism and mysticism. He wrote significant articles in every area of trance-induced altered-state theory. Although the ramifications of his work pervade all areas of hypnotism, Erickson did not develop any general explanatory positions.

There is no "Milton Erickson Theory of Hypnosis." He did less to revolutionize the field of hypnosis than he did to advance its credibility as a discipline worthy of scientific study.

Erickson's contributions to the study of hypnosis included founding the American Society of Clinical Hypnosis and serving as the first editor of the *American Journal of Clinical Hypnosis*—an editorship that extended from 1958–1968. These professional activities as well as his scholarly contributions were recognized by numerous awards and honors. He was a Life Fellow of the American Psychiatric Association, the American Psychological Association, and the American Association for the Advancement of Science, and he was named a Diplomate by the American Board of Psychiatry. In 1976, he was the recipient of the only award presented by the International Society of Hypnosis: the Benjamin Franklin Gold Medal. The inscription on the medal provides a valid description of his lifetime contribution to the study of hypnosis. It reads as follows:

> To Milton H. Erickson, MD—innovator, outstanding clinician, and distinguished investigator whose ideas have not only helped create the modern view of hypnosis but have profoundly influenced the practice of all psychotherapy throughout the world.

The July 1977 issue of the *American Journal of Clinical Hypnosis* was dedicated solely to his work in honor of his 75th birthday. The following statement by Lewis R. Wolberg, MD (Clinical Professor of Psychiatry, New York University School of Medicine) constitutes an appropriate conclusion to this article: "Dr. Erickson is perhaps the most creative and imaginative contemporary worker in the area of hypnosis and his inspired writings in this series rank among the enduring classics in the field." (Rossi, 1980a)

REFERENCES

Brenman, M., & Gill, M. (1947). *Hypnotherapy*. New York: International Universities Press.

Cooper, L. & Erickson, M. (1950). Time distortion in hypnosis: II. *Bulletin of the Georgetown University Medical Center, 4,* 50–68.

Cooper, L., & Erickson, M. (1954). *Time distortion in hypnosis*. Baltimore: Williams & Wilkins.

Elliotson, J. (1843). *Numerous cases of surgical operations without pain in the mesmeric state.* Philadelphia: Lea & Blanchard.

Erickson, M. (1928). A study of clinical and experimental findings on hypnotic deafness: I. Clinical experimentation and findings. *Journal of General Psychology, 9,* 127–150.

Erickson, M. (1936). *Migraine headache in a resistant patient*. Unpublished manuscript.

Erickson, M. (1938). A study of clinical and experimental findings on hypnotic deafness: II. Experimental findings with a conditioned response technique. *Journal of General Psychology, 19,* 151–167.

Erickson, M. (1939a). Experimental demonstration of the psychopathology of everyday life. *Psychoanalytic Quarterly, 8,* 338–353.

Erickson, M. (1939b). The induction of color blindness by a technique of hypnotic suggestion. *Journal of General Psychology, 29,* 61–89.

Erickson, M. (1943). Experimentally elicited salivary and related responses to hypnotic visual hallucinations confirmed by personality reactions. *Psychosomatic Medicine, 5*, 185–187.

Erickson, M. (1944). An experimental investigation of the hypnotic subject's apparent ability to become unaware of stimuli. *Journal of General Psychology, 31*, 191–212.

Erickson, M. (1959a). Hypnosis in painful terminal illness. *American Journal of Clinical Hypnosis, 1*, 117–121.

Erickson, M. (1959b). Further clinical techniques of hypnosis: Utilization techniques. *American Journal of Clinical Hypnosis, 2*, 3–21.

Erickson, M. (1964a). The confusion technique in hypnosis. *American Journal of Clinical Hypnosis, 6*, 183–207.

Erickson, M. (1964b). Initial experiments investigating the nature of hypnosis. *American Journal of Clinical Hypnosis, 7*, 152–162.

Erickson, M. (1964c). Pantomime techniques in hypnosis and their implications. *American Journal of Clinical Hypnosis, 7*, 64–70.

Erickson, M. (1965). The use of symptoms as an integral part of hypnotherapy. *American Journal of Clinical Hypnosis, 8*, 57–65.

Erickson, M. (1966). The interspersal technique for symptom correction and pain control. *American Journal of Clinical Hypnosis, 8*, 198–209.

Erickson, M. (1977). Control of physiological functions by hypnosis. *American Journal of Clinical Hypnosis, 20*, 8–19.

Erickson, M., & Erickson, E. M. (1938). The hypnotic induction of hallucinatory color vision followed by pseudo-negative after-images. *Journal of Experimental Psychology, 22*, 581–588.

Erickson, M., & Rossi, E. (1974). Varieties of hypnotic amnesia. *American Journal of Clinical Hypnosis, 16*, (4), 225–239.

Esdaile, J. (1847). *Mesmerism in India and its practical application in surgery and medicine*. Hartford: Silas Andrus.

Haley, J. (1973). *Uncommon therapy: The psychiatric techniques of Milton H. Erickson, MD*. New York: Norton.

Haley, J. (Ed.). (1985). *Conversations with Milton Erickson, MD: Volume III. Changing children and families*. New York: Triangle Press.

Hull, C. L. (1933). *Hypnosis and suggestibility*. New York: Appleton-Century-Crofts.

Rossi, E. (Ed.). (1980a). *The collected papers of Milton H. Erickson: Volume I. The nature of hypnosis and suggestions*. New York: Irvington.

Rossi, E. (Ed.). (1980b). *The collected papers of Milton H. Erickson: Volume IV. Innovative hypnotherapy*. New York: Irvington.

Chapter 12

Zing-Yang Kuo:
Radical Scientific Philosopher
and Innovative Experimentalist

Gilbert Gottlieb

This chapter describes the turbulent professional career and private biography of the most prominent anti-instinct scholar and researcher of the 20th century. Zing-Yang Kuo had the brilliant intuition that the adaptive behavior of newborn animals and humans was reconstituted from their prenatal activities, and that positing instinct as an explanation for the adaptive behavior of newborns (or adults, for that matter) was an empty exercise at best and a block to developmental understanding at worst. He translated these thoughts into a career-long research program, which I describe in this chapter along with details of his personal life that I obtained from his unpublished autobiography, which he sent to me shortly before he died in 1970. Kuo's intellectual legacy persists today in my own research and that of others on the prenatal experiential antecedents to postnatal behavior, and a much more circumspect concept of instinctive behavior.

SCIENTIFIC PHILOSOPHY

Public Biography

In his first paper, published in 1921, Zing-Yang Kuo assaulted the concept of *instinct*. His attack was based on the insight that the use of instinct as an explanatory concept is harmful to a genuine understanding of behavior because it makes the

---

* Photograph of Zing-Yang Kuo supervising the author in making an observation window in the shell of a duck egg (Dorothea Dix Hospital, Raleigh, North Carolina, Fall, 1963). Courtesy of Gilbert Gottlieb.

analysis of development superfluous and, therefore, unnecessary. For Kuo, a psychology based on instinct was an armchair psychology and, as such, was not an investigative science. Throughout his career, he remained keenly sensitive to concepts that served as facile substitutes for experimental analyses, especially those concepts that divert attention from an investigation of developmental processes, whether these processes be anatomical, physiological, or behavioral. This is not to say that Kuo was antitheoretical—he simply made a strong distinction between hypotheses that promote investigation and those that do not. For him, the concept of instinct fell in the latter category. There is, after all, a very significant difference between positing, say, a reproductive instinct to account for nest building in birds and undertaking a developmental analysis of nest-building behavior.

In his critique of the instinct concept, Kuo acknowledged that animals perform all manner of activities without the opportunity for prior learning or imitation—for him, these performances were not simply to be taken as demonstrations of the wonderful workings of instinct; rather, they posed interesting and significant problems for ontogenetic analysis. It was his lifelong conviction that an explanation of an animal's behavior could be derived entirely from (a) its anatomy and physiology, (b) its current environmental setting, and (c) its individual developmental history. His own research and critical writings can be comprehended only in the light of his belief that any analysis of behavior is incomplete if it relies mainly or exclusively on only one of these factors—all three must be taken into consideration in a comprehensive account of animal and human behavior.

In two of his lesser known works, published in the *Psychological Review*, Kuo (1928, 1929a) criticized concepts such as habit formation, trial-and-error learning, and purpose for the same reasons he had criticized instinct. These notions, too, are ones that short-circuit an empirical analysis of behavior and its development. It was now clear, if it had not been before, that Kuo was not merely an anti-instinctivist. He took the behaviorists to task, along with the nativists, for using any concept that serves as "a lazy substitute for energetic and painstaking work in experimental psychophysiology and developmental psychology" (Kuo, 1924, p. 447).

As has already been noted, in Kuo's view, a complete account of behavior includes anatomy and physiology, as well as developmental history and environmental setting. In this view, he was clear on the essential and strategic relations among behavior, physiology, and anatomy, and he was critical of those in his area of research who saw their task as merely establishing neuroanatomical correlates to behavior. In the search for the undergirdings of behavior—in order to avoid possibly erroneous conclusions—one must proceed through physiology to neuroanatomy:

> We must bear in mind the fact that physiological interpretations on the basis of neural structures is [sic] sometimes a dangerous thing as neuro-anatomy may not give the true picture of physiology. Furthermore, unless the beginning and development of the function of the parts of the nervous system concerned are definitely known, structural

correlations with behavioral development may not be dependable. It is not my intention here to minimize the importance of anatomical study of the development of the nervous system, but rather, to caution against any attempt to base physiological interpretations on anatomical data. (Kuo, 1939d, p. 104)

In his last published article, which appeared as a chapter in a book titled *Development and Evolution of Behavior*, Kuo (1970) reiterated his criticism of nativistic approaches to behavior on the one hand, and of black-box or empty organism approaches on the other. The first approach is best exemplified by the more traditional ethologists and the second one by the more conservative conditioning theorists. These approaches tend to reinforce the notion that there are two components to behavior, one of which is ascribable to the animal's own experience (learning) and the other of which is attributable to the experience of the species (instinct). Kuo believed it was useful to regard all behavior as being acquired during individual development—in this way, one is forced to come to grips directly with an analysis of the anatomico-physiological maturational events, as well as the environmental contingencies that determine behavior. From an ontogenetic viewpoint, all behavior has to be acquired during development—unless, that is, one cares to make a case for preformation.

Private Biography

At the time of Zing-Yang Kuo's birth in 1898 in a small town near Swatow on the southern coast of China, the country was still under the rule of the Manchu Dynasty. Men wore pigtails, women minced about with their feet bound, young girls served as slaves, temples were built for the worship of idols, shrines were erected for the worship of ancestors, and only about 1 person in 10 could read and write. With the overthrow of the Manchu Dynasty and the founding of the Chinese Republic by Sun Yat Sen in 1911, China was wracked by a period of continuous political unrest, characterized by revolutionary episodes and revolts, and periodic changes in leadership, all dedicated to bringing China into the 20th century. This political unrest and instability persisted and greatly hampered Kuo's attempt to practice and promulgate modern science in China.

Several things favored young Zing-Yang's survival and gradual emancipation from this unpromising beginning. He was born into an educated and well-to-do family, which, coupled with Zing-Yang's extreme precocity, allowed him an extraordinary measure of independence in thought and action. As a young teenager, for example, he removed his pigtail—a symbol of subservience to foreign rule—and campaigned for social reform in the village of his birth. In an attempt to fight the superstition implied by idolatry, he and his classmates, in an episode which would have delighted Tom Sawyer and Huckleberry Finn, stole into the temples at night and removed the outer garments of the gods and goddesses, thereby exposing their straw and clay innards. Later, when Zing-Yang stepped on a broken dish and severely cut his foot while wading barefooted in a creek, the old women of the village used such behavior as the basis for their whispers that, "The gods are not blind after all"; they warned their children not to follow Zing-Yang's ways lest they, too, get punished by the offended images.

"Out-Watsoning Mr. Watson"

In 1918, Zing-Yang sailed from China to the United States, where he enrolled in the University of California at Berkeley. After some vacillation, he settled on psychology as his major and graduated magna cum laude in 1921. He remained at Berkeley and completed requirements for the Ph.D. in 1923.

It was during his senior year that Zing-Yang wrote his first critique of the instinct concept, which was published in the *Journal of Philosophy* in 1921. Although other critiques of instinct appeared around this same time, Kuo's article attracted the widest attention and raised the greatest furor. Knight Dunlap (1919–1920), for example, in a well-reasoned article, attacked the teleological and nonpsychological implications of the various classifications of instinct. Kuo, on the other hand, denied the very existence of instinct, no matter how it was conceived or classified. This article was followed by no less forceful and radical ones on the same topic. "How Are Instincts Acquired?" appeared in the *Psychological Review* of 1922, and "A Psychology Without Heredity" and "The Net Result of the Anti-Heredity Movement in Psychology" appeared in the same journal several years later (Kuo, 1922, 1924, 1929b, respectively).

A number of rebuttals to the first article soon began to appear, the most significant of which were, perhaps, William McDougall's (1921–1922) 48-page retort in the *Journal of Abnormal and Social Psychology*, in which Kuo was described as "out-Watsoning Mr. Watson," and Tolman's (1922) sympathetic unraveling of young Kuo's hidden assumptions, alongside a confession of his "own faith that *instincts cannot be given up in psychology*," which also appeared in the *Journal of Abnormal and Social Psychology*. At that time, it was just as unusual as it is now for an undergraduate to publish a provocative paper or for such an article to elicit extended published replies from senior scientists—Tolman was Kuo's academic advisor and McDougall held the chair previously occupied by William James at Harvard. As can be imagined, these eventualities did not lessen the already brimming self-confidence of young Mr. Kuo.

RESEARCH THEMES

Public Biography

Although Kuo published a number of articles on topics such as the genesis of the cat's response to the rat and the factors that determine fighting in animals, he regarded these as sidelights to his most serious research, that on the behavior and physiology of the embryonic nervous system. For this work, he developed a technique that allowed him to observe directly the activities of the chick embryo in situ, without disturbing its circulatory membranes. In this research, he attempted to give a comprehensive account of the embryo's behavior in terms of its anatomico-physiological condition, the immediate environmental context, and the embryo's developmental history. Although the work was comprehensive at the descriptive-observational level, it was admittedly deficient in manipulative experiments designed to test the numerous hypotheses that were developed in the course of the investigation.

One of the most striking of Kuo's hypotheses held that certain of the early behaviors observed in the chick after hatching, such as locomotion and pecking, represent an extension and reorganization of movement patterns already present in the embryo. The reorganization of the components of embryonic behavior in the hatchling—the chick embryo does not peck or locomote inside the egg—is prompted by the changes in environmental context, structure, and physiology that occur in the transition from prenatal to postnatal existence. Thus, along with Holt (1931), Kuo was a staunch expositor of the view that prenatal development exerts a strong influence on postnatal behavior, in the specific sense that embryonic movements are the elements out of which postnatal behavior is constructed. Kuo, however, rejected Holt's idea that postnatal movement patterns or "reflexes" are the result of habits formed by prenatal conditioning—for Kuo, this conception was too static; it did not adequately account for the dynamic interrelationship between the embryo and its environment, or the neonate and its environment.

On the basis of his embryonic studies, Kuo also challenged Coghill's (1929) view that embryonic behavior begins as a relatively undifferentiated total pattern of movement, out of which local patterns become emancipated later in development. In the chick embryo, Kuo observed local and gross movement side by side in his undisturbed preparations. Coghill had used stimulation to provoke movement in his larval amphibians—in fact, the total pattern-partial pattern sequence was based on the larvae's response to stimulation—these forms being otherwise quite inactive during the early stages of development. In utilizing stimulation with his chick embryos, Kuo found that gross or local responses could be elicited at almost any stage of development, depending on the time interval and intensity of simulation. Embryonic behavior was a complicated affair—it would take time and patience to unravel the problem. For Kuo, and for certain other investigators of the time, it was clear that Coghill had not only severely overgeneralized his findings, but also had oversimplified the story. Although Coghill had correlative neuroanatomy in support of his behavioral findings, he had not bolstered his research with physiology. Kuo (1939d) cautioned the great neuroembryologist that physiological interpretations on the basis of neural structure alone are a tenuous affair. When it comes to an understanding of behavior, anatomical study must be based on physiology.

After completing his long series of behavioral studies on the chick embryo, Kuo embarked on a series of physiological studies, the aim of which was to provide what he regarded as the proper undergirding for his behavioral observations. By using the method of curarization, he was able to demonstrate that the earliest movements of the embryo are of a neurogenic character. (With his characteristic thoroughness, he calculated a dose–response curve for each age, determining the degree of motor paralysis for various concentrations of the drug at each age.) He augmented this work by using calibrated electrical stimulation and measuring the threshold of the embryo's response at various ages. He also assayed for the first appearance of acetylcholine in the embryo's nervous system. Finally, in order to get a clear picture of the neuroanatomical loci of embryonic motility (Kuo, 1939a, p. 371), he planned to do transections of the nervous system as well as electrophysiological recording when, in 1939, his physiological series was abruptly discontinued.

Private Biography

It was with the express purpose of justifying his anti-instinct critiques with research on development that Zing-Yang, on his return to China in 1923, accepted a position as professor of psychology at Fuh Tan University in Shanghai. His publications in the United States had created a reputation for him in China, and several months after his return certain wealthy relatives gave him a substantial sum of money with which to build a laboratory. Kuo supplemented these funds with his own fund-raising campaign. A three-story steel and reinforced concrete structure, designed by a German architect, resulted from Zing-Yang's efforts. Before completion of the laboratory, however, he was forced to secure additional funds from banks. Zing-Yang's success as a fund raiser, coupled with his popularity as a lecturer and teacher, soon resulted in his assuming the role of president of Fuh Tan University.

During this period (1923–1927), Shanghai was in great political turmoil. The various sectors of this great city were under the rule of foreigners (British, French, and American), and the Chinese inhabitants, particularly the students, were becoming overtly restless and directly challenged the authorities on the question of their second-class status in their own country. Moreover, the revolutionary tide of the Nationalists, headed by Chiang Kai-shek, was surging northward. Correctly foreseeing bloody times in Shanghai, which would have placed his family and himself in possible physical danger, Zing-Yang resigned his posts and left Fuh Tan in September 1926, before he had begun to exploit the resources of his new laboratory. Fortunately, certain books he wrote for Chinese consumption were paying handsome royalties, so Zing-Yang was able to buy a small piece of land in a more peaceful section of the country, where he constructed modest research facilities for himself and his several assistants and technicians.

During 1928 and 1929, at his private research facility, away from the distractions of Shanghai, Zing-Yang began his first serious work on the development of behavior in mammalian fetuses and avian embryos. As a sidelight, he designed a curious study for his assistants to carry out: one in which kittens and young rats were reared together. The results of this particular study became quite well known after they were published in an article in the *Journal of Comparative Psychology*

(Kuo, 1930), in which Kuo reported that these cats not only tolerated their companions, but also demonstrated some affection for them. This was an anti-instinct argument that even lay readers could comprehend, and the international press brought reports of it back to China, where, alas, only a few intimates recognized Dr. Kuo's "American" name (Zing-Yang). Faced with the necessity of selecting an Anglicized version of one of his various Chinese names, Dr. Kuo chose "Zing-Yang," which, roughly translated, means "Enduring Mission." This was a rendition of only the first and fourth components of the name by which he was known throughout his student years in China, so only his close friends would be apt to recognize this name when it appeared in the Chinese press. The whole matter amused Zing-Yang greatly—after all, in a manner of speaking, he was hiding out at the time.

Other sidelights in Kuo's program of research included the basic factors (glandular, dietary, training, social, and broadly environmental) involved in the development of animal fighting, which were belatedly summarized in serial fashion (I–VII) in the *Journal of Genetic Psychology* (Kuo, 1960a, 1960b, 1960c, 1960d, 1960e, 1960f, 1960g). During this period in the late 1920s, he also examined certain developmental factors contributing to sexual abnormalities in dogs, monkeys, and pigeons, some of the results of which are alluded to in his book, *The Dynamics of Behavior Development* (Kuo, 1967).

In attempting to study the prenatal ontogeny of behavior, Zing-Yang could never convince himself that the mammalian fetuses that had to be exteriorized for observation were normal preparations. They had, after all, been removed from their usual environment, and there was also some doubt about the normalcy of their physiological functioning. He, therefore, concentrated on perfecting a technique to observe the avian (chick) embryo inside the egg, without disturbing its surrounding circulatory membranes. The fruits of this labor appeared in a number of different journals under the general title "Ontogeny of Embryonic Behavior in Aves," numbered serially I through XII (VII,VIII, and IX were not published), beginning in 1932 and terminating in 1938 (Kuo, 1932a, 1932b, 1932c, 1932d, 1932e, 1933, 1938; Kuo & Shen, 1936, 1937). In 1939, he published three articles in his new series, titled "Studies in the Physiology of the Embryonic Nervous System" (Kuo, 1939a, 1939b, 1939c). He was forced prematurely to terminate this series in 1939. World War II was on the horizon, and events in the United States, as well as in China, no longer permitted Zing-Yang Kuo to do laboratory work.

INTELLECTUAL LEGACY

The studies on embryonic behavior and physiology consolidated Zing-Yang's reputation as a first-rate scientist. In addition, he became one of the few psychologists whose work was known to biologists—a rarer feat in those days than it is today. Two other rarities deserve mention. Zing-Yang had virtually no *students*, as that term is understood today. Throughout his career, he worked and published primarily by himself. Although his research spanned the nervous system and behavior, Kuo had co-authors on only four of his articles. He collaborated twice with T. C. R. Shen (Kuo & Shen, 1936, 1937), once with his good friend Leonard Carmichael (Kuo & Carmichael, 1937), and once with me (Gottlieb & Kuo, 1965).[1] He influenced his peers from afar, and some of his peers were influential scientists. For example, the well-known comparative psychologist T. C. Schneirla made strong and consistent use of Kuo's embryonic research over a period of 30 years, beginning with the chapters he wrote for a textbook, *Principles of Animal Psychology* (Maier & Schneirla, 1935) and ending with a review published in 1966 in the *Quarterly Review of Biology*. The critique of K. Z. Lorenz's theory of instinctive behavior, written by Schneirla's student D. S. Lehrman and published by the *Quarterly Review of Biology* in 1953, is in the intellectual tradition initiated by Kuo's early anti-instinct articles, and has as its main empirical basis Kuo's research on the chick embryo. It is through the writings of Schneirla and Lehrman that many of the European ethologists were introduced to Kuo's viewpoint and his work. More recently, Kuo's work on the chick embryo was reintroduced to psychologists by J. McV. Hunt (1961) in his book, *Intelligence and Experience*. Most recently, I, hardly his peer, have tried to give a thorough account of his theoretical views in a chapter for the previously mentioned volume on *Development and Evolution of Behavior* (Gottlieb, 1970) and in a recent book recounting his and my own contributions to the topic: *Synthesizing Nature–Nurture: Prenatal Roots of Instinctive Behavior* (Gottlieb, 1997).

This is not to say that Kuo's writings or his research have convinced anyone of the nonexistence of instinct or the related concept of innateness—on that topic, scientists, like people in general, seem at the outset to be believers or skeptics, so matters like semantics and faith loom large. What Kuo's research and writings have made clear is the significance of developmental analysis for the problems of behavior, particularly species-typical behavior, and that is, after all, what he set out to accomplish in his first article written and published when he was a senior at Berkeley (Kuo, 1921).

Although the concepts of instinctive behavior and innateness are still in use, most scientists now recognize that they are merely descriptive terms for species-typical behavior and have no explanatory status. That change in connotation, to use Kuo's terms, could be said to be "the net result of the anti-heredity movement in psychology." Kuo (1967) acknowledged that genes play a role in development along with many other influences, but genes in and of themselves do not determine behavior.

Along with Kuo's research and theorizing, and Schneirla's (1966) writings, three other critiques that brought about a more circumspect view of instinct are

---

[1]Dr. Kuo was overly generous in insisting that my name be placed first in this publication. He did more than his fair share of the observations, data analysis, and writing of the final report. After he returned to Hong Kong in 1964, I compiled a film of our research project, "Development of Behavior in the Duck Embryo," which is still available for rental from the Psychological Cinema Register of Pennsylvania State University.

Lehrman's (1953, 1970) and Beach's (1955) articles. Birney and Teevan (1961) assembled a useful collection of articles on *Instinct,* both pro and con.

Foreshortened Academic Career

Although Zing-Yang was not an admirer of Ivan Pavlov's approach to the study of behavior, partly because it was nondevelopmental and partly because it was concerned exclusively with only one acquisition process (conditioning), he admired Pavlov's ability to continue his research, relatively undisturbed, during the various revolutionary episodes and political upheavals in Russia during the early part of the 20th century. After the communist takeover of the czarist government in the early 1900s, the stability of Pavlov's situation in Russia was ensured by Lenin's belief that Pavlov's continuation of Sechenov's work was "of enormous significance for the working people of the world" (cited in Sechenov, 1965, p. 138). Kuo was not so fortunate. In light of his pillar-to-post academic career in China and the United States, it is remarkable that he accomplished anything of note in science.

In 1929, Zing-Yang was persuaded to leave his private animal farm and take up the position of research professor in the National University of Chekiang at Hangchow. The president of the University offered to build him a small laboratory, and he was to have no teaching or administrative duties. By that time, the royalties from his books had begun to decline, so it was clear to Zing-Yang that he could not continue indefinitely to finance his own research. So, he went to Hangchow, where, for the next 2 years, he worked from 12 to 14 hours daily, 7 days each week, to accomplish his research on the chick embryo, goaded by the sense that Chiang Kai-shek's regime, now ensconced in Nanking, would soon topple. There were cries of misrule and internal corruption on the one hand, and sounds of agitation from the Chinese communists on the other. The National University was funded by the Nationalist government in Nanking—when the government got into trouble, as Zing-Yang believed it would, the financial support of this small state-run university could be suspended indefinitely.

In the fall of 1931, while Chiang Kai-shek was attempting to put down a communist revolt in Kiangse Province and cope with the great Yangtze flood that had engulfed the country, the Japanese invaded Manchuria. By this time, the government was already several months in arrears in its remittances to the university, and Zing-Yang had barely enough money to buy feed for his chickens. When he learned of the apparent hopelessness of the situation from the president of the university, who himself was resigning, Zing-Yang made arrangements to move to Nanking, where he was given laboratory space in the biology building of the large National Central University, an institution that still received some limited financial support from the government.

At Nanking, Zing-Yang was able to continue his research on the chick embryo until 1933, at which time he was sent back to Hangchow to assume the presidency of the National University of Chenkiang. During the period from 1931 to 1932, the

Nationalist Government's weak response to the Japanese invasion, as well as the closing of some universities, fomented large-scale student unrest and protest, culminating in a general student strike. It was on the basis of his previous success in handling student unrest, when he was acting president of Fuh Tan University some 10 years earlier, that Zing-Yang was sent back to Hangchow. On his return, Zing-Yang was swamped with administrative duties and forced to severely curtail his research on the chick embryo. Political unrest and student uprisings throughout China continued more or less unabated and, in 1936, Zing-Yang decided to return to the United States. His first stop was Berkeley, where he was invited to lecture on psychobiology. From 1937 to 1940, he continued his studies on embryology at the University of Rochester, the Osborn Zoological Laboratory of Yale University, and the Carnegie Institution of Washington.

With the advent of World War II, despite his excellent scientific reputation, high productivity, and good connections, Zing-Yang had no promise of permanent employment anywhere in the United States. Thus, he was forced to discontinue his research and return to China, which was then under invasion by the Japanese. Except for a period in 1963, when he graciously consented to come to Raleigh, North Carolina, to help me begin my research on the duck embryo, Zing-Yang Kuo never again had the opportunity to work in a laboratory (see chapter opening photograph).

Final Sojourn in Hong Kong

In 1946, Zing-Yang and his family left China and took up residence in Hong Kong. Although he was made a member of the Board of Trustees of the Chinese University of Hong Kong, Zing-Yang had no formal employment in Hong Kong. With his wife, a practicing physician, he lived in an apartment in Kowloon. For 15 years or so, operating out of his apartment, he occupied himself with his first studies of human behavior: a social-psychological analysis of Chinese national character. For contemporary material he interviewed hundreds of Chinese adults and children, including those who arrived daily from China. In this way he kept up to date on the current behavior and attitudes of the Chinese peoples. His background material—the developmental history of Chinese national character—came from the writings of Confucius and other political and ethical philosophers, including Mao Tse-tung. (Prior to World War II, in his status as an educator, he had known Chou En-lai and other Chinese communist functionaries, as well as Chiang Kai-shek and his Nationalist group.)

At the time of his death, on August 14, 1970, Zing-Yang Kuo was working on a book-length manuscript integrating his autobiographical notes with his social-psychological studies of Chinese national character. At this writing (July 1997), an American scholar of Chinese science is preparing that manuscript for possible publication, which will add yet another dimension to Dr. Kuo's intellectual legacy. In addition, Kuo's (1967) book recently received a restrospective review in *Contemporary Psychology* (Rodkin, 1996).

ACKNOWLEDGMENT

This chapter is reproduced, with a number of additions and modifications, from an article published in the *Journal of Comparative and Physiological Psychology*, 1972, vol. 80, pp. 1–10.

REFERENCES

Beach, F. A. (1955). The descent of instinct. *Psychological Review, 62*, 401–410.

Birney, R. C., & Teevan, R. C. (1961). *Instinct: An enduring problem in psychology.* Princeton, NJ: Van Nostrand.

Coghill, G. E. (1929). *Anatomy and the problem of behaviour.* Cambridge, England: Cambridge University Press.

Dunlap, K. (1919–1920). Are there any instincts? *Journal of Abnormal Psychology, 14*, 35–50.

Gottlieb, G. (1970). Conceptions of prenatal behavior. In L. R. Aronson, E. Tobach, D. S. Lehrman, & J. S. Rosenblatt (Eds.), *Development and evolution of behavior* (pp. 111–137). San Francisco: Freeman.

Gottlieb, G. (1997). *Synthesizing nature–nurture:Prenatal roots of instinctive behavior.* Mahwah, NJ: Lawrence Erlbaum Associates.

Gottlieb, G., & Kuo, Z. Y. (1965). Development of behavior in the duck embryo. *Journal of Comparative and Physiological Psychology, 59*, 183–188.

Holt, E. B. (1931). *Animal drive and the learning process.* New York: Henry Holt.

Hunt, J. McV. (1961). *Intelligence and experience.* New York: Ronald.

Kuo, Z. Y. (1921). Giving up instincts in psychology. *Journal of Philosophy, 18*, 645–664.

Kuo, Z. Y. (1922). How are instincts acquired? *Psychological Review, 29*, 344–365.

Kuo, Z. Y. (1924). A psychology without heredity. *Psychological Review, 31*, 427–448.

Kuo, Z. Y. (1928). The fundamental error of the concept of purpose and the trial and error fallacy. *Psychological Review, 35*, 414–433.

Kuo, Z. Y. (1929a). Purposive behavior and prepotent stimulus. *Psychological Review, 36*, 547–550.

Kuo, Z. Y. (1929b). The net result of the anti-heredity movement in psychology. *Psychological Review, 36*, 181–199.

Kuo, Z. Y. (1930). The genesis of the cat's response to the rat. *Journal of Comparative Psychology, 11*, 1–35.

Kuo, Z. Y. (1932a). Ontogeny of embryonic behavior in Aves: I. The chronology and general nature of the behavior of the chick embryo. *Journal of Experimental Zoology, 61*, 395–430.

Kuo, Z. Y. (1932b). Ontogeny of embryonic behavior in Aves: II. The mechanical factors in the various stages leading to hatching. *Journal of Experimental Zoology, 62*, 453–483.

Kuo, Z. Y. (1932c). Ontogeny of embryonic behavior in Aves: III. The structural and environmental factors in embryonic behavior. *Journal of Comparative Psychology, 13*, 245–271.

Kuo, Z. Y. (1932d). Ontogeny of embryonic behavior in Aves: IV. The influence of embryonic movements upon behavior after hatching. *Journal of Comparative Psychology, 14*, 109–122.

Kuo, Z. Y. (1932e). Ontogeny of embryonic behavior in Aves: V. The reflex concept in the light of embryonic behavior in birds. *Psychological Review, 39*, 499–515.

Kuo, Z. Y. (1933). Ontogeny of embryonic behavior in Aves: VI. Relation between heart beat and the behavior of the avian embryo. *Journal of Comparative Psychology, 16*, 379–384.

Kuo, Z. Y. (1938). Ontogeny of embryonic behavior in Aves: XII. Stages in the development of physiological activities in the chick embryo. *American Journal of Psychology, 51*, 361–378.

Kuo, Z. Y. (1939a). Studies in the physiology of the embryonic nervous system: I. Effect of curare on motor activity of the chick embryo. *Journal of Experimental Zoology, 82*, 371–396.

Kuo, Z. Y. (1939b). Studies in the physiology of the embryonic nervous system: II. Experimental evidence on the controversy over the reflex theory in development. *Journal of Comparative Neurology, 70,* 437–459.

Kuo, Z. Y. (1939c). Studies in the physiology of the embryonic nervous system: IV. Development of acetylcholine in the chick embryo. *Journal of Neurophysiology, 2,* 488–493.

Kuo, Z. Y. (1939d). Total pattern or local reflexes? *Psychological Review, 46,* 93–122.

Kuo, Z. Y. (1960a). Studies on the basic factors in animal fighting: I. General analysis of fighting behavior. *Journal of Genetic Psychology, 96,* 201–206.

Kuo, Z. Y. (1960b). Studies on the basic factors in animal fighting: II. Nutritional factors affecting fighting behavior in quails. *Journal of Genetic Psychology, 96,* 207–216.

Kuo, Z. Y. (1960c). Studies on the basic factors in animal fighting: III. Hormonal factors affecting fighting in quails. *Journal of Genetic Psychology, 96,* 217–223.

Kuo, Z. Y. (1960d). Studies on the basic factors in animal fighting: IV. Developmental and environmental factors affecting fighting in quails. *Journal of Genetic Psychology, 96,* 225–239.

Kuo, Z, Y. (1960e). Studies on the basic factors in animal fighting: V. Inter-species coexistence in fish. *Journal of Genetic Psychology, 97,* 181–194.

Kuo, Z. Y. (1960f). Studies on the basic factors in animal fighting: VI. Inter-species coexistence in birds. *Journal of Genetic Psychology, 97,* 195–209.

Kuo, Z. Y. (1960g). Studies on the basic factors in animal fighting: VII. Inter-species coexistence in mammals. *Journal of Genetic Psychology, 97,* 211–225.

Kuo, Z. Y. (1967). *The dynamics of behavior development: An epigenetic view.* New York: Random House.

Kuo, Z. Y. (1970). The need for coordinated efforts in developmental studies. In L. R. Aronson, E. Tobach, D. S. Lehrman, & J. S. Rosenblatt (Eds.), *Development and evolution of behavior* (pp. 181–193). San Francisco: Freeman.

Kuo, Z. Y., & Carmichael, L. (1937). A technique for motion-picture recording of the development of behavior in the chick embryo. *Journal of Psychology, 4,* 343–345.

Kuo, Z. Y., & Shen, T. C. (1936). Ontogeny of embryonic behavior in Aves. X. Gastric movements of the chick embryo. *Journal of Comparative Psychology, 21,* 87–93.

Kuo, Z. Y., & Shen, T. C. R. (1937). Ontogeny of embryonic behavior in Aves: XI. Respiration in the chick embryo. *Journal of Comparative Psychology, 24,* 49–58.

Lehrman, D. S. (1953). A critique of Konrad Lorenz's theory of instinctive behavior. *Quarterly Review of Biology, 28,* 337–363.

Lehrman, D. S. (1970). Semantic and conceptual issues in the nature–nurture problem. In L. R. Aronson, E. Tobach, D. S. Lehrman, & J. S. Rosenblatt (Eds.), *Development and evolution of behavior* (pp. 17–52). San Francisco: Freeman.

Maier, N. R. F., & Schneirla, T. C. (1935). *Principles of animal psychology.* New York: McGraw-Hill.

McDougall, W. (1921–1922). The use and abuse of instinct in social psychology. *Journal of Abnormal and Social Psychology, 16,* 285–333.

Rodkin, P. C. (1996). A developmental, holistic, future-oriented behaviorism: Kuo's *The Dynamics of Behavior Development* revisited. *Contemporary Psychology, 41,* 1085–1088.

Sechenov, I. M. (1965). *Reflexes of the brain.* Cambridge, MA: MIT Press.

Schneirla, T. C. (1966). Behavioral development and comparative psychology. *Quarterly Review of Biology, 41,* 283–302.

Tolman, E. C. (1922). Can instincts be given up in psychology? *Journal of Abnormal and Social Psychology, 17,* 139–152.

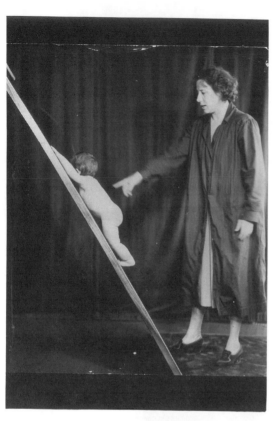

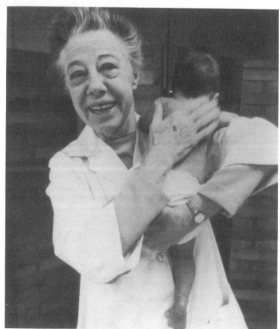

Chapter 13

Myrtle McGraw: Pioneer in Neurobehavioral Development

Thomas C. Dalton
Victor W. Bergenn

In her reminiscences that follow, Myrtle McGraw describes her studies of infant behavior that began when that topic was a recent arrival in the experimental laboratory.[1] It was a time when the theory of evolution was in the air and when it was assumed that, if a basic principle of behavior could be established for one species, that principle would apply to all species. McGraw and other young investigators of infant development had to contend with these and other conceptual challenges, along with various practical and ethical difficulties and the constraints of experimental procedures.

The limitation of this perspective was vividly underscored by McGraw in an anecdote. She reported that she and another experimenter at the Columbia-Presbyterian Medical Center entered an elevator together, he with a monkey on his shoulder and she with a baby in her arms. Both were headed for laboratories to conduct some physiological measurements. As the elevator ascended, the young

---

* Photograph of Myrtle McGraw with Johnny, 1932, at Babies Hospital Columbia University (top) courtesy of Mitzi Wertheim. Photograph of Myrtle McGraw in her laboratory at Briarcliff College, 1969 (bottom), courtesy of Mitzi Wertheim.

[1]In the main, this chapter presents, verbatim, selections from the unpublished memoirs and essays that McGraw wrote between the 1960s and 1980s. These writings were among the papers she left in possession of Victor Bergenn. McGraw's papers are now located in the special collections of Millbank Memorial Library, Teacher's College, Columbia University. We have exercised limited editorial judgment to ensure chronological continuity and to put the events she narrates into scientific perspective. For other accounts of McGraw and her career, see McGraw (1983, 1985, 1990). With Lewis P. Lipsitt, the authors of this chapter also published an article about McGraw for the Centennial Celebration of the American Psychological Association (Bergenn, Dalton, & Lipsitt, 1992).

man asked her why she was studying babies. She answered, "Well, really, I am not studying babies: I am interested in the processes of growth." He asked, "Then why do you use human babies and not animals for subjects? You can do more with animals, and they aren't nearly so messy." "Yes, I know," she answered, "but when your monkey grows up it will still be a monkey, while my baby will be a human; I want to learn how he does it."

McGraw concluded early on that the theories she learned in her graduate courses about salivary conditioning in dogs and maze learning in rats did not provide the theoretical basis to explain, to her satisfaction, how wiggly bits of protoplasm could, in 3 short years, become remarkable, articulate human beings able to ask and answer relevant questions. To her way of thinking, no baby achieved that state merely through the processes of classical and operant conditioning. Throughout here career, and even in her retirement, she was interested in understanding how the child got to where he or she was going. That was Myrtle McGraw's legacy: the analysis of growth and processes of change.

AN ALABAMA SCHOOLGIRL'S
DREAM COME TRUE

In the following, Myrtle McGraw's own words, which do not do full justice to her illustrious career and pioneer status in developmental neuropsychology, do manage to convey her unpretentious, diffident personality.

I was born on August 1, 1899, during a period that has come to be known for the decline of the "kinship family." There were, however, seven children in my family; I was the fifth. The family lived on a small farm in Boas on the outskirts of Birmingham, Alabama. My grandparents were of the Civil War generation, my parents of that war's first postwar generation, so it can be said that I and my siblings were of the second postwar generation. It was not uncommon to find persons of success and distinction in that post-Civil War generation who could not read or write. Nevertheless many members of that generation, including myself, became motivated toward formal education.

Early Education

Because I was born in the south at a time when it had not yet recovered sufficiently from the war to have enough public schools, my basic education was haphazard. I entered the public school in the first grade in Birmingham, Alabama, at about the age of 6. The first 3 years were a complete bore. What I learned then was the art of daydreaming, wondering what it would be like when

I really grew up. I managed to finish the sixth grade and then I became what would in these days be called a drop-out. I did not complete the eight grades that were at the time considered sufficient for a formal education. Instead, I registered for a course in typing and shorthand in a local school for business training. After finishing that course, I was employed in a small law office where I worked for more than 2 years. A law partner who noticed my interest in reading suggested that I should further my formal education. He arranged for me to be admitted to Snead Seminary, a Methodist boarding school, where I could work in the office of the head mistress to cover expenses.

During my sophomore year there, I received a copy of a magazine called The Independent (long since defunct), which contained an article about John Dewey (chap. 4, Pioneers II) entitled, "The Teacher of Teachers." At the time John Dewey was a professor at Columbia University in New York City. I wrote him a fan letter. I assume he was so puzzled that a young teenage girl in the mountains of Alabama had even heard of him that he answered. We corresponded for well over a year until he left for a sojourn of several years in China.

I am sure that some of the Snead staff wondered about those letters. Once I wrote to Dewey saying that I felt as if he were my intellectual godfather. After that he signed his correspondence "GF." Finally he wrote that he would not he able to write to me for some time because he was going on a long trip to the Orient—China and elsewhere—and would not be back for several years. I received one envelope from him while he was in China. It had only a pressed flower and a tiny piece of paper on which was written, "from the Great Wall of China."

Another event that was to affect my education and career immeasurably occurred when I was a senior at Snead Seminary. It was customary for outside speakers to give an address at Snead Chapel. One such speaker was Ralph A. Felton, Secretary of the Home Mission of the Methodist Church. We met at lunch. Afterward he asked if I would like to work in his office. I was so excited by the thought that I almost jumped out of my skin. I checked that urge and answered, "Of course." He replied that when he got back to his office he would write to me.

College Years

Finally, Felton wrote back that he was attending a conference at Ohio Wesleyan University in Delaware, Ohio, and asked me to come there to see him. We met and, after explaining his offer further, he asked what I thought about it. I answered, "I think I should go to college." He asked how I liked Ohio Wesleyan, and then he spent most of the day investigating how I could obtain scholarships and a work appointment. Applications for scholarships were written and signed with his recommendations. A professor of education offered to take me on as a secretary in his office during nonclass hours. That September I returned to Ohio Wesleyan and remained through the 4 years of college.

While staying with the Feltons the summer after my junior year in 1922, I ran across an announcement that John Dewey was teaching at Columbia. Both Feltons had degrees from divisions of Columbia—Blanche from Teachers College and Ralph from Union Theological Seminary. For the first time, I told them about the correspondence I had had with John Dewey before he went to the Orient and asked if we could invite him to come down there. My memory of Blanche Felton's reply is as clear today as when she spoke it: "Myrtle, you and I are not qualified to invite a John Dewey to come to us; we must go to see the professor." So the Feltons cooperated in making plans for me to go to New York City to see him.

I have not the vaguest idea how I managed to get from Grand Central Station to my appointment at Columbia University. Somehow I made it without mishap. With the Feltons' direction and guidance, I went to Teachers College first and asked for John Dewey's office. They steered me to the Schermerhorn building on campus and someone there directed me to the philosophy library. When I asked the man at the desk for Dewey's office, he casually pointed and said, "That door." The library was occupied with summer students reading. On the door a sign read "Office Hours: 3:30 to 4:30" and it wasn't yet noon. I went back to the desk and mentioned the office hours. The man at the desk seemed utterly unconcerned and replied, "Knock on the door."

I went back and timidly knocked on the door. A mild-mannered man answered and I said, "Dr. Dewey?" The voice answered "Yes." I said, "I know this isn't your office hours, but I wonder if I could see you?" He said, "Come in." I did and said, "Well, don't you know me?" Apparently he had just opened my telegram that had been sent to his office and was standing there thinking still, I guess, about this 16-year-old girl whom he was supposed to meet and had not. After that Dewey took me to a Chinese restaurant for lunch. Some weeks later I received a note from Dewey saying he'd get out to visit with us but only briefly. My only memory is that the visit was, indeed, brief but delightful.

Graduate Education

John Dewey and I wrote infrequently during my senior year. I probably mentioned my desire for graduate study and he probably understood my circumstances better than I realized. Dewey made it possible for me to attend Teachers College at Columbia University after my graduation from Ohio Wesleyan by hiring me to type the manuscript of a book he was writing, Experience and Nature (Dewey, 1981). During that first graduate year, I lived in a tiny room with a table where I could place my typewriter, a chair, and a cot-size bed. From time to time, Dewey would drop in to review the typewritten manuscript for corrections. I can remember myself thinking, "What can I do to get him to talk a bit?" During that first year, I never had occasion to meet any of his family; I was just a hired typist.

At Teachers College, I majored in religious education, but it was a confusing and disappointing year. I did not want to disappoint the Feltons, who had been so kind to me, but I could not stay in harmony with their recommendations. I was busy rethinking my choice of a religious education, realizing it was unsuitable for me. I had been through two Methodist schools—secondary and undergraduate—and I did not want or need more of it just then. I solved the problem by teaching in Puerto Rico the following year. I had not been in Puerto Rico more than 3 months before I wrote the Feltons that I did not think I qualified for foreign missionary work.

In September 1925, I returned to Columbia University and registered for a postgraduate course with a major in the relatively young discipline of psychology. It was a favorable time for such an undertaking. During the mid-1920s, new institutes and centers were being established for the study of infancy and early child development at many academic institutions throughout this country and in Europe, notably Austria (see Frank, 1962). The one at Teachers College had just been inaugurated. Helen Woolly was overall director, with Bess Cunningham as the director of research. She had two graduate research workers. The staff also included a pediatrician and a nursery school teacher for the young children. I applied for a job at the Institute and was given the position of secretary to Bess Cunningham. It was a full-time position but I managed to take courses during nonoffice hours, and I certainly gained information at the weekly staff meetings, seeing techniques demonstrated and hearing staff discussions. Listening in did not qualify me to pass courses, but it did help me pass with perhaps less intensive reading than I otherwise would have needed.

During this time, I met Lawrence K. Frank, an officer of the General Education Board of the Rockefeller Foundation. In 1927, Frank offered me a Laura Spelman Rockefeller fellowship so that I could finish the required coursework without the diversion of holding a full-time job. I completed the course requirements for the Ph.D. during that year but still needed to do research for the thesis. Consequently, in 1927, I accepted a teaching job in the psychology department at Florida State College for Women in Tallahassee. The position provided me with teaching experience and the possibility to conduct my thesis research.

The problem was, how could I find time to do experiments for a thesis while teaching? I sought the advice of Director Woolly. She had just returned from Austria and was impressed with the standardized infant test designed by Charlotte Bühler of Austria. She suggested I take that test and make a comparative study of White and African-American infants for my thesis research while in the south. Once classes started and I became acquainted with my students, I turned my thoughts to gathering material for the thesis. I did not think the college would provide me campus space to test the babies. I consulted my roommate and she agreed that the testing could be done in our apartment.

The next question was how to locate the infants for my study. In Florida in those days it was not customary to register the birth of babies, especially African-American babies. Fortunately I had bought a second-hand car. One of my students and I would drive out into the African-American district and look for diapers on the clothesline. Then we would rap on the door and ask the mother if we could borrow her baby (provided it was of the appropriate age), for a test. We had no difficulty getting cooperation, and we had no protest from the White community, not even from the White mothers who were cooperating.

When I left for Tallahassee, I was told that Dr. Woolly would be head of my thesis committee and that Professor Harold Pintner of Teachers College and Professor Henry Garrett, a statistician, would be the other two members. When I returned, I discovered that Dr. Woolly had withdrawn because of illness and Dr. Lois Meek had taken her place as director of my committee. The thesis was turned over to the committee for appraisal. Dates were set for the committee to meet, but the meeting was postponed each time, because Lois Meek was too busy with her directorship to read the manuscript.

Finally there was a meeting, but Professor Garrett told me that Dr. Meek had made the other faculty members angry with her many postponements. She also disapproved of the thesis—not because there were too few subjects or because the findings were misinterpreted—but because she did not trust the Charlotte Bühler test. Pintner then blurted out, "any student who goes out searching for diapers on the clothesline to get subjects for an experiment has the potential for becoming a good scientist." The thesis was then accepted.

THE NEUROLOGICAL INSTITUTE

During my year of thesis writing, from 1928 to 1929, I worked as an intern with the Institute of Child Guidance at Columbia University. During that time, I decided that clinical psychology was not something I wanted to adopt as a profession. Hence, my most urgent need was to find a new job before the clinical fellowship ended. Because I had taken a beginning course in neurology at Physicians and Surgeons of Columbia University, I decided to get help from my former neurology professor, Dr. Thomas Elwyn. He listened to my story and my doubts about a career in clinical psychology and recommended that I consult Dr. Frederick Tilney, Director of the Neurological Institute (see Elsberg, 1944; Pool, 1975). Tilney had a number of different investigations going on under his supervision (see Tilney, 1923; Tilney & Casamajor, 1924, Tilney & Kubie, 1931).

My first interview with Dr. Tilney was delightful; mostly he inquired about my background. When I started to leave, he commented that he would phone me, but added, "You understand that you have not been hired." Nevertheless, I went back to the Institute assured. A month or more passed without a call. My anxiety became intolerable, so I called his office. The secretary told me that Dr. Tilney would like to see me and she made an early date. The second appointment was pleasant, but brief. Tilney explained that he planned to extend his animal studies on the correlation of the nervous system and behavior to the human level and he needed someone to provide the protocol for observing infant behavior development beginning with the newborn. Then Dr. Tilney told me that I was hired and should come for work on September 1, 1930. Weeks later I had a call from Tilney's secretary again telling me to meet Dr. Tilney and Dr. Herbert Wilcox, head of Pediatrics, who was offering Tilney floor space for a laboratory.

Direct Observation of Infant Behavior

Once the laboratory had been equipped with facilities and personnel, Tilney did the most marvelous thing for my education. He appointed an advisory council of distinguished persons from different disciplines, including neuroanatomist C. E. Coghill, John Dewey, psychologists Robert Woodworth and John Watson (chap. 12, *Pioneers I*), pediatricians, and so forth. At our monthly meetings, I would demonstrate some performance of the infants and a lively discussion would follow. No member requested or received an honorarium. No classroom could have matched that type of instruction for me. In addition, as soon as we were operating as a laboratory, Dewey arranged for his eldest daughter, Evelyn Dewey (1935), to obtain and review the literature on the general area of infant development, which she later published (see Dalton & Bergenn, 1996, for more details about Dewey's role in McGraw's studies).

Arnold Gesell's (1924) developmental scales had already been published. I went to Yale hoping to spend a couple of weeks while his associates, Helen Thompson or Joan Halverson, would give me instruction in administering and interpreting those tests. Unintentionally, but in the long run, Gesell did me a great favor. I was shown the Yale laboratory but he gave me the brush-off on the request to stay for instruction. So I returned to the Medical Center empty-handed. I was on my own. Not knowing what to do next for months on end, I spent hours in the delivery room and the laboratory just looking at babies, always asking, what can they teach me? As I watched the babies, I became a little disenchanted with the method of checking off behavior achievements and plotting them against chronological age. It was like taking an inventory of performance. The minute changes in the quality of the behavior fascinated me, but I also wanted to understand how one developing function influences another. To do this, I needed to have at least a couple of babies, the same babies in the laboratory every day, to detect the subtle signals of behavioral growth.

Maturation Versus Learning

You will recall that at this time the primary debate in developmental psychology was maturation versus learning (see Dalton & Bergenn, 1995). I saw no reason whatsoever to question the maturation theory. Naive as I was, I thought that if I took a newborn and exercised it every day in any activity of which the baby was capable I would discover that magic time, that magic age, at which the baby could profit from practice and learning. Great! I thought I would be able to tell parents not to bother trying to teach babies anything until they reached the favorable age. Also, as soon as a new function appeared in the infants' behavior repertoire, I tried to find ways to make it a little more difficult or challenging for them. For example, when they began to crawl, we provided inclines for them to go up and down. I had already reached the conclusion that during infant development one could not adequately appraise an overt performance in any experimental situation without taking into account the physiological, neurological, and anatomical changes as significant factors. Thus, I set myself the task of reading the literature in embryology, physiology, and neurology to the extent of my ability (see Oppenheim, 1995).

Coghill (1929, 1930) visited our laboratory several times and I had become somewhat knowledgeable of his embryological studies of salamanders. I was particularly impressed with his description of the "S" movement of the spinal axis of embryonic vertebrates and his theory of individual development. I had observed that some of the newborn infants could progress several feet across the bed by using that kind of S-shaped spinal movement. Watson had stated, on the basis of his earlier studies, that there was no evidence of a swimming reflex in the behavior of the newborn infant. When he saw me demonstrate the reflex by putting the babies in the water and letting their heads go under, he said, "Girl, you have a lot more courage than I had." It was those observations and thoughts that triggered our studies of the swimming reflex in the infant (McGraw, 1939a).

Having been indoctrinated with the scientific idea of objectivity and measurement, the fact that I was so dependent on direct observation of overt behavior of the infant continued to bug me. Psychology was intent on becoming scientific. Standardized testing was an acceptable instrument for that purpose, but I was making no use of that technique. My focus was not following standardized testing but trying to describe oscillations of growth. I called that *process*. My psychology colleagues considered what I was doing to be interesting but not scientific. That troubled me. I always discussed my concerns and doubts with Dewey, but on one occasion he responded, somewhat harshly. "Look here," he said, "I have told you dozens of times that your method of investigation is sound, so lay off your concern."

Lawrence Frank gave a needed boost to our project when he dropped in one day to see how things were going. He told me that he would provide two interns to work with us for a year. He also urged me to consolidate our study plans and submit an application to the General Education Board of the Rockefeller Foundation for long-term funding. A couple of young men were added to our staff—a biochemist/mathematician and a physiological psychologist. They and I vigorously pursued the development of instruments that would yield objective data. One day the young men came into my office grinning like two cats that had eaten a canary. They had a platform mounted on ball-bearing rollers at each of the four corners. The corners were to be attached to a kymograph so we would have four recordings of the baby's balancing stability in the development of walking.

That device, I said, might give us a measure of balancing, but it would not tell us anything about the child's propulsion or stepping aptitude. The way these two forces work together is what is important. Ball bearings! A thought: "Why don't we put him on ball-bearing roller skates?" I asked. We had to have the skates custom made because no one had ever heard of putting a 1-year-old infant on skates. We did just that, and that was the beginning of our study of the skating behavior of infants.

THE METHOD OF CO-TWIN CONTROL: STUDIES OF JOHNNY AND JIMMY

I undertook the study of the twins, Johnny and Jimmy, because I wanted to determine the effect that daily practice and challenges would have on performance (McGraw, 1935, 1939b). The reason for using twins and the method of co-twin control was that this made it possible to determine the effects of environmental interventions with biological factors controlled as well as possible. In that investigation, Johnny received special practice and exercise that Jimmy did not.

The type of exercise given Johnny during the early months was simple. He was encouraged to make crawling and stepping movements; he was held by his feet in an inverted position to stimulate activity of the spinal muscles; his grasping and other reflexes were stimulated daily. As he grew older and became capable of more complex behavior, his practice schedule was expanded. For example, when he began to reach for toys held in front of him, he was given daily practice in that function. When he began to creep on his hands and knees, he was given daily exercise in creeping up and down inclines of varying steepness. As soon as he could sit on a stool and turn himself around, he was exposed to daily practice in getting off pedestals of various heights. When he began to stand on his two feet and take a few steps, he was placed on roller skates not with the thought of teaching him to roller skate, but primarily to make the job of balancing a little more difficult for him and to stimulate activity of certain muscle groups and nerve centers that were just beginning to work together. Because the spontaneous movements of newborn babies simulate swimming movements, Johnny was supported in a tank of water to stimulate the use of muscles involved in swimming. When he was a little older, it was observed that he, like most toddlers, enjoyed pushing furniture around the room. So the situation was set for him to push pedestals of different heights around and arrange them to climb up and get a piece of banana or cracker suspended from the ceiling.

The outcome of such practice in motor activities is well known. A baby of less than a year was scaling slopes of unbelievable steepness. At 15 months Johnny was doing a credible job of roller skating and, in less time swimming 12 to 15 feet with his face under water. These are the achievements that attracted popular notice. However, press reports and magazine articles confused the techniques of stimulation I employed with conditioning. Journalists also incorrectly concluded that my studies supported maturationism when, in fact, my work challenged the notion that neural and behavioral development occur in an invariable and uniform sequence (see Dennis, 1989, 1995).

What did that outcome actually mean? The answer is clear and simple. Like most controversial issues, the truth is somewhere between the extreme claims. The development of children is not merely a matter of waiting for the nerves to grow, nor can one take any little boy and make him anything one wants to merely by controlling the environment in which he shall live. In training young children, one must wait until the nervous system matures—until it achieves a state of readiness to perform. The child does not achieve this state of readiness in all things at the same time, nor do all children achieve it at the same age. However, once children have attained a state of nerve and muscle preparedness, they will profit much by an opportunity to exercise those muscle groups that have just begun to work together. By putting Johnny on roller skates just at the time his balancing and locomotor systems were beginning to work together, we were able to graft the roller-skating performance on the act of walking. Johnny not only exceeded the accomplishment of Jimmy in this activity, but he exceeded our expectations of any baby of comparable age. It is probably safe to say that toddlers will learn to roller skate with less expenditure of energy than older children. Although babies have a less mature nervous system to work with, they have a less difficult mechanical task to accomplish.

I reached these conclusions by studying the effects of growth on behavioral development. Let me reiterate what I said in the concluding chapter of *Growth*:

A behavior-course is not an isolated unit growing in every direction all at once. It is comprised of many aspects, each of which has its own growth rate and rhythm. While each aspect of a growing action-pattern has its own identifiable way of developing, it is at the same time an integral part of the total behavior-pattern, in the same fashion that the behavior-pattern in question is an integral part of the total action-system of the individual. One aspect of a behavior-pattern goes through a period of rapid development, then pauses as another aspect moves rapidly forward. But the growth of each aspect of development influences and determines the growth of the other. The development of one aspect overlaps with the development of another so that there are no sharp lines of demarcation separating the phases of a developing pattern, but the connection of one phase or one pattern with another is more than a mere overlapping. There is a close interdependence in the growth of the various aspects of a pattern. Development works back and forward; here and there it strikes rapids, in other spots it pauses or regresses. The appearance of a new movement or aspect of a pattern facilitates or inhibits the growth of a previously developing movement and also determines the emergence and organization of a succeeding one. It is the gradual twining and interweaving of movements and phases of developing patterns which make it difficult to allocate the rhythms and spurts of growth. (McGraw, 1935, pp. 305–306)

I went on to point out that:

In fact and in principle the underlying processes which obtain in the development of behavior also apply to the modification of behavior. Development is a process of modification, and it is really impossible to draw a distinction between the two; but when we speak of modified behavior we usually mean that it has been modified in such a way as to change it from a course of development which occurs under the usual circumstances. It is in this sense that we have used the term modified behavior. Behavior-patterns can be modified by (1) speeding up the growth process, (2) prolonging or reducing the rate of development, or (3) in some way altering the form or sequence of the pattern which ordinarily occurs during development. Changes in any of these ways may be brought about through deliberate manipulation of the factors involved in the growth process. In so doing, it is not the principles of development which are altered but merely the relationship between the ingredients which make up the growth compound. There are many ways of artificially or deliberately altering the relationship of the factors which activate the growth process. One very obvious method is to increase or restrict the amount of exercise or use the growing behavior-pattern is allowed. In this way it is possible to estimate the effect repetition of function may have upon its development.

The extent to which exercise of an activity may alter the development of a particular behavior-course in infancy is contingent upon the following conditions: (1) the neuro-structural level at which the activity is controlled; (2) the state of plasticity or fixity of the behavior-course at the time increased exercise or use is introduced; (3) the state of fixity attained by the behavior pattern at the time the factor of special exercise is withdrawn; and (4) the phylogenetic origin and importance of the behavior-pattern. (McGraw, 1935, p. 309)

BRAIN WAVES AND BEHAVIOR

The studies I reported in *Growth* and *The Neuromuscular Maturation of the Human Infant* were initiated in 1930 for the express purpose of determining the relationship between behavior development and the maturation of neural tissues, particularly that of the brain. That goal was never experimentally achieved due to Tilney's untimely death in 1938. However, an interpretation of developing motor activities common to the human infant was presented in light of available literature on the cellular structures of the nervous system. Early in the program, we became aware that histological studies of dead tissues could not disclose the whole story of function and the neural counterparts that mediated the behavior. Histological and reconstructive techniques were the established neurological methods of investigations at that time.

How vividly I recall many hours in Dr. Tilney's laboratory, as I watched him bending over his microscope and shared his excitement when he found a new layer of cells in the fetal brain of a cat. It was exciting because we had recorded on movie film the behavior of that same animal specimen. It was frustrating that we had no tangible method of estimating neural maturation of the same infants whose overt behavior I was studying. Even then we felt the final answer to our problem would not be found in the shape and processes of nerve cells but in the electrical and chemical components of neural functioning. We were thrilled and thought we had found the answer to our dreams when we first heard of the Berger rhythm.

Neurologists discovered that an infant's brain emits alpha waves in a characteristic pattern called a *Berger Rhythm*. I had my staff contact experts at the nearby Bell Laboratory to find out how to record these brain waves. My future husband, Rudy Mallina, a Bell inventor, helped my staff assemble the necessary apparatus for making these recordings. In 1935, Dr. Roy Smith, a neurophysiologist, was added to our research staff to collect data and study brain waves of the growing infants from whom we were gathering behavioral data. Insofar as I have been able to ascertain, ours was the first laboratory to record electroencephalograms (EEGs) of infants. We quickly learned that the dream of obtaining cinematographic records of overt behavior and EEGs simultaneously on the same child subjects was beyond realization. Hence, over the years, Dr. Smith accumulated yards of tape recordings from the electrodes placed on the skulls of our infants. The real difficulty arose in trying to evaluate all those records because, as Dr. Smith (1938a, 1938b, 1939) pointed out, slow waves and other frequencies often became superimposed and masked the particular frequency with which the experimenter was concerned. Now electroencephalographers have at their disposal giant computers that can sort out the significant frequencies from the background electrical noises of the brain.

At the time, the preponderance of neurological studies supported the general idea that awareness is located in the cerebral cortex. Available histological information on the newborn brain justified the assumption that the cerebral cortex is not functioning at the time of birth. Therefore, it seemed reasonable to assume that the emergence of conscious awareness would signify that the cerebral cortex entered into the pattern of behavior under consideration.

It is precisely the question of cortical involvement that indicates a need for reassessment of the behavior data in the light of advanced neurological knowledge. Karl Lashley (1930, chap. 20, *Pioneers I*) had shown that the cerebral cortex was almost expendable in the learning process of the rat. At that time, psychologists were too prone to overlook or disregard both the phyletic position and the individual maturity of their experimental animals. For that reason, we did not believe that Lashley's findings on the cortex of the rat should overrule the histological data of Tilney (1931) and Conel (1939; 1941) on the brain of the newborn. We appraised the descriptive data in terms of cortical and subcortical functioning. Despite the difficulties in descriptive recording and other problems, the basic configurations in the motor activities discussed have been well delineated (see Weinbach, 1938a, 1938b) and may be useful to modern investigators. It is in the *organization* of neural functioning (not in cellular structures) and the *organization* of behavior (not in achievements) that we may hope to find the relationship between the two systems.

Advanced knowledge in biology and physics will indubitably have great significance for future studies of behavior development. First of all, there are the fantastically revolutionary scientific breakthroughs in the field of genetics. Latest reports indicate that the decoding of the information stored in the DNA will be forthcoming in the not-too-distant future. If the geneticists can decode the DNA, the neurologists will surely be able in time to decode information transmitted from nuclei to nuclei, and from brain to behavior.

THE BRIARCLIFF YEARS

The decade from the early 1940s to early 1950s was for me a period of domesticity and diversity. I was preoccupied with rearing my daughter, Mitzi, who briefly had been involved in my experimental studies. I was invited to give an address to the New York Academy of Medicine in 1943 in which I described Coghill's contribution to my research (McGraw, 1943b). I completed a second book in 1943 (McGraw, 1943a) summarizing and synthesizing my studies, and I contributed a review article on "The Maturation of Behavior" in 1946 for Leonard Carmichael's *Manual of Child Psychology* (McGraw, 1946). I also wrote several feature articles for popular newspapers and magazines, such as *The New York Times* and *Parents Magazine*. In addition to these, I wrote about two dozen unpublished essays that attempted to place my infant studies in an anthropological and cultural perspective. Finally, an invitation to an international conference on sports medicine in Moscow in 1958 enabled me to travel extensively in eastern Europe. This trip stimulated me to submit a major research proposal to the National Institutes of Health for the comparative investigation of infant rearing and emotional development, but it was never funded.

Then one day in the early 1950s, there came an unexpected phone call requesting that I come to see the president, Clara Tead, of Briarcliff College, at Briarcliff Manor—only a short drive from my home in Hastings-on-Hudson, New York. I went as requested. I knew nothing about that small college, and I never learned how they ever heard about me. On my first visit, Mrs. Tead explained the nature of a vacancy in psychology at the college and asked me to come back for an evening appointment to meet her husband, Ordway Tead, who was president of the Board of Trustees. I was quickly offered the position. I appeared for duty the following fall of 1952.

The design of my laboratory at Briarcliff was based on that developed during the 1930s at Babies Hospital, but it was significantly different. In the Briarcliff laboratory, it was the students not the teacher who handled and focused observation on the infant's behavior. Mothers of infants or toddlers were solicited to bring their offspring in for study. A cooperative mother and child were assigned to each particular student for the duration of the course. A partition topped with one-way glass was arranged so that members of the class could observe while the student worked with her child subject. In class meetings afterward we discussed the pros and cons of each student's performance with her assigned child subject.

REFLECTIONS
ON THE DISCIPLINE OF PSYCHOLOGY

My husband died in 1970 and I retired from Briarcliff College in 1972. Throughout my retirement, Dr. Victor W. Bergenn, an educational psychologist who taught at Briarcliff College while I was there, has enabled me to sustain an interest in public education and extend my acquaintances with distinguished researchers in the field of psychology. Victor and his wife Marlene have been my closest and most watchful friends during these years of retirement. Victor invited me to collaborate with him in the creation of the Council on Educational Psychology in 1972 and I served as its first President from 1972–1988. The Council's mission is to influence policies affecting public education in the New York metropolitan area concerning such issues as effective learning processes, appropriate methods of educational testing, and equitable access to educational resources.

I also had the pleasure of becoming acquainted with some of the most provocative contemporary psychologists and neuroscientists in development, infancy, and early childhood. Ronald Oppenheim, a neurobiologist, and Gilbert Gottlieb, a psychologist who invited me to speak at North Carolina in the early 1970s, shared their views with me about basic developmental processes. Jerome Bruner had a lot to do with the resurgence of interest in the young child and process. Bruner said that I should join the Harvard crowd, but I declined. We were great friends. Jerome Kagan invited me to speak to a class at Harvard, as did T. Barry Brazelton. Brazelton remarked to me, "Do you know that they are beginning to say what you have been saying for years." I told him that my work at Babies Hospital did not get the attention then because the timing was bad. Psychology, infant development, and pediatrics were all so indoctrinated with behaviorism that they could not get the point of process going on all the time. Finally, Lewis Lipsitt provided invaluable assistance in getting me involved in scholarly publication and writing my memoirs. Lipsitt (1979) and I had the occasion to discuss his research on sudden infant death syndrome (SIDS). I think he found some interesting connections to my idea that a baby's first 4 months is a critical period in the transition from reflexive to voluntary motor control.

When reading current literature in the biological sciences, one cannot escape the feeling that we are on the brink of a new and exhilarating scientific era, or perhaps it is just another phase in the spurt of science that burst forth in the mid-19th century. The late 19th and early 20th centuries might appropriately be called the *Age of Scientific Cleavages*. New sciences, trying to cut the umbilical cord from the mother, philosophy, were asserting themselves and trying to find their own identity. Sometimes they were rather quarrelsome over territory and property rights, and they were often scornful of the mother from which they sprung.

Now we seem to be entering the *Age of Scientific Integration*, when the findings in one discipline synthesize with those of another. What the biological sciences need now is an Einstein who can abstract the fundamentals from all disciplines and formulate a theory of growth and development that will transcend the particulars of the growing organism. Formulation of the theory would generate new visions and stimulate new techniques for the study of organization in both behavioral and neural functioning. This exciting new day, reflecting as it does the forces of confluence rather than divergence, would also benefit if there appeared in our midst a timely, perceptive philosopher who could interpret, articulate, and give meaning and inspiration to the Age of Scientific Integration, as did the empiricists and pragmatists in the dawning decades of the scientific era.

REFERENCES

Bergenn, V. W., Dalton, T. C., & Lipsitt, L. P. (1992). Myrtle B. McGraw: A growth Scientist. *Developmental Psychology, 28,* 381–395.

Coghill, G. E. (1929). *Anatomy and the problem of behavior.* New York: Cambridge University Press.

Coghill, G. E. (1930). Individuation verses integration in the development of behavior. *Journal of Genetic Psychology, 3,* 431–435.

Conel, L. J. (1939). *The postnatal development of the human cerebral cortex: Vol. 1. The cortex of the newborn.* Cambridge, MA: Harvard University Press.

Conel, L. J. (1941). *The postnatal development of the human cerebral cortex: Vol. 2. The cortex of the one month infant.* Cambridge, MA: Harvard University Press.

Dalton, T. C., & Bergenn, V. W. (1995). *Beyond heredity and environment: Myrtle McGraw and the maturation controversy.* Boulder, CO: Westview.

Dalton, T. C., & Bergenn, V. W. (1996). John Dewey, Myrtle McGraw and *Logic*: An unusual collaboration in the 1930s. *Studies in History and Philosophy of Science, 27,* 69–107.

Dennis, P. (1989). "Johnny's a gentleman, but Jimmy's a mug:" Press coverage during the 1930s of Myrtle McGraw's study of Johnny and Jimmy Woods. *Journal of the History of the Behavioral Sciences, 25,* 356–370.

Dennis, P. (1995). Johnny and Jimmy and the maturation controversy: Popularization, misunderstanding, and setting the record straight. In T. C. Dalton & V. W. Bergenn (Eds.), *Beyond heredity and environment: Myrtle McGraw and the maturation controversy* (pp. 67–76). Boulder, CO: Westview.

Dewey, E. (1935). *Behavior development in infants: A survey of the literature on prenatal and postnatal activity, 1920–1924.* New York: Columbia University Press.

Dewey, J. (1981). Experience and nature. In J. A. Boydston (Ed.), *John Dewey: The later works: Vol. 1* (pp. 1–409). Carbondale, IL: Southern Illinois University Press.

Elsberg, C. (1944). *The story of a hospital: The Neurological Institute of New York, 1909–1938.* New York: Paul F. Hoeber.

Frank, L. K. (1962). The beginnings of child development and family life education in the twentieth century. *Merrill-Palmer Quarterly, 8,* 207–227.

Gesell, A. (1924). *Infant behavior: Its genesis and growth.* New York: McGraw-Hill.

Lashley, K. (1930). Basic neural mechanisms in behavior. *Psychological Review, 97,* 1–24.

Lipsitt, L. P. (1979). Critical conditions in infancy: A psychological perspective. *American Psychologist, 34,* 973–980.

McGraw, M. B. (1935). *Growth: A study of Johnny and Jimmy.* New York: Appleton-Century-Crofts.

McGraw, M. B. (1939a). Swimming behavior of the human infant. *Journal of Pediatrics, 15,* 485–490.

McGraw, M. B. (1939b). Later development of children specially trained during infancy: Johnny and Jimmy at school age. *Child Development, 10,* 1–19.

McGraw, M. B. (1943a). *The neuromuscular maturation of the human infant.* New York: Columbia University Press.

McGraw, M. B. (1943b). *Let babies be our teachers: Lecture to the laity*. In New York Academy of Medicine, *March of medicine* (pp. 100–118). New York: Columbia University Press.

McGraw, M. B. (1946). The maturation of behavior. In L. Carmichael (Ed.), *Manual of child psychology* (pp. 332–369). New York: Wiley.

McGraw, M. B. (1983). Myrtle B. McGraw. In A. N. O'Connell & N. F. Russo (Eds.), *Models of achievement: Reflections of eminent women in psychology* (pp. 43–54). New York: Columbia University Press.

McGraw, M. B. (1985). Professional and personal blunders in child development research. *Psychological Record, 35*, 165–170.

McGraw, M. B. (1990). Memories, deliberate recall, and speculations. *American Psychologist, 45*, 934–937).

Oppenheim, R. (1995). Myrtle McGraw's nascent and pioneering use of embryology to understand human development. In T. C. Dalton & V. W. Bergenn (Eds.), *Beyond heredity and environment: Myrtle McGraw and the maturation controversy* (pp. xv–xvii). Boulder, CO: Westview.

Pool, L. (1975). *The Neurological Institute of New York, 1909–1974*. Lakeville, CT: Pocketknife.

Smith, J. R (1938a). The electroencephalogram during normal infancy and childhood: Rhythmic activities present in the neonate and their subsequent development. *Journal of Genetic Psychology, 53*, 431–453.

Smith, J. R. (1938b). The electroencephalogram during normal infancy and childhood: The nature of the growth of the alpha waves. *Journal of Genetic Psychology, 53*, 455–459.

Smith, J. R. (1939). The "occipital" and "pre-central" alpha rhythms during the first two years. *Journal of Psychology, 7*, 223–227.

Tilney, F. (1923). Genesis of cerebellar functions. *Archives of Neurology and Psychiatry, 9*, 137–169.

Tilney, F., & Casamajor, L. (1924). Myelinogeny as applied to the study of behavior. *Archives of Neurology and Psychiatry, 12*, 1–66.

Tilney, F., & Kubie, L. (1931). Behavior in its relation to the development of the brain. *Bulletin of the Neurological Institute, 1*, 226–313.

Weinbach, A. P. (1938a). Some physiological phenomena fitted to growth equations: II. Brain potentials. *Human Biology, 10*, 145–150.

Weinbach, A. P. (1938b). Some physiological phenomena fitted to growth equations: III. Rate of growth of brain potentials (alpha frequency) compared with rate of growth of the brain. *Growth, 2*, 247–251.

Chapter 14

Henry W. Nissen: Quiet Comparative Psychologist

Donald A. Dewsbury

Many scientists' lives are instructive in one way or another. From the life of Henry Nissen, we learn something about the kind of personality that it takes to make a visible, lasting impact on psychology. Nissen was both a creative and successful psychologist and a highly modest and self-effacing man. Lashley (1958; chap. 20, *Pioneers I*) called him "one of the most lovable persons that I have ever known." He added, however, that Nissen was "too kindly, too modest, too sensitive to make a success of life" (p. 1). Whether one shares Lashley's view depends on one's criteria for success. It is true that, although Nissen's contributions were substantial and some have had lasting effects on comparative psychology, few are highly visible today.

Henry Wieghorst Nissen was an honored and respected comparative psychologist who, in 1953, was elected to the National Academy of Sciences. Serving as director of the Yerkes Laboratories of Primate Biology in Orange Park, Florida, he probably knew more about the biology and behavior of chimpanzees than any person then alive. He had significant impact on the psychology of his time. Yet when I examined the indexes of 14 relatively recent textbooks in the history of psychology, Nissen's name appeared in only three: in one for co-editing the selected papers of Karl S. Lashley, in one for his early field work on chimpanzees (Hearnshaw, 1987), and in one for his efforts to solve problems of comparison in comparative psychology (Hilgard, 1987). I explore the life of Henry Nissen, his contributions to psychology, and some of the reasons he is not often cited today.

THE LIFE OF HENRY NISSEN

Henry Wieghorst Nissen was born on February 5, 1901, in Chicago, Illinois. His father, Adolph, was "an old fashioned book-keeper by occupation, who could easily

---

*Photograph of Henry W. Nissen courtesy of Dora Nissen Mann.

have been cut out of a Dickens tale" (Koehler, 1960, p. 2). His mother, Marie, was described as "a nice looking, plumpish personification of an adoring and highly emotional mother" (Koehler, 1960, p. 3). When Heinz, as he was then called, was young, his father worked for the Pabst Chemical Company. The family lived on the northeast side of Chicago and Heinz attended public grammar school and high school there. During Heinz's early high school years, Adolph Nissen invested in an aluminum utensil factory in LaSalle, Illinois, and the family moved to LaSalle, where Heinz attended LaSalle-Peru Township High School (Carmichael, 1965; Koehler, 1960).

Education

After a year working as a bookkeeper and newspaper reporter, Nissen attended the University of Illinois in Champaign–Urbana. He received his BA in English in 1923 (Nissen, 1929b). His mother moved to Champaign to care for him while Henry was a student there. A highlight of Nissen's undergraduate career was a course in which Nissen and two close friends, all three of whom had grown up in German families and learned to speak German before English, participated in an intensive reading course in classic German literature. These three young men also played the three kings in a Christmas play. A psychology course with Madison Bentley was also pivotal.

With the death of Adolph Nissen in 1920, the family finances were strained. Thus, Nissen took time off before attending graduate school, working as a sales correspondent and statistician for the Tupman Thurlow Company in Chicago and New York from 1923 to 1926. While working for the Thurlow Company in New York, Nissen enrolled in night school at Columbia University and there met comparative psychologist Carl J. Warden. He later switched to full-time study as an assistant under Harry Hollingworth (chap. 9, *Pioneers II*) and on a university fellowship. Warden (1960) recalled Nissen doing extra work in the laboratory during a 1927 course in comparative psychology and recruited him to his research program in which they used the obstruction box method to assess the strengths of animal drives. In these experiments, rats had to cross grids bearing shocks of varying intensities to reach incentives at the other end of the box. The measure of the strength of motivation was the amount of punishment the animals would endure to reach that goal. This work led to Nissen's first publication (Warden & Nissen, 1928). In 1929 Nissen received his PhD (Nissen, 1929a).

Professional Career

After hearing a presentation by Nissen at a scientific meeting, Robert M. Yerkes (chap. 7, *Pioneers II*) invited him to join his research program in primate biology at Yale University. Nissen spent most of his remaining career at either Yale or the primate station, which was founded by Yerkes in Orange Park, Florida in 1930 and named the Yerkes Laboratories of Primate Biology on Yerkes' retirement in 1942.

From 1939 to 1955 Nissen was the assistant director of the Yerkes Laboratories. From 1955 to 1958, he was the director. Nissen also had a series of academic appointments at Yale and, when the Yerkes Laboratories were taken over by Emory University in 1956, he became nominally a professor of psychobiology at that university. His work with the Yerkes Laboratories provides the basis for most of this chapter.

Interludes in the primate work included a term as a research associate at the Psychiatric Institute and Hospital in New York City in 1944 and as the director of the Unit for Research in Biopsychology at the Rockland State Hospital in Orangeburg, New York from 1946 to 1947. During World War II, Nissen supervised a program under the Applied Psychology Panel of the Office of Scientific Research and Development on the selection and training of oscilloscope operators for the Army and Navy that entailed expenditures of over $172,000 administered through the Orange Park laboratories.

Personal Problems

Nissen's life was often difficult. Two marriages—one to Jane Marian Stowlby and one to Cathy Hayes—ended unsuccessfully. He contracted malaria while in Africa and was in ill health through much of his adult life. On one occasion, he almost died from a ruptured appendix; on another, he had a critical case of pneumonia. In the summer of 1957, he suffered a back injury. While attempting to separate an infant chimpanzee from its mother, he inadvertently got himself into an awkward position relative to the partially sedated mother and was pushed over on his back when she reached for the infant (C. Rogers, personal communication, July 31, 1996). Nissen was diagnosed with stomach ulcers in 1958. Late in life, he suffered from an advanced and debilitating emphysema that produced such a marked shortness of breath that it made many simple activities difficult for him. The condition was aggravated by his persistent habit of smoking cigarettes. Nissen died by his own hand on April 27, 1958.

HENRY NISSEN'S COMPARATIVE PSYCHOLOGY

Nissen's comparative psychology was eclectic. There is no cohesive theory or catch phrase that can be associated with his work. He preferred interesting questions to slick answers, yet the ideas he formulated were fundamental and foreshadowed many of the later trends in comparative psychology.

Broad Biological Perspective

A first characteristic of Nissen's work was his emphasis on breadth of understanding. Although he was trained as a psychologist and carried out his research exclusively in a psychological laboratory prior to going to Orange Park, he came to fully appreciate the importance of a comprehensive biological understanding of his anthropoid subjects. This meant the study of behavior, as well as physiology, endocrinology, morphology, ecology, evolution, and all other aspects of chimpanzees (see Denniston, 1958). His writings reflect both the breadth of the naturalist's interest of and the experimental scientist's careful attention to detailed accuracy and measurement (Riesen, 1958). Nissen liked parametric designs for experiments, perhaps to a fault. He believed in a hands-on approach to research and, in his work with others, participated in the observations and data collection.

Nissen was uniquely able to care for a complex colony of chimpanzees at a time when procedures had to be worked out through trial and error. Nissen's was a true, broad psychobiology (see Dewsbury, 1991). A facility like the Yerkes Laboratories requires considerable effort in day-to-day maintenance and trouble shooting. With his abilities and temperament, it is not surprising that Nissen accepted many of the responsibilities that lead to a successful program but not to individual accomplishment and recognition. Indeed, Lashley (1957) admitted that "Yerkes and I both used him to do the dirty work at the labs" (p. 1).

Nissen became the leading expert on all aspects of chimpanzee biology, including physiology, anatomy, and maintenance procedures, largely through self-education. With Robert Yerkes, he worked out the best procedures for the care, handling, and testing of chimpanzees. Nissen was originally to co-author a book portraying the story of the first years of the laboratory with Yerkes, but other pressures prevented him from fulfilling the assignment and the book eventually appeared under single authorship (Yerkes, 1943). Nissen did pass some of his expertise onto others through publications (e.g., Nissen, 1952a) in addition to extensive personal contacts. Some people seem to have a way with animals; they understand the animals and the animals appear to like them. It is something like the green thumb of the expert gardener. Nissen was one with that touch.

Field Research

An important accomplishment in the early part of Nissen's career was his completion of a major field study of the biology and behavior of chimpanzees. In 1924, Yerkes visited the Kindia Laboratories maintained by the Pasteur Institute of Paris in what was then French Guinea in Africa. Yerkes established a cooperative agreement that would enable a scientist from the Yale Laboratories to conduct a naturalistic study of chimpanzees in their native habitat. Henry Nissen, Yerkes' man, sailed from New York for Africa on December 26, 1929. He conducted a 2-month study. When he returned in June, he brought back 16 chimpanzees to be divided between the Yale Laboratories and the Orange Park facility that opened that month.

Although Nissen's study was primitive by today's standards for such research, nearly 30 years after it was conducted Riesen (1958) could still call it "the most adequate naturalistic study of anthropoid life in the scientific literature today" (p. 796). He patiently stalked the chimpanzees in the forest, observing groups of chimpanzees on 49 of his 64 days in the field. Nissen observed that the chimpanzees lived in a favorable habitat, where food, water, and other resources were readily available and enemies were not often troublesome. Thus, he believed that much of their energy is devoted to emotional expression as, for example, in the "stupendous amount of vocalization and drumming heard in the bush" (Nissen, 1931, p. 104). Further, their more intellectual and cognitive capacities seemed minimally taxed in securing resources and thus minimally developed in the field; Nissen proposed that they might best be developed and studied under conditions of captivity. In this respect, Nissen may have underestimated what has since been revealed—that there are appreciable cognitive demands on the animals in maintaining their complex social relationships (e.g., Cheney, Seyfarth, & Smuts, 1986). Nevertheless, the view that cognitive capacity was most highly developed in captivity was a persistent part of Nissen's psychology (e.g., Nissen, 1951a). Nissen (1931) concluded his field study in typical modest Nissen fashion, noting that "the story of the chimpanzee in his native habitat has only been started" (p. 104), that his was "so far ... an ill-balanced, uneven narrative" (pp. 104–105), and that "the major share of the task remains to be done" (p. 105). Throughout his career, Nissen believed that comparative psychology needed both the laboratory and the field emphases.

Motivation

The concept of *motivation*, which was at the heart of Nissen's psychology, dated back to his early work with Warden. In his later writing, and true to his Columbia heritage, Nissen emphasized the dynamic characteristics of drive. There was a close affinity etween his approach and the concepts of others of his generation, including the central motive state of Morgan (1943). Drives sensitize all behavior, but especially those for fairly specific chains of action. "the effect of drives is to organize longer sequences of unit acts into instinctive, habitual, or insightful patterns of response" (Nissen, 1954a, p. 317). "Behavior in general is not chaotic; it is organized, and the organization comes from what we call drives or sensitizing factors" (p. 314).

Nissen believed that drives are innately determined and that the structures subserving all motivational processes are inherited. He cautioned against models based on a half-dozen or so global instincts. Nissen used his careful observations of the behavior of chimpanzees in making this point. For example, he noted that many behavioral elements of sexual encounters occur in several quite different motivational contexts. Nissen thought it a mistake to label them *primary sex activity*. Rather, he treated sequences of behavior as composed of sets of independent acts, each of which has its own intrinsic motivation (e.g., Nissen, 1953, 1954a). He took the words of a then-popular song, "Every little movement has a meaning all its own," and changed them to, "Every little action has a motive all its own" (Nissen, 1953, p. 294).

This view of motivation is interesting because it unites Nissen, in different ways, with several other theorists with similar formulations. These include Robert S.

Woodworth's (1918) proposals that mechanisms become drives, Gordon Allport's (1937) theory of the functional autonomy of motives, and Konrad Lorenz's (1957) notion of action-specific energy. Nissen (1954a) wrote that, "Capacity is its own motivation. A function or capacity of the sense organs and brain is to perceive and to know, and this is one of the more important drives of all " (p. 318). This comes close to the self-actualization theories that have been prevalent from Aristotle to Jung and Abraham Maslow (who started his career in psychology as a student of the behavior of nonhuman primates).

In addition to their sensitizing powers, a second component of motives that any theory of motivation must account for is their capacity to determine the direction of behavior. Nissen advocated an approach–avoidance psychology, in which animals develop tendencies to approach and avoid stimuli or situations according to their positive or negative valences (Nissen, 1950, 1951a, 1954a). Thus, "the response is oriented, and it is always the external stimulus—or more correctly, the spatial relation of the object or stimulus to the organism—which determines the orientation or directionality" (Nissen, 1954a, p. 288). He maintained that this conception applies to learning and that much of the performance of animals in learning tasks might be explicable in terms of modifications in approach and avoidance tendencies, rather than more cognitive processes.

Comparative Psychology: Theoretical Positions

Nissen's conception of comparative psychology was so insightful that one can retrospectively, and with some admitted presentism, read his most important article, his chapter in Stevens' *Handbook of Experimental Psychology* (Nissen, 1951a), as virtually a blueprint for what would happen in comparative psychology in the next few decades. Nissen (1951a) defined *comparative psychology* broadly, "as the science concerned with similarities and differences of behavior at various phylogenetic levels" (p. 347). On the question of the most useful type of scientific investigation, he advocated a genetic method where the word *genetic*, as was usual in his time, referred to the evolution and development of behavior, which share an emphasis on the historical determinants of behavior—across generations in the first case, within the life of single organisms in the second (see Dewsbury, 1992). Nissen's aim was to understand the full historical background of behavior.

For Nissen, construction of a sound comparative psychology had to start with patient and careful attention to problems of description. The core of the problem of description is that of determining the appropriate units of which complex behavior is built. The comparative psychologist must carefully specify the fundamental units of behavior "before plunging ahead, hastily and precipitously, into logical and mathematical elaboration of terms whose validity, reality status, or relations to observed fact are still obscure" (Nissen, 1954a, p. 282). It is perhaps this emphasis on description that made Nissen appreciate the work of the European ethologists (e.g., Nissen, 1954a), although he could be critical of their theoretical models (e.g., Nissen, 1953).

There was a strong evolutionary component in Nissen's psychology. He emphasized the importance of evolutionary history of behavior and he viewed behavior as a mechanism for the adaptation of organisms to their environments (e.g., Nissen, 1958). Adaptation can be attained by either structural or behavioral mechanisms. Nissen believed that if we wish to order species along a scale, it is the behavioral characteristics that are more striking than the physical ones. The behavioral units are not adaptive; it is only the more complex psychological unit that manifests purpose (Nissen, 1958).

As for the evolutionary history of behavior, Nissen believed that, although phylogenetic levels are realities, there are discontinuities at different levels of the scale. Thus, new capacities are apparent as emergent properties at different levels and each level shows increasing complexity. He argued that two elements are essential for good comparisons among species: appropriate units of behavior and appropriate axes along which to compare them. In particular, he was concerned to identify the dimensions along which that variation among species would be most interesting and informative. He proposed that, although species could be compared with respect to receptors, effectors, and motivational mechanisms (Nissen, 1958), it is on the dimensions of central integration or cognitive capacity that the most meaningful differences occur. Thus, when we compare species, it is always the cognitive rather than the sensorimotor or motivational differences that show the greatest change: "Differences among animals with respect to what they want are trifling by comparison with differences in the means by which they satisfy their wants" (Nissen, 1951a, p. 380).

Development

Although Nissen promoted the notion of a strong innate component to behavior, he did not accept the all-or-none definition of the nature–nature issue that was promoted by many others. For Nissen, the nature–nurture axis was a continuum rather than a dichotomy: "Reflexes, instincts, and the inherited capacity to learn may be distributed on a continuum. What is inherited may be a more or less specific readiness to learn" (Nissen, 1953, p. 292).

Perhaps Nissen's most substantial research dealt with the development of behavior in chimpanzees. Beginning in 1939, with support from the Samuel S. Fels Fund, Nissen and his colleagues, especially Austin Riesen, initiated an ambitious infant studies program designed to study the physical and psychobiological growth and development of parasite-free chimpanzees beginning at birth and to establish norms for these developmental processes. This was a major long-term project that provided baselines for many other studies, although such normative data rarely generate results that make substantial observable impact on the field. Rather, they provide an essential, firm foundation.

Nissen learned X-ray techniques so that he could document skeletal development. He had to work out procedures for rearing the animals in captivity at a time when no guides were available. Data that were collected ranged from daily readings of body weight through 50 monthly measurements of bodily dimensions, pulse rates taken three times weekly, behavioral tests with a modified Gesell schedule, and various other behavioral records (Nissen, 1942).

In addition to collecting normative data, in some of their research, Nissen and his associates imposed experimental manipulations on their animals so that they could determine the effects of specific events on their subjects' development. For example, in one often-cited study, Nissen, Chow, and Semmes (1951) raised one chimpanzee with its limbs encased in cardboard cylinders from the age of 4 weeks to 31 months to determine the effects of tactual, kinesthetic, and manipulative experience on development. Much of the behavioral development of this chimpanzee, including learning ability, seemed normal, but there were numerous specific deficits—in learning tactual discriminations, tactual-motor coordination, and such patterns as clinging to the attendant, grooming, and standing.

Beginning in 1954, with support from such sources as the Ford Foundation and the National Institutes of Health, Nissen and his colleagues conducted a substantial program in which different experimental groups of chimpanzees were reared under different conditions of early experience. These included being reared with no social contact, with one companion, or with human mothering and rearing with a monotonous versus a varied environment. Eventually, a group of wild-born animals was used for comparison with the laboratory-reared chimpanzees. Although the program generated numerous publications (e.g., Davenport & Rogers, 1970), some aspects of the project were never fully reported. The effects of restricted rearing on sexual behavior in chimpanzees were found to be considerable and confirmed the importance of social learning in the development of social and sexual behavior in these apes (see Riesen, 1971). Nissen's observations have special value because he had such a solid baseline against which to interpret his effects and because he understood his animals so well. Because of the difficulty in obtaining large numbers of animals, frequent delays in preparing written reports, and the style in which articles were written, this work never received the publicity received by similar studies with rhesus monkeys done by Harlow and his associates at about the same time (e.g., Harlow, Harlow, & Suomi, 1971).

Nissen was interested in the effects of enrichment, as well as deprivation. Earlier work on the home rearing of chimpanzees by the Kelloggs and by Glen Finch provided the basis for the project conducted by Keith and Cathy Hayes (e.g., Hayes, 1951), which was conducted "under Nissen's watchful eye" (Riesen, 1958). This work helped to round out the entire developmental program.

Learning

Nissen conducted experiments on learning throughout much of his career. In general, as one might expect, his positions were somewhat middle of the road with respect to some of the issues of the day, such as the controversy between the peripheralist interpretation of learning, characteristic of stimulus–response theorists, and the more centrist position of Lashley (chap. 20, *Pioneers I*) and others. Nissen (1950) argued that the perceptual and motor elements that go into complex learning are either innate or learned early in life. He then argued that much learning is better described as the animal learning to approach some objects and avoid others using these preestablished perceptual and motor systems than as learning a response (e.g., to turn left or right). This precipitated one of Nissen's few published controversies. It dealt with the issue of the description of learned behavior in terms of approach–avoidance learning, which he favored, versus movement learning, which he thought often inadequate as an explanation of learned behavior (e.g., Bitterman, 1952; Nissen, 1952b).

Much of Nissen's research on learning dealt with relatively complex tasks, such as discrimination learning, delayed response learning, and delayed alternation learning. In this research, Nissen and his coworkers sought evidence of symbolic processes in studies of delayed response, discrimination learning, and delayed reward. They reported the results of several related experiments. All involved variations of basic discrimination learning between two different panels, one of which led to food. In general, chimpanzees were found to do better with spatial cues, such as left versus right, than with visual cues, such as red versus green (e.g., Nissen, Riesen, & Nowlis, 1938).

Nissen and his associates also studied reversed discrimination learning, in which first one and then the other stimulus would be correct, either for a fixed number of trials or until a given performance criterion was reached. They found that, after initial declines, the performance improved progressively with successive reversals, with one chimpanzee reaching the level of one-trial learning. This finding demonstrates the phenomenon of *learning to learn,* later to be made famous by Harry Harlow (e.g., Harlow, 1949). Such performance, at least under some circumstances, can be viewed in the context of Nissen's views on the orientation of approach–avoidance behavior in the natural life of the animal, rather than as a cognitive achievement (e.g., Menzel & Juno, 1982).

Nissen and his colleagues (1938) then studied the delayed response learning of three chimpanzees in an apparatus in which the two stimuli of different colors could be presented either vertically (one above the other) or horizontally (side by side). In these experiments, the chimpanzee might observe one stimulus being baited when the two stimuli were in a vertical orientation, but tested for their memory of the baited stimulus when the two were presented horizontally. The idea was that the subjects would have to respond to the color of the stimulus, thus eliminating positional cues, because the positions were changed between baiting and the opportunity to respond. The three subjects experienced great difficulty in learning delayed response tasks with even minimal delays. After the first 400 trials, however, scores reliably above chance were obtained and generalized to color or brightness differences, but not pattern differences different from those on which extensive training had been given. Nissen et al. believed that a symbolic mechanism was necessary for the subjects to solve the problem as they did. However, they concluded that this mechanism is highly developed for spatial cues, but not for visual stimuli.

The work was followed up by Nissen and Taylor (1939) with tests of delayed alternation with nonpositional cues. The subject, Moos, succeeded in the task, thus providing further evidence of some symbolic capacity when dealing with visual stimuli. Nissen's conservative interpretations of much of this research are reflected in the conclusions of Yerkes and Nissen (1939) that, "symbolic processes occasionally occur in the chimpanzee" but "they are relatively rudimentary and ineffective" (p. 587).

Cognition

It is often written that the field of cognition was dead during the time that Nissen did most of his work. It was not dead in Orange Park, as personified in the work of both Robert Yerkes (chap. 7, *Pioneers II*) and Henry Nissen. In Nissen's (1951a) chapter in Stevens' *Handbook of Experimental Psychology*, we find over 40% of a chapter on phylogenetic comparisons devoted to a section on cognitive aspects of behavior. Here Nissen discussed such issues as the genesis of perception, pattern specificity, the selective process of attention, concept formation, and symbolization and language. Note the date—1951, which is long before the so-called *cognitive revolution*.

Nissen was not so much interested in the mechanisms active under ordinary circumstances as he was in assessing the upper limits of animals' capacities under ideal conditions. Thus, in the laboratory, he created conditions enabling the study of phenomena that might not be apparent in everyday life. True to his times, however, Nissen opposed a mentalistic approach (e.g., Nissen, 1954b). Although he was convinced that his chimpanzees showed evidence of intentions, expectations, and satisfactions, and he believed that such notions were useful when he formulated experiments, Nissen believed that they had no place in the data of psychology. Although he believed that the chimpanzees had an awareness much like that of human beings, Nissen felt that the only way to build a sound psychology was to focus on the study of behavior as the basis for the formulation of general principles.

Other Research Interests

Nissen's research interests reached into a variety of areas. Some of his work touched on matters of social behavior (e.g., Nissen, 1951b; Nissen & Crawford, 1936). He was also interested in the physiological correlates of behavior (e.g., Jacobsen & Nissen, 1937). Typically, however, Nissen remained in the background, supervising and consulting while younger associates conducted the research in these areas and got credit for it.

HENRY NISSEN AS A PERSON

Nissen was a shy man, but also friendly and willing to sit down to talk through problems with his staff and colleagues. He also was a patient and a careful man. He wrote (Nissen, 1954a) that, "it pays to be patient, to be sure one's I-beams and rivets are sound before building a skyscraper" (p. 282). This is Henry Nissen, the careful man—a veritable model of the metaphor he selected. Regrettably, it is those who try to build skyscrapers with I-beams and rivets not fully in place who are remembered in the field.

Away from psychology, Nissen enjoyed social occasions, liked boating and fishing, appreciated music, and was an avid chess, poker, and table tennis player. When my numerous interviewees spoke of Nissen, they almost always referred to him as a kind, decent, and human person. There were virtually no criticisms of a man who seems to have been beloved by all who knew him.

THE IMPACT OF HENRY NISSEN'S WORK
ON PSYCHOLOGY TODAY

We return to the question—mentioned previously in this chapter—of why Nissen's work is not often cited today. Although the answer developed here is incomplete, several factors can be mentioned.

First, comparative psychology is less prominent on the general scene in psychology today than it was 40 years ago. The issues that Nissen dealt with were much more central to the psychology of his day than to that of our day. In an era of cognitive neuroscience and managed care, interest in the problems addressed in Nissen's work has receded.

Second, comparative psychology has changed and comparative psychologists have undervalued their own history. They usually attribute the development of post-World War II comparative psychology to such external influences as European ethology and sociobiology. The links to comparative psychology's internal history have often gone unnoticed (Dewsbury, 1984). In actuality, many of the recent trends in comparative psychology are consistent with Nissen's interests and emphases. For example, comparative psychologists have shown a renewed interest in field research and in the problems of adaptation, evolution, development, and cognition. Nissen's work in the latter two areas is worthy of reexamination.

Third, for their literature searches, young researchers rely on computerized databases that only go back a few years. They rarely cite much of the old research simply because they do not know about it.

Fourth, there were problems with the ways in which Nissen communicated his science. A self-effacing man with a writing style that was less than sparkling, his work was less flashy than his contemporaries. To be a visible scientist, one needs to do good research, and publicize and sell it in an effective manner. As a result, marginal science with good salesmanship sometimes becomes more prominent than more solid research less effectively promoted. Self-promotion was not a strength of this careful and modest researcher.

Fifth, the nature of Nissen's science was not amenable to wide dissemination. His messages of breadth, care of observation, and parametric design were not the kind of material with which one could produce a catch phrase that would forever be associated with a psychologist.

Was Lashley (1958) correct when he wrote that Nissen was "too kindly, too modest, too sensitive to make a success of life?" Phrased another way, was baseball manager Leo Durocher correct that nice guys finish last? If evaluated by his visibility in today's psychology, Nissen's life would appear to fit such a view. It might be noted in passing that this is also true of many of Nissen's prominent contemporaries. To evaluate Nissen according to our 1990s criteria for longevity in our world is to ignore Nissen's goals for his own life. Nissen was a man of principle. He played his own game by his own rules, not ours. I think that if we could ask him, Nissen would regard his scientific life as a success. His game was not to maximize the career-building visibility that so often generates recognition in posterity. Rather, it was the careful and conservative construction of a solid, broadly based science of psychology aimed at solidarity rather than visibility. Even so, he played the game well enough to earn election to the National Academy of Sciences. Judged by his goals, Nissen's scientific career was a success. Regardless of whether contemporary comparative psychologists acknowledge it, they are in the debt of Henry Nissen for building a significant part of the structure of comparative psychology.

ACKNOWLEDGMENTS

I thank Dora Nissen Mann, William Mason, Emil Menzel, Vincent Nowlis, Lee Peacock, Charles Rogers, and Gregory A. Kimble for their comments on an earlier draft of this manuscript.

REFERENCES

Allport, G. W. (1937). The functional autonomy of motives. *American Journal of Psychology, 50,* 141–156.

Bitterman, M. E. (1952). Approach and avoidance in discriminative learning. *Psychological Review, 59,* 172–175.

Carmichael, L. (1965). Henry Wieghorst Nissen February 5, 1901–April 27, 1958. *Biographical Memoirs, National Academy of Sciences of the United States of America* (Vol. 38, pp. 205–222). New York: Columbia University Press.

Cheney, D., Seyfarth, R., & Smuts, B. (1986). Social relationships and social cognition in nonhuman primates. *Science, 234,* 1361–1366.

Davenport, R. K., & Rogers, C. M. (1970). Differential rearing of the chimpanzee: A project survey. In G. H. Bourne (Ed.), *The chimpanzee* (Vol. 3, pp. 337–360). Basel: Karger.

Denniston, R. H., II. (1958, October). [Obituary for Henry Nissen]. Newsletter, Section of Animal Behavior and Sociobiology. *Ecological Society of America, 3*(2), 4–5.

Dewsbury, D. A. (1984). *Comparative psychology in the twentieth century.* Stroudsburg, PA: Hutchinson Ross.

Dewsbury, D. A. (1991). Psychobiology. *American Psychologist, 46,* 198–205.

Dewsbury, D. A. (1992). On the problems studied in ethology. *Ethology, 92,* 89–107.

Harlow, H. F. (1949). The formation of learning sets. *Psychological Review, 56,* 51–65.

Harlow, H. F., Harlow, M. K., & Suomi, S. J. (1971). From thought to therapy: Lessons from a primate laboratory. *American Scientist, 59,* 538–549.

Hayes, C. (1951). *The ape in our house.* New York: Harper.

Hearnshaw, L. S. (1987). *The shaping of modern psychology.* London: Routledge & Kegan Paul.

Hilgard, E. R. (1987). *Psychology in America: A historical survey.* San Diego, CA: Harcourt Brace.

Jacobsen, C. F., & Nissen, H. W. (1937). Studies of cerebral function in primates IV. The effects of frontal lobe lesions on the delayed alternation habit of monkeys. *Journal of Comparative Psychology, 23,* 101–112.

Koehler, E. G. (1960, April 18). [Letter to Leonard Carmichael]. *Leonard Carmichael Papers.* Philadelphia, PA: American Philosophical Society.

Lashley, K. S. (1957, May 15). [Letter to Leonard Carmichael]. *Leonard Carmichael Papers.* Philadelphia, PA: American Philosophical Society.

Lashley, K. S. (1958, May 1). [Letter to Mrs. Ada Yerkes]. *Robert M. Yerkes Papers.* New Haven, CT: Yale University Library.

Lorenz, K. (1957). The nature of instinct: The conception of instinctive behavior. In C. S. Schiller (Ed.), *Instinctive behavior: The development of a modern concept* (pp. 129–175). New York: International Universities Press.

Menzel, E. W., Jr., & Juno, C. (1982). Marmosets (*Saguinus fuscicollis*): Are learning sets learned? *Science, 217,* 750–752.

Morgan, C. T. (1943). *Physiological psychology.* New York: McGraw-Hill.

Nissen, H. W. (1929a). The effects of gonadectomy, vasectomy, and injections of placental and orchic extracts on the sex behavior of the white rat. *Genetic Psychology Monographs, 5,* 451–550.

Nissen, H. W. (1929b). [Letter to Robert M. Yerkes]. *Box 36, folder 688, Robert M. Yerkes Papers.* New Haven, CT: Yale University Library.

Nissen, H. W. (1931). A field study of the chimpanzee. *Comparative Psychology Monographs, 8*(1)(No. 36), 1–122.

Nissen, H. W. (1942). Studies of infant chimpanzees. *Science, 95,* 159–161.

Nissen, H. W. (1950). Description of the learned response in discrimination behavior. *Psychological Review, 57,* 121–131.

Nissen, H. W. (1951a). Phylogenetic comparison. In S. S. Stevens (Ed.), *Handbook of experimental psychology* (pp. 347–386). New York: Wiley.

Nissen, H. W. (1951b). Social behavior in primates. In C. P. Stone (Ed.), *Comparative psychology* (3rd ed., pp. 423–457). Englewood Cliffs, NJ: Prentice-Hall.

Nissen, H. W. (1952a). Care and handling of laboratory chimpanzees. *Carworth Farms Quarterly Letter, 25, 26, 27.*

Nissen, H. W. (1952b). Further comment on approach–avoidance as categories of response. *Psychological Review, 57,* 161–167.

Nissen, H. W. (1953). Instinct as seen by a psychologist. *Psychological Review, 60,* 291–294.

Nissen, H. W. (1954a). The nature of drive as innate determinant of behavioral organization. *Nebraska Symposium on Motivation, 2,* 281–321.

Nissen, H. W. (1954b). Problems of mental evolution in the primates. *Human Biology, 26,* 277–287.

Nissen, H. W. (1958). Axes of behavioral comparison. In A. Roe & G. G. Simpson (Eds.), *Behavior and evolution* (pp. 183–205). New Haven, CT: Yale University Press.

Nissen, H. W., Chow, K. L., & Semmes, J. (1951). Effects of restricted opportunity for tactual, kinesthetic, and manipulative experience on the behavior of a chimpanzee. *American Journal of Psychology, 64,* 485–507.

Nissen, H. W., & Crawford, M. P. (1936). A preliminary study of food-sharing behavior in young chimpanzees. *Journal of Comparative Psychology, 22,* 383–419.

Nissen, H. W., Riesen, A. H., & Nowlis, V. (1938). Delayed response and discrimination learning by chimpanzees. *Journal of Comparative Psychology, 26,* 361–386.

Nissen, H. W., & Taylor, F. V. (1939). Delayed alternation to non-positional cues in chimpanzee. *Journal of Psychology, 7,* 323–332.

Riesen, A. H. (1958). Henry Wieghorst Nissen: 1901–1958. *American Journal of Psychology, 71,* 795–798.

Riesen, A. H. (1971). Nissen's observations on the development of sexual behavior in captive-born, nursery-reared chimpanzees. In G. H. Bourne (Ed.), *The chimpanzee* (Vol. 4, pp. 1–18). Basel: Karger.

Warden, C. J. (1960). A few brief notes on Dr. Henry Wieghorst Nissen. *Leonard Carmichael Papers.* Philadelphia, PA: American Philosophical Society.

Warden, C. J., & Nissen, H. W. (1928). An experimental analysis of the obstruction method of measuring animal drives. *Journal of Comparative Psychology, 8,* 325–342.

Woodworth, R. S. (1918). *Dynamic psychology.* New York: Columbia University Press.

Yerkes, R. M. (1943). *Chimpanzees: A laboratory colony.* New Haven, CT: Yale University Press.

Yerkes, R. M., & Nissen, H. W. (1939). Pre-linguistic sign behavior in chimpanzee. *Science, 89,* 585–587.

Carl R.
Rogers

Chapter 15

Carl Rogers
and the Culture of Psychotherapy

Martin Lakin

Carl R. Rogers probably influenced modern psychotherapy in this country and beyond its borders as much as, and perhaps more than, any other American-born psychologist or psychiatrist. Now, a decade after his death, many mental health professionals in and outside the field of psychology still acknowledge his orientation to psychotherapy as their own. Rogers' career spanned the years that witnessed the international trials of World War II, the turbulent reactions to the war in Vietnam, the massive public dissatisfaction with public education, and the social activists' consciousness raising campaigns for affirmative action that were intended to erase discrimination against gender, ethnic, and economic groups.

During these times of crisis, rapid change, and mounting levels of personal confusion and frustration, the practice of psychotherapy was flourishing. In the decades following World War II, American psychologists and other mental health professionals were emerging as practitioners of psychotherapy alongside psychiatrists. The major therapeutic frameworks available to them were psychoanalysis and its multiple offshoots, the various behavioral methods, and Rogers' client-centered approach.

BIOGRAPHICAL SKETCH

Carl Rogers was born on January 8, 1902, in Chicago, Illinois. He grew up as the middle child in a closely knit family that subscribed to fundamentalist religious beliefs and the virtue of hard work. When his family moved to a farm in Wisconsin, Rogers became interested in scientific agriculture. Later, in his studies at the

---

* Photograph of Carl Rogers courtesy of Carl Rogers Memorial Library.

University of Wisconsin–Madison, Rogers enjoyed the physical and biological sciences. After his undergraduate degree, Rogers explored a liberal religious outlook at Union Theological Seminary for a time and then switched to psychology at Teachers College, Columbia University, where he became acquainted with Leta Hollingworth's (chap. 16, *Pioneers I*) commonsense approach to the study of human behavior. He was deeply influenced by John Dewey's (chap. 4, *Pioneers II*) pragmatism through the teaching of William Kilpatrick. In the course of his clinical internship, he was also exposed to Freudian concepts.

After receiving a PhD in clinical psychology in 1931, Rogers took a position as a staff psychologist at a community child guidance clinic in Rochester, New York. During this period, he wrote his first book, *The Clinical Treatment of the Problem Child* (1939). Roughly at the same time, he became much impressed with the writings of Otto Rank, Jesse Taft, and Frederick Allen, whose thinking about psychotherapy had a strong impact on his evolving formulation of the therapeutic situation and on his efforts to understand help seekers' developing readiness for self-understanding.

In 1940, Rogers moved to Ohio State University, where he continued to develop his conception of the counseling relationship. In 1945, he accepted the directorship of the Counseling Center at the University of Chicago. The situations at Ohio State and Chicago turned out, intellectually, to be most productive. It was also during his stay at Ohio State that the formulation that first became known as *nondirective* therapy and ultimately as *client-centered* therapy took tentative shape. His second book, *Counseling and Psychotherapy* (1942), provided an initial description of the theory, with sufficient illustrative case material to make it possible to see both the conception and its realization in sequential therapy sessions. For the next 20 years, he endeavored to validate the conception and prove the effectiveness of this approach.

During his tenure at Chicago, Rogers (1951) wrote *Client-Centered Therapy*, which spelled out his theory of psychotherapy more formally and illustrated its uses with children as well as adults. It was also during the Chicago years that he most fully articulated the conception of personality that guided his applications of individual psychotherapy and his philosophy of individual and group change. Together with his associates and colleagues in both settings, he formulated the bases of the theory and practice of psychotherapy that are still identified with him. These books reflect Rogers' phenomenological view that a person's behavior can be understood only from that person's own perspective. It is the perception of events, rather than the events themselves, that is crucial to the alteration of a help seeker's behavior. Rogers described his enduring ideas most fully in his contribution to Sigmund Koch's *Psychology: A Study of a Science* (Rogers, 1959).

Attracted by the challenge of applying client-centered psychotherapy to a population of schizophrenics, Rogers left the University of Chicago in 1957 to take a joint professorship in psychology and psychiatry at the University of Wisconsin. After several years in Madison, he joined Richard Farson, a former student at

Chicago, in a new venture in California. Farson had received funding to start the Western Behavioral Sciences Institute and invited Rogers to join him. Collegial relationships at Wisconsin had not prospered and Rogers was ready to move on. Several years later, Rogers and his associates of the time founded the Center for the Study of the Person in La Jolla, California. Working in these institutes until his death in 1987, he enlarged the application of his therapeutic approach to include small and larger groups and institutions and the amelioration and even resolution of intergroup conflicts. He also showed how his principles of psychotherapy might apply to broader issues of education and social change.

CLIENT-CENTERED THERAPY

The central concept in client-centered psychotherapy is that of the self. For the purpose of helping people overcome their problems, self-perceptions and self-experiencing—not the evaluations of outsiders no matter how expert—are the major forces for beneficial therapeutic change. The self, as Rogers conceived it, is both a filter that selects the aspects of the outside world that the individual perceives and, simultaneously, an instrument that determines how the individual interprets and responds to that input. The self is also the origin of a person's sense of esteem and competence. Especially in the early stages of development, the development of this latter attribute of self may be adversely influenced by those who represent authority and security.

Inevitably, the conditions laid down by others will play a positive or negative role in establishing, maintaining, or enhancing self-esteem. In particular, the expression of needs or desires that are at odds with the wishes or values of authority figures, or figures on whom one is dependent, can be dangerous in terms of personal security. When developing individuals become aware of such urges, and of the fact that important others are reacting negatively, they may distort or suppress them and their developing selves may suffer.

In Rogers' view, such self needs and desires and their fulfillment are basic to self-realization. In healthy environments they will be met or at least not suppressed to the point of denial. In developmental situations, where maintenance of the image of self is too dependent on internalization of standards of behavior that require distortion of self needs and wishes, denial or distortion can result in psychological dysfunction of varying levels of severity. A more benign developmental experience would allow self needs to be experienced and expressed so that the individual feels worthy and lovable without distorting inner experiences.

Implications for Psychotherapy

Although this formulation of problem etiology is similar in a number of respects to that of psychoanalysis, the resolution of problems takes a different form. By contrast with those therapies in which the approval of the therapist is contingent on the patient's behavior, the client-centered therapist avoids such conditional approval and responds to the behavior of the client with unconditional positive regard. By the exercise of this accepting and nonjudgmental attitude—hence the designation *nondirective therapy*—the therapist becomes a facilitator who helps but does not direct the therapy of the client. The designation *client,* rather than *patient,* reflects Rogers' intent to establish a more egalitarian relationship than that between *bewildered sufferer* and *knowledgeable expert* in more traditional talk therapies. The client-centered therapist neither instructs nor interprets, but encourages the help seeker to identify areas of exploration, choose personal goals, and set the pace of the therapy.

A central component of Rogers' conception of therapy is that clients can solve their personal psychological problems through self-exploration, which leads them to better self-understanding, provided that the therapist establishes and maintains the essential conditions of therapy. Proper therapeutic technique requires the therapist to be sensitive, accurate, empathic, and personally involved, and to frequently express comprehension of the person's utterances and emotional substrate. The responses of the therapist must remain congruent with the feelings expressions of the client. These matchings of the therapist's reactions to those of the client facilitate self-discovery and recovery and permit resumption of the tendencies toward personal growth that are associated with mental health. Successful therapy means recovering self-understanding and a sense of inner self. Acting in accord with the demands of that true self is to act in ways that are self-realizing (i.e., in ways that are productive and self satisfying because they represent correspondence between the person's real self and its behavioral expressions).

Guiding Values

Although the emphases in Rogers' programs shifted during the more than 50 years of his professional activity, all of them were guided by an enduring set of values. In his public addresses and in his writings, Carl Rogers was always an outspoken advocate of personal freedom and self-determination. He believed that being true to oneself requires the development of personal standards and the ability to behave in ways that are based on inner impulse and conviction rather than on the wishes of others. He detected these developments in his own life and explained them (Rogers, 1980) as at least in part reactions to the proscriptions and prescriptions implicit in his family's fundamentalist Protestant religion. Whatever their sources, however, the theme of personal freedom was dominant in Rogers' therapy, which emphasized the processes of discovering or recovering one's true inner self.

An American Dynamic Psychotherapy

The psychotherapy that Rogers created was uniquely American—the first viable alternative to European psychoanalytic therapy. By comparison with most versions of analytic therapy, the client-centered approach was decidedly less doctrinaire. It concentrated on no particular diagnostic categories—the *neuroses* in analytic theory. It gave no special significance to any particular psychological process—early memories, dreams, sexual proclivities, or expressions of defensiveness. It was refreshingly free of the obscure language and constructs that were difficult to validate, either in the laboratory or in persons' life experiences—Oedipal conflict, penis envy, inferiority complexes, collective unconscious, and the like. To many therapists, the procedure seemed reassuringly straightforward. Understand the feelings and meanings inherent in the client's communications, accept these communications without criticism or reservation, and you have created the conditions in which a person can engage in progressively deeper self-exploration and, ultimately, arrive at corrective self-discovery. The earnest and skillful application of these methods enables the therapist to facilitate desired change.

Rogers' ideas were especially attractive to the psychologists who were repelled by the apparent *soullessness* of behaviorism. Client-centered therapy was a therapy with human values and an emphasis on life's meanings, to which even secular seekers for spiritual sustenance could relate. For example, a substantial number of pastoral counselors, ministers, and Catholic priests came to Rogers' Counseling Center for study. It is also significant that Rogers was honored by Columbia University for having developed a democratic psychotherapy. The implied comparisons, of course, were with the more authoritarian imported European therapies, orthodox psychiatry, and the approaches that derived from behavioral psychology. Although no psychotherapy can be truly democratic, Rogers consistently emphasized what he considered to be the egalitarian aspect of client-centered therapy.

ADVANCING RESEARCH IN PSYCHOTHERAPY

Carl Rogers initiated a considerable amount of research that opened the psychotherapeutic process to systematic observation, analysis, and evaluation, not only for client-centered therapy but for the field as a whole. At a time when psychotherapy was regarded as virtually inaccessible to the scientific method and psychotherapeutic practice was dominated by medically trained psychiatrists, his demonstration that psychological treatment was amenable to systematic inquiry was especially valued by psychology's scientist practitioners who were struggling to establish their legitimacy in that endeavor.

It was in his Chicago days that Rogers made his most systematic efforts to validate his conception of psychotherapy. In conducting his research, he tried to develop methods that remained within the client's frame of reference. In this effort, Rogers found an intellectual partner in William Stephenson, a colleague at the University of Chicago. Stephenson's original work using Q-sort methodology promised to reveal the pathways that transitions in the client's self-feelings followed, which Rogers regarded as one legitimate avenue for studying therapeutic change. For clients it involved the simple task of sorting cards with personal characteristics listed on them from *least like me* to *most like me*. Pre- and post-therapy comparison of sortings yielded a measure of subjectively experienced change.

Although Q-sort methodology formed a natural union with the phenomenological characteristics of client-centered theory, the psychological community inevitably called for the more objective judgments provided by external evaluations. When such evaluations were solicited from clients' close friends, they appeared to support the clients' claims of benefit. In 1954, Rogers and Dymond published *Psychotherapy and Personality Change*, in which they reported the results of many studies that employed such methodology and substantiated the effectiveness of client-centered therapy.

At Chicago, Rogers attracted a number of colleagues who enthusiastically cooperated in establishing empirical bases for confidence in the methods he developed. They also helped him move the methods forward by examining the conditions and processes of therapeutic change and exploring other contexts where the therapy could be applied. Among these colleagues were John Butler, who helped evaluate therapeutic effects and enlarge the theory; John Shlein, who developed a brief version of client-centered therapy (long before managed care mandated shorter durations for all kinds of psychotherapy); Eugene Gendlin, who continued to refine the conditions of therapeutic process; Thomas Gordon, who applied client-centered ideas in education and parenting; Laura Rice and Geoffrey Barrett-Leonard, who continued to explore the humanistic aspects of the theory's applications; and Nat Raskin and Julius Seeman, both of whom carried on Rogers' work in different academic and service settings.

PROFESSIONAL CONTROVERSY

During his years at Chicago, Rogers' work came under attack both from psychologists who were committed to other orientations and nonpsychologists who regarded the practice of psychotherapy by psychologists as a threat. Psychologists in his own department were ambivalent about Rogers' theorizing, research, and therapeutic methods, and psychiatrists in the Chicago department of psychiatry were agitating against the activities at the Counseling Center. Elsewhere, the psychoanalysts criticized Rogers' idea of the really free and self-aware individual as a concept that left the individual not only without defensiveness but also without normal controls. Once when he returned from an invited address to the then psychoanalytic Menninger Clinic, Rogers reported that, ironically, his conception of the fully functioning person had been termed a *recipe for the production of psychopaths.*

It was also in Rogers' Chicago days that uncomfortable caricatures of client-centered responses became well known. In client-centered therapy, the therapist does not interpret the client's behavior; strive to promote insight; offer advice, praise, or blame; or explore topics beyond those initiated by the client. The role of the therapist is that of accepting and clarifying the client's statements; often the therapist does little more than restate them. Poking fun at these echoings of client sentiments by the therapists, the critics questioned the value of mere mimicry as a means to promote the patient's welfare. Actually, these nondirective repetitions of responses were intended to help clarify the meaning and emotion in the client's responses. They were considered to be essential for therapeutic effectiveness. Elias Porter (1950), one of Rogers' early associates, wrote a guidebook of such responses that even today, could serve as a model of technically correct responses to client utterances. In many contemporary programs of clinical training, supervisors still follow examples modeled on such responses, now termed exercises in the techniques of *active listening*. Eventually, Rogers came to regret the stylization of therapist's responses, complaining that its use implied a routinization of the therapeutic interaction that was completely at odds with the essentials of spontaneity and authenticity.

"Gloria"

In 1965, Everett Shostrom began to distribute the film that he had made with the collaboration of Carl Rogers, Fredrick Perls, and Albert Ellis depicting a therapeutic session conducted by each of these well-known psychotherapists with a patient code named *Gloria*. Shostrom's production was the first film to demonstrate comparative therapeutic concepts and techniques of mainstream schools of psychotherapy. Although the representation was limited to only three systems of psychotherapy and the actions of three therapists in one short session each, those who have viewed the film over the intervening years (mainly students in courses on abnormal psychology or psychotherapy) have invariably been intrigued by the marked differences among the three practitioners, their characteristic types of intervention, and the responses of Gloria to each of them.

In the previous decades, Frederick Perls and his colleagues had formulated the principles and strategies of Gestalt therapy, a dynamic psychotherapy focused on an ahistorical, here-and-now experiencing and expression of feelings. The idea is that one often dissembles one's real attitudes by behaving in accordance with social convention, even with one's therapist. This is to be corrected through confrontation—by ceaselessly unmasking and exposing the dissembled feelings. The goal is greater self-honesty and consequently greater comfort with oneself as well as greater self-fulfillment. Perls tried to encourage Gloria to express herself more authentically—to be less of a phony.

Albert Ellis, the only one of the three therapists still living, is credited with the creation of rational–emotive psychotherapy, the antecedent of what is currently known as *cognitive–behavioral* treatment. It focuses on bringing perceptions and feelings in line with needs and wants, with the aim of diminishing needless self-castigation and guilt and coming to act in ways that are enjoyable and useful to oneself and others. Ellis endeavored to get Gloria to take greater risks in energetically seeking what she seemed to want for herself rather than feeling like a perennial loser. For his part, Carl Rogers consistently appealed to Gloria's inner experiential self, trying to help her make her own judgments about deeply personal matters for which she had sought advice from him.

THE CHALLENGE OF WISCONSIN

Rogers' main reason for leaving the University of Chicago and moving to the University of Wisconsin–Madison and its department of psychiatry was the challenge offered by the opportunity to apply client-centered therapy at Mendota State Hospital. Another reason was the mixed appraisals his therapy had been receiving. Some of the skeptics held that client-centered therapy was a superficial type of counseling and that the population served by the Counseling Center was basically healthy folks who needed little or no treatment—"just let him try to work in that simple way with really disturbed people!" Clearly, the chance to do so with the backing of a major department of psychiatry represented a unique opportunity. The challenge of Wisconsin was attractive and Rogers was eager and felt ready to take advantage of the promised free hand in Madison.

The State Hospital Experience at Mendota

Rogers' work in the Mendota State Hospital and at the University of Wisconsin has been described in a number of publications. One of them (Rogers, Gendlin, Kiesler, and Truax, 1967) revealed the extent to which Rogers had expanded his horizons by using the diagnostic label, *schizophrenia,* which he had always been reluctant to employ. Another (Rogers & Stevens, 1967) described some of the compelling human interactions that were experienced with individuals thus categorized. Persons whose status as clients was not self-chosen, as distinct from those who sought treatment at the Counseling Center, did indeed present a different sort of challenge. The therapeutic consequences of the experiment as a whole may be said to have been equivocal. Certainly there were successes, but there was sufficient experience of failure to discourage sustained efforts to extend this species of talk therapy to other hospitalized populations on a large scale. One small example of the multitude of obstacles confronting the therapists who worked with schizophrenic patients was that merely getting them to keep appointments for their therapeutic sessions posed a significant difficulty.

The Shift to Group Therapy

It seems probable to me that Rogers was more than a little disappointed by his lack of success in extending individual psychological treatment to grossly disturbed patients at Mendota and that he regarded the Wisconsin experiment as a failure. I suspect that he may have even become discouraged about dyadic treatment in general because it was at about this time that he became active in promoting his conception of *group encounters*. From that point in his career, there is little more in Rogers' publications about further development of his ideas about dyadic psychotherapy. Encounter groups, rather than individual therapy, seem to have become Rogers' major activity from that time on. This shift raises many questions about the similarities and differences between what transpires in encounter groups versus individual therapy. Rogers made no systematic efforts to make the indicated comparisons. Such unresolved questions complicate efforts to evaluate Rogers' influence in the realm of group therapy theory and practice.

THE HUMAN POTENTIAL MOVEMENT

Despite the change from single- to multiple-person therapy, the uniquely Rogerian mode of being open and expressive apparently worked its magic. Participants in these groups were overwhelmingly positive in their endorsement of their experiences. Moreover, subsequent research (see Lieberman, Yalom, & Miles, 1973) seemed to suggest that effects of participation in at least certain types of groups may not differ substantially from those of successful individual therapy.

Therapy for Institutions?

When he was at the Center for the Study of the Person in La Jolla, Rogers and his associates launched a program of institutional psychological therapies based on experiences in encounter groups. It seems that some participants, themselves administrators of sizable organizations, became convinced of the desirability of cultural change in their organizations and institutions. They wanted to implement some of Rogers' ideas for creating more person-centered environments that would facilitate creative activity and productive interpersonal relationships. No doubt some of these institutional interventions were successful, but the ones that are more widely known were not. Indeed, these efforts to introduce programs of institutional change and revolutionize interpersonal relationships in certain highly bureaucratized and traditionally authoritarian systems seem to have precipitated a number of problems that had serious consequences for individuals and their institutions.

On the educational scene, Rogers has been credited with (and blamed for) the wave of diversity training that has swept over many American college campuses. Some of these programs involve intergroup sessions designed to alleviate interracial conflict. Sometimes the methods entail the use of sensitivity training sessions during which participants (typically, African-American and White students, but increasingly including others as well) attempt to communicate their feelings to one another.

Questions of Ethics and Efficacy

In the view of some mental health professionals, certain aspects of these group activities seemed problematic, and with some justification. The popularity of group therapy during the late 1960s and early 1970s led to an undisciplined increase in the number of groups that were created and, in some groups, gross distortions of their purposes. In particular, the behavior of certain leaders and participants in some groups called *encounter groups* strikingly illustrated the degree to which the therapeutic purposes of groups had been eroded. Critics (including some of the participants in these groups) protested that, too often, the groups were conducted by ill-trained and/or doctrinaire leaders and that they were a kind of psychological brain washing rather than an equal opportunity for honest exchange of sentiments. Other critics noted that Rogers seemed increasingly to emphasize the interpersonal expression of feelings, to the point that his group experiences were becoming denigrated as *touchy-feely*. Rogers seemed less and less concerned about any particular group's dynamics, electing instead to assess the impact of a group by the extent or degree to which it provided an emotionalized experience. Beyond that, he seemed more and more to use his own reactions as the sole index of a group's effectiveness.

Rogers was clearly disturbed by reported excesses in encounter groups. Whenever possible, he would take occasion to reemphasize the serious purposes of groups and rearticulate their therapeutic intentions. He argued that what he did personally and how he conducted himself in groups should be evaluated from that perspective. Although he could not be held responsible for what others did, he condemned group leaders' behaviors that were even marginally unethical.

A THERAPEUTIC APPROACH
TO INTERGROUP CONFLICT

Rogers had always had a significant following overseas, especially in Japan and Western Europe. Traveling in Japan in the 1970s, I met a number of Japanese "Rogerians," several of whom had continued to work with Rogers long after their initial contacts. In visiting the former USSR, I discovered that Rogers' visits to St. Petersburg (then Leningrad) had resulted in the formation of an institute designed to carry on the legacy of his therapy. *Dom Garmoniya* or Harmony House, as it is called, to which Rogers' daughter Natalie is reported to come as a frequent consultant, is considered to be a bastion of Rogerian therapy in Russia. However, I must acknowledge that I found little evidence of a recognizably client-centered orientation in my conversations with the resident psychotherapists. Nevertheless, ideas about Rogers were prominent features of the institute. It is noteworthy that there was such enthusiasm in Russia for a therapy, long reputed to be ideologically anti-authoritarian, in a country that had usually been characterized by authoritarian rule.

In the later years of his life Rogers, became increasingly involved in what might be considered his most ambitious undertaking or, from a critic's perspective, his most quixotic endeavor. This was the attempt to apply the principles of client-centered therapy to some of the most enduring, seemingly intransigent, and lethal intergroup conflicts of the time. He traveled to a number of hot spots in the world and applied what he called his *large-group intervention* strategies, enlisting the participation of representatives of antagonistic ethnicities, races, religious affiliations, and polities. They included nongovernmental members of conflicting groups in Northern Ireland, Israel, Brazil, the former Soviet Union, South Africa, and others.

Reactions to these intergroup experiences throughout this range of nations were suffused with an enthusiasm for personal openness and feelingful communication that was similar to those elicited by his individual therapy sessions. The impact of these reactions is attested to by the fact that advocates for Rogers' ideas about psychotherapy are now found in many of those same countries where he practiced large-group interventions. In his book *A Way of Being*, Rogers (1980) provided a number of anecdotal accounts of these group experiences that persuade the reader that emotional intensity was one of their most characteristic aspects. The personal testimonials were remarkably similar to the kinds of declarations that intense and gratifying psychotherapy elicits, despite the differences in contexts and ostensible purposes. Unfortunately, there is no record of what effects, if any, these large-group interventions had on the actual conflicts to which they were presumably addressed

CONCLUSION: A SPARK THAT CONTINUES TO KINDLE FLAMES

Carl Rogers left an enduring legacy of contributions, of which even the most controversial continue to stimulate thought and activity in psychology. One might even say that a part of that legacy was a rebellion against official orthodox psychotherapy and psychology. He espoused humanistic values in an era when logical positivism was the ruling philosophy of science. He rejected the increasingly entrenched professionalism that defined psychotherapy in narrow and self-serving terms. He offered the possibility of therapy oriented toward personal growth—a therapy that could give people a more vital sense of self and self-realization. On the larger scene, Rogers believed that self-directing human beings could and would create a healthier society. In the field of education, he held that free and self-directing learners would become better educated people and good citizens. As an academic psychologist, he pioneered in the systematic study of the processes of psychotherapy and in the quantitative and the qualitative evaluation of its outcomes.

It was not his scientific efforts that brought Rogers to the attention of the general public, however. Rather it was his view of human potentialities, which was later to characterize the human potential movement, with its emphasis on personal growth, personal choice, and liberated emotionality.In large part because of this appealing orientation, Rogers' influence extended far beyond the bounds of academic and applied psychology. In response to the problems associated with the unpopular war in Vietnam, the slow pace of change toward racial equality, and the intransigent intergroup conflicts in various places in the world, he developed a sense of mission that eventually led him to attempt to apply his therapeutic methods in what he called *conflict-resolution workshops.* Although Rogers was not unique among psychologists and psychiatrists in seeing connections between pathology and aggression and between psychotherapy and peacemaking, his attempt to adapt the ideology of individual to larger treatment programs was a pioneering effort to move away from an exclusively dyadic conception of the therapeutic process.

The appeal of Rogers' message was so powerful that it is easy to understand why he became something of a guru for people in the broader society as well as a model for many psychotherapists. At the end of his life, Rogers was viewed with a kind of veneration by many, but with skepticism by others. Perhaps the latter reaction occurred because of the far-reachingness of his group encounters, his large-scale interventions in organizations, and his attempts at peacemaking. Looking beyond the adulation and criticism, objective evaluation of Rogers' impact on psychotherapy and clinical psychology would have to credit him with a seminal role in determining the shape and scope of psychotherapeutic theory and practice in this country and well beyond its borders.

POSTSCRIPT: THE AUTHOR'S PERSONAL RELATIONSHIP TO ROGERS

As a way to conclude this assessment of Rogers and his work, it may be appropriate for me to describe my own relationship to this pioneer in the history of psychotherapy. In 1950, I returned from study in Jerusalem, where I had received an undergraduate degree, to the University of Chicago to do graduate work in psychology. For something like the next 2½ years, I was Rogers' student and his client in therapy. This kind of complex relationship was not unusual for the time.

Rogers Versus the Establishment

When I came to Chicago, I had had little preparation for graduate studies but was determined to become a clinician. Looking forward to studying with Rogers, I naturally gravitated toward the counseling center of which he was director. At that time in my career, I had no conception of the tensions and conflicts associated with clinical psychology as an academic specialty. However, I quickly became aware of them when the then department chairman warned us newcomers that those of us who aspired to be clinicians were out of place at Chicago and that we might find ourselves out of the program come spring. I recall how those of us who planned to specialize in clinical psychology sought support from Rogers, hoping that he would champion our interests in a campaign against such narrow-minded interpretations of academic psychology's mission.

Usually we were not disappointed. During my graduate days at Chicago, Rogers effectively promoted clinical psychology as no less legitimate than other aspects of the discipline that were represented in the university. Moreover, in the verbal and written battles being waged at that time among the various schools of psychology, we Rogerians particularly relished the outcomes of the debates that took place at various professional meetings where Rogers seemed, at least to us, to effectively demolish the opposition's arguments. We were particularly delighted to see our hero take on and (so we thought) defeat B. F. Skinner (chap. 16, this volume) at an American Psychological Association Convention in November 1956.

Not every such public appearance was so triumphant, however, either in Rogers' view or ours. A particularly disappointing occasion was a well-attended dialogue (see Rogers, 1960) with the famed Israeli philosopher, Martin Buber, whom Rogers admired and whose theories about personal relationships he considered similar to his own. In his philosophy, Buber emphasized the personalistic, subjective, egalitarian I–Thou relationship as an ideal for human interaction. Rogers had felt that his own conception of how therapy should be conducted was close to, if not identical with, Buber's philosophy. For Rogers, phenomenally experienced status differential between therapist and client was characteristic of inept practice. Successful therapy had to be egalitarian—something like Buber's ideal I–Thou interaction.

On this occasion, however, Buber rejected Rogers' contention that a therapeutic relationship could be egalitarian. Describing the therapeutic relationship as an expert-to-help seeker contract, Buber said to Rogers, "You see, you are the doctor for this person." Rogers' reactions (and ours in the audience) were a mixture of disappointment, bewilderment, and feelings of betrayal because in this pronouncement Buber seemed to endorse the classic medical model of doctor–patient relationship, in which an egalitarian, I–Thou psychotherapy is not even possible.

Ambivalent Personal Relationships

Even while I was Rogers' graduate student and client, we had certain disagreements, particularly with respect to what I considered to be the inevitable ambivalence of the therapeutic relationship and the potential coerciveness of therapists' emotional reactions. As the years went by, I became more and more convinced that Rogers somehow never fully understood the potentially compelling aspects of his own emotional reactions. Although he was always keenly aware of clients' responses, especially to himself, and tried to express his feelings as faithfully as he could, he was so convinced of the positive and constructive effects of emotional interactions that he remained relatively blind to their destructive possibilities, whether in the dyadic or group context.

Although I continue to question certain aspects of Rogers' theoretical and professional attitudes, I do not believe that what I say about him in this chapter is an undue expression of negative transference. I also continue to have great respect for him, and the lasting effects of my personal relationship with Rogers may contain residuals that led me to write about him more positively, as well as more critically, than I might have otherwise. Thus, this postscript ends with the message of admiration, mixed with criticism, that must be the lot of many contributors to human endeavor. Carl Rogers' legacy of spirited humanism and the confidence that human beings could, if appropriately helped, develop toward greater self-direction and personal control is a worthy inheritance for psychology. So, however, is the understanding that self-satisfied good intentions, even in the service of the human good, carry the potential for harming those that they intend to help.

REFERENCES

Lieberman, M. A., Yalom, I. D., & Miles, M. B. (1973). *Encounter groups: First facts.* New York: Basic Books.

Porter, E. H., Jr. (1950). *An introduction to therapeutic counseling.* Boston: Houghton-Mifflin.

Rogers, C. R. (1939). *The clinical treatment of the problem child.* Boston: Houghton-Mifflin

Rogers, C. R. (1942). *Counseling and psychotherapy.* Boston: Houghton-Mifflin.

Rogers, C. R. (1951). *Client-centered therapy: Its major practice, implications, and theory.* Boston: Houghton Mifflin.

Rogers, C. R. (1959). A theory of therapy, personality, and interpersonal relationships, as developed in the client-centered framework. In S. Koch (Ed.), *Psychology: A study of a science* (Vol. III, pp. 184–256). New York: McGraw-Hill.

Rogers, C. R. (1960). Dialogue between Martin Buber and Carl Rogers. *Psychologia, 3,* 208–221.

Rogers, C. R. (1980). *A way of being.* Boston: Houghton-Mifflin.

Rogers, C. R., & Dymond, R. F. (Eds.). (1954). *Psychotherapy and personality change.* Chicago: University of Chicago Press.

Rogers, C. R., Gendlin, E. T., Kiesler, D. J., & Truax, C. (1967). *The therapeutic relationship and its impact: A study of psychotherapy with schizophrenics.* Madison: University of Wisconsin Press

Rogers, C. R., & Stevens, B. (1967). *Person to person.* Moab, UT: Real People Press.

Chapter 16

Burrhus Frederick Skinner: The Contingencies of a Life[1]

Daniel W. Bjork

Burrhus Frederick Skinner ("B.F." to the public and "Fred" to those who knew him) may well go down in history as the individual who had a greater impact on Western thought than any other psychologist. Taken with the seriousness he intended it to be taken, Skinner's conception that human conduct is under the control of contingencies of reinforcement is revolutionary. It clashes head on with the cherished view that the causes of behavior are internal dispositions like intelligence, motivation and free will. This chapter explores the human side of this revolutionary giant's life and contributions to the science of psychology.

BOYHOOD

Fred Skinner was born in 1904. He grew up in a small American town, Susquehanna, Pennsylvania, 30 miles north of Scranton, a few miles from the New York state line. He was the eldest son of an ambitious attorney for the Erie Railroad, which sustains Susquehanna's economic vitality. His beautiful but demanding mother was once the town debutante. Having a lovely contralto voice, she sacrificed a singing career to marry an up-and-coming lawyer whose family was socially beneath her own. Fred's only sibling was a younger brother, athletic and popular.

---

* Photograph of Burrhus Frederick Skinner courtesy of Archives of the History of American Psychology, Akron, Ohio.

[1] At the time the materials for this chapter were being collected, the Skinner Archives, referred to in this chapter, were located in the basement of the Skinner home. The Hamilton College Library Archives and Harvard Archives are located at Hamilton College and Harvard University, respectively.

Skinner attended grammar and high school in the same building and was one of only eight graduating seniors. Intellectually astute and aware of his powers, he challenged friends and even teachers when he thought that he was right, sometimes giving the impression that he did not respect the targets of his comments. He had profound respect for one special teacher, Mary Graves (Skinner, 1970), who recognized his potential, lent him books, and chatted with him about literature and Darwinism. She, more than anyone else in Susquehanna, moved him toward an intellectual way of life.

The situation in the town of Susquehanna had many positive aspects. It stimulated a boyhood of exploration and invention. Beyond the Erie Railroad tracks and Main Street were the thickly wooded hills of northeastern Pennsylvania. Young Fred's forays into those woods yielded generous quantities of honeysuckle, dogwood, arbutus, blackberries, acorns, and walnuts. He trapped eels in the Susquehanna River and dammed a creek to make a swimming hole. He brought home chipmunks, rabbits, bees, and pigeons. Once, he and a friend tried to make pigeons drunk by feeding them alcohol-soaked corn.

What Fred liked even more than tramping and collecting was building things. He made roller skates, scooters, wagons, seesaws, tops, model planes, kites, and even a cannon that shot potatoes and carrots over neighborhood houses. At age 10, he constructed a private place in which to read and dream—a box that shut out distractions. He enjoyed books about people who invent things not just for fun, but for survival—*Robinson Crusoe*, *The Swiss Family Robinson*, and especially Jules Vernes' *Mysterious Island*. Fred had more in common with Benjamin Franklin than other American inventors such as Thomas Edison and Henry Ford because he loved the world of books as much as that of nuts and bolts. Although Skinner's first 18 years in Susquehanna were indelible in the sense that his fundamental character was clearly etched, the village setting became increasingly restrictive. His parents' intellectual complacency and the town's limited horizons made him restive. Escape became essential.

LIFE AS AN UNDERGRADUATE STUDENT

When Fred escaped, it was not to New York City or Boston, but to another small town, Clinton, New York, 9 miles west of Utica, the site of Hamilton College, where in 1922 he became 1 of 111 entering freshmen. In contrast to his experience in Susquehanna, at Hamilton he found that he had nothing that made him appear exceptional. He had no athletic ability, a quality that would have given him status even though all freshmen wore green caps and were derisively called *slimers*. His father, William Skinner, unlike the fathers of many of Fred's classmates, was not a Hamilton man. Fred did not join a prestigious fraternity, have close friends, or date.

Moreover, Fred's sense of being academically superior was immediately undercut. The speech professor criticized his countrified accent. Pronouncing *tremendous* as *tremenjous* was unacceptable. Nor was it proper to say *forhorrid* for *forehead.* One never ended sentences with *up.* Fred was insecure, disappointed, and generally miserable: "They're making me do too many things I don't want to do," he complained. "They don't know half as much about *me* as I do" (Skinner Archives, Spring, 1923). He looked forward to the summer and returning to Susquehanna, where at least there were several friends who appreciated his uniqueness. In the spring of 1923, just before semester's end, a tragedy occurred that deepened his unhappiness. While Fred was at home, spending a few days with his family, his brother, Edward, suddenly collapsed and died. Fred now became the sole center of parental attention and was drawn back into being a family boy.

At the beginning of his sophomore year, Fred entered a college social circle that encouraged individual expression and ended his isolation. He began tutoring the youngest son of a distinguished Hamilton chemistry professor, Arthur Percy Saunders. Percy Saunders had remarkably varied interests. He raised prize-winning peonies, was an amateur astronomer, played the violin, and loved literature. The professor was also a political liberal who subscribed to radical magazines and criticized American businessmen for their shallow, Philistine values. The Saunders' home was a salon for area literati and artists who gathered in the music room for conversation and musical ensembles. Writers of the caliber of Robert Frost, Ezra Pound, Alexander Wollcott, and James Agee had enjoyed the conviviality of the music room.

This was a novel and exciting world for young Skinner. He saw Percy Saunders as the living antithesis of his Kiwanis Club-oriented father. Saunders became Fred's confidante and mentor, encouraging his intellectual independence and burgeoning literary ambition. Here, too, was a relaxed yet intellectually stimulating setting where he could forget his mother's rigid moral code and unending admonition: Grace Skinner never tired of reminding Fred to be aware of what people think. During the summer between his junior and senior years, Skinner attended the Bread Loaf School of English in Vermont. There he met Robert Frost, who offered to read several of his short stories. Two months before graduation, Fred received a letter of praise from Frost. It was the determining factor in his decision to be a writer. "I ought to say you have the touch of art," wrote the great poet. "You are worth more than anyone else I have seen in prose this year" (Skinner, 1976, pp. 248–249). His parents reluctantly agreed to let Fred try for a career they believed would only bring improvidence and, worse, tainted social status for them all.

THE UNSUCCESSFUL WRITER

Fred did not move to New York City as did so many aspiring American writers. He felt guilty about leaving his parents because the burden of Edward's death still weighed heavily. Thus, he made plans to spend the next year, 1926–1927, writing at home. Home was now Scranton, where William had taken a position as an attorney for a local coal company.

Skinner began to write by making a special place to write. In a small third-floor room, he built a bookcase, a work table, and a rack on which he stacked books while he was in his reading chair. Indeed, the would-be-author did far more reading than writing, digesting, among others, the novels of Sinclair Lewis, Dostoyevsky, Proust, and H. G. Wells. He also delved into literary journals such as the *Saturday Review of Literature, American Mercury, The Dial, New Masses, Two Worlds Monthly,* and *Exile.*

Yet none of his reading was catalytic enough to help produce anything but a few short stories, let alone a great American novel. After 2 months, he had written virtually nothing. Just to write was not enough; he wanted a special kind of writing—objective writing. Objective writing was pure literary description that avoided the thoughts and feelings of characters. Much later, looking back on what he called his *dark year,* Skinner reflected that, "A writer might portray human behavior accurately, but he did not therefore understand it. I was to remain interested in human behavior but the literary method had failed me" (Skinner, 1976, p. 291).

While he struggled to write, Fred also wanted to express a philosophy of life.Writing should announce some truth beyond objective writing and yet encompass it. This truth emerged from two sources: acute descriptive powers and reading.An opportunity to exercise his descriptive powers arose as he cared for his maternal grandfather who was dying of prostate cancer. When the complication of bronchial pneumonia brought the old man to his final hours, Fred was at bedside. He wrote to Saunders,

> All night long this organism—worn out beyond repair—lay there. Certain muscles of his diaphragm went on functioning—a little air was pulled spasmodically into the remaining lung space. An overtaxed heart—sustained on strychnine—pumped impure blood—and gave out under the strain. His pulse weakened—he coughed a bit and lay still. I listened to his heart—it was still. I lifted him up—a little black fluid ran from his lips. (Hamilton College Library Archives, August 16, 1926)

However, to describe the dying was not enough. What had really happened?

> I am very sure that my grandfather—all of him—all that I knew of him and felt—his character, personality, emotions, skill, desires—all—everything went as soon as the physical condition of his body became unfit for certain nervous coordinations. Just as the dreary character of the clock I now hear will vanish when the parts which give forth its ticking shall stop. (Hamilton College Archives, August 16, 1926)

Traditional religious and metaphysical supports were not required to understand his grandfather's demise, or for that matter anyone's death. It was only necessary to focus on observables: One observed and recorded what happened. That was all. In August 1926, Fred Skinner was expressing himself from the behaviorist standpoint (D. Bjork 1993).

That very month he read a book review in *Dial* in which Bertrand Russell made favorable reference to behaviorist John B. Watson. Skinner did not recall actually reading Watson's (1925) *Behaviorism* until early 1928. In fact he was not sure he ever read Watson's (1919) *Psychology From the Standpoint of a Behaviorist* (Skinner Archives, n.d.). Skinner's letters to Saunders showed that his shift to the behaviorist perspective occurred in the summer and autumn of 1926. "We go on thinking—yet do we live by thinking?—not by a damn sight!" (Hamilton College Library Archives, August 16, 1926). Fred had discovered a fundamental paradox of behaviorism: By using the mind, that theory reduces mind to behavior.

DISCOVERIES AT HARVARD

When Skinner entered Harvard as a graduate student in psychology in the fall of 1928, he viewed mental explanations as fictions and was therefore predisposed to treat psychological phenomena as behavior. However, he was not yet an experimentalist. He had done no scientific work and had certainly not discovered a new science. He was scientifically ambitious: "I expect to settle down and solve the riddle of the universe," he announced to Saunders (Hamilton College Archives, September 26, 1928).

No one at Harvard influenced Fred's experimental approach more than physiologist William Crozier. Crozier specialized in studying the movement or tropisms of lower organisms. He was a no-nonsense professor who had a reputation for kicking shins and refused mediocre graduate students. Skinner adopted Crozier's scientific prerequisite: Unless one could control experimental conditions one did not have experimental science (Pauly, 1990, pp. 41–47, 195–196). Crozier allowed Fred to do experiments in the physiological laboratory and, as co-editor of the *Journal of General Psychology*—in those days, one of the most prestigious journals in psychology (see chap. 11 on Murchison in *Pioneers II*)—helped him publish his research. Skinner was so impressed with Crozier that he almost switched to physiology. However, his best friend, Harvard classmate and fellow behaviorist Fred S. Keller, convinced Skinner that he could stay in psychology and still produce a science of behavior (Personal interview with Keller, April 26, 1990).

In late 1929 and early 1930, Skinner worked on the modification of an apparatus that Yale behaviorist Clark L. Hull (chap. 14, *Pioneers I*) first called the *Skinner Box*. Earlier, Fred had built a silent release box. A rat released into an apparatus entered through the silent release box, which insulated the animal from distracting noise, hence making experiments more controllable. Skinner was apparatus-minded and he remembered that, in late 1929, he "began to be unbearably excited. Everything I touched suggested new and promising things to do" (Skinner, 1979, p. 38).

Skinner built a spruce board run. The rat was fed at the end of this run and then hand carried back to the silent release box for another trial. Because hand carrying seemed inefficient, he constructed a back alley so the rat could return untouched to the straightaway. The stimulus of eating the food elicited another run. Now came an unexpected effect: The rat did not always immediately make another run after eating. It waited a while before the next trial, and the animal's delay interested Skinner. Perhaps he could study the time between eating and the beginning of a run. Time became the variable he would soon be able to control experimentally. Skinner then reduced the run to a tilted board. When the rat ran down this shortened track, it tilted the board and the tilt turned a disk that dropped a pellet into a cup. As the rat sated itself, it made fewer runs and the kymograph marks were farther and farther apart. By connecting lines to the marks, he could graph the time between runs—the most reliable measure yet.

One thing led to another and then, suddenly, the happy, break-through accident—perhaps the greatest of Skinner's experimental career. The disk of wood from which he had made the food dispenser had a central spindle that he had not cut off: "One day it occurred to me that if I wound a string around the spindle and allowed it to unwind as the [disk] was emptied ... I would get a different kind of record" (personal interview, December 15, 1989). Instead of marks, he got a curve—a curve that revealed changes in the rate of response that the marks missed. Skinner had invented the cumulative recorder, which recorded curves remarkably free from variation. He had an ingestion curve and "the tangent of the curve told you exactly how hungry the rat was at a given moment" (personal interview, December 15, 1989).

Now the tilted board was unnecessary; just a box with a wire bent into a lever that released a pellet would suffice. When the rat pressed, the cumulative recorder produced curves recording lawful behavior. On his 26th birthday, Fred wrote his parents: "What heretofore was supposed to be 'free behavior' on the part of the rat is now shown to be just as subject to natural laws as,... the rate of his pulse" (Skinner Archives, late March 1930). The wonder of young Skinner's science was in seeing what he predicted actually happen.

There were two more experimental surprises in the spring of 1930. Skinner recalled that "I didn't decide in advance I wanted to prove that one reinforcement conditioned behavior. To my amazement I discovered it." The rat would eventually press the lever and the pellet dropped and was eaten. Yet it was not the food that provided the immediate reinforcement. Instead, it was the sound of the magazine as the pellet was released: "If you give an animal food, that is not instantaneous. When [the rat] pushes down [the lever] and it goes BANG, that BANG is the thing. It is absolutely instantaneous with the [rat's] movement, and that is what makes [immediate reinforcement] possible." He did not hypothesize different schedules of reinforcement. Rather, "I was running out of pellets and decided I would only reinforce now and then"—another happy accident (personal interview, March 9, 1990). Skinner had the acuity to understand the significance of experimental accidents; he saw possibilities that most others would have missed. Contingencies produced astonishing scientific results.

Skinner was more than a clever inventor experimenter, however. His ability to define the dimensions of a new science also made him special. Fred's dissertation on "The Concept of the Reflex" marked him as a bold theorist. The history of the reflex from Descartes to Pavlov had been the history of inference. Past attempts to distinguish between involuntary and voluntary reflexes were unconvincing. Constructs such as the *reflex arc* or *synapse* were reducible to a simple correlation: the correlation of stimulus to response. Hence, the focus of Skinnerian science was not on happenings inside the organism but on events outside it. The implication was that one could study the reflex without studying physiology. This was a radical departure from traditional reflexology (Skinner, 1932).

The departure was unacceptable to Edwin G. Boring, the head of the Harvard Psychological Laboratory and the most powerful figure in the department. In a five-page typed letter, Boring accused Skinner of pretending to write a history of the reflex while really dismissing that history and substituting his own interpretation as scientific fact. For this polemical cleverness, Skinner did not need science; he needed "propaganda and a school." Fred was not daunted. He penciled in the margin: "I accept the challenge" (Harvard University Archives, October 13, 1930). Boring reluctantly approved the dissertation perhaps because the *Journal of General Psychology* had already accepted it for publication.

By 1931, Skinner had a doctorate in psychology and a rising reputation as an original experimentalist. However, he would not leave Harvard until 1936. Instead, he accepted a prestigious Junior Fellowship from the recently formed Harvard Society of Fellows. The fellowship allowed him to continue lever box experiments and to further distinguish Skinnerian behavioral science from Pavlovian reflexology, or what became *operant conditioning* from *classical conditioning*.

Skinner had read Pavlov's (chap. 3, *Pioneers I*) *Conditioned Reflexes*, admired his ability to control experimental conditions, and readily admitted borrowing the term *reinforcement* from the great Russian physiologist. Nonetheless, he took special care to distinguish his science from Pavlov's. Beyond Skinner's focus on the behavior of the whole organism rather than on the reflexes of a surgically altered animal, there was a difference in the effect of intermittent reinforcement: "Pavlov found it very hard to sustain salivation if food was not always paired with a conditioned stimulus, but rats pressed a lever rapidly and for long periods even though reinforcement was infrequent" (Skinner, 1987, p. 189). Skinner produced different lever pressing behaviors by introducing different schedules of reinforcement; he studied the behavior of lever pressing and the variables of which pressing was a function. A difficulty arose from this new emphasis. Pavlov always linked a specific stimulus to a specific response—the sound of a bell to the flow of saliva. Yet when Skinner observed a rat in a lever box, there were behaviors that could not be directly linked to specific stimuli. What specific stimuli produced the exploration of the box, standing on hind legs, moving forelegs, and first pressing the lever? He had discovered lawful behavior, but much of it could not be explained as a correlation of stimulus to response because he could not identify the specific eliciting stimulus.

Skinner, however, was not discouraged. In 1934, he prepared an essay on the *generic nature* of lever pressing (Skinner, 1935). Frankly admitting that some rat behavior appeared spontaneous because specific eliciting stimuli could not be identified, he then clarified the dimensions of what his science studied. All the specific movements involved in lever pressing were viewed as classes of behavior that could be brought under the control of reinforcers, which in turn yielded repeatable, predictable responses. Hence, lever pressing was every bit as generic a subject for scientific study as the reflex: "The difference between operant and non-operant research is ... almost entirely one of the dimensions of the thing studied" (Harvard University Archives, October 28, 1970). Skinner did not actually call lever pressing an *operant* until 1937, but he was discussing it as such in 1934. An operant was an operation (a behavior) emitted without any readily identifiable eliciting stimulus. Yet it could be brought under the control of reinforcers just as surely as could responses to identifiable stimuli, such as conditioned responses to conditioned stimuli of Pavlov's laboratory.

The Behavior of Organisms (Skinner, 1938) was the definitive experimental proof that distinguished Skinner's behavioral science from Pavlov's. The book became the basis for all future operant science. Moreover, Skinner never doubted that operant research could be applied to human beings. *The Behavior of Organisms*, which dealt exclusively with white rats, ended with a firm conviction about where Skinnerian science was headed: "The importance of a science of behavior derives largely from the possibility of an eventual extension to human affairs" (Skinner, 1938, pp. 441–442).

THE SOCIAL INVENTOR

Although Fred began attending to this relevance to human conduct, he did not simply drop research on rats and turn to people. He remained interested in operant animal behavior but switched from rats to pigeons. His interest in pigeons began inauspiciously in April 1940 while aboard a train bound for Chicago. Gazing at the passing countryside, he watched birds lifting and wheeling in formation as they flew alongside the train. He envisioned the birds as devices with extraordinary vision and maneuverability. Why could they not be used to guide missiles to intercept enemy bombs— bombs that were killing and maiming thousands of innocent civilians? This was the imaginative beginning of what became a government-funded program to develop a bird-guided missile called *Project Pigeon.* Although the government eventually rejected pigeon technology, Skinner's efforts to develop such a technology launched his career as a social inventor. Pigeons were conditioned to peck a target inside a missile that would then intercept a bomb. Pigeon technology was simply the means to achieve the social effect of minimizing loss of human life from wartime bombing (see Skinner, 1960).

There were other reasons he shifted to social invention than the inventive opportunities that World War II provided. When Skinner left Harvard in 1936 for his first teaching position at the University of Minnesota, he was no longer a bachelor, having married Yvonne Blue, the daughter of a well-to-do Chicago ophthalmologist. By 1944, the Skinners had two daughters, Julie and Deborah. Fred's most intimate social circle, his family, had considerable influence in stimulating social invention (R. K. Bjork, 1996).

Yvonne had not especially wanted children. Skinner recalled that, when Julie was born in 1938, Yvonne was scared to death of the baby (personal interview, December 12, 1989). How could he make baby care easier for his wife? Fresh from the disappointment of the government's rejection of Project Pigeon in the summer of 1944 and with the arrival of his second child, Deborah, he began to build an apparatus. First called the *baby tender* and later marketed as the Aircrib, Skinner's cubicle provided a unique living space for his infant daughter—a thermostatically controlled, enclosed crib with a safety glass front and a stretched canvas floor that could be rolled clean when soiled. The baby was kept in perfect comfort without the restraining paraphernalia of zippered pajamas or even diapers. Deborah enjoyed remarkable freedom of movement and developed into a strong, healthy child. Moreover, the crib freed Yvonne. She did not constantly need to worry about Debbie's well-being, yet she could remove the baby from the tender for cuddling or play at any time.

Fred was also excited about the commercial future for his crib, but his hopes were was ill-founded. General Mills Corporation decided against marketing the baby tender. What if something went wrong with the thermostat? As a company spokesman, A. E. Bennett, put it: "One underdone baby, one frozen youngster, or one smothered child ... charged to General Mills, could be a pretty bad thing from the publicity standpoint" (Harvard University Archives, October 27, 1944). So Fred decided to let an enterprising individual manufacture and market the "Aircrib." Unfortunately, the entrepreneur proved to be a fraud and a personal embarrassment to Skinner, who had to inform disappointed customers that their orders for Aircribs would never be filled. Between 1957 and 1967, a small business, Aircrib Corporation, sold perhaps 1,000 cribs. However, with the death of the company president, sales ceased, although individuals continued to write Skinner for specifications to build their own cribs (D. Bjork, 1993).

Despite its commercial failure, the baby tender brought Skinner his first taste of national notoriety. The *Ladies' Home Journal* bought "Baby Care Can Be Modernized," Fred's article describing the crib's virtues, for $750. The editor retitled the piece "Baby in a Box." The association between the "Skinner Box" and the "Baby Box" suggested that the professor was doing operant experiments on his own daughter, Deborah. Stories still circulate that Deborah Skinner committed suicide or suffered insanity because of 2 years internment in "the Box." Deborah, however, is not only alive and sane, she is an accomplished painter and writer living in London. The only effects she remembers from her 2 years in the baby tender are unusually prehensile toes and the habit of sleeping with only a sheet (telephone interview, February 1993).

Deborah Skinner was the catalyst for another invention with considerable social potential. After 9 years at Minnesota and 2 years at Indiana University, Skinner returned to Harvard in 1947 as a William James Lecturer. His topic was "Verbal Behavior: Psychological Analysis," which eventually appeared as *Verbal Behavior* (1957)—a difficult inquiry not into language per se, but into the contingencies that shaped verbal behavior. Fred's interest in verbal behavior peaked as he observed his daughters developing verbal skills after the family moved permanently to Cambridge, Massachusetts, in 1948. Deborah learned to read more slowly than her sister, Julie, causing both Debbie and her father considerable frustration. Fred quite naturally was concerned about the quality of instruction at Shady Hill, the private school attended by many Harvard faculty children, including Deborah.

One day in 1953, Skinner visited his daughter at Shady Hill and was appalled at how a mathematics class was being taught. Some children finished problems quickly and were left with nothing to do; other students struggled without success; test results were not available until the next day. There had to be a better way to teach. Thus, Fred built a crude teaching machine—a device in which mathematical problems were printed on pleated tape and later on cardboard disks. The questions were sequential, designed to ensure success. A lever was moved that covered the student's answer with a Plexiglas plate, which revealed the correct answer and also prevented altering it. If the question was answered correctly, another lever was moved, exposing the next question. If the question was answered incorrectly, the lever could not be moved and the student would have to try again (D. Bjork, 1993).

The machine could not *read* a right or wrong answer; all it could do was cover the answer under the Plexiglas as it showed the correct response. The key component in Skinner's invention was the preparation of frames, beginning with the simplest problem in arithmetic or spelling and proceeding so gradually in degree of difficulty that the student seldom erred. The reinforcement of getting the right answer prompted the student to move on to the next question, and the next, and ultimately to mastery of the subject. Hence, the student learned a subject not through trial and error, but by the reinforcing effect of answering questions correctly.

Skinner assembled a group of bright young behaviorists who developed a broad spectrum of teaching machine programs with varied degrees of difficulty. He also spent considerable time and effort dealing with large corporations, especially IBM and Rheem, that showed interest, but failed to develop and market efficient and reasonably priced teaching machines. Neither company was willing to risk producing a teaching machine until they were sure that a mass market for the product existed. The failure of American big business to take a chance on a technology of teaching that Fred was sure would revolutionize the quality of American education was a bitter disappointment—the most disheartening of his career as a social inventor. He blamed himself for not persuading business representatives to embrace his invention: "My wilted-shirt attitude, my willingness to go on...a first-name basis was a mistake. If I...acted the 'Professor' according to the businessman's script, I would probably [have been]...listened to" (Skinner Archives, November 20, 1962).

Skinner never fully understood that the businessman's script was not as adventuresome as he had imagined. Indeed, behind the vaulted myth of the spirit of

American free enterprise was the conservative reality of ensuring safe, profitable enterprise. Also, and quite paradoxically, Fred was compelled to deal with men who identified with the Kiwanis Club creed that he had rejected as an undergraduate at Hamilton College. The commercial fate of both the Aircrib and the teaching machine as marketable social inventions rested with corporate executives with whom Skinner, despite his efforts, could never identify.

After scores of public lectures promoting teaching machine education, Skinner eventually realized that it was not just his inappropriate approach to American business that prevented his invention from succeeding. Teachers and school administrators were afraid that the teaching machine would deprive them of their jobs. When The Technology of Teaching (1968) appeared, Fred was convinced that only behaviorists would find it useful. At the end of his life, although convinced that computers had made teaching machines antiques, he still became quite agitated when discussing the tragic failure of America's educational establishment to use a technology of teaching to solve otherwise intractable problems of mass education (personal interview, March 9, 1990).

Skinner's career as a social inventor involved literary creations as well as gadgetry. Only 1 year after building the baby tender, he invented a much more ambitious social application of a science of behavior. It was a utopian novel written in "a white heat" during the summer of 1945. Walden Two (1948) described a community under the control of positive reinforcement. Babies were raised in Aircribs in a common area. All adult members of the community were parents to the children. Private property was abolished. There was virtually no government. Work was not determined by gender and competition was discouraged.

Although Walden Two initially made a stir, especially in a review in Life that described the novel as "a corruption" of Henry David Thoreau's classic, Walden, few copies of Skinners's book were sold until the counterculture era in the 1960s and early 1970s (Jessup, 1948). By then several experiments in communal living more or less based on behavioral engineering were launched, but only two persisted—Twin Oaks in Virginia and Los Horcones (the Pillars) in Sonora, Mexico.

These developments made Skinner something of a counterculture guru to those who joined the early communities. One enthusiastic Twin Oaks member known simply as Josh depicted Fred as a secular savior:

> And it came to pass [that] ... there arose among the scribes and wise men a prophet named B. F. Skinner and Skinner did speak unto the elders and scribes, saying, "Your teachings are false. Listen unto me and I will tell thee of the science of human behavior." And they did scoff at him ... but he did keep his cool ... saying, "Thou lackest understanding." (D. Bjork, 1993, pp. 258–259)

Skinner was partly responsible for the aura. He had given Frazier, his alter ego in Walden Two, a God complex. Fred was painfully aware that he had occasionally exhibited God-like conceit since boyhood. Indeed, his supporters tended to treat him as a secular deity, whose science would save the world, whereas detractors depicted him as a secular devil whose science would destroy human freedom.

If *Walden Two* brought a taste of fame and the cross winds of both criticism and praise, *Beyond Freedom and Dignity* (1971) hurled him into a firestorm of controversy. With the commercial failure of his last great mechanical invention, the teaching machine, Skinner once again tried literary invention. Again, an accident—a spur of the moment decision—helped determine effects. The original title was *Freedom and Dignity*, but Fred's editor at Knopf pointed out that after one read the book there was precious little of freedom and dignity left to talk about. Immediately Skinner suggested *Beyond Freedom and Dignity*. The revised title infuriated many readers who began the book with the assumption that Skinner's objective was to destroy freedom and dignity: They read the *Beyond* as *In Place Of*.

Yet there was no mistaking his major point: The concepts of autonomous human action and the "literature of freedom and dignity" were blocking scientific solutions to lethal social problems such as overpopulation, pollution, and the prospect of nuclear holocaust. Time was running out on the human species. The best hope for survival lay in applications of behavioral science by behavioral scientists.

Although there were a few positive reviews, most were negative, some outrageously so. Well-known intellectuals such as the linguist, Noam Chomsky, and the novelist, Ayn Rand, were deeply offended. Chomsky (1971) suggested that Skinnerian behavioral engineering was not "incompatible with a police state." Rand (1984), writing sometime between 1971 and 1973, accused Skinner of being obsessed with a "hatred of man's mind and virtue...reason, achievement, independence, enjoyment, moral pride [and] self-esteem." Dozens of public appearances, including a particularly contentious one on William Buckley's *Firing Line* (October 17, 1971) and a *Time* magazine cover story (September 20, 1971), transformed B.F. Skinner into an infamous scientific Darth Vader.

Skinner never quite understood the source of national outrage. He had criticized the utilitarian value of individual freedom in a nation that viewed that tradition as its cultural bedrock. Moreover, he had argued that controlling individual behavior through positive reinforcement would produce a better world. To a nation that had less than three decades earlier defeated the ultimate controller, Hitler, and his diabolic designs for a better future, Skinner's behavioral engineering was both a disturbing echo and an alarm. To a nation in the early 1970s that was caught in the vortex of antiwar militancy, the civil rights movement, and rising feminine and gay consciousness, *Beyond Freedom and Dignity* seemed obscenely out of step with the march of human liberty. Although he fought back with more public appearances and another book, *About Behaviorism* (1974), to clarify his position, he was no longer so much the social inventor as the aging defender of a science.

CONCLUDING CONTINGENCIES

At age 86 and 8 days before his death in August 1990, Skinner delivered a 20-minute speech to a standing room only crowd at the APA annual meeting in Boston. Most knew that this would probably be his last public appearance because he had been suffering from leukemia since November 1989. The frail, white-haired founder of operant science and of several interesting if not wholly successful social inventions addressed his audience with a strong, resonant voice. He spoke without notes and his focus was unmistakably clear. Psychologists had generally failed to adopt the science of behavioral analysis, preferring instead to embrace the mythical power of mentalism. Skinner drew an analogy that evoked gasps of disbelief, dismay, and/or approval: Creationist resistance to Darwinian natural selection paralleled the contemporary resistance of cognitive psychologists to behavioral analysis.

The juxtaposition of creationist cognitive nonscience to the Darwinian operant science was timely. Much of Skinner's intellectual attention during the late 1970s and 1980s was focused on attacking cognitive psychology and relating the selection of behavior to natural selection. Those who adopted the new mentalism had forgotten why introspection had failed as science. Although introspection, as the preferred way of studying sensation and perception, was no longer popular, cognitive psychologists were still looking inside the brain as a processor of information to describe what the mind did. Indeed, the cognitivists were relying more and more on brain science to reveal the nature of the mind.

> Cognitive psychologists like to say that "the mind is what the brain does," but surely the rest of the body plays a part. The mind is what the *body* does. It is what the *person* does. In other words, it is the behavior, and that is what behaviorists have been saying for more than half a century. To focus on an organ is to rejoin the Homeric Greeks. (Skinner, 1989, p. 67)

Although brain science was important, neurology would never reveal the nature of the mind. The cognitive psychologists had not progressed much beyond William James. They were in deep difficulty when they relied on another science—neurology—as the basis for their own inferences.

Skinner had built operant science on experimental analysis that did not rely on physiology. Behavior could be scientifically studied for itself alone. In the 1930s, Skinner had delivered the science that John B. Watson had promised—and one that, as we have seen, was distinct from Pavlov's. By the 1960s, Skinner was not only responding to the challenge of the cognitive revolution, but he was also aware that ethology and genetics were bringing Darwinian concerns into new perspective. His 1966 article, "The Phylogeny and Ontogeny of Behavior," asserted that a science of behavior was more adept at analyzing ontogenic (individual) contingencies than phylogenic (species) contingencies. Nonetheless, he readily acknowledged that, "parts of the behavior an organism … have always been accepted as 'inherited.'" He firmly maintained that only past effects, whether genetic or cultural, determine behavior—behavior was shaped by prior consequences (Skinner, 1966).

The key evolutionary emergence that allowed humans to command complex verbal behavior, and hence build culture, was vocal musculature. However, as Skinner neared the end of his life, he became increasingly pessimistic about the ability of humans to shape a liveable future. "Our evolutionary history has prepared us for the past," he said, repeatedly. "I've always known I was going to die," he remarked with a slight smile; but at the end he was also certain that the world would end and rather quickly:

> I think that the world is going to do what Shakespeare put in that line in his sonnet, "the world is going to be consumed by that which it was nourished by." I think evolution is random, accidental, no design in it at all. I think [that] the evolution of vocal musculature which made it possible for human beings to talk about the world, to have science and culture [was not] enough to take the future into account. And I am sure, quite sure, we have already passed the point of [no] return. (Personal interview, March 9, 1990)

However, Skinner did not end his life in a slough of despair. Even with leukemia he worked defending his science, answering correspondence, and tinkering in his basement workshop. Every day was engineered so his most productive hours could be devoted to writing. He was awakened by a timer and wrote with circadianlike rhythm from 5 a.m.to 7 a.m. He was indeed the organism he knew best. His personal history and cultural heritage produced a remarkable man and a still more remarkable science, yet Skinner wanted no personal credit. Fortuitous contingencies explained his successes. As he remarked in the last volume of his autobiography, "By tracing what I have done to my environmental history rather than assigning it to a mysterious, creative process, I have relinquished all chance of being called a Great Thinker" (Skinner, 1983, p. 411).

REFERENCES

Bjork, D. W. (1993). *B.F. Skinner: A life*. New York: Basic Books.

Bjork, R. K. (1996).The personal culture of Yvonne Blue Skinner. In L. D. Smith & W. R. Woodward (Eds.), *B.F. Skinner and behaviorism in American culture* (pp. 179–198). Bethlehem, PA: Lehigh University Press.

Chomsky, N. (1971, December). The case against B.F. Skinner. *New York Review of Books*, pp. 18–24.

Jessup, J. K. (1948, June 28). The newest utopia. *Life*, p. 162.

Pauly, P. J. (1990). *Controlling life: Jacques Loeb and the Engineering ideal in biology*. Berkeley: The University of California Press.

Rand, A. (1984). *Philosophy: Who needs it?* New York: Signet.

Skinner, B. F. (1932). The concept of the reflex and the description of behavior. *Journal of General Psychology, 6,* 427–458.

Skinner, B. F. (1935). The generic nature of the concepts of stimulus and response. *Journal of General Psychology, 9,* 40–65.

Skinner, B. F. (1938). *The behavior of organisms: An experimental analysis.* New York: Appleton-Century-Crofts.

Skinner, B. F. (1948). *Walden Two.* New York: Macmillan.

Skinner, B. F. (1957). *Verbal behavior.* New York: Appleton-Century-Crofts.

Skinner, B. F. (1960). Pigeons in a pelican. *American Psychologist, 15,* 28–37.

Skinner, B. F. (1966). The phylogeny and ontogeny of behavior. *Science, 153,* 1205–1213.

Skinner, B. F. (1968). *The technology of teaching*. New York: Appleton-Century-Crofts.

Skinner, B. F. (1970). B. F. Skinner: An autobiography. In P. W. Dews (Ed.), *Festschrift for B. F. Skinner* (pp. 1–21). New York: Irvington.

Skinner, B. F. (1971). *Beyond freedom and dignity*. New York: Knopf.

Skinner, B. F. (1974). *About behaviorism*. New York: Knopf.

Skinner, B. F. (1976). *Particulars of my life*. New York: Knopf.

Skinner, B. F. (1979). *The shaping of a behaviorist*. New York: Knopf.

Skinner, B. F. (1983). *A matter of consequences*. New York: Knopf.

Skinner, B. F. (1987). *Upon further reflection*. Englewood Cliffs, NJ: Prentice-Hall.

Skinner, B. F. (1989). *Recent issues in the analysis of behavior*. Columbus OH: Merrill.

Watson, J. B. (1919). *Psychology from the standpoint of a behaviorist*. Philadelphia: Lippincott.

Watson, J. B. (1925). *Behaviorism*. New York: People's Institute.

Chapter 17

Kenneth W. Spence:
Theorist With an Empiricist
Conscience

Gregory A. Kimble

Although most psychologists today do not remember who Kenneth Spence was or what he stood for, in the middle decades of the 20th century he was one of the most important psychologists in the world. He was a member of the National Academy of Sciences and the Society of Experimental Psychologists. In 1953, he received the Howard Crosby Warren Medal from the Society of Experimental Psychologists. In 1955, he delivered the Silliman Lecture at Yale, a prestigious series that had been given previously by such distinguished scientists as Ernest Rutherford, Enrico Fermi, and Charles Sherrington, but never by a psychologist. In 1956, the first year it was given, he received the Distinguished Scientific Contribution Award from the American Psychological Association. From 1962 to 1967, he was the most widely cited author in psychology's most prestigious journals (Myers, 1970). After his death in 1967, the University of Iowa dedicated in his memory the Spence Laboratories of Psychology, a new six-story structure attached to the building in which he had spent most of his productive life.

Unlikely as it may seem given all this recognition, psychology's reactions to Spence in his own time were often negative and sometimes downright hostile. After a review of Spence's life and work, this chapter considers the reasons for these reactions and speculates on their implications for the future of psychology.

BRIEF BIOGRAPHY

Kenneth Wartinbee Spence was born in Chicago on May 6, 1907. At the age of 4, he moved with his family to Montreal in Canada, where his father (an electrical engineer who worked for the Western Electric Company) had been transferred. Spence attended West Hill High School in Montreal and McGill University.

In high school and college, Spence was active in athletics. When he was at McGill, he injured his back in a track meet and went to LaCrosse, Wisconsin, to live with his grandmother during his period of convalescence. While there, he attended LaCrosse Teachers College and met his first wife, Isabel Temte.Returning to McGill, Spence declared a major in psychology. That institution awarded him the AB and MA degrees in 1929 and 1930, respectively.

From McGill, Spence transferred to Yale University, where he received his PhD in 1933. His doctoral dissertation on visual acuity in the chimpanzee (Spence, 1934) was sponsored by Robert M. Yerkes (chap. 7, *Pioneers II*), not by Clark L. Hull, as is commonly believed, although Spence's ties to Hullian theory do in fact date to his years in New Haven.

From the beginning of his career as a psychologist, Spence believed that a science of psychology must be expressed in terms of mathematics. Like most psychologists of his generation, however, he was not well grounded in that subject. After finishing his graduate work, he applied for a postdoctoral fellowship to study mathematics, but his application was rejected by a biologist who felt that psychology would never be sufficiently precise to require such methods. Denied that fellowship in mathematics, on the completion of his doctoral degree, Spence spent the next 4 years as a National Research Council Fellow at the Yerkes Laboratories of Primate Biology in Orange Park, Florida.

Spence's first academic job, in 1937 to 1938, was a 1-year assistant professorship at the University of Virginia. After that, in 1938, he went to the State University of Iowa (now the University of Iowa) as an associate professor and in 1942, became professor and head of the department there. Spence remained at Iowa until 1964, when he moved to the University of Texas. He died of cancer in Austin on January 12, 1967, at the age of 59.

EARLY CONTRIBUTIONS

Spence came into psychology at a time when the discipline seemed on the verge of developing a comprehensive theory of behavior. The most important of these theories were those of Kurt Lewin (chap. 7, this volume), E. C. Tolman (chap. 15, *Pioneers I*), Edwin R. Guthrie (chap. 10, *Pioneers II*), Clark L. Hull (chap. 14, *Pioneers I*), and B. F. Skinner (chap. 16, this volume). Spence's position in this scheme of things was established early. Beginning when he was a graduate student at Yale and for most of his career, he was identified with the development of an empirically based theory of behavior within the general framework of Hull's neobehavioristic system, which combined Pavlov's (chap. 3, *Pioneers I*) concept of conditioned associations with Thorndike's (chap. 10, *Pioneers I*) law of effect.

The Backward Order of Elimination of Blinds in Maze Learning

In a paper he prepared for Hull's seminar at Yale, Spence analyzed some data obtained by Tolman and Honzik (1930) on the order in which rats learning a complex maze eliminated the blind alleys they encountered on their way to the goal. The analysis assumed the validity of Hull's (1932) goal-gradient hypothesis ("...the goal reaction gets conditioned most strongly to stimuli preceding it, and other reactions of the behavior sequence get conditioned to their stimuli progressively [more weakly] as they are remote" [p. 25]), which implied that animals should learn to make the correct turns that are near to the goal more quickly than the earlier correct turns because they are rewarded sooner. Combining this hypothesis with the assumption that rats have tendencies to move in the general direction of food, Spence gave numerical values to the pathways at each choice point and calculated a theoretical order in which they should be eliminated. The correlation between these calculated values and the actual order of elimination was over +.90. The published version of this article (Spence, 1932) illustrates the style that was characteristic of Spence's writings throughout his long career. With the aid of simple mathematical statements of the interactions among hypothetical processes, it presented a theoretical analysis of empirical data. The argument was set forth in lucid prose that was the product of clear thinking and hard work.

Theory of Discrimination Learning

Only a few years later, while he was an NRC Fellow at Orange Park, Spence published his influential theory of discrimination learning (Spence, 1936). Experiments on discrimination learning employ some procedure that makes reward contingent on a response to one of two stimuli presented together or in succession. Responses to one of these stimuli (S+, a card with a large square on it) are reinforced and responses to the other (S–, a card with a smaller square) are not. Spence's theory explained such learning as the result of an interaction between excitatory and inhibitory processes. The theory hypothesized that: (a) every reinforcement of a response to S+ leads to an increment in the excitatory tendency to respond to that stimulus, (b) every nonreinforcement of a response to S– leads to an increment in the inhibitory tendency not to respond to that stimulus, (c) the magnitude of the inhibitory tendency conditioned to S– is less than that of the excitatory tendency conditioned to S+, (d) the excitatory and inhibitory tendencies generalize to stimuli neighboring S+ and S–, and (e) in their choices between two stimuli organisms select the stimulus that has a stronger net excitatory tendency (excitation minus inhibition) conditioned or generalized to it. This analysis set the "battle lines" for a great deal of research on reversed discriminations and transposition that was designed to support the theory or to refute it.

Discrimination Reversal. When animals learn to differentiate between two stimuli, they may take 40 or 50 trials without showing any consistent tendency to choose S+ instead of S–. According to Spence's continuity theory, during this "presolution period," the habit of responding to S+ gains strength gradually with every reinforcement of a response to that stimulus. According to an alternative, noncontinuity theory, championed by David Krech (chap. 18, this volume), during the presolution period, animals test and discard a series of wrong hypotheses about the card to choose untilthey happen on the correct solution. If the animal could put them into words, these incorrect hypotheses would be summarized in sentences like, "The right response is to the card on the right," "It's the card on the left," or "If the correct response was to the card on the right on the last trial, it will be to the card on the left of this trial." After entertaining a series of such wrong hypotheses, the animal finally discovers the correct solution—"it's the card with the larger square"—suddenly and "insightfully."

To illustrate the methods used to decide between these two interpretations, suppose that after 20 trials in such an experiment—before the animals are responding consistently—the contingencies of reinforcement are reversed: S+ becomes S– and vice versa. According to Spence's theory, the prior reinforcements of responses to S+ (now S–) should slow up learning following the reversal because, to learn to choose the new S+, the previously conditioned tendency to select the stimulus that is now S– would have to be extinguished. In contrast, according to noncontinuity theory, the earlier experience should not impede postshift learning because the discarded wrong hypotheses are just as wrong for the reversed discrimination as for the original one. Although the results are not totally consistent, experiments of this type supported Spence's theory more often than the alternative.

Transposition. Spence's (1937) theory also implied an ingenious explanation of the phenomenon of transposition—the fact that when animals are presented with a pair of different stimuli after they have learned a discrimination they choose the novel stimulus that has the same relationship to the other stimulus as S+ had to S– in original acquisition. The name of the phenomenon, *transposition*, suggests an analogy to music, where the relationships among notes allow a listener to recognize a familiar melody when a musician plays it in a new key and every note is changed.

To describe the phenomenon as it was studied in the laboratory, imagine an experiment where animals first learn to choose the larger of two squares, with areas of 160 and 100 cm^2. After mastering this discrimination, they are presented with the original S+, 160 cm^2, and a still larger square with an area of 256 cm^2. In such

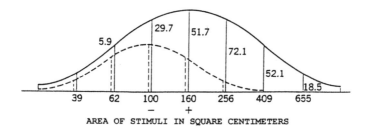

AREA OF STIMULI IN SQUARE CENTIMETERS

FIG. 17.1.   Generalization of excitation and inhibition in discrimination learning. In this experiment, S+ is a large square with an area of 160cm² and S- is a small square with an area of 100 cm². The strength of the excitatory and inhibitory tendencies are represented, respectively, by the solid and dashed curves. The numerical values are net excitatory tendencies (excitation–inhibition) at the stimulus values on the baseline, which is on a logarithmic scale.
Note. From "The Basis for Solution by Chimpanzees of the Intermediate Size Problem," by K. W. Spence, 1942, *Journal of Experimental Psychology, 31*, p. 259. Copyright © 1942 by the American Psychological Association. Adapted with permission.

experiments, most animals choose stimulus 256, although they have never been reinforced for responding to it and they had been rewarded for responding to stimulus 160. Such data suggest that, in discrimination learning, animals respond to relationships between training stimuli, rather than to the absolute differences between them, as Spence's theory implies.

Spence's explanation of transposition employed a model like that shown in Fig. 17.1. This figure depicts the generalization gradients of excitation and inhibition generated by reinforcement of S+ and nonreinforcement of S- in the experiment just described (Spence, 1942). From a set of hypothetical values for excitation and inhibition, Spence demonstrated that, in the test situation, the advantage of excitation over inhibition developed in the original discrimination would yield a generalized difference that favored Stimulus 256 when it was paired with Stimulus 160. The same kinds of analyses also predicted when transposition would not occur. For example, confronted with Stimuli 409 and 655, the animal would choose 409—the smaller square. This explanation was another example of the style of theorizing that Spence had used in his analysis of the backward order of elimination of blinds in maze learning. Again, he used a simple mathematical model to account for available experimental data.

Tests of Spence's theory with laboratory rats usually supported it, but experiments with children (e.g., Kuenne, 1946) raised questions. Although young children responded as the theory predicted, those who were old enough to verbalize the relationship between S+ and S- did so and their responses to the test stimuli were relational. Such data did not particularly bother Spence, however. Anticipating a position that would take on more importance in his later work, he took it for granted that the responses of human beings would involve verbal mechanisms that were not included in the original theory.

Later modifications of the theory by two of Spence's students, Howard and Tracy Kendler (Kendler & Kendler, 1962), made room for such mechanisms. They postulated that discrimination learning is a two-level process that varies with age and evolution. In the first, lower level (essentially Spence's model), nonverbal organisms (young children and infrahuman animals) respond to stimuli directly. In the second, higher level, they transform incoming stimuli into an internal, often verbal representation of the relationship between S+ and S–, and this internal transformation is what guides overt behavior. This model, which had its origins in Spence's discrimination learning theory, could account for differences between the behavior of human beings and other animals and for the developmental changes in such learning that occur in children. Tracy Kendler (1995) refined and extended this theory to cover a broad range of developmental changes in learning and problem-solving behavior.

THE HULL–SPENCE THEORY OF LEARNING

During his first years at Iowa, Spence was deeply involved in the development of the general theory of learning described in *Principles of Behavior*, which Hull (1943) was writing at the time. For some time, Spence and Hull had carried on a correspondence in which they commented on each other's theoretical ideas and formulated new ones. This interchange continued throughout the preparation of the *Principles*, with Spence taking on the dual roles of contributor and critic. Spence's efforts, which were not always successful, were aimed at broadening the foundations of the theory and strengthening its connections to behavior. He urged Hull to relate his conceptions to those of other theorists and to eliminate the irrelevant *physiologizing*. Hull felt compelled to offer some problematic physiological analogues to his theoretical constructs, but Spence believed that such speculations were unnecessary and contributed little more than confusion.

Essentials of the Hull–Spence Theory

Although Hull and Spence disagreed on such specifics, their original positions were so similar that psychology at midcentury saw them as a single Hull–Spence theory. The most general idea in this theory was that two intervening variables—habit strength (learning) and drive (motivation)—interact multiplicatively and that another (inhibition) subtracts from the resulting product in determining the strength of a response:

Response strength = f(excitatory potential) = [f(Habit strength X f(Drive)] – [f(Inhibition)]

Habit strength is a long-term potential for performance, an associative process that increases gradually with practice to some upper limit—the greatest strength a habit can attain given the existing magnitude and delay of reinforcement—at a rate that depends on individual differences.

Drive is a more temporary energizing process that makes this potential manifest in overt performance. The energizing process is one in which drive multiplies with habit strength to produce a higher order concept, *excitatory potential*. Drives are a function of drive conditions such as deprivation from food or water or the delivery of noxious stimulation. Some drives, like the need for food, are largely unlearned or primary; others, like the need for praise and money, are learned or secondary. Like Freud's concept of libido, drives are general dispositions that may energize any habit.

Inhibition is a consequence of nonreinforcement (e.g., of responses to S– in discrimination learning) that suppresses behavior and works against the expression of a habit.

Spence's Theory

As time went by, Spence made a series of modifications of this theory. Sometimes Hull accepted them, but sometimes he did not.

1. In the case of habit strength, in Principles of Behavior, Hull (1943) assumed that reinforcement, in the form of drive reduction, is necessary for all learning. In his Silliman Lecture, Spence (1956) tentatively proposed a two-factor theory in which reinforcement is necessary for classical conditioning but not for instrumental conditioning.

2. In the case of inhibition, Hull proposed an elaborate theory that involved two inhibitory factors. The first, reactive inhibition, develops with the mere elicitation of a response. It is a fatiguelike state with motivational properties. The consummatory response for this drive is resting, which leads to fatigue reduction. When reactive inhibition gains sufficient strength, it forces the organism to rest—a reaction that is rewarded because it reduces reactive inhibition (a drive) and, therefore, is learned. This learned resting response, which Hull called conditioned inhibition, becomes anticipatory. Elicited by conditioned stimuli, it inhibits the response that produces reactive inhibition. These two inhibitions add together before they subtract from the product of habit strength and motivation. By contrast, Spence continued to postulate the simpler inhibitory process mentioned in connection with his theory of discrimination learning. He treated inhibition as a learned suppression of responding that increases with the number of nonreinforced trials in conditioning.

3. In the case of motivation, Hull (1943) noted in *Principles of Behavior* that motives have two aspects: drive, which is "characteristic of primary needs," and incentive motivation, which "corresponds roughly to the common-sense notion of reward." Spence accepted this general conception, but his treatment was both different from and broader than Hull's. The most important difference was that Spence defined *incentive motivation* as a function of the amount and delay of

reinforcement—variables that Hull assigned the role of determining the upper limit of habit growth. The greater breadth came from Spence's extension of the incentive motivation concept to include negative incentives, fear and anxiety, which correspond to punishment, whereas for Hull this concept was confined to the effects of reward. Such concepts began to make Spence's theorizing relevant in contexts that were outside the range of the traditional theories of learning—a point that is discussed after we describe the methodology that permitted a behavioristic theory to make such extensions.

METHODOLOGICAL CONTRIBUTIONS

Both Spence and Hull were behaviorists in the tradition of John B. Watson (chap. 12, *Pioneers I*). They insisted that the basic data of psychology derive from public observations, which can be verified by other scientists rather than from personal experience and intuition, which belong exclusively to the individual who has them. The inescapable implication of this dictum is that, in the final analysis, a science of psychology must be a stimulus–response (S–R) behaviorism because the only observables available are the things that organisms do (responses) and the situations in which they do them (stimuli). For many psychologists, of course, this point of view is unattractive because it appears to rule mental processes out of psychology, thus excluding everything of interest in the field.

The Intervening Variable Approach

In his dealing with this issue, Spence was greatly influenced by the Iowa philosopher Gustav Bergmann, who promoted logical positivism as the most useful philosophy of science for psychology. The bottom line commitment of logical positivism is to operationism—the proposition that the meanings of scientific concepts reside in the observations that define them. This view makes mental processes acceptable to science if they are operationally defined—if they are tied to public operations. Put a different way, they are acceptable if they figure in laws that describe the relationships among independent and dependent variables.

Stimulus–Response (S–R) and Response–Response (R–R) Laws and Concepts

One of Kenneth Spence's contributions to clear thinking in this area was his elaboration of the idea that the intervening variables of psychology are of two different kinds that participate in two different kinds of laws, which Spence called *stimulus–response (S–R)* and *response–response (R–R)* laws. The concepts in S–R laws link behavior to objects and events in the environment. For example, the concept of habit ties changes in performance (dependent variable, R) to reinforced practice (independent variable, S). The concepts in R–R laws make their most obvious appearance in the field of psychometric psychology, where concepts intervene between predicted from and predicted to behavior. For example, the concept of intelligence connects (predicted from) performance on an intelligence test (R$_1$) with (predicted to) performance elsewhere—in school or in an occupation (R$_2$). Spence also noted that laws in Kurt Lewin's field theory were R–R laws because the quasiphysical concepts—valence, vector, tension system, permeability of boundaries, and the rest—are defined by reference to behavior, not in terms of physics. In those days more than today, this contrast made the R–R science of psychology seem inferior because R–R laws were seen as merely correlational, whereas the laws of S–R science were taken to be causal.

The Limits of Logical Positivism

Contrary to the accusations of some of his critics, Spence never claimed that logical positivism and operationism could serve as a blueprint for the science of psychology. In his many published articles (often with Bergmann), which interpreted the positivistic philosophy of science to the psychological community, Spence took positions that now seem obviously correct. There is no God-given recipe for formulating fruitful concepts and developing viable theories in science. No matter how precise they are, operationally defined concepts have no value in and of themselves. They gain that status only when they are embedded in significant empirical relationships (i.e., in S–R or R–R laws). Although logical positivism enables psychologists to gain penetrating insights into theoretical formulations, and to make sophisticated judgments about their strengths and limitations, it is no substitute for originality, ingenuity, and persistence as the essential ingredients in creative scientific effort.

KENNETH SPENCE, THE GENERALIST

Returning now to a discussion of the generality of his position, Spence believed that the laws of simple learning are basic: They apply to complex behavior and they are the same for human beings and other organisms. His research on anxiety and learning and on the role of cognition in conditioning serve to illustrate the sort of generality he had in mind.

Anxiety and Learning

Because of the importance he assigned to classical conditioning, where the acquisition and extinction of responses can be studied in relative isolation, Spence began a program of research on classical eyelid conditioning soon after he arrived at Iowa.

In these experiments, there were 50 or 60 trials consisting of pairings of a conditioned stimulus (CS), often a dim light or a soft tone, and an unconditioned stimulus (US), a puff of air delivered to the cornea. The interval between the two stimuli was brief—typically between half a second and a second. Initially, these experiments were investigations of habit acquisition as a function of such variables as the interstimulus interval (e.g., Kimble, 1947), but later Spence began to use them as a tool to show how motivation (anxiety) influences learning.

In the first of these experiments, Janet Taylor (1951)—later Janet T. Spence—developed *The Taylor Manifest Anxiety Scale*, a personality inventory made up of items that clinicians judged to describe the behavior of anxious people. This test defined individuals' chronic levels of anxiety in terms of the number of test items they accepted as describing themselves. In her experiment, Taylor (1951) found that subjects with high scores on her test learned faster and reached a higher level of conditioning than those with low anxiety. She took these results to mean that the motivation provided by high anxiety facilitated performance in this simple situation.

For more complex situations, where learning requires participants to overcome established habits, Spence's theory predicted that anxiety would impede performance if these habits led to error. One study supporting that prediction found that high-anxiety subjects learned a maze (in which, blindfolded, they traced the correct patterns of right and left turns with a stylus) more slowly than low-anxiety subjects (Farber & Spence, 1953). According to Spence's theory, the reason for this outcome is that, when subjects come to choice points in a maze, they have previously learned biases toward turning right or left. The greater motivation of the high-anxiety subjects energizes these habitual tendencies more than it does for low-anxiety subjects, making them more difficult to abandon when they are errors. Later research carried out in this tradition revealed that the influence of anxiety on learning is more complex than this early work suggests (see Kimble, 1961). Particularly in human beings, anxiety may evoke cognitive activity (thoughts and strategies) that facilitates or interferes with learning depending on such factors as sex and intelligence.

The Role of Cognition

Although Spence believed that human behavior involves cognitive mechanisms that the behavior of other animals often does not, he did not totally neglect these processes in his interpretations of animal learning. As part of a never-published theory of perception, Spence emphasized the importance of what he called *receptor-exposure acts*. For example, he argued that the speed with which rats learn to discriminate between two stimuli will be faster if the to-be-discriminated stimuli are located near the bottom of the cards on which they are presented. Rats tend to look downward (receptor-exposure act) in that direction and, thus, they will attend to them sooner (Amsel, 1995).

In another recognition of the influence of cognition, Spence (1966) suggested that their better understanding of the procedures explains why human participants often cease responding after only one or two nonreinforcements in the extinction phase of experiments in conditioning, whereas other animals extinguish slowly. His speculation (an early expression of the notion that experiments have demand characteristics) was that the participants in these experiments—most often undergraduate students in introductory psychology classes—know that they are in a conditioning experiment and understand what is supposed to happen there. When they perceive the transition from acquisition to extinction, they inhibit their responses as their understanding of these procedures requires.

In one of his last articles, Spence (1966) obtained data that supported this interpretation with the aid of an ingenious technique that masked the transition from acquisition to extinction. In this procedure, eyelid conditioning trials were embedded in a light-guessing experiment: A light, located centrally on the wall before the subject, came on and then went off, followed in a few seconds by a different light to the right or left of the first light, 70% of the time on the left and 30% on the right. Participants were told that their task was to learn to predict which light would come on—registering their predictions by pressing buttons on the right- or left-hand arm of their chairs—and that the purpose of the experiment was to determine the effect of a distraction on the accuracy of their performance. The "distraction" was the conditioning trial consisting of a tone (CS) followed by an air puff (US), which began as the central light went off. Using this procedure, Spence was able to show that the extinction of the human eyelid response proceeded at the same slow rate as it does in other organisms.

THE CHANGING SCIENTIFIC SCENE

Early during World War II, psychologists in increasing numbers began to find careers in the clinic and in industry, where complex behavior involving mentalistic concepts cried out for study. Spence's work on anxiety and cognition should have been accepted as a pioneering effort in that direction but the Zeitgeist was against it. By midcentury, psychologists with different agendas had joined forces and launched a revolution, of which the so-called *cognitive revolution* is the best-known part.

The Revolt Against Positivism

The actual target of this revolt was the methodology with which Kenneth Spence was so closely identified. One group of dissidents felt (*thought* is the wrong word here) that those methods destroyed the warmth and richness of human experience and dehumanized the individual. Egged on by the gossip that back home in philosophy they were in trouble, they abandoned logical positivism and operationism in favor of undisciplined subjectivism. They began accepting intuition as a source of data, common sense as theory, and personal dispositions as the causes of behavior. The announcements of these sentiments cluttered the literature of psychology with feeling/thinking and jargon/substance ratios that are more appropriate for art criticism than science.

Other psychologists with harder scientific noses had objections of another kind. They thought of intervening variables as immaterial fictions that have no place in science. Rejecting the view that operational definitions make them legitimate, these critics took a dim view of such concepts as consciousness, volition, purpose, and self-esteem because they were not directly observable properties of stimuli and responses. In some quarters, even habit, incentive, and inhibition were suspect unless psychologists who used them alleged that they were entities with physical existence in the nervous system. In an extreme expression of that attitude, some physiological psychologists, in effect, left psychology. They turned their energies to research on anatomical structures and physiological processes without much concern for the relevance of their studies to behavior.

A Pox on Both Their Houses

Spence reacted negatively to both these trends, accusing the humanists and scientists alike of mistaking words for actuality. He reminded them of the operational rule that the meanings of psychology's concepts are in the operations that define them. Those without defining observations are no better than the concept of the soul. Those with the same defining operations are identical no matter what you call them.

To make this last point more specific, in his own specialty—learning theory—Spence saw that many of the differences among theories were merely verbal. The alternative to Hull–Spence theorizing that interested him the most was Tolman's cognitive theory, in which the key concept was sign-gestalt expectation. Spence recognized that this mentalistic-sounding neologism was essentially identical to his own concept of habit strength. Both were intervening variables defined in terms of similar independent variables (e.g., amount of practice) and expressed as changes in behavior (e.g., the probability that a rat will make a right turn at a choice point in a maze). Many of Tolman's cognitively oriented supporters rejected this reasoning because they could not ignore the different surplus meanings that live in concept names as different as *habit* and *expectancy*. Spence criticized this epistemic blindness and (in something like words he might have used himself) observed that the most rudimentary understanding of the nature of scientific concepts seemed to have eluded those psychologists, who came to the discipline under the mistaken impression that it is one of the arts. As such language indicates, Spence sometimes offered his opinions in ways that some psychologists would find offensive.

PERSONALITY

No doubt Kenneth Spence would have preferred that this portrait of him as one of psychology's pioneers be completely impersonal. If it were, it would be incomplete: Without some sense of what Spence was like as a person, it is impossible to understand why he had such an influence on his students and why he was so thoroughly disliked by so many of his contemporaries.

Spence As a Teacher

Both in and out of the classroom, Spence's impact on his students was enormous. By a quaint and charming mixture of childish enthusiasm and stern parental demands, he was able to transmit to students the excitement of theoretical psychology and the essential role that experimentation played in such a science. Most students attended Spence's seminar on learning every year in their careers at Iowa. These seminars were exciting. Their focus was on the debates that raged between the advocates of Hull–Spence theory and its opponents—chiefly Guthrie and Tolman—whose theories the students were expected to know in some detail. This context provided Spence with a forum for the presentation of his newest theoretical ideas just as they were beginning to take form. In the process, he made students think of themselves as participants in the creation of a new and important science of behavior.

Outside the classroom, Spence served as a model of dedication to his science. He loved to talk about psychology and often dropped into student offices in the evening—students worked at night in those days—for scientific discussion. He went over the drafts of dissertations with a fine-toothed editorial comb, praising creativity when he found it and showing students how to say what they were trying to say better than they had said it. On their oral examinations for the PhD degree, he was an ally instead of an inquisitor. On my own examination, he gave me a chance to make a good impression by asking me to describe a statistical interpretation of the interstimulus-interval function that I had not included in my dissertation.

No doubt every one of Spence's 75 doctoral students carry with them some of his ideas and a desire to achieve a quality in their own work that would be acceptable to their professor. Many of these students went on to make important contributions to psychology, almost always in areas that were different from the one in which they had been trained. An important aspect of Spence's influence on his students was that they left him with the knowledge and skills they needed to strike out on their own.

How to Make Enemies and Alienate Psychologists

There was nothing vague, half-way, or tentative in the way that Spence presented himself and his theorizing to the psychological public. He had strong attitudes, powerful opinions, and prodigious energy. He was very demanding and critical of others, but even more demanding and critical of himself. Everything he published went through numerous revisions, and what seemed acceptable to most psychologists often failed to meet his standards. Once he honed in on a problem, his powers of concentration were awesome. Nothing could distract him from pursuing his line of thought. In the arguments over theoretical issues at conventions and in the literature, which were so important in midcentury American psychology, Spence typically had thought his position through more carefully than had his opponents. He usually emerged from these debates as the winner, often making his defeated adversaries look like students who had failed to do their homework.

Predictably, these victories did not endear Spence to his colleagues. Moreover, the acid tone of many of his negative comments alienated psychologists in almost every nook and cranny of the discipline. He slighted the physiological psychologists by insisting that the creation of a science of psychology required the development of the abstract mathematical statements that relate behavior to its determining antecedent conditions—a program for which physiology is irrelevant. He offended the psychometric psychologists and an important group of social psychologists by showing that their R–R laws were merely correlational and, thus, inferior to the causal S–R laws of experimental psychology. He irritated the dust-bowl empiricists by promoting the intervening variable approach, thus opening the door to topics that were, for them, taboo. He annoyed the operant conditioners by ridiculing their aversion to theory and their infatuation with cumulative response curves. I recall his asking once in class, "How can you take them seriously? They don't even know how to draw a learning curve." He antagonized the humanists in psychology's two cultures (Kimble, 1984)—who already were a majority in the field—by challenging their knowledge, belittling their methods, and questioning their values.

CONCLUSION: FORGOTTEN BUT NOT GONE

Against this background, contemporary psychology's amnesia for Kenneth Spence and his psychology (mentioned at the beginning of this chapter) begins to look like the Freudian mechanisms of denial and repression. More realistically, however, it seems probable that psychology's forgetfulness in this case reflects the cyclic pattern that has characterized the history of psychology. Its shifting theoretical allegiances and expanding practical commitments have often led the discipline to jettison orientations that it returns to later.

It is difficult to penetrate the future and predict Kenneth Spence's position in the history of psychology. So much depends on the direction psychology will take and whether it retains its integrity as a single discipline. If this psychology of the future is to fulfill its destiny and contribute to human betterment by applications of scientific knowledge, it will have to recover the ambition to be a science of behavior because the problems of the world today (poverty, prejudice, psychopathology, etc.)

are rooted in behavior. Such a psychology will have to embody a broad conception of the interactions among motivational, associative, and inhibitory variables—the basic concepts in Spence's theorizing. What goes around comes around, and the psychology yet to come will acknowledge and give high honor to the memory of Kenneth W. Spence.

ACKNOWLEDGMENTS

This chapter began as a joint contribution, by Howard H. Kendler and me, with Howard as the senior author. The plan was to make it a revision of Kendler's (1967) biography of Kenneth W. Spence, supplemented by materials that appeared in his article (Kendler, 1992) on Spence in Squire's *Encyclopedia of Learning and Memory*. I was responsible for the initial draft. As the manuscript developed, the connection to those sources became increasingly remote, and Howard and I finally agreed (without a hint of malice) that I should be the single author. The chapter as it now appears retains some of Howard's language. For example, the title was his idea, but more important, it owes much to the many wise suggestions Howard made along the way. This chapter also benefited from two other published appreciations of Spence (Amsel, 1995; Hilgard, 1967). I delivered a version of this chapter (with Kendler as co-author as an address at the APA Convention in Toronto in 1996.

REFERENCES

Amsel, A. (1995). Kenneth Wartinbee Spence. *Biographical Memoirs* (Vol. 66). Washington, DC: The National Academy Press.

Farber, I. E., & Spence, K. W. (1953). Complex learning and conditioning as a function of anxiety. *Journal of Experimental Psychology, 45*, 1220–1225.

Hilgard, E. R. (1967). Kenneth Wartinbee Spence. *American Journal of Psychology, 80*, 314–318.

Hull, C. L. (1932). The goal gradient hypothesis and maze learning. *Psychological Review, 39*, 25–43.

Hull, C. L. (1943). *Principles of behavior*. New York: Appleton-Century-Crofts.

Kendler, H. H. (1967). Kenneth W. Spence: 1907–1967. *Psychological Review, 74*, 335–341.

Kendler, H. H. (1992). Spence, Kenneth. In L. R. Squire (Ed.), *Encyclopedia of learning and memory* (pp. 603–606). New York: Macmillan.

Kendler, H. H., & Kendler, T. S. (1962). Vertical and horizontal processes in problem solving. *Psychological Review, 69*, 1–16.

Kendler, T. S. (1995). *Levels of cognitive development*. Hillsdale, NJ: Lawrence Erlbaum Associates.

Kimble, G. A. (1947). Conditioning as a function of the time between conditioned and unconditioned stimuli. *Journal of Experimental Psychology, 37*, 1–15.

Kimble, G. A. (1961). *Hilgard and Marquis' conditioning and learning*. New York: Appleton-Century-Crofts.

Kimble, G. A. (1984). Psychology's two cultures. *American Psychologist, 39*, 833–839.

Kuenne, M. R. (1946). Experimental investigation of the relationship of language to the transposition behavior of young children. *Journal of Experimental Psychology, 26*, 471–490.

Myers, C. R. (1970). Journal citations and scientific eminence in contemporary psychology. *American Psychologist, 25*, 1041–1048.

Spence, K. W. (1932). The order of eliminating blinds in maze learning. *Journal of Comparative Psychology, 14,* 9–27.

Spence, K. W. (1934). Visual acuity and its relation to brightness in chimpanzee and man. *Journal of Comparative Psychology, 18,* 333–361.

Spence, K. W. (1936). The nature of discrimination learning in animals. *Psychological Review, 43,* 427–449.

Spence, K. W. (1937). The differential response in animals to stimuli varying within a single dimension. *Psychological Review, 44,* 430–444.

Spence, K. W. (1942). The basis for solution by chimpanzees of the intermediate size problem. *Journal of Experimental Psychology, 31,* 257–271.

Spence, K. W. (1956). *Behavior theory and conditioning.* New Haven, CT: Yale University Press.

Spence, K. W. (1966). Cognitive and drive factors in the extinction of the conditioned eye blink in human subjects. *Psychological Review, 73,* 445–451.

Taylor, J. A. (1951). The relationship of anxiety to the conditioned eyelid response. *Journal of Experimental Psychology, 41,* 81–92.

Tolman, E. C., & Honzik, C. H. (1930). "Insight" in rats. *University of California Publications in Psychology, 4,* 257–275.

Chapter 18

David Krech:
Scientist and Social Activist

Nancy K. Innis

David Krech first appeared on the academic scene in psychology shortly after the end of World War II, when he accepted an appointment as assistant professor of psychology at Swarthmore, a small co-educational liberal arts college near Philadelphia founded by the Religious Society of Friends (Quakers) in 1864. By 1945, when he accepted the Swarthmore appointment, Krech had become a social psychologist, trained in this emerging discipline not in the university but through his experiences during the previous decade. Before developing those interests, Krech had lived another life, in which he attempted to make his mark as an experimental psychologist. However, things had not turned out as he had hoped, in part, because his name was Isadore Krechevsky. During the first half of the 20th century, many in the academic community were prejudiced against Jews (Krech, 1974). Schools were not always open to them, university professorships were not easy to obtain, and social activism was interpreted as communistic radicalism. Following a succession of disheartening experiences in the 1930s and 1940s, brought on both by his ethnic background and his political activities, Krechevsky left psychology. After World War II, however, he returned to the discipline with his name changed to David Krech. With this new identity, he was able to turn away from his disillusioning past. He did not deny his history or try to hide it, but he now felt comfortable and optimistic. The pages to follow include a description of some of that stormy history.

BRIEF BIOGRAPHY

David Krech was born Yitzhok-Eizik Krechevsky on March 27, 1909, the second youngest of the nine children of Zadie Krechevsky and Sarah Rabinowitz. He was

---

* Photograph of David Krech courtesy of Archives of the History of American Psychology, Akron, Ohio.

named for his maternal great grandfather, Yitzhok-Eizik Haver, a scholar descended from a "long line of rabbis and Talmudic scholars" (Krech, 1974, p. 222). His father, whose main interest was Talmudic study, was "the descendant of a long line of successful...Jewish merchants" (p. 222).

Krechevsky was not Krech's original family name. It had been Epstein until one of the family ancestors made a deal with a Polish nobleman who, in return for being forgiven a large debt, agreed to adopt the Epstein sons so that they would not be subject to conscription into the Tsar's army. Krech became Isadore Krechevsky when his family settled in New Britain, Connecticut, in 1913. At his mother's insistence, they had left their home in Swiencianke, a village near the border between Lithuania and Belarus, for "the land of opportunity where Jewish students were not subjected to the *numerus clausus* (quotas) of the Russian universities" (Krech, 1974, p. 223), or so she believed. Although America was not Tsarist Russia, Krechevsky's Jewish heritage did result in significant adversity.

Undergraduate Education

The town of New Britain provided its citizens with good schools. Young Isadore Krechevsky, who enjoyed his studies, became the first member of his family to attend a university. In 1926, he enrolled at the Washington Square campus of New York University (NYU). He chose NYU because he wanted to live in New York City and because it accepted Jewish students. Initially he wanted to be a scientist, but decided on law—a program in which he believed he could easily succeed. He set out with great expectations and ambitions, hoping as he claimed in his autobiography that a law degree would allow him "to do well" (achieve financial success) but also "to do good"—as he had been taught by his religious parents (Krech, 1974, p. 222). During his sophomore year, however, Krechevsky took a course in introductory psychology that was required by the pre-law program. It captured his interest and eventually became a love that he could not abandon, even in the face of a series of discouraging experiences.

Psychology was a science, but a "science without tears—no memorizing" (Evans, 1976, p. 136), as he would later claim. It was a science that would allow him to realize both of his ambitions: to do well and also to do good. He soon switched his major. Krechevsky's psychology teachers at NYU, including Theodore Schneirla, were behaviorists—a perspective that he too adopted—and it was not long before he was engaged in animal research. During his senior year, one of his professors, Frances Holden, suggested that he carry out an independent research project and provided him with the apparatus to study discrimination learning in rats (Krech, 1974). Then, as he lay sick with the flu, he received a copy of Karl Lashley's (1929, chap. 20, *Pioneers I*) *Brain Mechanisms and Intelligence*. Having nothing else to do, he read the book carefully and was especially intrigued by Lashley's description of the performance of rats during the "presolution period" in discrimination experiments. Lashley did not suggest how to study this behavior systematically, but Krechevsky thought that such an investigation would be possible using his discrimination setup. Thus began his studies of attempted solutions, later to be referred to as *hypotheses*, in rats.[1] Krechevsky completed his BA in 1930 and remained at NYU, receiving his master's degree under the supervision of T. N. Jenkins in 1931 (Krechevsky, 1932b).

Graduate Education at Berkeley

Although it had not been a problem at NYU, Krechevsky was aware that being Jewish would limit his choice of graduate schools. Also aware of this, Frances Holden encouraged him to apply to the University of California to work with Edward C. Tolman (chap. 15, *Pioneers I*). She knew that Berkeley would provide a comfortable, yet stimulating, environment in which to expand his ideas. She was right. When Krechevsky told Tolman about his research at NYU, Tolman "caught fire and jumped out of his seat and practically shouted out 'Hypotheses in rats!'" (Krech, 1974, p. 229). Tolman would become his mentor and later his friend—"a great teacher, a great scientist, and a man to love" (Krech, 1974, p. 232).

Tolman's weekly seminars, which he recalled as "superb educational *happenings*," were the highlight of Krechevsky's 2 years at Berkeley. In these seminars, Tolman and the students "would all go to it, spouting and talking and planning new experiments" (Krech, 1974, p. 229). It was an exhilarating atmosphere and one most suited to Krechevsky's argumentative disposition. During his years at Berkeley, Krechevsky impressed Tolman[2] as "very brilliant, tremendously articulate, very industrious," but also as "cocksure," which did not always endear him to his fellow students. When he returned to Berkeley as a faculty member years later, Krech was once again center stage at Tolman's seminar, where his "sharp wit, incisive criticism, and the incredible range of information he could bring to bear on a question" (Petrinovich & McGaugh, 1976, p. 6) inspired "awe and respect" in the graduate students. By then, discussion centered on issues emerging from "the Berkeley–Yale–Iowa conflict" (Petrinovich & McGaugh, 1976, p. 2). One of these issues, the continuity–discontinuity debate, was the result of Krechevsky's early work on hypotheses in rats (Krechevsky, 1938).

As a graduate student at Berkeley, Krechevsky continued his research on hypotheses and worked with fellow students on other animal learning projects. This predilection to collaborate with colleagues was evident throughout his career. Over the next 2 years, Krechevsky published 10 articles—an energetic beginning for the young scientist. The logic behind his hypotheses hypothesis was described in an article in the *Psychological Review*, in which Krechevsky (1932a) briefly discussed

---

[1]There is some controversy over the question of who was the first to use *hypotheses*. Krech (1974) attributed it to Tolman; Tolman (1948) attributed it to Krech.

[2]E. C. Tolman to E. G. Boring, January 1934. Boring papers, Harvard University Archives, Pusey Library, Harvard University.

the results of three studies, including his MA thesis research. By *hypotheses*, he was referring to the fact that rats, when faced with a discrimination problem, do not respond randomly; rather, they adopt systematic strategies from the outset. In one study carried out at Berkeley, he used an apparatus in which the rats were required to enter four successive boxes, each requiring a choice between two alternatives. The situation was set up so that the correct alternatives were, in fact, randomly assigned. Results showed that the "rat, when placed in an unsolvable situation, does not respond in a helter-skelter chance fashion, but makes a series of integrated, unified attempts at solution" (Krechevsky, 1932c, p. 63). For example, on a series of trials it would always choose left, then adopt an alternation strategy, and so forth. This contradicts the S–R theorists' position that "the animal is a plastic individual whom the environment molds as it will." The rat's choices were not forced by the environment, but rather "initiated...by the animal himself"(Krechevsky, 1932a, p. 532)—a result of his nature and his past experience (see Krechevsky, 1933a,1933b). Krechevsky's ideas fit nicely with Tolman's (1932) purposive behaviorism and his findings provided support for Tolman's theory.

Early Scientific Career

In contrast to Tolman, whose focus was on the rat's behavior, Krechevsky was interested in the brain mechanisms underlying that behavior. He was able to pursue this interest when, in 1933, as a new PhD, he received a National Research Council (NRC) fellowship that permitted him to spend a year in Karl Lashley's laboratory at the University of Chicago becoming "a neurological psychologist" (Krech, 1974, p. 231). Soon after he arrived at Chicago, Krechevsky learned how to make cortical lesions and embarked on a series of studies examining the hypotheses of brain-damaged rats in an attempt to understand "the process of learning" (Krechevsky, 1935, p. 426). Lashley's (1929, chap. 20, *Pioneers I*) equipotentiality theory of brain function maintained that the amount of brain tissue destroyed, rather than the location of the lesion, determined the nature of behavioral deficits. Krechevsky's (1935) studies, for example those on the number and nature (spatial or visual) of hypotheses displayed by lesioned rats, indicated that both area and amount were important.

THE PSYCHOLOGIST AND SOCIAL ISSUES

Krechevsky's NRC fellowship came to an end in 1934 during the Great Depression. There was still no opportunity for a teaching appointment so he was forced to stay on at Chicago—first as Lashley's research assistant (1934–1935) and then, after Lashley moved to Harvard, as a research associate (1935–1937) running the laboratory.

As the Depression deepened, employment opportunities for psychologists, particularly recent graduates, worsened. In 1934, Krechevsky, who now believed that his "failure to get an academic job was not only a reflection of bad economic times, but also of a bad society" (Krech, 1974, p. 235), joined New America. New America was a radical organization combining "elements of Marxism and progressivism" (Finison, 1986, p. 24) that "attracted a number of social scientists, educators, and religious leaders to its ranks" (Finison, 1979, p. 29). Krechevsky was soon involved, along with Ross Stagner and other New America psychologists, in organizing a petition urging the American Psychological Association (APA) to take some action to help unemployed psychologists find work. Their petition was ignored (Finison, 1979; Stagner, 1986). The following year, along with Lorenz Meyer, Ward Halstead, and Walter Lurie, he began to work toward setting up a society to "stimulate more psychologists to direct their efforts toward the making of a new and better America" (Krech, 1974, p. 236; see also Finison, 1986). In January 1936, an announcement describing this plan was printed on the front page of the American Guardian, a radical newspaper, and copies of the paper were mailed to over 700 psychologists.

Psychologists from around the country expressed interest in such a society. At the 1936 APA meeting at Dartmouth College, the Society for the Psychological Study of Social Issues (SPSSI) was born. Goodwin Watson from Columbia University was elected chairman of the society and Krechevsky was named secretary–treasurer. There were 333 charter members, including a number of well-established, liberal psychologists such as Gardner Murphy, Gordon Allport, and Edward Tolman, whose presence added respectability to the organization. When APA was reorganized in 1945, SPSSI became Division 9 of the association. Although its founders "clearly viewed the formation of the Society itself and the increased possibility of influencing American psychology as political action," this "component was downplayed in Society publications" to attract a larger membership (Finison, 1979, p. 31). Krechevsky remained secretary–treasurer until 1939, when, disillusioned both by world conditions and his treatment by the academic community, he left psychology to work full time for New America. He continued to support the aims of SPSSI and was SPSSI chairman in 1950–1951 (Capshew, 1986).

Academic Trials and Tribulations

In 1937, Krechevsky's association with the University of Chicago came to an end in part because he had signed a statement protesting the action of the Chicago police in what is known as the *Memorial Day Massacre*. Krechevsky had been present when police opened fire on a group of steel workers who, along with their wives and children, were peacefully picketing the Republic Steel Corporation. Fortunately, Krechevsky was not without a job. Although it was not what he felt he deserved, he accepted a research associateship at Swarthmore College. At Swarthmore, the "rich Gestalt ambiance" provided by Wolfgang Köhler (chap. 17, *Pio-*

neers I), Karl Duncker (chap. 10, this volume), and Hans Wallach, along with their many visitors, and exposure to the phenomenology of Robert MacLeod, brought new and lasting influences (Krech, 1974).

Naturally, what Krechevsky really wanted was a regular academic appointment and, in the summer of 1938, it seemed that he had found one: a half-time appointment as assistant professor at the University of Colorado. Even before he arrived in Boulder, however, Krechevsky's appointment had been reduced to an instructorship. In a letter to George Norlin, president of the University of Colorado, President Taliaferro of the University of Chicago had written that Krechevsky "showed a decided tendency toward the extreme left" and was secretary of a society whose members had "rather radical tendencies" (G. Norlin; cited in Krech, 1974, p. 239). Despite this inopportune beginning, Krechevsky had a reasonably good year at Colorado. He collaborated with Karl Muenzinger on a textbook of learning that incorporated Tolman's purposive behaviorism, Lashley's field theory, and the Gestaltist views of perception. The book was never completed. The following year, although Krechevsky was highly recommended for promotion to an assistant professorship, the University Regents were adamant in rejecting the promotion. Adding insult to injury, they noted that, given his Jewish heritage, he should be thankful for an instructorship because few university appointments were open to Jews (Krech, 1974). This was the last straw—it drove Krechevsky out of psychology, the science he loved so much.

Krechevsky then worked for New America until the organization was dissolved in the summer of 1941. During the next 4 years, he devoted his energies to the war effort in various capacities. His first job, for the Department of Agriculture, involved assessing the attitudes of the urban poor to the food stamp program. He then worked for the War Office in the Division of Program Surveys, where he "learned to respect the scientific integrity, methodological sophistication, psychological thinking, and social utility" of those engaged in survey research (Krech, 1974, p. 241). Indeed, this experience would prove to be the beginning of Krech's career as a social psychologist.

The War Years

On November 28, 1942, Isadore Krechevsky was inducted into the U.S. Army and before long, on the recommendation of Robert Choate Tryon (chap. 22, *Pioneers I*), one of his teachers at Berkeley, he was assigned to the Office of Strategic Services (OSS; now the CIA) in Washington. At the OSS Assessment Station, headed by Harvard psychologist Henry Murray, he joined Donald MacKinnon and other psychologists, including many friends from his Swarthmore and Berkeley days, to evaluate recruits who had volunteered for espionage assignments (Krech, 1974). Here he acquired the fundamental techniques of personality assessment. The war years brought changes to Krechevsky's perspective on psychology and his personal life. In September 1943, he married Hilda Gruenberg and the following May they filed a petition to change their name to Krech. Krech was discharged from the army early in 1945 so that he could join the U.S. Strategic Bombing Survey, an attempt to assess the morale of German citizens following the American invasion. Most of the survey team were fellow members of SPSSI. While abroad they spent their free time "plotting and planning the postwar future of social psychology in America and the role SPSSI could play" (Krech, 1974, p. 243).

LATER CAREER

The fall term of 1945 marked the beginning of a new career in psychology for David Krech. Once again he was at Swarthmore College, but this time—for the first time—he had a respectable faculty appointment. Krech was back in form, writing papers, collaborating with colleagues, and critically evaluating his discipline, but now as a social psychologist. The major publication from this period was a textbook, *Theory and Problems of Social Psychology*, written with Richard S. Crutchfield, a war-time associate who had also studied with Tolman at Berkeley. The book was greatly influenced by the ideas of Robert MacLeod (e.g., MacLeod, 1947), at that time still department chair at Swarthmore and a man who would continue to be a close friend and a respected mentor for Krech throughout his life (Krech, 1973). Over the next three decades, Krech and Crutchfield would continue their collaboration, which included a popular introductory textbook, *Elements of Psychology*.

Social Psychology

Theory and Problems of Social Psychology was unlike any previous textbook in the field. The authors were determined to present a "theoretically sound social psychology" that was also "practically valid and useful" (Krech & Crutchfield, 1948, p. vii). Their approach was to (a) systematically set out the theoretical principles of motivation (dynamics), perception (organization), and learning (Tolman style) and then show how these could be applied to social situations; (b) determine the principles involved in belief formation; and (c) consider a number of current social problems to which the theoretical ideas could be applied to understand, and perhaps even solve, them (Krech & Crutchfield, 1948). The problems dealt with included racial prejudice, industrial conflict, and international conflict—issues that had long been the concern of SPSSI members. "The book represented a major step toward organizing the subject matter and theory of social psychology and was widely recognized as a major achievement" (Petrinovich & McGaugh, 1976, p. 3).

Berkeley and the "Loyalty Oath"

When Isadore Krechevsky left the University of California in 1933, his ambition was to return some day as a professor (Krech, 1974). In 1947, David Krech was offered an appointment as associate professor of psychology at that institution. Edward Tolman, who hated departmental administration, had taken on the role of chair so that he could make sure that the appointment went through. Krech, of course, was delighted to accept and would remain at Berkeley for the rest of his career.

Not long after Krech's return to Berkeley, the university faced a moral crisis. The cold war and reactions to it had prompted the University of California Regents, in 1949, to require all faculty to sign an anti-communist loyalty oath as a condition for the renewal of their annual contracts. There was widespread opposition among the faculty, eloquently expressed by Tolman in an address to the Academic Senate deploring the oath as an infringement on academic freedom. Many faculty did not sign, but the Regents remained adamant. What followed was a year of division and suspicion on the Berkeley campus (Stewart, 1950), during which a diminishing group of faculty continued to oppose the threat of the oath (Innis, 1992). Krech, who of course deplored the Regents' action, was spared the anguish of participating in that year of controversy. In 1949–1950, he was promoting social psychology in Norway as a visiting professor at the University of Oslo. However, the controversy continued and, in the spring of 1950, the Regents issued an ultimatum indicating that all those who did not sign would be fired. Krech again was saved from having to take a stand at Berkeley when his friend Jerome Bruner arranged a visiting appointment in the Department of Social Relations at Harvard for 1950–1951. Although Krech accepted the position, he soon discovered that if he wished to retain his job at Berkeley, he would have to sign the oath and, ultimately, he did (Krech, 1974). Edward Tolman supported and encouraged this painful decision on the ground that he and a few others, who were more secure financially, would continue to fight the oath for all who supported academic freedom. They did so in the courts and eventually were vindicated (Innis, 1992).

Physiological Psychology

During the late 1940s, a diverse group of psychologists was arguing for a *New Look* in the psychology of perception. This movement, which only lasted for about 10 years, tried to unite perception, learning (cognition), and motivation (Bruner & Postman, 1950). The "real send-off for...the New Look" (Hilgard, 1987, p. 161) was a symposium on perception and personality held at the 1949 APA convention in Denver. Krech was in at the start of this movement. During his year at Harvard, he and Jerome Bruner collaborated on the editing of a book that reprinted the papers from the symposium (Bruner & Krech, 1950).[3] In his chapter in this volume,

---

[3]The papers had been previously published in 1949 in Volume 18 of the *Journal of Personality*.

entitled "Notes Toward a Psychological Theory," Krech (1950a) declared that psychology had "reached the stage where it has accumulated sufficient data and understanding to reformulate, explicitly, its entire theoretical framework," and he proposed "to point to the proper direction in which the theoretician in psychology should move" (p. 66). Given the importance of the determination of all-encompassing laws in any science, he suggested the idea of a "dynamic system" and indicated that "*every* experience or behavior of man is correlated with, or is determined by, or is congruent with, or is a function of a Dynamic System" (p. 68). He went on to claim:

> There can be no laws relating to "learning," to "perception," to "motivation." The laws concerning the functioning of Dynamic Systems must involve *all the parameters of Dynamic Systems simultaneously*. And since experience and behavior are controlled by the functioning of Dynamic Systems, the only laws which enable us to understand and predict behavior must be laws of Dynamic Systems. (p. 80)

Aware of inconsistencies in his original approach, Krech (1950b) soon offered a definition of a *dynamic system* that, in the terminology of MacCorquodale and Meehl (1948), made it less like an immaterial "intervening variable" and more like a "hypothetical construct;" that is, "a postulated actually existing structure which eventually might be described by direct experimentation" (Krech, 1950a, p. 74). *Dynamic systems* were defined as "molar organizations of specific neural events" (Krech, 1950b, p. 289). The task of the psychologist (as opposed to that of the neurologist) was "to spell out the relationships between postulated neurological attributes of a Dynamic System and the observable psychological data of experience and behavior" (p. 290).

Krech soon embarked on a new and productive field of research relating brain events and behavior. Because of his commitment to a dynamic approach, he rejected the (static) lesion method of assessing brain function and began to carry out studies examining the relationships between brain chemistry and behavior. Characteristically, this research was collaborative. In addition to David Krech, the team consisted of Edward Bennett, a biochemist and student of Melvin Calvin, Mark Rosenzweig, a young physiological psychologist, and (a few years later) Marion Diamond, an anatomist (Evans, 1976; Krech, 1974). The earliest of their studies looked for correlations between cortical levels of the enzyme cholinesterase (ChE) and adaptive behavior and discrimination learning in the rat (e.g., Krech, Rosenzweig, Bennett, & Kreukel, 1954; Krech, Rosenzweig, & Bennett, 1962). The studies that attracted the most attention, however, involved comparisons of the brains of rats raised in enriched environments (i.e., with the opportunity to interact with numerous objects and with other rats) with those of rats housed alone and/or in impoverished environments (e.g., Krech, Rosenzweig, & Bennett, 1960). These studies obtained evidence of both chemical and structural differences in the brain (Diamond, 1976; Rosenzweig & Bennett, 1976). The differences could not be attributed to genetics because littermates had been assigned to the comparison groups in these experiments. Other possibly confounding variables were also systematically eliminated, providing "definite evidence that the result of an enriched early environment was literally a better brain" (Evans, 1976, p. 141).

CONCLUSION

In 1971, for health reasons, David Krech took early retirement (Ghiselli, 1978), but he remained in Berkeley as Professor Emeritus. A few years later, former graduate students honored him with a *Festschrift*. In the introduction to the book, Petrinovich and McGaugh (1976) pointed to the four major threads that run through Krech's work: (a) a concern for the importance of individual differences, (b) "an insistence on the primary importance of the Big Question," (c) an attempt to discover the basic mechanisms underlying molar behavior, and (d) a strong "commitment to the essentials of Gestalt psychology" (pp. 3–4). Krech died in 1977.

In 1970, David Krech was honored with the Distinguished Scientific Contribution Award from the APA. The opening sentences of the Citation (1971) cogently characterized the man:

> The friends of David Krech will say that his career has been brilliant, varied, and consistently creative. His enemies will say that he has been destructive and provoking. Both judgments are correct. He has been provoking and destructive when he has downed his opponents, but he has always been gentle with them afterwards. His career has been varied: animal psychology, social psychology, physiological psychology, and some undisclosed activities during World War II. In all of these he has been brilliant and creative. (pp. 81–82)

Isadore Krechevsky, alias David Krech, did well and he did good.

ACKNOWLEDGMENTS

The author thanks the Canadian Social Sciences and Humanities Research Council for supporting her research on Edward C. Tolman and his students.

REFERENCES

Bruner, J. S., & Krech, D. (Eds.). (1950). *Perception and personality: A symposium.* Durham, NC: Duke University Press.

Bruner, J. S., & Postman, L. (1950). Perception, cognition, and behavior. In J. S. Bruner & D. Krech (Eds.), *Perception and personality: A symposium* (pp. 14–31). Durham, NC: Duke University Press.

Capshew, J. H. (1986). Networks of leadership: A quantitative study of SPSSI presidents, 1936–1986. *Journal of Social Issues, 42,* 75–106.

Citation. (1971). David Krech. *American Psychologist, 26,* 81–86.

Diamond, M. C. (1976). Anatomical brain changes induced by environment. In L. Petrinovich & J. L. McGaugh (Eds.), *Knowing, thinking, and believing: Festschrift for Professor David Krech* (pp. 215–241). New York: Plenum.

Evans, R. I. (1976). *The making of psychology: Discussions with creative contributors.* New York: Knopf.

Finison, L. J. (1979). An aspect of the early history of the Society for the Psychological Study of Social Issues: Psychologists and labor. *Journal of the History of the Behavioral Sciences, 15,* 29–37.

Finison, L. J. (1986). The psychology of insurgency: 1936–1945. *Journal of Social Issues, 42,* 21–33.

Ghiselli, E. E. (1978). David Krech: 1909–1977. *American Journal of Psychology, 91,* 731–734.

Hilgard, E. R. (1987). *Psychology in America: A historical survey.* New York: Harcourt Brace.

Innis, N. K. (1992). Lessons from the controversy over the loyalty oath at the University of California. *Minerva, (30,* 337–365.

Krechevsky, I. (1932a). 'Hypotheses' in rats. *Psychological Review, 6,* 516–532.

Krechevsky, I. (1932b). "Hypotheses" versus "chance" in the pre-solution period in sensory discrimination-learning. *University of California Publications in Psychology, 6,* 27–44.

Krechevsky, I. (1932c). The genesis of "hypotheses" in rats. *University of California Publications in Psychology, 6,* 45–64.

Krechevsky, I. (1933a). The docile nature of "hypotheses." *Journal of Comparative Psychology, 15,* 429–443.

Krechevsky, I. (1933b). The hereditary nature of "hypotheses." *Journal of Comparative Psychology, 16,* 99–116.

Krechevsky, I. (1935). Brain mechanisms and "hypotheses." *Journal of Comparative Psychology, 19,* 425–462.

Krechevsky, I. (1938). A study of the continuity of the problem-solving process. *Psychological Review, 45,* 107–133.

Krech, D. (1950a). Notes toward a psychological theory. In J. S. Bruner & D. Krech (Eds.), *Perception and personality: A symposium* (pp. 66–87). Durham, NC: Duke University Press.

Krech, D. (1950b). Dynamic systems, psychological fields, and hypothetical constructs. *Psychological Review, 57,* 293–290.

Krech, D. (Ed.). (1973). *The MacLeod symposium, June 2–3, 1972.* Ithaca, NY: Cornell University Press.

Krech, D. (1974). David Krech. In G. Lindzey (Ed.), *A history of psychology in autobiography* (Vol. VII, pp. 221–249). Englewood Cliffs, NJ: Prentice-Hall.

Krech, D., & Crutchfield, R. S. (1948). *Theory and problems of social psychology.* New York: McGraw-Hill.

Krech, D., Rosenzweig, M. R., & Bennett, E. L. (1960). Effects of environmental complexity and training on brain chemistry. *Journal of Comparative and Physiological Psychology, 53,* 509–519.

Krech, D., Rosenzweig, M. R., & Bennett, E. L. (1962). Relations between brain chemistry and problem-solving among rats raised in enriched and impoverished environments. *Journal of Comparative and Physiological Psychology, 55,* 801–807.

Krech, D., Rosenzweig, M. R., Bennett, E. L., & Kreukel, B. (1954). Enzyme concentrations in the brain and adjustive behavior patterns. *Science, 120,* 994–996.

Lashley, K. (1929). *Brain mechanisms and intelligence.* Chicago: University of Chicago Press.

MacLeod, R. (1947). The phenomenological approach to social psychology. *Psychological Review, 54,* 193–210.

MacCorquodale, K., & Meehl, P. E. (1948). On a distinction between hypothetical constructs and intervening variables. *Psychological Review, 55,* 95–107.

Petrinovich, L., & McGaugh, J. L. (1976). Introduction. In L. Petrinovich & J. L. McGaugh (Eds.), *Knowing, thinking, and believing: Festschrift for Professor David Krech* (pp. 1–8). New York: Plenum.

Rosenzweig, M. R., & Bennett, E. L. (1976). Enriched environments: Facts, factors, and fantasies. In
L. Petrinovich & J. L. McGaugh (Eds.), *Knowing, thinking, and believing: Festschrift for Professor David Krech* (pp. 179–213). New York: Plenum.

Stagner, R. (1986). Reminiscences about the founding of SPSSI. *Journal of Social Issues, 42,* 35–42.

Stewart, G. (1950). *The year of the oath.* Garden City, NY: Doubleday.

Tolman, E. C. (1932). Purposive behavior in animals and men. New York: Appleton-Century-Crofts.

Tolman, E. C. (1948). Cognitive maps in rats and men. *Psychological Review, 55,* 189–208.

Chapter 19

Benton J. Underwood:
A Tribute of Memories

Joel S. Freund

The goal of this chapter is to give the reader a sense of who Benton J. Underwood was, as his students and his colleagues saw him—no easy task. As I hope to make clear, Ben Underwood was a man of many facets. He was an extremely productive researcher, a superb methodologist, and an incomparable teacher. If I were to make such statements within Ben's hearing, however, he invariably would ask, with a twinkle in his eye, "Where are the data?" Well, Ben, here they are.

THE SCIENTIST

Presenting the entirety of Ben Underwood's influence on the science of verbal learning and memory would require more space than is available, so I touch on just a few broad topics: (a) component analysis of paired-associate learning, (b) mediation and implicit associative responses, (c) attributes of memory, and (d) interference theory of memory. In this summary of his contributions, I have drawn extensively from Postman's (1972) talk honoring Ben's 25th year at Northwestern University.

The Functionalist Orientation

Functionalism was characterized by three orienting attitudes. The first was a behavioristic point of view expressed in stimulus–response (S–R) terminology in the specification of associated events (e.g., excitation, inhibition, extinction, and generalization). The second might be called *pragmatic associationism*. Function-

---

* Photograph of Benton J. Underwood courtesy of Joel S. Freund's collection.

alists accepted the assocationistic theory of the time and used the standard methods (serial learning, paired-associates learning), but modified them as necessary to meet scientific purposes. The third attribute was an insistence that simple and complex phenomena could be analyzed into component processes, the effects of which could be determined. Recombination of the components would produce the original phenomenon.

When Ben began his career, psychologists studied rote verbal learning to understand the nature of the association—the connection between S and R. At that time, learning was conceived as a passive process: Each repetition of the S–R pair strengthened the associative bond between them until the stimulus came to elicit the response. Underwood's research on stimulus selection (Underwood, 1963; Underwood & Erlebacher, 1965; Underwood, Ham, & Ekstrand, 1962; Underwood & Keppel, 1963; Williams & Underwood, 1970) was instrumental in changing the conception of subjects in experiments from that of passive learners to that of active participants, although Ben recognized that some associations could be established simply through contiguity—essentially a passive form of learning (Spear, Ekstrand, & Underwood, 1964).

Historically, the conception of an association was that of a mental representation of the connections between events (e.g., between the nonsense syllables used stimulus and response terms in a list of paired associates). This conception did not necessitate a distinction between the functions of these syllables as stimuli and responses. The interest was in the connections. Although it had long been recognized that syllables differ in their meaningfulness (Glaze, 1928), psychologists did not realize that variations in meaningfulness might have different consequences when syllables were used as stimuli or responses.

Two-Stage Theory

It was Underwood's discovery that manipulation of response meaningfulness has a greater effect on learning than the manipulation of stimulus meaningfulness that led to the development of the two-stage theory of paired-associate learning. In the first or response learning stage of this theory, response terms become available as units. In the second or associative stage, these responses are associated with their stimuli. For Underwood, this theory raised two factual questions: "What conditions determine response availability, and how do variations in availability influence the course of associative learning?" (Postman, 1972, p. 6).

The commonly accepted answer to the first question was that differences in the difficulty of learning verbal units depended on their meaningfulness, which was operationally defined in various ways, including (a) the percentage of subjects who reported having an association in a limited period of time, (b) the number of associates elicited in a given period of time, (c) the number of associates the subject thinks would be elicited, (d) ratings of relative speed of learning, (e) rated familiarity, and (f) rated pronunciability. Underwood and Schulz (1960) reduced these measures to complementary manifestations of a single variable: frequency of everyday linguistic usage. Their principal conclusion was the spew hypothesis. According to this hypothesis, the "order of emission of verbal units is directly related to frequency of exposure with those units" (p. 86).

Mediation and Implicit Associative Responses

The second (associative) element of the S–R link has also undergone considerable transformation as a result of Underwood's research. He demonstrated that not only are rote connections difficult to form but that research participants typically employ mediating associations of various sorts (Barnes & Underwood, 1959; Twedt & Underwood, 1959). These unverbalized reactions are responses to the stimulus terms that serve as mediators to aid subjects in connecting the overt stimuli and responses. One type of mediating association is the implicit associative response (IAR), the existence of which was demonstrated in a false-recognition experiment (Underwood, 1965). Students listened to a long list of words and, to each, indicated whether that word had been in the list before. Some of the list words were new, some were repetitions, and some were new words with associations to previous words in the list. The evidence for IARs was that subjects falsely identified the associates as old words more often than they did new words without those associations.

Underwood's subsequent research has demonstrated that IARs may underlie the effects of conceptual similarity on acquisition (Underwood, Ekstrand, & Keppel, 1965; Underwood & Freund, 1969; Wood & Underwood, 1967). Postman (1972) summarized the effect of Underwood's research in this area as follows:

It can no longer be taken for granted that the nominal and functional stimulus are identical; response learning and associative learning have been shown to be analytically separable processes that bear different relations to task variables and to the conditions of practice; and the establishment of the prescribed associations is seen as the end product of a sequence of mediating events. (p. 9)

Attributes of Memory

A second major line of related research began with the question of how subjects discriminate among the stimuli and responses. Research on this question led to the development of the frequency theory of verbal-discrimination learning (Ekstrand, Wallace, & Underwood, 1966) and subsequently to a modification of the role assigned to frequency in various tasks (Underwood 1971). Because he postulated that frequency of occurrence is the primary discriminative attribute that influences learning and retention, he examined its effects in many different experimental situations (Underwood & Freund, 1970; Underwood, Zimmerman, & Freund, 1971). The results of this research led to the notion that memory is composed of many attributes—not just frequency—only a few of which are tapped by any given test (Underwood, 1969, 1983). The view of memory as a complex of attributes led to another major theoretical shift in the field of verbal learning, with regard to the function and effect of repetition. According to the attribute theory, repetition increases the probability of recall, not by increasing the strength of associative connections, but by establishing multiple retrieval attributes. This conception of memory continues to be an assumption underlying many major theories of memory.

Interference Theory

The final contribution to be discussed here, of the many that Underwood made to verbal learning, concerns the role of interference in forgetting. Ebbinghaus (chap. 4, this volume) obtained substantial amounts of forgetting after short periods of time. For example, his data showed savings of only 58% after 20 minutes, 44% after 1 hour, and 34% after 24 hours. The generally accepted explanation for this rapid forgetting was retroactive interference—the blocking of the S–R associations learned in the laboratory by associations developed more recently, either in the laboratory or outside of it. For example, in paired-associate learning, associations are formed between a set of stimuli (A) and a set of responses (B). Once these A–B associations are learned, the presentation of a particular stimulus, A, tends to elicit a particular response, B. Retroactive interference occurs when later learning leads to the formation of A–C associations (a new response to the original stimulus), so that in a memory test A elicits C instead of B.

There was considerable controversy concerning the mechanisms underlying retroactive interference. The theoretical alternatives included response competition between B and C, the unlearning, or extinction of A–B associations, and suppression of all B responses. Underwood's theoretical analyses and methodological contributions to the understanding of the phenomenon were substantial (see Barnes & Underwood, 1959, for examples; see Postman, 1972, for an evaluation).

An even more important contribution began with Underwood's classic and oft-cited 1957 article, which shifted the research emphasis of the entire field. In that article, Underwood organized the results of published studies according to the number of lists participants had mastered prior to learning and attempting to recall the critical list. These analyses clearly indicate that the massive forgetting obtained over a 24-hour interval by Ebbinghaus and others was more the result of proactive interference produced by the associations acquired in those earlier experiments than it was retroactive interference. In his own research, Underwood demonstrated that, for a naive subject learning only one list, there was only about 20% forgetting after 24 hours.

The importance of proactive interference in forgetting was not restricted to long-term memory. In 1962, Keppel and Underwood demonstrated that proactive interference (PI) plays a major role in short-term memory. The well-known curve, showing that short-term memory has a life span of only about 20 seconds, occurs only after several trials; on the first trial in such experiments, retention is essentially perfect after 20 seconds. It is the cumulative proactive effect of associations developed on the earlier trials that produces rapid short-term forgetting. The demonstration that PI had similar effects in long- and short-term memory argued for abandoning the distinction between short- and long-term memory.

Another suggestion from this history of research is that, although proactive interference is responsible for forgetting in both long- and short-term memory, the sources of the interference differ. For short-term memory, the source of interference is within the experiment, whereas for long-term memory, the source is extra-experimental, preexisting language habits. Utilizing this idea, Underwood and Postman (1960) developed an elegant theory to explain forgetting and Underwood and his colleagues put this theory to rigorous tests. "The outcome of such empirical tests can be summarized only too briefly. With a few scattered exceptions, the deductions from the theory failed to be supported" (Postman, 1972, p. 19). Inquiry into the reasons for the failure of the theory led to comparisons of the conditions under which language habits are normally acquired (i.e., widely spaced practice, high degree of learning) and laboratory conditions. Thus, Underwood turned again to the investigation of the effect of distributed practice on long-term retention, which cannot be described here because of space limitations (Underwood & Ekstrand, 1966, 1968; Underwood & Freund, 1968).

THE TEACHER

In 1987, Ben Underwood was awarded the American Psychological Foundation Award for Distinguished Teaching in psychology. The citation that accompanied that award read, in part:

> For incomparable lifetime contributions in research and practice to the advancement of the teaching of psychology, and to the evaluation and improvement of college teaching generally.... An excellent and respected teacher, he has demonstrated a commitment to the education of generations of students.... His teaching was simple and straightforward, and he had a way of drawing everyone out and getting each person to do his or her best. All of his students agree that his enthusiasm was contagious. As a teacher, he gave generously of his time and his energy, and he showed his love of teaching in countless ways. (American Psychological Association, 1988, p. 264)

Although the citation is accurate, it does not convey a true feeling of the time and energy that Ben put into his teaching or how much fun he, and subsequently his students, had.

My first encounter with Dr. Underwood was at 8:00 a.m. on Tuesday, September 9, 1964, at Northwestern University, in Kresge Centennial Hall, Room 330. The room was filled with about 30 undergraduates enrolled in B05 Experimental

Psychology, the first part of a two-quarter sequence. At the front of the room paced this tall, good-looking man with sandy hair. He looked and acted like a championship athlete awaiting the big race. After the bell rang and the class settled down, he began to call roll from the computer registration cards. As he called each name, he looked intently at the person and then back to the card. After one cycle through the cards, he seldom referred to them that day. By the second class period, he knew the names, first and last, of all of us. I later learned that this feat of memory was simply, but by no means a simple, application of some of his research. Having obtained the cards on Monday, he had proceeded with the response learning stage of his two-stage theory— he had learned our names—so that during class he *merely* had to hook up or associate the names with the faces.

During that and the subsequent quarter (about 20 weeks total), my fellow students and I performed and wrote formal reports on seven original experiments, took six extraordinary exams (more about those later), and were forced to think during class. A master of the Socratic method, Dr. Underwood would quietly and politely ask a question. Every time you gave an answer, he would respond with another question, each one more and more pointed and searching, until you were backed into a corner with no recourse but to think your way out. I worked harder, was more challenged, and enjoyed that class more than any other in my undergraduate career.

From here on in this chapter, I often use the reports of Underwood's students and his colleagues—putting them in italics—as they describe their memories of Ben as a mentor, colleague, and friend. Although their words have been edited to fit this chapter, their essential meaning has been retained. One of his former students described the atmosphere in Ben's classroom this way:

His enthusiasm for the material and for our learning it was clear from the outset. A videotape of the class would have led to the conclusion that Ben was teaching human sexuality and not A–B, A–Br transfer designs (John J. Shaughnessy).

In the methods course, it was clear that Ben was training us to think like psychologists. He tried to convey his love for research in the examples he used. The examples required the students to critically examine research studies—to explore alternative answers and in many cases alternative research designs. He had the ability to correct students when needed, but yet encourage them to provide what we felt were "insights" into psychology. I remember a research project that Ben assigned to our class that was based on a study he had just completed. The findings were puzzling and although I am sure he had an explanation for them, he presented the findings to us and asked us to develop studies to test various hypotheses. We each developed our ideas and tested them in separate studies. We felt that we were part of the research enterprise in psychology, even in an undergraduate methods course (Ronald Nowaczyk).

In his research methods classes, Ben challenged students to think analytically and critically. He was unafraid to admit when he was wrong (which was rare) or when he did not know. In fact, he was the only professor I ever had who admitted that he did not know the answer to some question raised by students. He conveyed the attitude that learning was important even if it entailed disciplined hard work, and that it could even be fun. His intensity and involvement with his classes were contagious. He was not reluctant to criticize our work when it was inadequate, and he held exacting standards, but even these experiences served to make us want to learn more. However, he was generous with his positive reinforcements and praise whenever we showed occasional flashes of brilliance (John Jung).

I enrolled at Northwestern as an undergraduate with the intention of majoring and eventually going on to get a PhD in physics. It was Ben Underwood's course in experimental psychology that convinced me to change my major to psychology. I consider that course to be the most important intellectual event in my undergraduate education. Similarly, it was the hours of listening to and working with Ben on research that made graduate education the tremendously rewarding experience that it was for me.

I never looked on Ben as a surrogate father, but he was as devoted to his students and gave them as much attention as would have been appropriate for a parent to give a child. Ben Underwood piqued my interest in psychology, nurtured me intellectually, convinced me that academics was the best life possible, and provided a role model for how I might try to conduct myself as a professor. By far, he was the best undergraduate teacher I had at Northwestern. He was also the most giving professor I have ever known. I am still trying after 9 years of teaching to give back to my students what Ben Underwood gave to me in just 3 (Charles S. Reichardt).

Dr. Underwood's exams in B05 were infamous. By any measure other than time spent thinking, they were relatively short. Each exam had only a few questions totaling less than 100 points. Every test started with what Ben called *remarkably discriminating* identification of terms. The remainder was a series of thought problems that he generated anew for each test in each class. Most of the exam questions required only short answers for a complete answer. For example, each of the two midterms I took that first quarter contained seven question worth a total of 60 points. On my first exam I wrote a total of 727 words, 182 (25%) of which were on the eight identifications in the first question. We were allowed, and most of us usually took, the entire 2-hour class period for the exam. Thus, my effective writing speed was about 6 words per minute.

When I worked with Ben as his teaching assistant, he worked at home on Wednesdays. When I saw him one Thursday, I asked him what he had done the day before. He said he had worked on the upcoming test in his experimental psychology class. Knowing how much Ben could get done in a day, I asked what else he had worked on. Ben gave me that wonderful quizzical look of his and said that he had spent the whole day making up the test. He commented that he typically spent an entire day to make up a test like that. I doubt that Ben's students knew or cared that they were taking a test that was made "fresh" for them. I know that Ben cared about his students so much that he wanted to make a test that would best teach them (John J. Shaughnessy).

Ben's enthusiasm was infectious, and as an undergraduate, I did not know, or care about the source of that enthusiasm. It took the words of another former graduate student to help me realize that Ben was teaching a dearly held philosophy rather than a subject.

Along with recent and complete information, Ben imparted his philosophy. This philosophy involved the importance of what we know as the scientific method, not simply as a tool of research but as a mode of thought and indeed—as a way of life. Interestingly, although Dr. Underwood spoke about objectivity, measurement, and verifiability, there was always an underlying fervor behind his statements. He instilled in us a passion to know and to use one's powers of reasoning. By the same token, this meant doing away with illusions, hypocrisy, wishful and fuzzy thinking, and all the other deceptions that we practice on ourselves as well as each other. To quote the poet John Keats, who was himself outstanding in his own field, "Beauty is truth, truth beauty..." (Concetta Romanow).

Although on the undergraduate level, student–faculty interactions occur primarily in the classroom, on the graduate level the opportunities are more diverse and more likely to involve incidental learning and modeling. It is these incidental learning situations that have lasting impact on students.

At any one time, Ben Underwood would have only one research assistant on the Office of Naval Research (ONR) contract, which funded his research for over 20 years, although he was always directing a number of master's theses and dissertations. In addition, he was a journal editor and an active participant on a number of grant review panels. Also, at the beginning of my second year of graduate school, William A. Hunt retired as chair of the department and Ben was asked to take over. Thus, he was extremely busy, yet he always had time for students.

Although he was a very busy man, he was easily approachable for consultation, advice, or simply informal discussion. A draft of a thesis turned in one day was invariably returned the next along with many constructive, detailed criticisms. At the time, I tended to take these things for granted, but in the interim I have come to realize how rare they are (John C. Abra).

We had been working on an interpretation of the effect of linguistic frequency on recall. Deese interpreted the effect in terms of interitem associations. Ben suggested that we write the data up independently and then see how the two versions aligned. I left his office, my expectation being that I would give him something in about a month. Either the day after or 2 days later, I happened on Ben in a Kresge corridor, at which time I was handed his version, pretty neatly typed with no great excess of penciled marginal notes (Kenneth L. Leicht).

In addition to showing respect for students by thoroughly reading and promptly returning written work, Underwood communicated his respect in more subtle ways.

During my tenure as his research assistant, Underwood arranged with Art Melton to get together with the relevant faculty and graduate students from the University of Michigan for a couple days to present papers. I remember at one of these joint meetings how one of the tenured faculty from Michigan not only interrupted his students' presentations, but repeatedly interrupted the presentation of his wife who was also a faculty member. In contrast, Underwood let each student fend for him or herself. If a student could not answer a question, Underwood only commented if asked by the student. I still remember the respect for students that Underwood showed in this and many other ways (Charles S. Reichardt).

Although Ben's relationship with his graduate students was really quite formal, it was one of mutual respect. Ben never talked much about mutual respect, but he taught it.

One way Ben communicated his respect for his students was that he was eager to learn from them. When I was working with Ben, he became intrigued with the "trees" that Al Erlebacher was teaching us as a way to break down the sources of variation in complex analyses of variance. Ben would work out the tree for an experiment he was analyzing and then bring it to one of us to look over. I suspect Ben knew well what a high it was for us to be teaching him (John J. Shaughnessy).

THE PERSON

I do not believe that it is possible to separate Ben Underwood the person from Dr. Underwood the teacher. I believe that he was a teacher, not by profession or vocation, but by nature. Every teacher teaches by example, either intentionally or unintentionally. Academicians also teach with words that sometimes do not match their incidental examples. In Ben Underwood's case, however, the teacher's example matched his words. I suspect that it was for this reason that he had a lasting influence on those whose lives he touched. Now, having made that statement in a situation where it is unlikely that I will be asked for evidence, I still feel that I must provide whatever data I have. Ben's influence was that strong. Apparently, I am not alone in that reaction.

More important than acquiring new knowledge about verbal learning or producing new data was what I learned from Ben about a style of thinking—an approach to problems of a scientific or other origin in an academic setting. For many years after I left Northwestern, my response to a wide variety of academic problems—on the design or interpretation of experiments, devising an explanation for students in a lecture, or settling a personnel issue in a faculty meeting—was to imagine Ben's response and, phenomenologically, to actually hear his voice and see his gestures. I know that seems pretty strange, but it did happen and still does. I find it sort of interesting behaviorally the "voice of consciousness" or "conscience" that Julian Jaynes describes (Norman E. Spear).

To say that Ben Underwood influences his students' professional lives is to say that a mother plays a role in the birth of her children. Ben has always been more than just a teacher; he has been a professional example, a model that his students strive to emulate. He teaches, but more important he embodies, all the traits for which we strive: superior technical knowledge, a keen sense for analysis, and dedication to scientific integrity. I share with Ben's other students a debt that never will, and never can, be repaid. We owe Ben Underwood a major share of the credit for our professional successes (Joel S. Zimmerman).

By the time they are seniors, most students majoring in psychology have some notion of what is meant by the term *functionalist* and the tenets of that school. However, few would be likely to understand what it means to be a functionalist. To my mind, the term *functionalist* and the name *Underwood* are synonymous.

I always had trouble figuring out the attributes that defined functionalism, but if it stood for anything, it was for the genuine priority of data. It held that when ideas, theories, or beliefs conflict with the data, the ideas have to be modified or jettisoned outright, no matter how logical or beautiful they might seem. What is so special about functionalists, and about Underwood in particular? My dominant free associate is integrity. Popper (cited in Magee, 1973) tells us that scientists should welcome disproof of their ideas because that is how science progresses. This sounds laudable on paper, but in practice most scientists I have run across hang on for dear life to their theories, in which they have time, energy, and ego invested. It is this rare readiness to admit error, this genuine commitment to empirical priorities, this well, integrity, that still makes me proud to have been nurtured within this tradition (John C. Abra).

For as long as I knew him, Ben not only smoked, but enjoyed cigarettes. My memories of the summers spent in the lab analyzing and writing up data include the noise of the Frieden calculators; the hours spent checking and analyzing thousands of numbers; the coffee; the writing, talking, and arguing over various interpretations; and Ben's cigarettes. The history of that habit provides evidence of Ben's commitment to data. After he had a pacemaker installed, the doctor presented him with data that indicated that continued smoking would, in all probability, kill him. The data took priority and Ben stopped smoking; he allowed himself one cigarette each day right after dinner.

Ben was also able to induce students to examine and change their own behavior using the same functionalist reliance on data to make appropriate decisions.

The scene was Ben's dimly lit office in Fayerweather Hall in late 1952, about 6:30 p.m. Ben was going over some notes, getting ready to teach D14 [graduate course in verbal learning]. I was an undergraduate "subject runner" on the ONR contract and a student in experimental psychology. I asked to have a word with Ben, who grunted and looked up from his notes, obviously annoyed over my intrusion. I asked a simple question: "Should I quit school and get a job?" I went on to say, "Since returning to school after a stint in the Navy, my studies are not going well no matter how hard I try. I just don't think I have what it takes any more."

Ben responded reassuringly, "Oh. Maybe you don't." I started to excuse myself and leave. Then evidently as an afterthought he added, "How long have you been back?" I said, "Six months." This prompted the question, "Do you think you have collected enough data in that time to answer your question?" I didn't know what to give as an answer. Ben concluded by telling me that I should probably collect some additional data. He also mentioned that maybe the data indicating learning-to-learn is not forgotten might be wrong because I seemed to be living proof of such a possibility given my premilitary record of excellent scholarship. I excused myself and collected the requisite data (Rudolph W. Schulz).

Although Ben drew admiration because of his insightful thinking, solid methodology, and captivating lectures, he evoked enthusiasm and affection because of the warmth and graciousness with which he treated everyone.

My first real encounter with Ben came at the Midwestern Psychological Association Convention a couple of years after I got my Ph.D. Ben came up to talk to me after I had given a paper on what later became known as the total time hypothesis (a label that came out of Ben's lab). I was a very young and green experimental psychologist, and I do not think I even took myself seriously, much less expected anyone else to do so. Ben started talking to me that day with a seriousness and intensity that took me by surprise and I suddenly realized that maybe he actually thought I was a grown-up. I have often thought that Ben's interest in my work at that moment really changed the way I viewed myself, and for that I will always feel a debt of gratitude.

I soon learned that what I had experienced was Ben's hallmark. It made no difference whether you were an unknown graduate student, a new Ph.D., or a senior scientist—Ben gave you the same attention and respect as he gave Leo Postman, Art Melton, or Bill Estes. Ben was a giant in his field, but he was very modest and totally unassuming. He was focused on what others had to contribute to our science and what he could contribute to their careers, rather than being focused on himself. Obviously that is not to suggest that Ben's interest in his own research lacked intensity. Rather, the point is that he listened to students and younger colleagues with the same intensity as he devoted to his own work. When you talked with Ben, he had a way of making you feel that he considered you to be a truly important contributor to his thinking.

Years later I once told him how much I appreciated all the support he had given me, even though I was not one of his students. His face brightened with a smile and he said, "That's right, you weren't one of my students were you—I keep forgetting that. I guess it is just an irrelevant technicality." The warmth and generosity underlying that comment was characteristic of Ben and reflected the giving relationship he had with everyone in our field (Neal F. Johnson).

In 1959, Sheila and I migrated from California to Evanston to begin my graduate training with Ben. We moved into a strange, Chicago-type apartment on Simpson Street about three buildings from the "El" and Ben and Louise Underwood became our adopted family. Ben introduced us to well-done steaks, potatoes, pork, and martinis. Sheila and I were both influenced by the Underwood's kindness and remember fondly and vividly the warmth of their family and the care with which Ben and Louise looked after two lonely and "homeless" people from California (Geoffrey Keppel).

I have a couple vivid memories that illustrate his versatility and graciousness as a person. I had known something about Ben's background as an athlete and coach—for example, how he had learned to pass left-handed so he could do so smoothly while running in either direction as a tailback. So I was particularly interested during my first year or so at Northwestern when Ben played with our softball team in a game against the University of Chicago's Psychology Department. I vaguely remember that they had rather a ringer as pitcher, that this was something other than slow pitch, and that practically all of us were shut out at bat. All the while Ben was joking very modestly about how he was too old for this sort of thing, he was, subtly, the only one to really hit their pitcher. The best hit of the day was Ben's, a beautifully placed shot to right center field that was especially impressive because it was so obviously planned due to the large open area in that part of their outfield.

Although there are many other examples, the one with perhaps the most impact on me was when I completed my draft of a paper reporting several experiments that Bruce Ekstrand and I had done in collaboration with Ben. The original version included many more experiments than were eventually published in this article, and it took me some time to write it. I thought my version was in great shape; in retrospect, I realize that it most definitely was not. I gave it to Ben and he seemed pleased, no doubt in spite of what he read. Twenty-four hours later, Ben asked me to look over the version he had, he said, "revised somewhat." In fact, it was completely rewritten, the entire manuscript generated practically from scratch and largely uncontaminated by my own attempts. It was of course superb. I was delighted to be associated with it in any way. Moreover, Ben resisted any suggestion that he had in fact done all the important intellectual work and insisted that I be first author (Norman E. Spear).

After Ben's nomination for the American Psychological Foundation distinguished teaching award was completed and sent in to the APA, I sent him a copy of the application and supporting materials. Soon after I received the following note from him:

Louise showed me the pack of letters dealing with my teaching. I ought to be provoked with you for taking your time to carry out this teaching thing, but I cannot. The truth is I am very appreciative of your effort and the efforts of all those who were willing to compose letters. My career was closely tied to the students who chose to work with me and I am indebted to all of them. If along the way some found my teaching to be above the mean, I will not complain. (B. J. Underwood, personal communication, April 15, 1987)

Another facet of this extraordinary man that also permeated every encounter was his humor and playfulness. Ben loved to play with words and ideas, and to argue. If you stated something was true, he might staunchly and passionately argue that it was false, even if he held no opinion or even believed that you were correct.

Soon after I became Dr. Underwood's research assistant, I was invited to his house for dinner. I have two distinct memories of that first dinner with Ben and Louise. The first was the excellent Manhattan served prior to dinner (I did not try Ben's martinis until a later dinner). The second was the discussion that started just as we sat down to dinner and continued for sometime during it. On the wall in the dining room was a framed copy of Grant Wood's "American Gothic"—a gift from the Keppel family. My innocent comment about the couple in the picture turned into a 20-minute discussion about what type and quality parents they would be and how their children might turn out.

The demarcation between work and play was less clear for Ben than it is for most people. Ben liked to play with words, ideas, data, and, most of all, people. One of the forms of intellectual play that Ben liked most was arguing. I remember one occasion when several graduate students were having dinner at the Underwoods' and someone mentioned that she had gone to the zoo that day. Seemingly out of the blue, Ben asked why anyone would want to go to a zoo. For several minutes we argued with Ben about the value of going to a zoo. I never did find out if Ben really believed that zoos served no useful purpose, but I did learn that Ben enjoyed arguing so much that he would argue about just about anything (John J. Shaughnessy).

Ben's debates or arguments had effects not only on the participants, but also on others, both students and faculty, who may have been present as observers.

I remember one occasion around 1960. Ben and Don Campbell carried on a spirited debate on operationalism at one of our regular morning coffee sessions. After it had gone on for an hour or so, with a very impressionable assistant professor (me) attending in awe, Bill Hunt, the Chairman, walked out saying, "If you guys were at the University of Chicago, you would call this a symposium and publish it" (Lee Sechrest).

Ben treated everyone he encountered with respect, graciousness, and good humor. No matter how busy he was and however little time he had to spend with you, he always gave you his full, undivided attention.

Busy as he was, Ben could make a visitor to his office feel that that office was precisely where the visitor belonged. When I succeeded Ben as department chair after years as his student and junior colleague, he eased the role reversal by regularly addressing me as boss. His sense of humor appeared not only in the jokes he told, but also in his ability to be amused by his own dedication—to appreciate how a career of research with the memory drum might not seem as exciting to everyone as it did to him (Winfred F. Hill).

In 1959, E. C. Tolman (chap. 15, *Pioneers I*) wrote:

The system [i.e., Tolman's theory] may not well stand up to any final canons of scientific procedure. But I do not much care. I have liked to think about psychology in ways that have proved congenial to me. Since all the sciences, and especially psychology, are still immersed in such tremendous realms of the uncertain and the unknown, the best that any individual scientist, especially any psychologist, can do seems to be to follow his own gleam and his own bent, however inadequate they may be. In fact, I suppose that actually this is what we all do. In the end, the only sure criterion is to have fun. And I have had fun. (p. 152)

In a letter to Ben, Jock Abra commented on Tolman's statement this way:

That's a supremely healthy attitude towards life and it could just as well have been written by Underwood. Detachment can make absolutely any human activity seem silly. That way lies madness. Let us not be mad. Let's instead lose perspective and live every moment with intensity. Underwood may not have realized it, and he might be horrified by the observation, but he is one of the few genuine existentialists I have ever met—not, I hasten to add, in his beliefs about the universe, but rather in his approach to the business of living. (John C. Abra)

In 1982, I called to talk to Ben about something, and he told me that he planned to retire at the end of that year. I expressed my amazement and asked why. Ben's answer exemplified his attitude toward his work and his life: "I don't have any graduate students to badger, and it just isn't fun any more." Never doing anything halfway, Ben went about the business of retirement without looking back. Once he fulfilled the obligations to his students and publishers, unlike some aging athletes, he did not try to stage a comeback. Retirement meant that he could read history, garden, and be with his grandchildren.

BIOGRAPHY OF BENTON J. UNDERWOOD

Ben Underwood was born in Center Point, Iowa, on February 28, 1915. He received his formal education (through high school) in Albion, Iowa, graduating with 18 classmates. His goal of becoming a high school athletic coach was almost put beyond reach by the Great Depression because he did not have the funds to go to college. Finally, however, a scholarship, loans from friends and relatives, and a board-and-room job allowed him to attend Cornell College in Mount Vernon, Iowa, where he graduated in 1936 with a BA in psychology and education.

After an initial lack of enthusiasm for his talents, late in the summer, Underwood was offered a position in the junior high school in Clarion, Iowa. A year later, he obtained the position of athletic coach in the junior college at Tipton, Iowa. As athletic coach, Underwood was required to teach any academic subject not covered by other faculty members. By the end of his second year at Tipton, that experience had made it clear to him that, "It was of much greater interest and challenge to teach a 'regular' academic subject to reluctant minds than to try to teach a pivot shot to would-be candidates for the basketball teams" (American Psychological Association, 1988, p. 264). Inevitably, this insight led to the decision to seek graduate training.

In 1939, Underwood and his new bride headed to the University of Oregon–Eugene for the summer session undecided as to his area of study. That indecision was resolved in favor of the field of learning after a few weeks in class with Professor John F. Dashiell, who was visiting Eugene from the University of North Carolina. When offered a position as research assistant to Arthur W. Melton at the University of Missouri, he accepted. Thus, at the end of the summer, Ben and his wife trekked back to the midwest.

Melton's influence helped Underwood to see the importance of using experimental techniques to understand behavior. Also, for the first time in his life, "Underwood began to realize what it meant to try to be a scholar" (American Psychological Association, 1988, p. 265). Melton also helped him obtain a position as research assistant to John McGeoch at Iowa—at that time, the University of Missouri did not offer a doctoral degree in psychology. Two and a half years later, in December 1942, Underwood received his PhD, his dissertation having been directed by Kenneth W. Spence (chap. 17, this volume) because of McGeoch's untimely death. From Spence, Underwood learned an analytic approach to problems, a part of which involved increasing the "tightness" of his experimental designs as knowledge in his field increased and theories became more pointed.

After completing his degree, Underwood was commissioned as an ensign and served as a Naval Aviation Psychologist from 1943 to 1946. After release from the navy, he joined the faculty at Northwestern University as an assistant professor. Within 2 years, he was promoted to the rank of associate professor and 4 years later to the rank of full professor. In 1976, he was appointed to the prestigious position of B. Stanley Hall Professor of Social Sciences, a post he held until his retirement in 1983. On June 15, 1989, the Underwoods celebrated their golden wedding anniversary and on November 29, 1994, with the death of Benton J. Underwood, psychology lost one of its foremost methodologists, and many people lost a friend.

CONCLUSION:
UNDERWOOD'S IMPACT ON PSYCHOLOGY

One index of Ben's influence on the field of learning and memory is in the quantity and quality of his publications. During a career that spanned 42 years, from 1941 to 1982, he had 193 publications—$M = 4.6$ per year—including 174 journal articles (47 as sole author, 127 with co-authors), 10 book chapters, and 9 books. The articles included 10 in Psychological Review, 2 in the Psychological Bulletin, 4 monographs, and 5 in places like the Annual Review of Psychology, Scientific American, and The Encyclopedia Britannica.

Ben Underwood's importance as a methodologist is particularly evident in his book-length publications. His 1949 Experimental Psychology and the 1966 revision helped define the field of experimental psychology in the years after World War II. That book was used as a college textbook for almost 20 years, until Ben revised it (actually rewrote it) in 1966. In addition, Ben wrote two books that dealt exclusively with research design. In Psychological Research, which was written for graduate students, Ben conveyed the "art and the logic of experimental design in a clear and exquisite manner. Without question, this book helped to set the standards of research design in psychology in general, not just in experimental psychology" (Keppel, 1994). In Experimentation in Psychology, published with John Shaughnessey, Ben not only laid out the basics of research methods in a clear, concise manner, he also attempted to teach students how to begin constructing theories. Other methodological contributions appeared as articles, such as "Speed of Learning and Amount Retained: A Consideration of Methodology" (1954), "An Evaluation of Two Problems of Method in the Study of Retention" (Underwood & Keppel, 1962), "Degree of Learning and Measurement of Forgetting" (1964), and "Individual Differences as a Crucible in Theory Construction" (1975). In the crucible article, Underwood outlined two necessary steps for developing and testing theories. The first step required correlational analyses of individual differences, and the second required the predicting and testing of interactions between subject variables and environmental independent variables.

The quality and importance of Ben's work is evident in the recognition bestowed on him by others in the field and by the fact that the phenomena he investigated are still being studied. In 1964, Ben was the recipient of the prestigious Warren Medal given by the Society of Experimental Psychologists. He was elected to the National Academy of Sciences in 1970, and in 1974 he was awarded the Distinguished Scientific Contribution Award from the American Psychological Association. In 1976, in recognition of his service to Northwestern and his scholarly contributions to the discipline of psychology, he was appointed Stanley G. Harris Professor of Social Science.

Ben had a knack for choosing important problems to study. As data on that point, I cite two examples. First, in 1965, he demonstrated the existence of implicit associative responses. Although completed 30 years ago, this research has been resurrected and forms one of the bases for current research on creation of false memories (see Roediger, 1996, for a review, Roediger & McDermott, 1995). Second, capitalizing on Ben's demonstration of the pervasive effect of proactive inhibition, Lynn Hasher and her colleagues (Hasher, Zacks, & May, in press; May, Kane, & Hasher, 1997) demonstrated that the typical age difference found in memory span tasks does not reflect age differences in capacity; rather, it reflects age differences in susceptibility to interference.

In the introduction to Ben's volume in the Centennial Psychology Series, the editor wrote:

For this volume, Professor Underwood has selected fifteen papers that provide a comprehensive overview of his important contributions to theory and research on human learning and memory. Based on four decades of systematic work, these papers highlight the evolving theory and empirical findings of a talented and dedicated investigator. (Spielberger, 1982, p. viii)

REFERENCES

American Psychological Association. (1988). American Psychological Foundation awards for 1987: Distinguished teaching in psychology. *American Psychologist, 43*, 264–265.

Barnes, J. M., & Underwood, B. J. (1959). "Fate" of first-list associations in transfer theory. *Journal of Experimental Psychology, 58*, 97–105.

Ekstrand, B. R., Wallace, W. P., & Underwood, B. J. (1966). A frequency theory of verbal-discrimination learning. *Psychological Review, 73*, 566–578.

Glaze, J. A. (1928). The association value of non-sense syllables. *Journal of Genetic Psychology, 35*, 255–269.

Hasher, L., Zacks, R. T., & May, C. P. (in press). Inhibitory control, circadian arousal, and age. In D. Gopher & A. Koriat (Eds.), *Attention and performance XVII, Cognitive regulation of performance: Interaction of theory and application.* Cambridge, MA: MIT Press.

Keppel, G. (1994, December 16). *Remarks presented at the memorial service for Benton J. Underwood.* Alice Millar Chapel, Evanston, IL.

Keppel, G., & Underwood, B. J. (1962). Proactive inhibition in short-term retention of single items. *Journal of Verbal Learning and Verbal Behavior, 1,* 153–161

Magee, B. (1973). *Karl Popper.* New York: Viking.

May, C. T., Kane, M., & Hasher, L. (1997) *The role of proactive interference in measures of working memory span.* Manuscript submitted for publication.

Postman, L. (1972). The experimental analysis of verbal learning and memory: Evolution and innovation. In C. P. Duncan, L. Sechrest, & A.W. Melton (Eds.), *Human memory: Festschrift in honor of Benton J. Underwood* (pp. 1–23). New York: Appleton-Century-Crofts.

Roediger, H. L. III. (1996). Memory illusions. *Journal of Memory and Language, 35,* 76–100.

Roediger, H. L. III., & McDermott, K. B. (1995). Creating false memories: Remembering words not presented in lists. *Journal of Experimental Psychology: Learning, Memory, and Cognition, 21,* 803–814.

Spielberger, C. D. (1982). Editor's introduction. In B. J. Underwood (Ed.), *Studies in learning and memory: Selected papers* (pp. vii–x). New York: Praeger.

Spear, N. E., Ekstrand, B. R., & Underwood, B. J. (1964). Association by contiguity. *Journal of Experimental Psychology, 67,* 151–161.

Twedt, H. M., & Underwood, B. J. (1959). Mixed vs. unmixed lists in transfer studies. *Journal of Experimental Psychology, 58,* 111–116.

Underwood, B. J. (1954). Speed of learning and amount retained: A consideration of methodology. *Psychological Bulletin, 51,* 276–282.

Underwood, B. J. (1957). Interference and forgetting. *Psychological Review, 64,* 49–60.

Underwood, B. J. (1963). Stimulus selection in verbal learning. In C. N. Cofer & B. S. Musgrave (Eds.), *Verbal behavior and learning* (pp. 276–282). New York: McGraw-Hill.

Underwood, B. J. (1964). Degree of learning and the measurement of forgetting. *Journal of Verbal Learning and Verbal Behavior, 3,* 112–119.

Underwood, B. J. (1965). False recognition produced by implicit verbal responses. *Journal of Experimental Psychology, 70,* 122–129.

Underwood, B. J. (1969). Attributes of memory. *Psychological Review, 76,* 559–573.

Underwood, B. J. (1971). Recognition memory. In H. H. Kendler & J. T. Spence (Eds.), *Essays in nonbehaviorism* (pp. 313–335). New York: Appleton-Century-Crofts.

Underwood, B. J. (1975). Individual differences as a crucible in theory construction. *American Psychologist, 30,* 128–134.

Underwood, B. J. (1983). *Attributes of memory.* Glenview, IL: Scott, Foresman.

Underwood, B. J., & Ekstrand, B. R. (1966). An analysis of some shortcomings in the interference theory of forgetting. *Psychological Review, 73,* 540–549.

Underwood, B. J., & Ekstrand, B. R. (1968). Linguistic associations and retention. *Journal of Verbal Learning and Verbal Behavior, 7,* 162–171.

Underwood, B. J., Ekstrand, B. R., & Keppel, G. (1965). An analysis of intralist similarity with experiments on conceptual similarity. *Journal of Verbal Learning and Verbal Behavior, 4,* 447–462.

Underwood, B. J., & Erlebacher, A. H. (1965). Studies of coding in verbal learning. *Psychological Monographs, 79* (whole no. 13).

Underwood, B. J., & Freund, J. S. (1968). Effect of temporal separation of two tasks on proactive inhibition. *Journal of Experimental Psychology, 78,* 50–54.

Underwood, B. J., & Freund, J. S. (1969). Further studies on conceptual similarity in free-recall learning. *Journal of Verbal Learning and Verbal Behavior, 8,* 30–35.

Underwood, B. J., & Freund, J. S. (1970). Retention of a verbal discrimination. *Journal of Experimental Psychology, 84,* 1–14.

Underwood, B. J., Ham, M., & Ekstrand, B. R. (1962). Cue selection in paired-associate learning. *Journal of Experimental Psychology, 64,* 405–409.

Underwood, B. J., & Keppel, G. (1962). An evaluation of two problems of method in the study of retention. *American Journal of Psychology, 75*, 1–17.

Underwood, B. J., & Keppel, G. (1963). Coding processes in verbal learning. *Journal of Verbal Learning and Verbal Behavior, 1*, 250–257.

Underwood, B. J., & Postman, L. (1960). Extraexperimental sources of interference in forgetting. *Psychological Review, 67*, 73–95.

Underwood, B. J., & Schulz, R. W. (1960). *Meaningfulness and verbal learning*. Philadelphia: Lippincott.

Underwood, B. J., Zimmerman, J. S., & Freund, J. S. (1971). Retention of frequency information with observations on recognition and recall. *Journal of Experimental Psychology, 87*, 149–162.

Williams, R. F., & Underwood, B. J. (1970). Encoding variability: Tests of the Martin hypothesis. *Journal of Experimental Psychology, 86*, 317–324.

Wood, G., & Underwood, B. J. (1967). Implicit responses and conceptual similarity. *Journal of Verbal Learning and Verbal Behavior, 6*, 1–10.

Chapter 20

Leon Festinger:
Beyond the Obvious

Jack W. Brehm

Suppose you were the head of the Search Committee in a psychology department that had a position for a young social psychologist to teach and do research, and that you received this letter of recommendation from the chair of one applicant's training program:

> Well, when this guy was an undergraduate, he did an experiment on level of aspiration that was published in the *Journal of Experimental Psychology*. He came here to work on social psychology with one of our professors, but he found that he wasn't interested in the research that professor is now doing. So he did another experiment on level of aspiration, a little theoretical paper on the same subject, and an experiment on the taste preferences of rats. He's developed a couple of statistical tests, and for his dissertation, he did a mathematical theory of decision making—so he hasn't done that much empirical research, and nothing in social psychology. Of course he's only been around for three years, and he spends an awful lot of his time playing games—chess, cribbage, pinball, whatever—two or three times as much as anyone else I ever saw.

Would you hire that candidate? Maybe, maybe not. The guy in question was, of course, Leon Festinger and, given his later history, it would have been fortunate if you had hired him. Even at this early stage of his career, it was clear that Festinger had a high ability to theorize, a tendency to do theoretically based experiments, an openness to different approaches, and an interest in methodology—and he did spend a lot of time playing games. His record after obtaining his PhD is quite clear: The amount of time he spent playing games was rivaled only by his research productivity. In the last four decades, his theoretical ideas probably led to more research in social psychology than those of any other scholar in the discipline.

---

* Photograph of Leon Festinger courtesy of Karen Zebulon's collection.

THE THEORY OF COGNITIVE DISSONANCE

Leon Festinger conceived the theory of cognitive dissonance, his major contribution to psychology, during the academic year 1953–1954, and published the theory in book form in 1957, together with bits and pieces of evidence gleaned from the literature and a little experimental data. Within the first decade after this meager publication, however, reports of research on dissonance theory began to fill the social psychological journals. At least five books describing further research on the theory, or in response to it, had been published. Altogether there were over 300 publications on or about the theory of cognitive dissonance (Margulis & Songer, 1969). Two decades later, the number of articles and books on or about the theory was approaching 1,000 and the field was still counting (Moentmann, 1979).

The Environment in Which the Theory Developed

So much research instigated by one theory was unprecedented in social psychology, perhaps in all psychology. What accounted for the tremendous influence of the theory? Certain characteristics of the place and time into which the theory was born, and certain qualities of the theory, are probably responsible.

In the 1950s, American academic psychology was dominated by behaviorism, particularly by learning theory. Although there were controversies among the different versions of such theorizing, two widely accepted premises were that (a) rewards (reinforcements) have a direct influence on the tendency to repeat behavior, and (b) thoughts and feelings are not permissible psychological processes because they are not observable (although, by that time, some behaviorists were positing internal states that were conceived as intervening variables; see chap. 17, this volume). Dissonance theory created problems for both of these assumptions. First, it held that, just as behavior can be induced by rewards, rewards can be induced by behavior. Indeed, it held that the tendency to repeat behavior is an inverse function of the amount of reward received and that the reward value of an action is a direct function of the magnitude of its negative consequences. These startling propositions were not easily accepted in many quarters. Rewards—pellets of food for bar pressing in rats and points for nonsense syllables remembered correctly by human beings—were the building blocks out of which most behavioristic theories were constructed. Such theories, which predicted behavior from rewards, could not permit the values of rewards to be affected by the behavior that was predicted. Second, to assert that behavior could induce rewards, dissonance theory proposed an internal cognitive and affective process. This proposal took strong implied exception to the assumption that unobservable events are not proper subject matter for psychology.

In addition, in those days, social psychology had become complacent with the view that its future was in the determination through research of which various commonsense hypotheses (grandmother psychology) were actually true. Much of its research concerned the conflicts that pervade common thinking on psychological issues—"absence makes the heart grow fonder" versus "out of sight, out of mind." That prevalent belief defined a rather stultifying future for a science. Dissonance theory came onto this scene as a breath of fresh air for those who were looking for excitement in their discipline. Because of its departure from the orthodox position, it provided an entirely new understanding for many of the common-sense phenomena to which social psychology was applied. To understand those applications, one must know the theory. For that reason, the theory is outlined here so that the reader can obtain some personal appreciation for its significance.

Essentials of the Theory

The theory of cognitive dissonance was generated in the context of a group of behavioral scientists and graduate students, organized by Festinger and supported by the Ford Foundation, for the express purpose of systematizing what was known about informal communication processes. In the course of their investigations, the group encountered an intriguing study in which people in a community that had experienced an earthquake—but one that did little visible damage—had circulated rumors to the effect that disastrous events would soon occur. Festinger suggested that because people felt fear from the earthquake but saw nothing fearful in their environment, they needed to justify their fear and did so by spreading rumors about impending disaster. The essence of Festinger's theory was that a dissonant, not-fitting relationship between people's knowledge about their behavior and their knowledge about the situation in which that behavior occurs creates a need for them to behave in ways that justify their actions.

Festinger's statement of the theory of cognitive dissonance, like all of his writing, is simple, clear, compelling, and concise. The whole theory is laid out in 31 readable pages in chapter 1 of *A Theory of Cognitive Dissonance* (1957), which present its five essential assumptions:

1. Two cognitions—two bits of knowledge about the physical or social environment or about oneself—may have any of three relationships to each other: (a) If one cognition follows from the other, the two are consonant. (b) If one follows from its opposite (Festinger used the term *obverse*), the two cognitions are dissonant. (c) The two cognitions may be unrelated and irrelevant to each other.
2. In some measure, every cognition is resistant to change. For example, it was not easy for people who experienced the earthquake to rid themselves of their fear.
3. Every cognition has some degree of importance to the person who holds it. Fear is an important cognition because it is related to personal safety.
4. The magnitude of dissonance is a direct function of the ratio of dissonant to consonant cognitions, where each cognition is weighted according to its importance.

5. Dissonance, a drivelike state (comparable, e.g., to hunger), can be reduced by the addition of consonant cognitions, elimination of dissonant cognitions, or changes in those cognitions that are least resistant to change.

That is all there is to the basic theory, but something more is needed to explain such surprising phenomena as people starting rumors predicting disasters. That something more is the additional imagination that Festinger provided.

Postdecision Dissonance

When a person makes a decision, dissonance is almost an inevitable consequence. For example, consider a woman with limited funds who is trying to decide whether to buy a new coffee maker or a toaster. She knows that she can make do with her old coffee maker, but that the new one would be more efficient and probably make better tasting coffee. However, she really loves toast, has no toaster, and must use her oven to make toast. Hence, a toaster would be wonderful to have but is really only useful in the morning, whereas a coffee maker is useful at all meals and even in between. If she finally chooses the coffee maker, then all of the positive thoughts about it and all of the negative thoughts about the toaster will be consonant with her decision, whereas all of the negative thoughts about the coffee maker and positive thoughts about the toaster will be dissonant.

The reader will recognize that this example lends itself to a variety of specific predictions about the magnitude of dissonance following the decision. For example, if the woman chooses the coffee maker, the more positive her thoughts are about the toaster— the more attractive she thinks it is—the greater will be the postdecision dissonance. The reader will also recognize that after the decision dissonance can be reduced by increasing the number and/or importance of consonant cognitions and/or by decreasing the number and/or importance of dissonant cognitions. For example, in her private thinking, the woman could magnify the importance of positive aspects of the coffee maker or develop negative thoughts about the toaster. Indeed, there are many ways for a person to reduce postdecision dissonance.

Forced Compliance

A similar conceptual analysis can be applied to what Festinger called *forced compliance*. Suppose, as part of a study in psychology, participants are required to perform a boring task for an hour and then asked to tell the next participant, who is waiting in the hall, that the task was fascinating. The first participant's knowledge of how boring the task really was would be dissonant with telling the next participant that the task was interesting. However, suppose that the first participant is paid for delivering the message to the next one. Receiving such a payment would be consonant with saying the task was fascinating. If the amount of payment were quite large, there would be relatively little dissonance from delivering the message. In the case where the participants are not paid for delivering the message, any dissonance created by delivering it could be reduced by persuading oneself that the task was really interesting. Thus, according to dissonance theory, the less one is paid for saying the task was fascinating, the more one would come to believe that the task really was fascinating. Of course, one also could reduce dissonance by magnifying the importance of the money ("an offer I could not refuse") or by finding other reasons for cooperating with the experimenter, such as helping science. As in the prior example, the possibilities for reducing dissonance are many and depend, in part, on the inventiveness of the individual experiencing the dissonance.

These two general implications from dissonance theory—postdecision dissonance and forced compliance—encompass the bulk of research generated by the theory. A third general implication of the theory is that, when experiencing dissonance, a person will tend to avoid further dissonant information and will instead seek out consonant information. This implication is fairly obvious, but its demonstration is complicated by the fact that there are multiple reasons for seeking all kinds of relevant information if there is the possibility of further action or decisions. The interested reader can find a discussion of the problems inherent in selective exposure to information in Wicklund and Brehm's (1976) *Perspectives on Cognitive Dissonance.*

Festinger's Creative Style

Any number of behavioral scientists might have come up with that interpretation of the study of rumor that gave rise to dissonance theory. The interesting observation concerns the nature of the argument by which Festinger got from that explanation to his theory, which was a tour de force and the major reason that he became an important figure in the history of psychology. The theory of cognitive dissonance, as originally described, did not automatically suggest its implications for postchoice dissonance and the effects of forced compliance. Festinger's provision of the imagination necessary to recognize these implications, once the theory had been proposed, is a demonstration of his particular theoretical style. Alternatively, what is possible is that Festinger conceived both implications first and then stated the theory in the most general possible terms to give it maximal power and generality.[1]

In either case, the link that Festinger provided between the theory and its implication was the recognition that cognitions about own behavior and the environment can easily differ in their resistance to change. In regard to one's own

---

[1]This is an interesting point to the investigator of scientific creativity. The published version of the theory is purely in terms of cognitions, whereas an early unpublished paper (Festinger, *Social Communication and Cognition*) defined *dissonance* in terms of the relationship between an item of cognition and an item of behavior. It seems possible, perhaps likely, that the conceptual implications involving behavior did in fact precede the published general statement.

behavior, and especially in regard to decision, it is difficult to distort or deny what one has done. If you sold your bicycle, it would be next to impossible for you to imagine that you still had the bicycle and could ride it to the park. Further, you could not undo the fact of having sold it if the person who bought it moved 1,000 miles away. In contrast, it is relatively easy to juggle the reasons for and against having sold the bicycle. It is easy to imagine that the bicycle would soon have had expensive mechanical problems—that it was not working well anyway, that it was not a mountain bike, and so forth. The limit of finding justifications for one's behavior is determined, in large part, by one's own mental inventiveness. In general, when dissonance occurs from having made a decision or having behaved in a certain way, it will be justifications for behavior that will be used to reduce dissonance, not denial of or undoing the behavior.

Range of Application

Another implicit aspect of the theory facilitated applications to a wide variety of important human problems. The theory accommodates the natural complexity that occurs in the human cognitive system. In the examples described earlier to illustrate the conceptual implications of the theory for postdecision dissonance and forced-choice behavior, the reader may have noted that one could easily have elaborated either example with additional possible consonant and dissonant cognitions. In a given decision situation, the potential dissonant cognitions could include the decision maker's physiological state (ambition, fear), recent past experience (passing an examination), achievement level, difficulty of instrumental behavior, one's values regarding the potential outcomes, knowledge of one's parents' or aunt Martha's attitude, a friend's advice, the implications of local or state law, and on and on. Without being terribly explicit about rules of combination, the theory allows one to analyze and make predictions about complicated situations.

Persuasive Argument

Because it lent itself to complex situations, the theory was broad enough to provide potential understanding of many of the traditional problems with which social psychologists were concerned. One of these applications was to the psychology of persuasion. For example, it predicted that the effectiveness of a persuasion would increase as the attractiveness of the communicator decreases and that children's liking for a toy would decrease as the threatened punishment that keeps them from playing with that toy decreases.

The theory also helped our understanding of when one person will try to persuade another. One of the earliest studies to be based on the theory (Festinger, Riecken, & Schachter, 1956) involved observations of a group that prophesied a cataclysm on a certain date. After making that prediction, some members of the group took irreversible actions. They quit their jobs, sold or otherwise rid themselves of their personal belongings, canceled travel plans, and so forth. Thus, if the cataclysm failed to occur, knowledge of that failure would be dissonant with those irrevocable actions. For the group members, denial—either that the cataclysm had not happened or that they had behaved as they had—would be nearly impossible. On these bases, Festinger, Riecken, and Schachter predicted and found (when the cataclysm actually failed to occur) that the group would reduce their dissonance by trying to persuade other people that they had saved humanity from disaster.

It was, then, the wonderful flexibility of the theory that made it applicable to a wide variety of social phenomena and its new and surprising hypotheses that made it the dominant theory of social behavior in the 1960s. Lest the reader infer that dissonance theory is no longer of interest to behavioral scientists, within the last few years, several articles have appeared in research journals, there have been reviews of specialized areas of dissonance research, and a new book on dissonance theory has appeared (Beauvois & Joule, 1996). Indeed, it seems that there is renewed interest just in time for the theory's 40th birthday.

BACKGROUND AND DEVELOPMENT
OF THE THEORIST

So who was this person who could take the simple idea that a drivelike state is created by having two items of knowledge that do not fit with each other and turn it into a relatively simple but powerful theory that increased our understanding of the decision process—of how attitudes can be changed and of why prophetic groups proselytize and, as we shall see, challenged accepted views of animal behavior? Who was Leon Festinger, what did he do before composing dissonance theory, and what did he do afterward?

Leon Festinger was born on May 8, 1919, in Brooklyn, New York, to Alex and Sara Solomon Festinger, who were Jewish immigrants from eastern Europe before World War I. After completing high school, he attended the City College of New York, where, after trying various science courses and finding them boring, he settled on psychology as a major and obtained a BS in 1939. It was at City College that Festinger first became acquainted with the work of the German psychologist, Kurt Lewin (chap. 7, this volume), and, under the supervision of Max Hertzman, carried out an experiment on aspiration level, which was later published (Hertzman & Festinger, 1940).

Festinger then went to the Iowa Child Welfare Station at the University of Iowa to do graduate work with Lewin, who had recently come to this country to escape from Nazi Germany. While still in Germany, Lewin had carried out an analysis of how, within a person, tension systems are created by goals, and how these tension systems affect the memory and behavior of individuals until and unless they are eliminated by goal attainment. Research by Tamara Dembo and Sybille Escalona on aspirations to attain a goal—working with Lewin's conceptual framework of goal valences, goal potencies, and restraining forces—was what interested Festinger, and he pursued that interest at the University of Iowa although Lewin had become interested primarily in social and political problems because of his recent experience in Germany. Also during his stay at Iowa, with the help of Kenneth Spence (chap. 17, this volume)—of Hull–Spence learning theory fame—Festinger carried out an experiment on taste preferences in rats. Further, he developed some important nonparametric statistical tests, and he wrote a mathematical decision theory for his PhD dissertation. At the time he obtained his doctorate—1942—Festinger clearly was not a social psychologist.

After holding the position of research associate in psychology at Iowa from 1941 to 1943, Festinger took an appointment as senior statistician, Committee on the Selection and Training of Aircraft Pilots, at the University of Rochester. This position was considered to be part of the war effort (World War II). He remained there from 1943 until the end of the war in 1945. By the end of the war, Lewin had managed to establish a Research Center for Group Dynamics at the Massachusetts Institute of Technology, and Festinger accepted an appointment as assistant professor of social psychology at MIT from 1945 to 1948 to participate in the Research Center. As Festinger said of this appointment, when he accepted it he became a social psychologist by fiat.

Festinger, the Social Psychologist

The Research Center—which, in addition to Kurt Lewin, had Ronald Lippitt, Marian Radke Yarrow, and Dorwin (Doc) Cartwright as faculty—enrolled an immensely talented set of graduate students, including Kurt Back, Morton Deutsch, Harold Kelley, Albert Pepitone, Stanley Schachter, and John Thibaut. The faculty and students worked closely together and carried out a number of experiments using methodology that permitted the examination of important variables in group influence processes without the sacrifice of precision in arriving at inferences and conclusions. This was pioneering work in experimental social psychology and was made possible only by the extraordinary talents of the participants.

Leon Festinger's initiation as a social psychologist of note occurred while he was at the MIT Center. He had been enlisted to help with a study of graduate student housing at the University. While helping with the analysis of data, he noticed a strong relationship between residents' opinions on certain issues and their scores on a measure of social contact in the housing area. This work, carried out in association with Stanley Schachter and Kurt Back (1950), led to the formulation of a number of ideas about social influence processes, more research, and Festinger's (1950) first important theoretical article in social psychology, in which he proposed the concept of *pressures toward uniformity* in groups. The idea was that disagreement within a group would create a pressure on members of the group to reduce the disagreement to the extent that the members were attracted to the group and the disagreement was on an issue relevant to the group. Disagreement could be reduced by deviant members moving toward the rest of the group, by the majority trying to persuade deviant members, and by redefining the group so that deviant persons were excluded. This article set the pattern for much of his later theorizing; it brought together a number of independent (causal) variables that determined a common process (pressure toward uniformity), which then had several possible consequences. It was an elegant way in which to understand a seemingly complex set of events.

Unfortunately, the Research Center met an unexpected crisis when Kurt Lewin died in 1947. The Center then lost some of its appeal to MIT, and the entire Center was moved to the University of Michigan, where it became part of the Institute for Social Research. Festinger went along as associate professor and program director. During the period that Festinger was at Michigan, from 1948 to 1951, a number of important experiments on group influence processes was carried out, and several graduate students, including those who had started at MIT, completed their doctoral work. After accepting a professorship at the University of Minnesota in 1951 and building on the recent research done at Michigan, Festinger proposed an imaginative new theory to account for many of the phenomena of group influence organized by the notion of pressures toward uniformity.

The new theory, called *social comparison processes*, was published in 1954. It assumed that people have a need to evaluate their own opinions and abilities and that, when they cannot obtain objective criteria for that evaluation, they will evaluate themselves by comparing their opinions or abilities with those of other people. By making the additional assumption that a good evaluation can be obtained only if the position of the comparison person is fairly close to one's own, Festinger was able to derive a pressure toward uniformity. This was an insightful theory. It generated a lot of fruitful research, and it led to an extension by Schachter (1959) to include emotions among social comparison processes.

Social comparison theory could hardly be called obvious. After reading it, one might have thought, "What next?" Of course we already know what was next because, as we have seen, dissonance theory had already been formulated by the time that social comparison theory was published. In fact, both of these theories and the pressure toward uniformity article were produced within a half dozen years.

From 1953 to 1963, Festinger devoted most of his attention to dissonance theory. In 1955, he left Minnesota to take a professorship at Stanford University. Most notably, during this period, he and his coworkers—mainly graduate or postdoctoral students—carried out a number of laboratory experiments, many of which were published in *Conflict, Decision, and Dissonance* (Festinger, 1964). They were designed to explore various facets of dissonance theory and rule out alternative explanations for some sets of findings.

Festinger, the Animal Experimental Psychologist

As if that were not enough to do, Festinger was simultaneously involved in a second major research effort in collaboration with Douglas Lawrence, an animal experimental psychologist at Stanford. This research program was intended to show that dissonance theory could be applied to understanding the behavior of laboratory rats and various phenomena of learning, such as the effects of partial or delayed reinforcement. Up to that time, these phenomena had been largely the province of animal experimentalists and learning theorists. For example, Lawrence and Festinger (1962) reasoned that once a rat had learned how to run a maze to reach a goal box where food was normally attained, the absence of food would be dissonant with having run to the goal box with the expectation that food would be there. They reasoned further that to reduce the dissonance the animal should tend to find some sort of extra attraction in carrying out this task. Furthermore, each time the rat ran to the goal box and found no food, more dissonance and dissonance reduction should take place. Therefore, Lawrence and Festinger concluded that the tendency to run to the goal box when it might contain no food should be a direct function of the absolute number of times the animal found no food. If the rat sometimes found food and sometimes did not (partial reinforcement), the accepted formulation was that the resistance to extinction (persistence of the rat in running to an empty goal box) is a direct function, not of the absolute number of nonreinforced trials, but of the proportion of previous runs on which the rat failed to find food. Lawrence and Festinger produced an impressive set of experiments in support of their argument that the critical factor is the absolute number of nonreinforced trials rather than the proportion. They also produced evidence that delay of reinforcement, as well as insufficient reward, could strengthen behavioral tendencies in a way consistent with a dissonance theory analysis.

During this same time period, Festinger and his coworkers also initiated work on some problems in attitude change that had no apparent connection with dissonance theory: the effectiveness of overheard persuasion and increased persuasion when the audience is distracted from persuasive intent. These research forays may have been indicators that Festinger was becoming bored with dissonance research.

Festinger, the Perception Psychologist

By 1963, Festinger had begun to focus on the veridicality of cognition (i.e., the correspondence between the cognition—what one knows—and the reality it represents). For example, if one sees a picture on the wall, investigation should confirm that there is a picture and it is on the wall, not on the floor or ceiling. Veridicality is an important link in the dissonance formulation, but it led Festinger not in the direction of further research on dissonance theory, but how the eye and brain work together to establish spatial location. After initiating research on perception, Festinger returned to New York in 1968 to take the Else and Hans Staudinger Professorship at the New School for Social Research.

For approximately the next 11 years, until he closed his laboratory in 1979, Festinger worked on problems of visual perception. He and his new set of coworkers demonstrated that visual location is determined, at least in part, by efferent rather than afferent signals. That is, visual location is determined by the messages that the brain sends to the eyes and other motor systems, rather than by signals received by the brain regarding the orientation of the eyes. Additional work done during this period concerned how color information is sent from the eyes to the brain.

If this research program in visual perception was productive, and it was, why did Festinger close his laboratory? Because, in his own words, "my laboratory. . . had become devoted to studying ever narrowing aspects of how the human eye moves" (1983, p. ix). He went on to say that it is appropriate for young investigators to be excited about small problems, but small problems tend not to be important in the long run and so they are not satisfying for the aging investigator who has necessarily acquired more perspective. Thus, Festinger sought another challenge for his inquiring mind. Evidence that he was concerned about larger issues in science and society was already apparent, not so much in his theorizing and research, but in other ways that he spent his time.

Festinger on the International Scene

World War II decimated the faculties and facilities of European universities. The late John Lanzetta, from Dartmouth University, was one of the first among the social psychologists in this country to take an interest in the problems of invigorating social psychology in postwar Europe. He instigated meetings in Italy, and one of those meetings gave rise to the European Association of Experimental Social Psychology (EAESP). However, according to the eminent French psychologist, Serge Moscovici (1989), their organization lacked the strength to tackle problems concerned with building research facilities, scheduling regular joint meetings with social psychologists from eastern Europe (then behind the Iron Curtain), and so forth. The support they needed was provided by the Committee for Transnational Social Psychology, created and directed for 15 years by Leon Festinger. Moscovici gave credit to Festinger for successfully dealing with some of their most important problems through his persistence and powers of persuasion.

Perhaps even more important, Festinger established the principle that the task was to locate and support talented European researchers in social psychology regardless of what subject matter they approached or how they approached it. Imitation of American social psychology, or cross-cultural replication, was not encouraged. Today the European Association is thriving as is social psychology in nearly every corner in Europe, with many impressive centers of research. EAESP publishes the *European Journal of Social Psychology*, and their psychologists are frequent contributors to journals in the United States. Festinger's active support of the reestablishment and strengthening of social psychology in postwar Europe stands as a clear indicator of his concern for both the science of social psychology, as well as the need to increase our understanding of social problems and how to handle them. It should not have been entirely surprising, then, that he eventually became impatient with his work on ever narrowing problems in vision.

Festinger, the Psychologist Paleontologist

It is clear that Festinger was searching for a more important problem, though why he chose to try to understand better what present-day human beings have inherited from their ancient ancestry is not so clear. It seems to be a difficult problem. In contrast to almost all of Festinger's earlier research, it did not lend itself to experimental investigation. In any case, with the help of various distinguished scholars, he plunged into archeology and paleontology in an attempt to gain some understanding of the kinds of problems humankind has confronted up to the beginning of civilization—up to one or two millennia B.C. He congregated groups of experts to fill gaps in his knowledge, and he raised questions concerning what was known and guessed about the nature of humans at the beginning of civilization. For example, he learned as much as he could about stone tool making and then examined the available evidence concerning the variability found in tools left by particular groups. Wide variability in quality from the same period indicated a lack of specialization, which implied that individual members of the group made their own tools. Because then as now there would have been advantages to specialization—all members would have had the best styles of stone knives or axes—the lack of it suggested that each member of a tribe was self-sufficient. Does that mean, Festinger asked, that a preference for self-reliance has been wired into the brains of people during the hundreds of thousands of years over which humanity has been evolving? What might that imply about modern humans' adjustment to civilization, in which it is impossible to be self-sufficient because we live in a technical world?

Other questions that Festinger raised concerned why human beings gave up the nomadic life of hunter–gatherers and what implications followed from settling permanently in a particular location. He asked why conflict between human groups followed, but apparently did not precede, permanent settlements. Another of Festinger's concerns centered on the wide-spread occurrence of slavery, the conditions that likely gave rise to it, and the conditions that led to its demise. Altogether, in one slim volume, Festinger (1983) presented a number of analyses of how human beings dealt with one major problem after another and argued convincingly that each problem solution led to new problems. In the end, Festinger gave credit to human beings for their inventiveness in solving each problem they confronted. He also lamented their lack of foresight regarding the problems their solutions created. His book sheds light on the potential of present-day human beings to cope with an increasingly complex world. If he has it right, human beings will survive as a species because of their inventiveness, but the process will be much more blind than would be necessary if only they had the imagination necessary to foresee implications of problem solutions prior to their implementation.

Finally: Festinger, the Psychologist Historian

For the last half dozen years before he died, Festinger was busy at work on a new problem, which was broader in scope than what was investigated in the previous endeavor and demanding yet more background knowledge and new skills in problem solving. The problem he became curious about was what accounts for cultural change. He focused on a question that had been asked by others—namely, why the cultures of western Europe, Byzantium, and the Islamic world had developed along different paths, given that they started out sharing pretty much the same base of knowledge and culture. Western Europe, by the medieval period, was embracing technology and change, whereas both the Byzantine and Islamic worlds seemingly were content with the status quo. What light Festinger might have been able to throw on this puzzle will never be known because he felt his analyses were still incomplete when he died on February 11, 1989. What is clear from his analyses of human behavior leading up to civilization, and his incomplete attempt to analyze cultural change during the medieval period, is that there are other, possibly more fruitful, ways for behavioral scientists to spend their analytic powers than on the problems that lend themselves to laboratory experimental work. Part of his inspiration for this turn in his efforts may have been his respect and admiration for Kurt Lewin, who was greatly concerned about social problems.

FESTINGER, THE PERSON

To students in psychology who had close contact with Leon Festinger, it was inspiring, exhilarating, and sobering to participate or watch this man at work and play—inspiring because of the research discussions; exhilarating because there was always something going on, be it research, distinguished visitors, or just playing games; and sobering because Leon was the role model one was supposed to emulate and emulation seemed impossible for ordinary mortals.

It would be easy to imagine that graduate students would have seen little of Leon in person or on a one-to-one basis. In truth, access was easy. His office door was usually open (if it was closed, that frequently signified that a game of cribbage was in progress) and he was always willing to talk about research or almost any other topic. Everyone called him by his first name, and he treated the students as equals, except of course if you disagreed with him. In that case, you had to be able to put up an awfully good argument. I remember that another graduate student and I had prepared a coding scheme for some research. When we presented it to Leon, he argued in favor of doing the coding a different way and won the argument. The next day, when we talked again about the coding, Leon reversed himself and convinced us that the way we had originally suggested was best. This was not playing games; these were serious arguments (but we rejoiced in having been right the first time). As Elaine Hatfield (personal communication, 1996) put it, Leon believed in a meritocracy. As long as you sacrificed everything for science, "he didn't notice if you happened to be male or female, Jewish, WASP, or Buddhist . . . . Maybe he assumed everyone was Jewish, but that was quite nice."

Because of his theoretically stimulating approach to research and his egalitarian style, Festinger attracted numerous highly talented students. Graduate students were frequently included at dinners with faculty members and, as far as I know, everyone was invited to his parties. These parties usually lasted until early morning hours and, by that time, sometimes included singing songs of the Lincoln Brigade from the Spanish revolution or group dancing. Finally the handful of people remaining might pile into Leon's car and head off to a delicatessen for cheesecake and coffee, with Leon driving much too fast and explaining that people are better drivers after they have had a few drinks.

It may seem odd, given his intellectual brilliance, but I do not remember Leon engaging in the rapid repartee in which many academics delight. That was not his style. He spent most of his time talking to people one on one. For me, it was an interesting experience, particularly at a party, convention, or bar, because I always had the impression that he was giving me his full attention, not just being social. For however long we talked, he would be completely engrossed in our conversation. Leon's powers of concentration and comprehension were enormous. He was the only person I ever talked to who, after 20 minutes, knew more about my research than I did.

Festinger, the Scientist[2]

Any serious attempt to understand complex human behavior must involve the interplay between theory and research, and rigor in either cannot be sacrificed especially when the theory is imaginative or takes exception to currently accepted thought. In this brief portrayal of Festinger's work, the rigor of his research has been neglected because a convincing case can only be made through detailed discussion of research design and methods. Suffice it to say that the rigor of his research matched the rigor of his theory and perusal of any of his published work will quickly satisfy a reader in this respect.

Most important was Festinger's ability to pose trenchant theoretical problems and research questions. According to Gazzaniga (1989), who participated in Festinger's investigations in prehistory and medieval history, he could elicit the interest

---

[2]An individual who is so creative and productive will have received honors and awards. Festinger received the Distinguished Scientific Contribution Award of the American Psychological Association in 1959. He was a member of the Society of Experimental Psychologists, a Fellow of the American Academy of Arts and Sciences, and a member of the National Academy of Sciences. He received an Honorary Doctorate from the University of Mannheim in 1978, the Distinguished Senior Scientist Award of the Society of Experimental Social Psychology in 1980, and, in 1980–1981, was an Einstein Visiting Fellow at the Israel Academy of Sciences and Humanities.

and cooperation of distinguished scholars from other fields because of his ability to master new material and see interesting questions that had not been examined before. As Schachter (1994), long-time associate and friend of Festinger, said, "He discovered things no one knew before; he made connections no one had made before, and he did it all with an éclat and an elegance that compel one to think of his work in aesthetic as well as scientific terms" (p. 107).

There are many difficulties in the way of understanding complex human behavior. One of the greatest, Festinger often said, is that we are trying to understand phenomena that we experience, and consequently we are burdened by the need to disentangle our experience from a dispassionate understanding. Eventually, perhaps, we will be visited by Martians who, by virtue of their unencumbered view, will be able to shed a great deal of light on why we behave as we do. Until that time, however, we are consigned to dealing with problems of human behavior in much the same way as we must deal with a cleverly written mystery story; we must assume that each aspect of a problem may not be what it appears to be. As with a good mystery, we must make that assumption about each of a string of events and suspend judgment until we can attach one or more new interpretations to each of the events, hopefully allowing us to see the whole in a different light from that with which we started. Gaining that last, integrating insight produces a thrill that cannot be manufactured in any other way.

Leon Festinger always said he was having fun with his current research. I think it is safe to say that he had fun for a while and then the insights became less frequent and he started looking for new mysteries. If it is in any sense appropriate to say he had an insatiable appetite, it seems not to have been for knowledge but rather for problems to solve. Having fun is solving those problems. However, solutions can be found only when problems have been identified; the creative process begins with the way the problem is formulated. In the words of Zukier (1989), psychologist and historian, "Throughout Festinger's work, there is a persistent refusal to understand the seemingly obvious, and a conviction that uncovering the question may indeed be harder than solving it" (p. xiii).

Some problems come in packages, like puzzles and games, and Festinger never ceased to enjoy them, but the problems that really turned him on as a behavioral scientist are those mysteries about why people behave as they do. Leon Festinger was perhaps without peer in identifying and solving the psychological mysteries of complex human behavior.

ACKNOWLEDGMENTS

I wish to thank the following, who responded to my inquiry in preparation for this biographical chapter: Elliot Aronson, Ofer Bar-Yosef, Dorwin Cartwright, Michael Gazzaniga, Harold Gerard, Elaine Hatfield, William J. McGuire, Judson Mills,

Serge Moscovici, Albert Pepitone, Jane Piliavin, Henry Riecken, Stanley Schachter, Peter Schoenbach, Robert Somerville, and, of course, Trudy Festinger.

REFERENCES

Beauvois, J.-L., & Joule, R.-V. (1996). *A radical dissonance theory.* Bristol, PA: Taylor and Francis.

Festinger, L. (1950). Informal social communication. *Psychological Review, 57,* 271–282.

Festinger, L. (1954). A theory of social comparison processes. *Human Relations, 7,* 117–140.

Festinger, L. (1957). *A theory of cognitive dissonance.* Stanford, CA: Stanford University Press.

Festinger, L. (1964). *Conflict, decision, and dissonance.* Stanford, CA: Stanford University Press.

Festinger, L. (1983). *The human legacy.* New York: Columbia University Press.

Festinger, L., Riecken, H., & Schachter, S. (1956). *When prophecy fails.* Minneapolis: University of Minnesota Press.

Festinger, L., Schachter, S., & Back, K. (1950). *Social pressures in informal groups.* New York: Harper.

Gazzaniga, M. (1989). *Lunch with Leon.* Unpublished manuscript, Dartmouth University.

Hertzman, M., & Festinger, L. (1940). Shifts in explicit goals in a level of aspiration experiment. *Journal of Experimental Psychology, 27,* 439–452.

Lawrence, D. H., & Festinger, L. (1962). *Deterrents and reinforcement: The psychology of insufficient reward.* Stanford, CA: Stanford University Press.

Margulis, S. T., & Songer, E. (1969). Cognitive dissonance: A bibliography of its first decade. *Psychological Reports, 24,* 923–935.

Moentmann, V. (1979). *Dissonance theory: a bibliography 1957–1978.* Mannheim, Germany: Sonderforschungsbereich 24.

Moscovici, S. (1989). Obituary: Leon Festinger. *European Journal of Social Psychology, 19,* 263–269.

Schachter, S. (1959). *The psychology of affiliation.* Stanford, CA: Stanford University Press.

Schachter, S. (1994). Leon Festinger, 1919–1989. *Biographical Memoirs, 64,* 98–110.

Wicklund, R.A., & Brehm, J.W. (1976). *Perspectives on cognitive dissonance.* Hillsdale, NJ: Lawrence Erlbaum Associates.

Zukier, H. (1989). Introduction. In S. Schachter & M.S. Gazzaniga (Eds.), *Extending psychological frontiers: Selected works of Leon Festinger* (pp. xi–xxiv). New York: Russell Sage Foundation.

Index